PURE LOVE

PURE LOVE

READINGS ON SIXTEEN ENDURING VIRTUES

Selected, with Reflections, by

MARILYN ARNOLD

DESERET BOOK COMPANY

SALT LAKE CITY, UTAH

Library of Congress Cataloging-in-Publication Data

Pure love : readings on sixteen enduring virtues / compiled by Marilyn Arnold.
   p.   cm.
  Includes bibliographical references and index.
  ISBN 1-57345-239-4 (HB)
   1. Literature—Collections. 2. Conduct of life—Literary collections. 3. Charity—Literary collections. 4. Virtues—Literary collections. I. Arnold, Marilyn, 1935–
PN6014.P87   1997
808.8'0353—dc21   97-23499
                                                CIP

Printed in the United States of America   72082

10 9 8 7 6 5 4 3 2 1

It is good also, to write, for our Father

in heaven was a writer.

He wrote with his own finger

on the tables of stone.

FROM "MORMON PROVERBS,"

TIMES AND SEASONS, MAY 15, 1845

CONTENTS

PREFACE

Although some of the pieces in this collection are contemporary, many are not. Some, in fact, are ancient. As a result, like scripture, they are not cognizant of matters such as gender-specific language and role stereotyping. Nevertheless, they contain valuable insights, artistry, and charm. I ask that the reader exercise charity in assessing their worth; take them as products of their time and enjoy their timeless wisdom.

A word of caution. Do not use this book as a guide to contemporary American spelling, grammar, capitalization, and punctuation conventions. Usage in all these matters changes over time, and practices vary from country to country. I have often preserved original spelling, capitalization, and punctuation because they contribute to the flavor of the pieces. At times, however, I have added clarifying punctuation and paragraphing. Middle English texts have been rendered in modern English, as have texts in languages other than English. Even today, conventions differ between Britain and America. The British, for example put an "e" after the "g" in judg[e]ment, but Americans leave it out. The British and earlier Americans use "-our" endings where modern Americans use "-or," as in "hono[u]r." The British also use "-ise" endings in some words where Americans use "-ice" or "-ize," or double "l" in some words where Americans use only one.

There are also multiple versions of a good many pieces, and in such cases, I have tried to find the most authentic. Failing that, I have gone with my personal preferences.

The publisher has exercised editorial privilege in reformatting many of the poems in this volume. The arrangement of lines and stanzas should not be regarded as definitive in any sense.

ACKNOWLEDGMENTS

I extend heartfelt thanks to the people who made this volume possible. Most important, of course, are the writers themselves who are represented here. Of those who are living, a good many gladly allowed the reprinting of their work without charge. In some cases, surviving relatives extended such permission. Many other people took interest in the project and made helpful suggestions or assisted in the search. Among those are Richard H. Cracroft, who knows the LDS sources perhaps better than anyone else; Milton Jones, who tracked sources and scanned hundreds of printed materials; Bonnie Ballif-Spanville, who offered encouragement and backup assistance; Maureen Ursenbach Beecher, who generously shared her research in the journals of early Mormon women; the staff of the Harold B. Lee Library at BYU; Audrey Shumway, then Director of Libraries at Dixie College; and the staffs of the Provo City and the Washington County libraries. Other individuals lent precious family documents and books. I thank also my mother, Rhoda C. Arnold, for the stories and poem borrowed from her memory. Without the work of Sheri Dew and her associates at Deseret Book, of course, there would be no book. Special thanks go to Jack Lyon, a sensitive and skilled editor who worked closely with me on the project. He is graciousness personified.

INTRODUCTION

Religion without morality, professions of godliness

without charity, church-membership without adequate

responsibility as to individual conduct in daily life,

are but as sounding brass and tinkling cymbals—noise

without music, the words without the spirit of prayer.

JAMES E. TALMAGE

Love is one of the leading characteristics of Deity, and

ought to be manifested by those who aspire to be the sons

of God. A man filled with the love of God, is not content

with blessing his family alone but ranges through the

world, anxious to bless the whole of the human family.

JOSEPH SMITH, LETTER TO THE TWELVE

APOSTLES, DECEMBER 15, 1840

According to the Apostle Paul, the greatest virtues can be described under the rubric of charity, what Mormon further defined as "the pure love of Christ." (Moroni 7:47.) Paul lists those sixteen virtues in 1 Corinthians 13, in quick succession in verses 4 to 8. That remarkable listing suggested to me a design for a "book of virtues" that would richly engage the Christian reader, and more particularly the Latter-day Saint. Following Paul's serendipitous prompting, I offer here a collection of writings, a unique and happy mixture from Latter-day Saint and non-Latter-day Saint sources. The reader may discover, as I did, that the various writings even seem to talk with each other at times. All of the pieces have been chosen for their moral, religious, and artistic qualities.

This collection has several purposes. It is intended to provide delightful and informative hours of just plain good reading—old favorites, little-known gems, thought-provoking commentaries, inspiring sermons, fanciful children's pieces. It is also intended to deepen the reader's spiritual understanding and to bend individual hearts toward the virtues taught and exemplified by Jesus Christ. May it lead all of us to practice more earnestly the virtues encompassed by true charity—pure Christian love.

At the same time, the collection offers useful resources to teachers, speakers, and parents throughout the Church. Over time there have been numerous smaller collections published for the latter purpose. Several years ago, for example, Preston Nibley compiled a good many books of inspiring stories by and about LDS leaders and members, and these books are still available in many libraries and homes. And he is only one of several compilers. More recently, a number of collections have focused on the lives and writings of LDS women.

Nationally known authors have also produced many anthologies of wholesome poems and stories—most notable in recent times *The Norton Book of Friendship,* by Eudora Welty and Ronald Sharp; *The Art of Growing Older,* by Wayne Booth; and *The Book of Virtues* and *The Moral Compass,* by William Bennett. These all, as we say, provide a "good read" and at the same time put forth healthy moral exempla. This sort of thing has always been popular, as the shelves of used book stores attest. In fact, within my gaze as I write this introduction is a somewhat ragged book, published in 1898, titled *The Twentieth Century Speaker.* One side of the cover advertises it as a source of material "for home, school, Sunday School, Easter greetings, Christian endeavor, entertainments, temperance, etc." The other side claims it to be equally valuable "for Christmas, Thanksgiving, Labor Day, pioneer gatherings, patriotic occasions, etc." Thus, unconsciously, the book merges religious and secular purposes, as though their compatibility simply goes without saying.

The present volume, although it bears a family relationship with the collections mentioned above, clearly has a character all its own. It draws from the great world body of moral wisdom and art, but it combines those texts with inspired wisdom and art originating in the body of The Church of Jesus Christ of Latter-day Saints. Elder Stephen L Richards spoke often of the spiritual brotherhood of humankind, and this is especially evident in the bond of virtue that unites all God-fearing people. In its selections and commentary, this volume portrays and affirms the principles taught in the thirteenth Article of Faith:

> We believe in being honest, true, chaste, benevolent, virtuous, and in doing good to all men; indeed, we may say that we follow the admonition of Paul—We believe all things, we hope all things, we have endured many things, and hope to be able to endure all things. If there is anything virtuous, lovely, or of good report or praiseworthy, we seek after these things.

This splendid statement describes not only our personal and communal aspirations but also our link to other mortals and the good things of the world, the things outside our faith that evidence the workings of the Light of Christ among humankind.

Joseph Smith's obvious allusion is to Paul's statement in Philippians 4:8, but Joseph also talks about belief (faith), hope, benevolence (charity), and endurance—the principal subjects of Paul's brilliant discourse in 1 Corinthians 13. Surprisingly, in his landmark collection, William Bennett does not list charity as one of the ten "virtues," though he does name compassion and friendship. In the present collection, like Joseph Smith, I have chosen to follow the admonition of Paul.

Just prior to chapter 13, Paul has been stressing the fact that Church members are unified as "the body of Christ." (1 Corinthians 12:27.) He concludes chapter 12 by indicating that he now intends to show the Saints "a more excellent way," specifically more excellent than the law of Moses. And that more excellent way is the way of Jesus Christ. It is the way he shows forth—in his love, his atonement, and his redeeming gospel. As Moroni teaches: "Wherefore, by faith was the law of Moses given. But in the gift of his Son hath God prepared a more excellent way; and it is by faith that it hath been fulfilled." (Ether 12:11.)

Paul is less direct than Moroni in linking Christ to the "more excellent way" of charity, but in light of what Moroni says, we can hardly mistake Paul's intent: "But when that which is perfect is come," meaning Jesus Christ, "then that which is in part shall be done away," meaning the law of Moses. "When I was a child" (immature in the gospel, having only the law), Paul continues, "I spake as a child, I understood as a child, I thought as a child: but when I became a man," that is, received the full gospel of Christ, "I put away childish things," the elementary details of the law. "For now," while we remain under the law, "we see through a glass, darkly" and "know [only] in part;" but then," after Christ comes, we shall see "face to face" and "know even as also [we are] known." (1 Corinthians 13:10–12.) Paul welds the link between Christ and charity by immediately ending the chapter with a reference to faith (in Jesus Christ), hope (our hope is in him), and charity, concluding emphatically that "the greatest of these is charity."

The choice to follow the outline suggested in Paul's listing of charity's attributes inevitably sets this collection in a different frame of reference from others in the genre. The reader will notice, however, that I have extended the possible applications of each virtue Paul names beyond the obvious. Exercising the editor's prerogative, from Paul I have taken the general categories; but I have not limited the material under those categories to what Paul may have specifically intended. Exercising the writer's prerogative, Paul suggests a good deal more than he specifies. Scripture has great power to suggest, and this passage from Paul's writings has obviously kindled my imagination.

This collection is meant to appeal to young and old and all persons in between. As I suggested earlier, there are children's pieces and there are thoughtful philosophical discourses and stories, many of which are excerpted because of space considerations. It is hoped that the extracts here will lead readers into libraries and bookstores to find the complete texts.

PROLOGUE

B y way of introduction to this volume and its subject, I offer Matthew Cowley's classic discourse on charity. Since he cites Paul, I will not repeat the passage from 1 Corinthians.

CHARITY

What is charity? Does it consist solely in the giving of bread to the hungry, clothes to the naked, or succor to the distressed?

> Though I bestow all my goods to feed the poor, and though I give my body to be burned, and have not charity, it profiteth me nothing. Charity suffereth long, and is kind; charity envieth not; charity vaunteth not itself, is not puffed up; doth not behave itself unseemly, seeketh not her own, is not easily provoked, thinketh no evil; rejoiceth not in iniquity, but rejoiceth in the truth; beareth all things, believeth all things, hopeth all things, endureth all things. Charity never faileth. (I Cor. xiii:3–8; emphasis added)

If to say that one has charity to any considerable extent requires the possession of all the foregoing characteristics, then we may truthfully admit that there is a great charity famine now prevailing throughout the world.

It is not difficult to find people who will impart of their substance to feed the poor; but too frequently many who do so will look with scorn upon those who differ from them in matters of religion, politics or other subjects. Modern history records many instances where people noted for their hospitality have shown intense hatred and bitterness toward some who have come into their midst preaching doctrines which were in conflict with the theories they and their fathers had espoused.

In many cases mobs have been headed by ministers of religion, who have instigated and participated in shedding the innocent blood of their fellow beings for no other reason than their hatred of a religion different from their own. Indeed, few if any in modern Christendom can be said to exemplify in their lives all the traits attributed to charity in the quotation from the sayings of the apostle Paul. Who "suffers long" without a murmur, especially if the suffering comes by oppression from an outward foe, and in return for evil? Who are kind to those who wrong them? Where is he who "envieth not" the possessions of his neighbor, or the honors and emoluments of office enjoyed by others? Who, under the wave of prosperity, in the lap of luxury, or dwelling in popular favor, "vaunteth not" himself, "is not puffed up" or "doth not behave himself unseemly?" Who "seeketh not" his own, "but rather" prefers his brother before himself? Who is not "easily provoked," and therefore does not retaliate against those who may give offense? Who "thinks not evil" of those who go contrary to his views, but the motives of whose hearts he knows nothing about?

. . . Few there are, even among the Saints, who fully and becomingly "bear all things" and prove themselves the true type of the Savior of mankind, who preferred ever to suffer wrong than to do wrong.

. . . Charity should be sought after and cultivated by the Saints above all other people. Our professions are greater. If our deportment contradicts our teachings, our ignorance is more apparent, or our hypocrisy is more pronounced.

It is stated in the Book of Mormon that "Charity is the pure love of God." By this plain yet comprehensive definition, we learn that unless the love of God dwells in our hearts we have not charity. This love for the salvation of mankind induces the true servants of the Lord to travel to the ends of the earth, without the shadow or hope of earthly reward, to preach the Gospel to the world. Not only that; with all the self-denial of home and its comforts which such a mission implies, we also esteem all the good which others have, not asking them to forsake one truth they now possess, but inviting them to receive more truth, pointing them to a greater light, and leaving them perfectly free from undue persuasion to receive the message or reject it as they may choose.

The Prophet Joseph instructed the Twelve and the Elders, in preaching the Gospel, not to tear down the tenets of other men's faith, but in the spirit of meekness explain the Gospel and bear testimony to its divinity, leaving all mankind absolutely the keeper of their own consciences, to do as they please and meet the responsibility of their own acts at the bar of eternal justice. Neither should it be forgotten that much of the labor of mankind, without a knowledge of the Gospel, in many respects has been directed by a divine Providence to ameliorate the condition of mankind. . . .

[Instances cited] serve as pointed lessons to the youth of Israel, teaching us to be broad and generous in viewing the labors of those not of us, so that if the hand of Providence is manifest we shall not be oblivious thereto, nor be found in the ranks of those who have not charity. ◄

Indeed, like the Savior, who encompassed "all the law and the prophets" in his injunctions to love God and neighbor, Paul gathered many virtues into charity's fold. Although I take my text from Paul, it is with the recognition that there are anticipations and echoes of Paul in the Book of Mormon and Doctrine and Covenants as well as elsewhere in the New Testament. The Lord teaches the same principles to all his children.

The Lord God hath given a commandment that all men should have charity, which charity is love. And except they should have charity they were nothing. (2 Nephi 26:30.)

And now I would that ye should be humble, and be submissive and gentle; easy to be entreated; full of patience and long-suffering; being temperate in all things. . . .

And see that ye have faith, hope, and charity, and then ye will always abound in good works. (Alma 7:23–24.)

Wherefore, there must be faith; and if there must be faith there must also be hope; and if there must be hope there must also be charity.

And except ye have charity ye can in nowise be saved in the kingdom of God; neither can ye be saved in the kingdom of God if ye have not faith; neither can ye if ye have no hope. (Moroni 10:20–21.)

Wherefore, if a man have faith he must needs have hope; for without faith there cannot be any hope.

And again, behold I say unto you that he cannot have faith and hope, save he shall be meek, and lowly of heart.

If so, his faith and hope is vain, for none is acceptable before God, save the meek and lowly in heart; and if a man be meek and lowly in heart, and confesses by the power of the Holy Ghost that Jesus is the Christ, he must needs have charity; for if he have not charity he is nothing; wherefore he must needs have charity.

And charity suffereth long, and is kind, and envieth not, and is not puffed up, seeketh not her own, is not easily provoked, thinketh no evil, and rejoiceth not in iniquity but rejoiceth in the truth, beareth all things, believeth all things, hopeth all things, endureth all things.

Wherefore, my beloved brethren, if ye have not charity, ye are nothing, for charity never faileth. Wherefore, cleave unto charity, which is the greatest of all, for all things must fail—

But charity is the pure love of Christ, and it endureth forever; and whoso is found possessed of it at the last day, it shall be well with him. (Mormon's words, recorded in Moroni 7:42–47.)

. . . add to your faith virtue; and to virtue knowledge;

And to knowledge temperance; and to temperance patience; and to patience godliness;

And to godliness brotherly kindness; and to brotherly kindness charity. (2 Peter 1:5–7.)

And faith, hope, charity and love, with an eye single to the glory of God qualify him for the work [of the kingdom].

Remember faith, virtue, knowledge, temperance, patience, brotherly kindness, godliness, charity, humility, diligence. (D&C 4:5–6.)

Behold, I will show unto the Gentiles their weakness, and I will show unto them that faith, hope and charity bringeth unto me—the fountain of all righteousness. (Ether 12:28.)

1

CHARITY SUFFERETH LONG

Blessed are the merciful:

for they shall obtain mercy.

MATTHEW 5:7

First on Paul's list of the attributes of charity is the phrase "*suffereth long*," a phrase that of itself suggests the Savior's loving forbearance and mercy as well as his great sacrifice for our sakes. The expression indirectly enjoins us to pattern our lives and characters after him. We are to be forgiving and patient, to harbor no enmity and seek no vengeance, to be tolerant of the shortcomings in others, and to accept in faith the sometimes trying vicissitudes of life.

Wilford Woodruff recorded these words of Joseph Smith, delivered with additional counsel to the Twelve and other missionaries, on July 2, 1839:

Ever keep in exercise the principle of mercy, and be ready to forgive our brother on the first intimations of repentance, and asking forgiveness; and should we even forgive our brother, or even our enemy, before he repent or ask forgiveness, our heavenly Father would be equally as merciful unto us. ❧

In the following letter to William W. Phelps, the Prophet Joseph demonstrates that he practiced the counsel he taught.

Nauvoo, Hancock County, Illinois, July 22, 1840

Dear Brother Phelps:—I must say that it is with no ordinary feelings I endeavor to write a few lines to you in answer to yours of the 29th ultimo; at the same time I am rejoiced at the privilege granted me.

1

You may in some measure realize what my feelings, as well as Elder Rigdon's and Brother Hyrum's were, when we read your letter—truly our hearts were melted into tenderness and compassion when we ascertained your resolves, &c. I can assure you I feel a disposition to act on your case in a manner that will meet the approbation of Jehovah, (whose servant I am), and agreeable to the principles of truth and righteousness which have been revealed; and inasmuch as long-suffering, patience, and mercy have ever characterized the dealings of our heavenly Father towards the humble and penitent, I feel disposed to copy the example, cherish the same principles, and by so doing be a savior of my fellow men.

It is true, that we have suffered much in consequence of your behavior—the cup of gall, already full enough for mortals to drink, was indeed filled to overflowing when you turned against us. One with whom we had oft taken sweet counsel together, and enjoyed many refreshing seasons from the Lord—"had it been an enemy, we could have borne it." "In the day that thou stoodest on the other side, in the day when strangers carried away captive his forces, and foreigners entered into his gates, and cast lots upon [Far West], even thou wast as one of them; but thou shouldest not have looked on the day of thy brother, in the day that he became a stranger, neither shouldst thou have spoken proudly in the day of distress."

However, the cup has been drunk, the will of our Father has been done, and we are yet alive, for which we thank the Lord. And having been delivered from the hands of wicked men by the mercy of our God, we say it is your privilege to be delivered from the powers of the adversary, be brought into the liberty of God's dear children, and again take your stand among the Saints of the Most High, and by diligence, humility, and love unfeigned, commend yourself to our God, and your God, and to the Church of Jesus Christ.

Believing your confession to be real, and your repentance genuine, I shall be happy once again to give you the right hand of fellowship, and rejoice over the returning prodigal.

Your letter was read to the Saints last Sunday, and an expression of their feeling was taken, when it was unanimously

Resolved, That W. W. Phelps should be received into fellowship.

"Come on, dear brother, since the war is past,
For friends at first, are friends again at last."
    Yours as ever,
        Joseph Smith, Jun.

As B. H. Roberts notes:

When the great offense of Elder William W. Phelps is taken into account—amounting as it did to a betrayal of the Prophet and the Church in Missouri, during the troubles of the Saints in that state—this letter is remarkable. The Prophet's frank forgiveness of his erring brother, gently chiding his wrong-doing, but at the same time remembering in a large way that brother's former devotion and labors; the Prophet's willingness to have the prodigal return and occupy his former high standing among the Saints—all this exhibits a broad-mindedness and generosity that can come only from a great soul, influenced by the spirit of charity enjoined upon his disciples by the teachings of the Son of God. One of the surest evidences of Joseph Smith's greatness of mind and of the inspiration of God upon him is to be seen in his treatment of those who had fallen but were willing to and did repent of their sins. His capacity to forgive under these circumstances seemed boundless. ✦

William Shakespeare's lines about the quality of mercy have become classic:

FROM *THE MERCHANT OF VENICE*

    The quality of mercy is not strain'd,
    It droppeth as the gentle rain from heaven
    Upon the place beneath: it is twice blest;
    It blesseth him that gives and him that takes:
    'Tis mightiest in the mightiest: it becomes
    The throned monarch better than his crown;
    His sceptre shows the force of temporal power,
    The attribute to awe and majesty,
    Wherein doth sit the dread and fear of kings;
    But mercy is above this sceptred sway;
    It is enthroned in the hearts of kings,

It is an attribute to God himself;
And earthly power doth then show likest God's
When mercy seasons justice. Therefore, . . .
Though justice be thy plea, consider this,
That, in the course of justice, none of us
Should see salvation: we do pray for mercy;
And that same prayer doth teach us all to render
The deeds of mercy. (iv.1.)

In her unpublished autobiography, early Mormon settler Mary Elizabeth Woolley Chamberlain remembers her meek child self, seeking the forgiveness of her Father in Heaven in prayer.

After I was old enough to say my prayers, away from mother's knee I would often forget them, some times for several nights, and then when I did think of them I would say them over and over and over, to pay up, always being sure that I repeated them enough to have a few times left over for interest so that the Lord would forgive me. We always repeated the Lord's prayer first, and then a simple individual prayer, asking for what ever we were in need of. If we ever lost anything of value we prayed about it, and on many occasions my prayers were directly answered, which greatly strengthened my faith. ❧

John Taylor recounts a personal experience with forgiveness.

I will tell you a circumstance that took place with me upwards of forty years ago. I was living in Canada at the time, and was a traveling Elder. I presided over a number of the churches in that district of country. A difficulty existed in a branch of the church, and steps were taken to have the matter brought before me for settlement. I thought very seriously about it, and thought it a very insignificant affair. Because we ought to soar above such things, and walk on a higher plane, for we are the children of God and should be willing to suffer wrong rather than do wrong; to yield a good deal to our brethren for the sake of peace and quietness, and to secure and promote good feelings among the Saints.

At that time I did not have the experience I now have, and yet I do not know that I could do anything better than I did then. Before going to the trial I bowed before the Lord, and sought wisdom from him to conduct the affair aright, for I had the welfare of the people at heart. When we had assembled I opened the meeting with prayer, and then called upon a number of those present to pray; they did so, and the Spirit of God rested upon us. I could perceive that a good feeling existed in the hearts of those who had come to present their grievances, and I told them to bring forward their case. But they said they had not anything to bring forward. The feelings and spirit they had been in possession of had left them, the Spirit of God had obliterated these feelings out of their hearts, and they knew it was right for them to forgive one another. (*Journal of Discourses* 21:366–67.) ❧

Heber J. Grant tells of another experience in which John Taylor wrought forgiving concord between two faithful older men. They had "suffered the drivings and persecutions of the Saints" in Nauvoo, "as well as the hardships of pioneering, incident to the early settlement of the west." But in Salt Lake City, they "quarreled over some business affairs." They asked John Taylor, then president of the Quorum of the Twelve Apostles, to mediate their differences, pledging to abide by his decision. Elder Grant continues:

President Taylor willingly consented. But he said: "Brethren, before I hear your case, I would like very much to sing one of the songs of Zion for you." Now President Taylor was a very capable singer, and interpreted sweetly and with spirit, our sacred hymns.

He sang one of our hymns to the two brethren.

Seeing its effect, President Taylor remarked that he never heard one of the songs of Zion but that he wanted to listen to one more, and so asked them to listen while he sang another. Of course, they consented. They both seemed to enjoy it; and, having sung the second song, he remarked that he had heard there is luck in odd numbers and so with their consent he would sing another, which he did. Then in his jocular way, he remarked, "Now, brethren, I do not want to wear you out, but if you will forgive me, and listen to one more hymn, I promise to stop singing, and will hear your case."

The story goes that when President Taylor had finished the fourth song, the brethren were melted to tears, got up, shook hands, and asked President

5

Taylor to excuse them for taking up his time. They then departed without his even knowing what their difficulties were. ❦

Oscar A. Kirkham tells a personal story about the moral rescue of three young men by their caring and merciful victim.

THE WORTH OF A BOY

My first Buick was a very wonderful car to my family and me and was bought at a real sacrifice. But having quite a group of small children I decided it was the best way to take care of them and give my wife a chance to get away from home once in awhile.

One night we parked our car on First South near State Street and took our two little girls to the Salt Lake Theater to see Maude Adams in *Peter Pan*, a great treat for all of us.

When we came out, the car was gone. I went over to the police station to investigate and found that the car had indeed been stolen and wrecked in the yards of the Union Pacific Railroad. This was a really serious loss to us.

Three boys had been apprehended. They were taken to Juvenile Court where it was recommended they be sent to reform school. I was not content, so I visited the homes of the boys. One mother, a widow, had recently come from Germany. She was very much concerned about her boy. From the other two home visits I could see part of the reason for the boys' action because there was neither law nor order there.

I then asked permission to talk to the boys and promised to get jobs for them and that each bring me three dollars every Saturday until the car repair bill was paid. They liked the idea so I persuaded the court authorities to allow me to assume the responsibility for the boys.

It was a great experience for all of us. The boys were happy to have work and paid me each week as they had agreed. We soon formed a friendly alliance and joined the gymnasium where we had fun together.

The parents were grateful and soon noticed a big improvement in the boys, who became my very good friends. I took a great deal of pleasure as time went on. They asked me to help in their decisions and solve their problems. They have grown into fine, upstanding men. ❦

The sequence of the following scriptural verses, capped by the admonition to be perfect like the Father, suggests that the Father is a model of forgiveness, and that forgiveness of one's enemies is an important step on the road to perfection.

Ye have heard that it hath been said, Thou shalt love thy neighbour, and hate thine enemy.

But I say unto you, Love your enemies, bless them that curse you, do good to them that hate you, and pray for them which despitefully use you, and persecute you. . . .

For if ye love them which love you, what reward have ye? do not even the publicans the same?

And if ye salute your brethren only, what do ye more than others? do not even the publicans so?

Be ye therefore perfect, even as your Father which is in heaven is perfect. (Matthew 5:43–44, 46–48.) ◆

Many who have written on the subject have warned against the cankering of an unforgiving soul.

Bitterness injures the one who carries it more than the one against whom it is directed. (Spencer W. Kimball.) ◆

This is certain, that a man that studieth revenge keeps his own wounds green, which otherwise would heal and do well. (Francis Bacon.) ◆

Unrighteous anger can never be excused,
For the weight of a man's anger drags him down.
(Sirach [the Apocrypha] 1:26.)

A POISON TREE

I was angry with my friend;
I told my wrath, my wrath did end.
I was angry with my foe;
I told it not, my wrath did grow.

And I watered it in fears,
Night and morning with my tears;
And I sunnèd it with smiles,
And with soft deceitful wiles.

And it grew both day and night,
Till it bore an apple bright—
And my foe beheld it shine.
And he knew that it was mine,

And into my garden stole
When the night had veiled the pole.
In the morning glad I see
My foe outstretched beneath the tree.
(William Blake.)

When you see a good man, think of emulating him; when you see a bad man, examine your own heart. (Confucius.) ❧

Him I call indeed a Brahmana who is tolerant with the intolerant, mild with fault-finders, and free from passion among the passionate.

Him I call indeed a Brahmana from whom anger and hatred, pride and envy have dropt like a mustard seed from the point of a needle. (Gautama Buddha.) ❧

Benjamin Franklin counsels against the impulse to revenge:

Doing an injury puts you below your enemy;
Revenging one makes you but even with him;
Forgiving it sets you above him. ❧

In a familiar Book of Mormon story, Pahoran's magnanimity leaves us in awe. Pushed to fury by extremes of war—both internal and external—and the apparent neglect of the Nephite troops by their government, young Captain Moroni fires an accusing and threatening letter to the chief judge, Pahoran. Moroni blames Pahoran for the suffering of the troops and the loss of Nephite cities. He implies that Pahoran is a traitor, and he threatens to march on

Zarahemla and set things right by force. What Moroni does not know is that the faithful Pahoran has been driven from office and forced to flee for his life. Pahoran's generous reply to Moroni's letter is a classic in Christlike forgiveness.

I, Pahoran, who am the chief governor of this land, do send these words unto Moroni, the chief captain over the army. Behold, I say unto you, Moroni, that I do not joy in your great afflictions, yea, it grieves my soul.

But behold, there are those who do joy in your afflictions, yea, insomuch that they have risen up in rebellion against me, and also those of my people who are freemen, yea, and those who have risen up are exceedingly numerous. . . .

And behold, they have driven me out before them, and I have fled to the land of Gideon, with as many men as it were possible that I could get. . . .

And now, in your epistle you have censured me, but it mattereth not; I am not angry, but do rejoice in the greatness of your heart. I, Pahoran, do not seek for power, save only to retain my judgment-seat that I may preserve the rights and the liberty of my people. My soul standeth fast in that liberty in the which God hath made us free. . . .

And now, Moroni, I do joy in receiving your epistle, for I was somewhat worried concerning what we should do, whether it should be just in us to go against our brethren.

But ye have said, except they repent the Lord hath commanded you that ye should go against them.

See that ye strengthen Lehi and Teancum in the Lord; tell them to fear not, for God will deliver them, yea, and also all those who stand fast in that liberty wherewith God hath made them free. And now I close mine epistle to my beloved brother, Moroni. (Alma 61:2–3, 5, 9, 19–21.) ❦

Such long-suffering forgiveness was taught by the Lord during his mortal ministry.

Then came Peter to him, and said, Lord, how oft shall my brother sin against me, and I forgive him? till seven times?

Jesus saith unto him, I say not unto thee, Until seven times: but Until seventy times seven.

Therefore is the kingdom of heaven likened unto a certain king, which would take account of his servants.

And when he had begun to reckon, one was brought unto him, which owed him ten thousand talents.

But forasmuch as he had not to pay, his lord commanded him to be sold, and his wife, and children, and all that he had, and payment to be made.

The servant therefore fell down, and worshipped him, saying, Lord, have patience with me, and I will pay thee all.

Then the lord of that servant was moved with compassion, and loosed him, and forgave him the debt.

But the same servant went out, and found one of his fellowservants, which owed him an hundred pence: and he laid hands on him, and took him by the throat, saying, Pay me that thou owest.

And his fellowservant fell down at his feet, and besought him, saying, Have patience with me, and I will pay thee all.

And he would not: but went and cast him into prison, till he should pay the debt.

So when his fellowservants saw what was done, they were very sorry, and came and told unto their lord all that was done.

Then his lord, after that he had called him, said unto him, O thou wicked servant, I forgave thee all that debt, because thou desiredest me:

Shouldest not thou also have had compassion on thy fellowservant, even as I had pity on thee?

And his lord was wroth, and delivered him to the tormentors, till he should pay all that was due unto him.

So likewise shall my heavenly Father do also unto you, if ye from your hearts forgive not every one his brother their trespasses. (Matthew 18:21–35.) ❧

Marion D. Hanks tells the story of a man who accosted him rather belligerently one day on Temple Square. In answer to Elder Hanks's inquiry, the man told his story:

At age nineteen he had been ejected from [an LDS meetinghouse] by a bishop's counselor who had been summoned because of the boy's trouble-making in class. One thing that had been said, this man remembered for nearly sixty years. As he was thrown out, someone objected. The answer that came from the counselor who had the task in hand was: "Ah, let him go, he is just one kid!"

He went, and he never came back, nor was there ever any visiting, never any outpouring or increase of the love that should follow reproof, according to the Lord. He moved to another area of the land, married, had a family; his wife passed away and he married again, his second wife died after bearing a family also. He had come to Salt Lake City at the insistence of his third wife, who having been taught by the missionaries and converted to the principles of the gospel, had brought him here hoping that somehow he might be touched—he, the member.

I asked him . . . how many living descendants he had. He counted them, and answered, "Fifty-four." I asked him then, how many of them are members of the Church, and I expect you know the answer, though perhaps not his interesting expression. He said, "Huh, ain't any of them members of the Church. They're a pretty hard lot."

Now, who was it the bishop's counselor propelled out the door that morning? Just one boy? Just one? This one has in his own lifetime become, in effect, a multitude, and the current has but begun to run, and every one of them denied, according to his own witness, the love of the gospel and the brotherhood of the Saints, the warmth and strength and direction of the programs of the Church.

Oh, I can understand a little more, why the Lord said that one soul was precious to him. ❧

A seventeenth-century Japanese philosopher offers sage advice:

FROM "SOCIAL INTERCOURSE"

When others are rude let us not blame them as long as they do not injure our honour. If we forgive discourtesy in others we do not lose the peace of our hearts. As an old saying has it: Gladness is the reward of patience. . . .

The way of dealing with impossible men is to treat them most gently. . . .

Do not bestow either rewards or punishments while you are in great joy or anger, but rather wait until your emotion has subsided, lest your award may be unjust. . . .

We often encounter treacherous men who distress us with detestable deeds and words. When we are placed in such an adverse circumstance, we should try to suppress our anger and resentment and control our countenance. This is a chance to improve our character and to make an advance in learning. Let us not let the chance slip by without availing ourselves of it. . . .

Do good toward others, but do not expect it to be reciprocated. I am I, and he is he; let me do what is right. That his justice is injustice does not concern me. (Kaibara Ekken.) ❧

Joseph F. Smith adds to this perspective by suggesting that charity does not require us to set aside discernment.

I feel in my heart to forgive all men in the broad sense that God requires of me to forgive all men, and I desire to love my neighbor as myself; and to this extent I bear no malice toward any of the children of my Father. But there are enemies to the work of the Lord, as there were enemies to the Son of God. There are those who speak only evil of the Latter-day Saints. There are those—and they abound largely in our midst—who will shut their eyes to every virtue and to every good thing connected with this latter-day work, and will pour out floods of falsehood and misrepresentation against the people of God. I forgive them for this. I leave them in the hands of the just Judge. Let him deal with them as seemeth him good, but they are not and cannot become my bosom companions. I cannot condescend to that. While I would not harm a hair of their heads, while I would not throw a straw in their path, to hinder them from turning from the error of their way to the light of truth; I would as soon think of taking a centipede or a scorpion, or any poisonous reptile, and putting it into my bosom, as I would think of becoming a companion or an associate of such men.

These are my sentiments, and I believe that they are correct. . . . If you can save a sinner from his wickedness, turn the wicked from the course of death that he is pursuing, to the way of life and salvation, you will save a soul from death, and you will have been an instrument in the hand of the Lord. . . . Some of our good Latter-day Saints have become so exceedingly good that they cannot tell the difference between a Saint of God, an honest man, and a son of Beelzebub, who has yielded himself absolutely to sin and wickedness. And they call that liberality, broadness of mind, exceeding love. I do not want to become so blinded with love for my enemies that I cannot discern between light and darkness, between truth and error, between good and evil, but I hope to live so that I shall have sufficient light in me to discern between error and truth, and to cast my lot on the side of truth and not on the side of error and darkness. The Lord bless the Latter-day Saints. If I am too narrow with reference to these matters, I hope that the wisdom of my brethren and the Spirit of Light from the Lord may broaden my soul. ✦

We need mercy; then let us be merciful. We need charity; let us be charitable. We need forgiveness; let us forgive. Let us do unto others what we would that they should do unto us. ✦

The following story, from the Zen Buddhist tradition, illustrates a rare kind of patience and forgiveness. The central character absorbs a great wrong and forgives both its perpetrators.

SHAME AND CONSCIENCE

There was a certain merchant who was deeply impressed by the lofty virtue of the Zen monk Hakuin. He used to present the monk with gifts of money and goods from time to time.

As it happened, the daughter of the merchant had a love affair with a family servant, resulting in the birth of a child. When the irate merchant demanded an explanation, his daughter said she had been impregnated by the monk Hakuin.

The merchant was furious: "To think that I gave alms to an evil shavepate like that for ten years!" Picking the baby up in his arms, the merchant took it right over to Hakuin. Laying it in the Zen master's lap, the merchant gave him a tongue-lashing and left in a huff.

Hakuin didn't argue. He began to take care of the baby as if it were his own. People who saw him also believed he had fathered the child.

One winter day, when Hakuin was out begging for alms from house to house in the falling snow, carrying the infant with him as he went, the merchant's daughter saw them and was filled with remorse. In tears, she went to her father and confessed the truth.

Mortified, the merchant was totally at a loss. He rushed over to throw himself to the ground at the feet of Zen master Hakuin, begging his forgiveness.

Hakuin simply smiled and said, "The child has another father?" ❦

The following lines were written on a bookmark found in the Breviary of a sixteenth-century religious figure, Teresa of Avila.

> Let nothing disturb thee,
> Nothing affright thee;
> All things are passing;
> God never changeth;
> Patient endurance
> Attaineth to all things;
> Who God possesseth
> In nothing is wanting;
> Alone God sufficeth.

A modern translation of John Wycliffe recommends patience.

FROM "OF VIRTUOUS PATIENCE"

Temptations are overcome by patience and meek suffering. What is patience?—a glad and willing suffering of troubles. He that is patient murmurs not at adversity, but rather, at all times, praises God with the prophet. . . . Sometimes there are reared against him despisings, reproofs, scorns, and slanders. Therefore it is needful that he take the shield of patience, and be ready to forget and to forgive all wrongs, and to pray for the turning to good of them that hate him and hurt him. No man is showed to himself whether he be strong or feeble, unless he be tempted when he is at peace. ❦

On a lighter note, this bit of rhymed whimsy suggests that it can be risky busi-ness to push the limits of another's forbearance over the brink, especially if that "other" is a crocodile.

THE CROCODILE'S TOOTHACHE

The Crocodile
Went to the dentist
And sat down in the chair,
And the dentist said, "Now tell me, sir,
Why does it hurt and where?"
And the Crocodile said, "I'll tell you the truth,
I have a terrible ache in my tooth,"
And he opened his jaws so wide, so wide,
That the dentist, he climbed right inside,
And the dentist laughed, "Oh, isn't this fun?"
As he pulled the teeth out, one by one.
And the Crocodile cried, "You're hurting me so!
Please put down your pliers and let me go."
But the dentist just laughed with a Ho Ho Ho,
And he said, "I still have twelve to go—
Oops, that's the wrong one, I confess,
But what's one crocodile's tooth, more or less?"
Then suddenly, the jaws went SNAP,
And the dentist was gone, right off the map,
And where he went one could only guess . . .
To North or South or East or West . . .
He left no forwarding address.
But what's one dentist, more or less?
(Shel Silverstein.)

Adult whimsy on the subject of forgiveness and patience is equally delightful.

To cancel wrong it ever was required
The wrong should be forgiven, and forgot

15

Ah, see, how well have thou and I conspired,
Since I forgive, and thou rememberest not!
(Edith M. Thomas.)

ENIGMA

A woman loves the boyhood of her lover,
And why, no man can hope to understand.
The frowsy fields he used to scamper over,
The hilltops where he ranged a freckled rover,
Are her enchanted land;
And all he said and did (little enough
Alas!) and all he dreamed, her eager heart
Has wrought into some bright preposterous stuff
With heaven knows what art.

This is an ancient riddle no sage may guess,
Though it be old as love and simple as man.
A little after Eden it began.
Ever she yearns above his hopes and fears,
And never he knows that half her tenderness,
Her patience with his shame-faced trespasses,
Her rueful laughter and her hard-held tears
Are meant, by some inexplicable law,
For a young fool he has not known for years,
A scalawag he thinks she never saw.
(Nancy Byrd Turner.)

As Mark Twain tells it, he exercised amazing patience and restraint—but only to a point—in the matter of a capricious timepiece.

MY WATCH

My beautiful new watch had run eighteen months without losing or gaining, and without breaking any part of its machinery or stopping. I had come to believe it infallible in its judgments about the time of day, and to consider its constitution and its anatomy imperishable. But at last, one night, I let it run down. I grieved about it as if it were a recognized messenger and forerunner of calamity. But by and by I cheered up, set the watch by guess, and commanded my bodings and superstitions to depart. Next day I stepped into the chief jeweler's to set it by the exact time, and the head of the establishment took it out of my hand and proceeded to set it for me.

Then he said, "She is four minutes slow—regulator wants pushing up." I tried to stop him—tried to make him understand that the watch kept perfect time. But no; all this human cabbage could see was that the watch was four minutes slow, and the regulator *must* be pushed up a little; and so, while I danced around him in anguish, and implored him to let the watch alone, he calmly and cruelly did the shameful deed.

My watch began to gain. It gained faster and faster day by day. Within the week it sickened to a raging fever, and its pulse went up to a hundred and fifty in the shade. At the end of two months it had left all the timepieces of the town far in the rear, and was a fraction over thirteen days ahead of the almanac. It was away into November enjoying the snow, while the October leaves were still turning. It hurried up house rent, bills payable, and such things, in such a ruinous way that I could not abide it.

I took it to the watchmaker to be regulated. He asked me if I had ever had it repaired. I said no, it had never needed any repairing. He looked a look of vicious happiness and eagerly pried the watch open, and then put a small dice box into his eye and peered into its machinery. He said it wanted cleaning and oiling, besides regulating—come in a week. After being cleaned and oiled, and regulated, my watch slowed down to that degree that it ticked like a tolling bell.

I began to be left by trains, I failed all appointments, I got to missing my dinner; my watch strung out three days' grace to four and let me go to protest; I gradually drifted back into yesterday, then day before, then into last week, and by and by the comprehension came upon me that all solitary and alone I was lingering along in week before last, and the world was out of sight. I seemed to detect in myself a sort of sneaking fellow-feeling for the mummy in the museum, and a desire to swap news with him.

I went to a watchmaker again. He took the watch all to pieces while I waited, and then said the barrel was "swelled." He said he could reduce it in three days. After this the watch *averaged* well, but nothing more. For half a day it would go like the very mischief, and keep up such a barking and wheezing and whooping and sneezing and snorting, that I could not hear myself think for the disturbance; and as long as it held out there was not a watch in the land that stood any chance against it. But the rest of the day it would keep on slowing down and fooling along until all the clocks it had left behind caught up again. So at last, at the end of twenty-four hours, it would trot up to the judges' stand all right and just in time. It would show a fair and square average, and no man could say it had done more or less than its duty.

But a correct average is only a mild virtue in a watch, and I took this instrument to another watchmaker. He said the kingbolt was broken. I said I was glad it was nothing more serious. To tell the plain truth, I had no idea what the kingbolt was, but I did not choose to appear ignorant to a stranger. He repaired the kingbolt, but what the watch gained in one way it lost in another. It would run awhile and then stop awhile, and then run awhile again, and so on, using its own discretion about the intervals. And every time it went off it kicked back like a musket. I padded my breast for a few days, but finally took the watch to another watchmaker.

He picked it all to pieces, and turned the ruin over and over under his glass; and then he said there appeared to be something the matter with the hair-trigger. He fixed it, and gave it a fresh start. It did well now, except that always at ten minutes to ten the hands would shut together like a pair of scissors, and from that time forth they would travel together. The oldest man in the world could not make head or tail of the time of day by such a watch, and so I went again to have the thing repaired.

This person said that the crystal had got bent, and that the mainspring was not straight. He also remarked that part of the works needed half-soling. He made these things all right, and then my timepiece performed unexceptionably, save that now and then, after working along quietly for nearly eight hours, everything inside would let go all of a sudden and begin to buzz like a bee, and the hands would straightway begin to spin round and round so fast that their individuality was lost completely, and they simply seemed a delicate spider's web over the face of the watch. She would reel off the next twenty-four hours in six or seven minutes, and then stop with a bang.

I went with a heavy heart to one more watchmaker, and looked on while he took her to pieces. Then I prepared to cross-question him rigidly, for this thing was getting serious. The watch had cost two hundred dollars originally, and I seemed to have paid out two or three thousand for repairs. While I waited and looked on I presently recognized in this watchmaker an old acquaintance—a steamboat engineer of other days, and not a good engineer either. He examined all the parts carefully, just as the other watchmakers had done, and then delivered his verdict with the same confidence of manner.

He said:

"She makes too much steam—you want to hang the monkey-wrench on the safety-valve!"

I brained him on the spot, and had him buried at my own expense.

My uncle William (now deceased, alas!) used to say that a good horse was a good horse until it had run away once, and that a good watch was a good watch until the repairers got a chance at it. And he used to wonder what became of all the unsuccessful tinkers, and gunsmiths, and shoe-makers, and engineers, and blacksmiths; but nobody could ever tell him. ❧

In a thoughtful sonnet on his blindness, John Milton admonishes himself to exercise patience, to suffer long his particular infirmity.

SONNET XIX

When I consider how my light is spent,
Ere half my days, in this dark world and wide,
And that one Talent which is death to hide,
Lodg'd with me useless, though my Soul more bent
To serve therewith my Maker, and present
My true account, lest he returning chide;
"Doth God exact day-labor, light denied,"

I fondly ask; But Patience, to prevent
That murmur, soon replies: "God doth not need
Either man's work or his own gifts; who best
Bear his mild yoke, they serve him best; his State
Is Kingly. Thousands at his bidding speed
And post o'er Land and Ocean without rest:
They also serve who only stand and wait."

Anne Morrow Lindbergh tells of patience, her own needed exercise in stand-ing and waiting, that she learned from the sea.

FROM *GIFT FROM THE SEA*

The beach is not the place to work; to read, write or think. I should have remembered that from other years. Too warm, too damp, too soft for any real mental discipline or sharp flights of spirit. One never learns. Hopefully, one carries down the faded straw bag, lumpy with books, clean paper, long over-due unanswered letters, freshly sharpened pencils, lists, and good intentions. The books remain unread, the pencils break their points, and the pads rest smooth and unblemished as the cloudless sky. No reading, no writing, no thoughts, even—at least, not at first.

At first, the tired body takes over completely. As on shipboard, one descends into a deck-chair apathy. One is forced against one's mind, against all tidy resolutions, back into the primeval rhythms of the sea-shore. Rollers on the beach, wind in the pines, the slow flapping of herons across sand dunes, drown out the hectic rhythms of city and suburb, time tables and schedules. One falls under their spell, relaxes, stretches out prone. One becomes, in fact, like the element on which one lies, flattened by the sea; bare, open, empty as the beach, erased by today's tides of all yesterday's scribblings.

And then, some morning in the second week, the mind wakes, comes to life again. Not in a city sense—no—but beach-wise. It begins to drift, to play, to turn over in gentle careless rolls like those lazy waves on the beach. One never knows what chance treasures these easy unconscious rollers may toss up, on the smooth white sand of the conscious mind; what perfectly rounded stone, what rare shell from the ocean floor. Perhaps a channelled whelk, a moon shell, or even an argonaut.

But it must not be sought for or—heaven forbid!—dug for. No, no dredging of the sea-bottom here. That would defeat one's purpose. The sea does not reward those who are too anxious, too greedy, or too impatient. To dig for treasures shows not only impatience and greed, but lack of faith. Patience, patience, patience, is what the sea teaches. Patience and faith. One should lie empty, open, choiceless as a beach—waiting for a gift from the sea. . . .

One cannot collect all the beautiful shells on the beach. One can collect only a few, and they are more beautiful if they are few. One moon shell is more impressive than three. There is only one moon in the sky. One double-sunrise is an event; six are a succession, like a week of school-days. Gradually one discards and keeps just the perfect specimen; not necessarily a rare shell, but a perfect one of its kind. One sets it apart by itself, ringed around by space—like the island.

For it is only framed in space that beauty blooms. Only in space are events and objects and people unique and significant—and therefore beautiful. A tree has significance if one sees it against the empty face of sky. A note in music gains significance from the silences on either side. A candle flowers in the space of night. Even small and casual things take on significance if they are washed in space, like a few autumn grasses in one corner of an Oriental painting, the rest of the page bare.

My life in Connecticut, I begin to realize, lacks this quality of significance and therefore of beauty, because there is so little empty space. The space is scribbled on; the time has been filled. There are so few empty pages in my engagement pad, or empty hours in the day, or empty rooms in my life in which to stand alone and find myself. Too many activities, and people, and things. Too many worthy activities, valuable things, and interesting people. For it is not merely the trivial which clutters our lives but the important as well. We can have a surfeit of treasures—an excess of shells, where one or two would be significant. ❦

Patience with people, especially little people, is sometimes difficult to muster, as Louisa Lula Greene (Richards) discovered when she began teaching youngsters in her home in Smithfield, Utah. Her journal records the ups and downs of her pioneer educational efforts. The entry for May 31, 1867, reads:

Friday evening. My school is done for this week and I am not sorry for it. No for five days shut up in the house with a lot of little children that cannot keep quiet, is enough to weary the stoutest heart I think and make anyone feel thankful to be released for a couple of days and see the glorious Sabbath day approaching.

After exclaiming (in a June 11 entry) at "what trying things children are!" she takes herself to task for her impatience:

Oh hush, for shame Lula! They are children, have not the wisdom, reason, forethought, nay, nor pride they will have when they are older. Must I not bear with their failings even as I ask my Heavenly Father to bear with mine? I want to but it is hard, very hard to be always patient & forbearing! Is it not also grievous unto God to see the sins of the world? Oh! let me strive more dilligently to love & serve the Lord. ✦

Heber C. Kimball tells the following story:

My wife, one day, when going out on a visit, gave my daughter Helen Mar charge not to touch the dishes, for if she broke any during her absence she would give her a whipping when she returned. While my wife was absent, my daughter broke a number of dishes by letting the table leaf fall, and then she went out under an apple tree and prayed that her mother's heart might be softened, that when she returned she might not whip her. Her mother was very punctual, when she made a promise to her children, to fulfil it, and when she returned she undertook, as a duty, to carry this promise into effect. She retired with her into her room, but found herself powerless to chastise her; her heart was so softened that it was impossible for her to raise her hand against the child. Afterwards, Helen told her mother she had prayed to the Lord that she might not whip her. ✦

GRANDDAUGHTER

Next to tears for the supposed naughtiness
Of tipping oatmeal from her pastel bowl
And spilling milk under our haughtiness,
She displays the repentance of her soul

Over there. Her gaze is tenuous with sorrow
As she looks at the world, hoping for the best,
Arms folded to gather herself for the harrow
Of scolding. "Amen," she says in a tentative test

Of our love, grace over, but willing to pray.
I saw that the lip of her tray had tipped her bowl,
She not knowing why her oatmeal in disarray
Was so, but feeling the sackcloth of her role.

And there stand I as well with her as anywhere,
Marvelling how to keep some order at hand,
Displaying my hope glossily to keep fair
Days of charity flowing like hourglass sand.
(Clinton F. Larson.)

John Donne makes a rather formal declaration of the human sympathy that binds us all in Christ's pure love.

FROM "MEDITATION XVII"

All mankind is of one author, and is one volume; when one man dies, one chapter is not torn out of the book, but translated into a better language; and every chapter must be so translated. God employs several translators; some pieces are translated by age, some by sickness, some by war, some by justice; but God's hand is in every translation, and his hand shall bind up all our scattered leaves again for that library where every book shall lie open to another.

As therefore the bell that rings to a sermon calls not upon the preacher only but upon the congregation to come, so this bell calls us all; but how much more me who am brought so near the door by this sickness! There was a contention as far as a suit—in which piety and dignity, religion and estimation, were mingled—which of the religious orders should ring to prayers first in the morning; and it was determined that they should ring first that rose earliest. If we understood aright the dignity of this bell that tolls for our evening prayer, we would be glad to make it ours by rising early, in that application, that it might be ours as well as his, whose indeed it is.

The bell doth toll for him that thinks it doth; and though it intermit again, yet from that minute that that occasion wrought upon him he is united to God. Who casts not up his eye to the sun when it rises? but who takes off his eye for a comet when that breaks out? Who bends not his ear to any bell which upon any occasion rings? but who can remove it from that bell which is passing a piece of himself out of this world?

No man is an island entire of itself; every man is a piece of the continent, a part of the main. If a clod be washed away by the sea, Europe is the less, as well as if a promontory were, as well as if a manor of thy friend's or of thine own were. Any man's death diminishes me, because I am involved in mankind, and therefore never send to know for whom the bell tolls; it tolls for thee. ❧

The following observations by Albert Schweitzer demonstrate the close tie between forgiveness, the subject of this chapter, and kindness, the subject of the next. The application extends beyond these two, however, to the innate power of what Paul delineates as the several faces of charity.

FROM MEMOIRS OF CHILDHOOD

The most valuable knowledge we can have is how to deal with disappointments. All acts and facts are a product of spiritual power, the successful ones of power which is strong enough; the unsuccessful ones of power which is too weak. Does my behaviour in respect of love effect nothing? That is because there is not enough love in me. Am I powerless against the untruthfulness and the lies which have their being all around me? The reason is that I myself am not truthful enough. Have I to watch dislike and ill-will carrying on their sad game? That means that I myself have not yet completely laid aside small-mindedness and envy. Is my love of peace misunderstood and scorned? That means that I am not yet sufficiently peace-loving.

The great secret of success is to go through life as a man who never gets used up. That is possible for him who never argues and strives with men and facts, but in all experience retires upon himself, and looks for the ultimate cause of things in himself.

. . . At the present time when violence, clothed in life, dominates the world more cruelly than it ever has before, I still remain convinced that truth, love, peaceableness, meekness, and kindness are the violence which can master all other violence. The world will be theirs as soon as ever a sufficient number of men with purity of heart, with strength, and with perseverance think and live out the thoughts of love and truth, of meekness and peaceableness.

All ordinary violence produces its own limitations, for it calls forth an answering violence which sooner or later becomes its equal or its superior. But kindness works simply and perseveringly; it produces no strained relations which prejudice its working; strained relations which already exist it relaxes. Mistrust and misunderstanding it puts to flight, and it strengthens itself by calling forth answering kindness. Hence it is the furthest-reaching and most effective of all forces.

All the kindness which a man puts out into the world works on the heart and the thoughts of mankind, but we are so foolishly indifferent that we are never in earnest in the matter of kindness. We want to topple a great load over, and yet will not avail ourselves of a lever which would multiply our power a hundred-fold.

There is an unmeasured depth of truth in that strange saying of Jesus: "Blessed are the meek, for they shall inherit the earth" (St. Matt. v,5). ✦

2

CHARITY IS KIND

Minds . . . are not conquered by arms,

but by love and generosity.

BARUCH SPINOZA

*C*harity, the pure love of Christ, reaches far beyond what we normally think of as romantic love or affection. Love has to do with our emotional responses to each other, yes, but it has perhaps even more to do with how we treat each other and serve one another. As Paul has said, charity is kind. By definition, to be kind is to be thoughtful, gentle, and loving. The Prophet Joseph Smith consistently exemplified charity's loving kindness.

E. H. Nye, who was President of the California Mission of the Latter-day Saints Church in 1898, tells of meeting and spending an evening with an aged gentleman who was, as a boy, a stage-driver between Nauvoo and Keokuk, with Carthage as a half-way station. . . .

"This man," says Elder Nye, "[spoke of arriving] in Nauvoo at night, a stranger, about a year prior to the death of Joseph Smith, without money or friends, a boy of about fourteen years of age, having understood that his brother lived there. On inquiring for his brother, he learned that it was eight miles to his home, with snow on the ground, and very cold. The gentleman of whom he inquired, took him over to a large house that he thought was a hotel and told the man of the house the situation, who said, 'Come in, Son; we'll take care of you.'

"He was taken in, warmed, fed and lodged. The next day was bitter cold and the man of the house, who he learned was Joseph Smith, told him to content himself in peace; it was too cold for him to go out to his brother's place alone; some teams would be in from there and then he could go out. The boy said he had no money, but he was told not to worry about that; they would take care of him. After this incident he became well acquainted with Joseph Smith, who always called him 'Sonny.'" ✦

B. F. Grant, son of Jedediah M. Grant, tells of similar kindness extended to him by Brigham Young. As a youngster of fourteen or fifteen, newly arrived in Salt Lake City, he heard that President Young wanted to see him. B. F. Grant says he went to the prophet's office and introduced himself.

I told him who I was, and he did not merely reach out his hand to shake mine, but he arose from his chair and gave me a father's handshake. In so doing, he discovered that the callouses on my hands were hard and thick, and he remarked, "My boy, what kind of work are you doing?" I replied, "I am unloading coal and chopping wood."

He then resumed his seat and continued his inquiry regarding my past life and what I had been doing. He remarked, "Isn't it pretty heavy work, shoveling coal and chopping wood, for a boy of your age?"

I replied, "No, sir, I have been used to hard work all of my life."

He answered, "Wouldn't you like to have somethng easier than your present work, for instance, a position in a store?"

I replied, "I haven't got sense enough to work in a store."

He said, "What do you mean by that?"

I replied, "I can neither read nor write."

I discovered this good and great man's heart was touched by this remark; I saw tears rolling down his cheek, and he took his handkerchief and wiped them off and said, "My boy, come and live with me; I will give you a home; I will clothe you; I will send you to school; and you can work during the vacation for me."

I accepted his kind offer. He became a father to me. He furnished a home; he clothed me; and provided an opportunity for me to attend school. . . .

In addition to his large family at the time I was living with him, there were six orphaned boys and girls who were being cared for by him. I lived with one of his families and was treated most royally by all the members; in fact, I felt I was indeed a real member of the family so far as treatment was concerned. ✦

Describing events of his first mission, Wilford Woodruff tells of contrasting acts of unkindness and kindness.

FROM *LEAVES FROM MY JOURNAL*

In the southern portion of Missouri and the northern part of Arkansas, in 1834, there were but very few inhabitants.

We visited a place called Harmony Mission, on the Osage River, one of the most crooked rivers in the west. This mission was kept by a Presbyterian minister and his family.

We arrived there on Sunday night at sunset. We had walked all day with nothing to eat, and were very hungry and tired. Neither the minister nor his wife would give us anything to eat, nor let us stay over night, because we were "Mormons," and the only chance we had was to go twelve miles farther down the river, to an Osage Indian trading post, kept by a Frenchman named Jereu. And this wicked priest, who would not give us a piece of bread, lied to us about the road, and sent us across the swamp, and we wallowed knee deep in mud and water till ten o'clock at night in trying to follow this crooked river. We then left the swamp, and put out into the prairie, to lie in the grass for the night.

When we came out of the swamp, we heard an Indian drumming on a tin pail and singing. It was very dark, but we traveled towards the noise, and when we drew near the Indian camp quite a number of large Indian dogs came out to meet us. They smelt us, but did not bark nor bite.

We were soon surrounded by Osage Indians, and kindly received by Mr. Jereu and his wife, who was an Indian. She gave us an excellent supper and a good bed, which we were thankful for after the fatigue of the day.

As I laid my head on my pillow, I felt to thank God from the bottom of my heart, for the exchange of the barbarous treatment of a civilized

Presbyterian priest, for the humane, kind and generous treatment of the [so-called uncivilized] Osage Indians.

May God reward them both according to their deserts. ❦

For David O. McKay, the principle of kindness extended to all living creatures. The story is told that after valuable saddles were stolen from his saddle house in Huntsville, Utah, the house was thereafter kept locked.

FROM "KINDNESS TO ANIMALS"

One day, during hot weather, when members of the family were at home in Huntsville, two of President McKay's sisters were out for a drive and decided to check on things at the farm. They found the door to the saddle house locked, but one of the windows open. They immediately corrected what they felt was a bit of carelessness, and went on their way with a feeling of satisfaction that another theft had been averted.

That afternoon President McKay drove up to keep an appointment at Huntsville, with barely enough time to return to Salt Lake City for a later engagement. Upon being told of the open window, he said, "I left that window open purposely because there is a bird's nest inside, and that is the only entrance the parent birds have to carry food to their babies. I think I shall just have time to run over."

When the sisters said they would correct the mistake, he insisted on doing it, saying, "I must pick up a halter that needs repairing, anyway." When he returned to the house after the two-mile drive, he said in his gracious way, "It was just as I expected—one little bird was outside trying to get in, and the mother was inside attempting to get out."

His kindness to everyone and to everything has given him a benign demeanor that is one of his great characteristics. It has made him more like the One who "marks the sparrow's fall." ❦

Indeed, kindness and gentleness have a power all their own, as do human affection and caring. Love expressed for and by children strikes a resonant chord in all of us. Joseph Smith's tender regard for children is well documented. Margaret McIntyre Burgess tells these two stories from her childhood in Nauvoo.

My older brother and I were going to school, near to the building which was known as Joseph's brick store. It had been raining the previous day, causing the ground to be very muddy, especially along that street. My brother Wallace and I both got fast in the mud and could not get out, and, of course, child-like, we began to cry, for we thought we would have to stay there. But looking up, I beheld the loving friend of children, the Prophet Joseph coming to us. He soon had us on high and dry ground. Then he stooped down and cleaned the mud from our little heavy-laden shoes, took his handkerchief from his pocket and wiped our tear-stained faces. He spoke kind and cheering words to us and sent us on our way to school rejoicing. ✦

Joseph's wife, Emma, had lost a young babe. My mother had twin baby girls, the Prophet came to see if she would let him [borrow] one of them. Of course it was rather against her feelings, but she finally consented for him to take one of them, providing he would bring it home each night. This he did punctually himself and also came after it each morning.

One evening he did not come with it at the usual time and mother went down to the Mansion to see what was the matter; and there sat the Prophet with the baby wrapped up in a little silk quilt. He was trotting it on his knee and singing to it to get it quiet before starting out, as it had been fretting. The child soon became quiet, when my mother took it and the Prophet came up home with her.

Next morning when he came after the baby, Mother handed him Sarah, the other baby. They looked so much alike that strangers could not tell them apart; but as Mother passed him the other baby he shook his head and said, "This is not my little Mary." Then she took Mary from the cradle and gave her to him and he smilingly carried her home with him. . . . After his wife became better in health, he did not take our baby away any more, but often came in to caress her and play with her. ✦

A friend of pioneer Briant Stringham wrote of the man's singular delight in children. Leonard Arrington describes him as "'practically religious,' generous in his secret donations to the poor, and preferring the society of children to adults."

30

I have seen him caring for a sick child in his arms, as tender and careful as a mother could be. He made the remark that he would like a piece of land—I have forgotten the number of acres it would contain—but he wanted it full of babies and he would lie down while they rolled and tumbled over him. ❧

THE CHILDREN'S HOUR

Between the dark and the daylight,
When the night is beginning to lower,
Comes a pause in the day's occupations,
That is known as the Children's Hour.

I hear in the chamber above me
The patter of little feet,
The sound of a door that is opened,
And voices soft and sweet.

From my study I see in the lamplight,
Descending the broad hall stair,
Grave Alice, and laughing Allegra,
And Edith with golden hair.

A whisper, and then a silence:
Yet I know by their merry eyes
They are plotting and planning together
To take me by surprise.

A sudden rush from the stairway,
A sudden raid from the hall!
By three doors left unguarded
They enter my castle wall!

They climb up into my turret
O'er the arms and back of my chair;
If I try to escape, they surround me;
They seem to be everywhere.

They almost devour me with kisses,
  Their arms about me entwine,
Till I think of the Bishop of Bingen
  In his Mouse-Tower on the Rhine!

Do you think, O blue-eyed banditti,
  Because you have scaled the wall,
Such an old mustache as I am
  Is not a match for you all!

I have you fast in my fortress,
  And will not let you depart,
But put you down into the dungeon
  In the round-tower of my heart.

And there I will keep you forever,
  Yes, forever and a day,
Till the walls shall crumble to ruin,
  And moulder in dust away!
  (Henry Wadsworth Longfellow.)

One of my favorite verses from childhood captures the sweet relationship that can flourish between loving parent and child. It appeared in the old book of Deseret Sunday School Songs, *used for many years as the LDS hymnbook, although designated on its title page particularly "For the use of Sunday Schools and Suitable for Primary Associations, Religion Classes, Quorum Meetings, Social Gatherings and the Home."*

Oh, I had such a pretty dream, mamma,
  Such pleasant and beautiful things;
Of a dear little nest, in the meadows of rest,
  Where the birdie her lullaby sings.

A dear little stream full of lilies
  Crept over the green mossy stones,
And just where I lay, its thin sparkling spray
  Sang sweetly in delicate tones.

And as it flowed on toward the ocean,
Thro' shadows and pretty sunbeams,
Each note grew more deep, and I soon fell asleep,
And was off to the Island of Dreams.

I saw there a beautiful angel,
With crown all bespangled with dew:
She touched me and spoke, and I quickly awoke:
And found there, dear mamma, 'twas you.
(J. S. Lewis.)

I note that in the 1909 edition, awarded to my mother, Rhoda Clark Arnold, August 21, 1931, by the "Lehi [Utah] Fourth Ward Sunday School Officers and Teachers for her Faithful Service," the following statement is published in both front and back covers. Happily, its message fits well among illustrations of kindness and gentleness.

I AM A
Sunday School Song Book
I was made to be *Used*,
Not to be *Abused!*

Before I am used, I should be gently laid upon a table with my cover laid out flat. My leaves should be held upright, then laid out one at a time, first from the front, then from the back, then firmly but gently stroked with thumb or finger. This will help to take the stiffness out of my back.

After this is done I should be gently handled. If my sides are forced back too far, my back will be broken, and I'll soon become an unsightly—useless bunch of leaves.

Treat me kindly and I'll stay with you.

I am a Song Book. I was made for the use of the Sunday School.

I am full of tender melodies and I cannot stand abuse or rough handling.

If tenderly and carefully handled I will stay together and help you for a long time. ✦

Many of those lines can be taken individually and applied to people as well as to books.

Early Christian writer Ignatius advised his devout colleague, Polycarp, by letter not to spend "all your affection on the cream of your pupils. Try rather to bring the more troublesome ones to order, by using gentleness. Nobody can heal every wound with the same unguent; where there are acute spasms of pain, we have to apply soothing poultices."

Emma Ray Riggs McKay, wife of David O. McKay, confirms what Polycarp advised.

FROM *THE ART OF*

REARING CHILDREN PEACEFULLY

Children respond favorably to praise. Let me give you an example. The first and only year I taught school, the principal came into my room the first day, which was midyear, and, pointing out a child twelve years of age, he said, before the whole roomful of pupils, "You'll have to watch out for that boy; he is the worst boy in school. He drove Miss B. away by throwing a bottle of ink at her."

What a blow for the boy, and for me, too! I thought, "Now Earl will show me that that record is true by being his worst. I'll try to nip it in the bud."

I wrote a little note, saying, "Earl, I think the principal was mistaken about your being a bad boy. I trust you and know you are going to help me make this room the best in school." As I walked down the aisle I slipped it to him without anyone's noticing. I saw his face light up, and afterwards his mother told me that he brought the note home and said in an excited tone, "Read this, Mother, but don't destroy it, for I want to wear it next to my heart." He was one of my best behaved boys the remainder of the year. Praise brings good results, not cruel criticism nor abuse. ✦

In the second of six "nonlectures" delivered by invitation at Harvard University (the Charles Eliot Norton lectures) in the early 1950s, poet e e cummings speaks of two of his early teachers who knew eminently well how to reach youngsters, "a Miss Maria Baldwin and a Mr. Cecil Derry":

Miss Baldwin . . . was blessed with a delicious voice, charming manners, and a deep understanding of children. Never did any demidivine dictator more gracefully and easily rule a more unruly and less graceful populace. Her very presence emanated an honour and a glory: the honour of spiritual freedom—no mere freedom from—and the glory of being, not (like most extant mortals) really undead, but actually alive. From her I marvellingly learned that the truest power is gentleness. Concerning Mr. Derry, let me say only that he was (and for me will always remain) one of those blessing and blessed spirits who deserve the name of teacher: predicates who are utterly in love with their subject; and who, because they would gladly die for it, are living for it gladly. From him I learned (and am still learning) that gladness is next to godliness. ◆

THE WIND AND THE SUN

A dispute once arose between the Wind and the Sun, which was the stronger of the two, and they agreed to put the point upon this issue, that whichever soonest made a traveller take off his cloak, should be accounted the more powerful. The Wind began, and blew with all his might and main a blast, cold and fierce as a Thracian storm; but the stronger he blew the closer the traveller wrapped his cloak around him, and the tighter he grasped it with his hands. Then broke out the Sun: with his welcome beams he dispersed the vapor and the cold; the traveller felt the genial warmth, and as the Sun shone brighter and brighter, he sat down, overcome with the heat, and cast his cloak on the ground.

Thus the Sun was declared the conqueror; and it has ever been deemed that persuasion is better than force; and that the sunshine of a kind and gentle manner will sooner lay open a poor man's heart than all the threatenings and force of blustering authority. (Aesop.) ◆

One poet has penned a delightful defense of kindness to frogs.

THE FROG

Be kind and tender to the Frog,
And do not call him names,
As "Slimy Skin," or "Polly-wog,"
Or likewise, "Ugly James,"
Or "Gap-a-grin," or "Toad-gone-wrong,"
Or "Bill Bandy-knees";
The Frog is justly sensitive
To epithets like these.
No animal will more repay
A treatment kind and fair,
At least so lonely people say
Who keep a frog (and, by the way,
They are extremely rare).
(Hilaire Belloc.)

Literary examples of enduring human love, whether romantic, platonic, or familial, are legion. And in some of them, such as the following, charity plays a large role. This funny and touching story of a day in the life of a Latter-day Saint mission president's wife captures the essence of conjugal love, but in doing so, Arta Romney Ballif focuses not on the "newlyweds" of her tale, but on the old hands, Arta and her husband, Ariel.

A WEDDING NIGHT

The long white cloud had been swelling all day. Toward evening it grew dark and burst. Rain poured on the roof of the mission home. I was alone when the telephone jangled. I looked at the clock. Seven-thirty P.M. Two more rings, long and even in length. Brrrr-brrrr. I set the milk on the table and turned the stove unit off. I hate being dictated to by a mechanical gadget. I took the butter from the refrigerator and set it on the table just to prove that I was my own boss. Brrrr-brrrr. Now answer it.

"Where have you been? Is dinner ready?" asked my husband, the dear *Tumuaki* (President), from his office downtown.

"Of course, two hours ago."

"I have to perform a marriage before eight o'clock."

"When will you be home for dinner?"

"The wedding will be at the mission home," he said.

"Here?"

"That's right. You'll have to be a witness."

"But the house is in a clutter. I've been sewing, and Bonnie's gone to a practice, and it's seven-thirty—"

"Fine. That will give me twenty minutes to get home and ten minutes to perform the ceremony before eight o'clock. The front door must be left open. That's the law. If the couple arrives, tell them I'm on my way."

I set the milk and butter in the refrigerator, left the meat in the oven. Potatoes? We always ate soggy potatoes and over-cooked vegetables. I frantically picked up pins, ravelings, scraps, patterns from floor, table, machine, chairs. I dropped the scissors, jabbing my big toe, the one with the split toenail. Blood oozed out from between the crack; pain rushed up my leg.

Brrrr. Let it ring. Put away the ironing board. Brrrr. Close the machine. Keep calm. Pick up fashion magazines. Brrrr-brrrr. All right. What do you want? "Hello."

"Mama, I can't come home until ten o'clock. Okay?"

"Okay."

Push the vacuum over the floor quickly. What's the terrible smell? You didn't turn the stove off under the carrots. Burnt black. What a smudge and the pan is ruined. Never mind, throw it outside. Why does the screen door stick? Kick it. Again, harder.

"Good evening, Mrs. Ballif, hasn't it been a lovely day today?" I was trapped. Remember who you are, a Mormon Mission President's wife, and the neighbors do not like Mormons. Keep calm and remember. The woman sat on steps over the low brick wall talking baby talk to her cat.

"As I was saying to my 'ittle pussy, isn't it a night? Well, you know how it is on days like this, I love to—I just can't settle to anything. First it rains, then it shines. Funny, isn't it? Well, I think, really, I do think, I—I forgot what I was going to think."

"I burnt the carrots," I said.

"Doesn't it make a smell, though? When you burn something, I mean. Oh, yes, I was going to say that my husband is very hard to cook for. I never can—You know, it looks like it is going to rain, doesn't it? I wish it wouldn't rain tonight. It has been raining all week and pussy gets so wet. Did you ever see a day like this? My, but it does get wet, doesn't it? Do you think it will rain?"

"Yes, I think it will rain," I said, dropping the carrots and saucepan into the garbage bucket. "It's raining now."

"When I burn something, I always—I mean. Oh, my pussy is so naughty. I'm sure it is going to rain. Would you believe I had to dry my clothes in—You can hardly get your clothes dry, can you? I mean, on days like this."

The stench of burnt carrots permeated every room. What to do? Light a match, that will take the odor away. Yes. Where are the matches? On the shelf above the stove. Not there. Where? On the mantel. But I never put them on the mantel. Look, anyway. No, I knew they wouldn't be there. Downstairs? No time to go downstairs. You have to go outside and around the house to get downstairs, and you'll meet Mrs. Danzy again. But the house does stink. And a wedding, too. Whose? Should be nice, no matter. Nicest time of their lives. Mine was lovely. No rain. But I was scared—Better get the matches. What a downpour. Pussy must be wet.

Oh, oh! I knew there was a step. My ankle. Oh, oh. Must be broken. Can't be. Get that match. Hop. Hurry.

"Have they come yet?" *Tumuaki* was home pushing open the front door, calling loudly. "Where are you? Mama? What's the smell?"

The basement was dark. The one electric bulb would not give light. My fingers felt the dusty shelf. Hammer, saw, wrench, spiders, slivers, ouch! No matches. Forget the awful odor. Get upstairs and feed your excited husband.

He greeted me with, "Haven't they come yet? It's ten to eight. Get ready. What's the matter? Why aren't you dressed? The ceremony has to be performed before eight o'clock. The law. Ten to, now. Hope they won't miss it this time." He munched a piece of dry meat and gulped a glass of milk.

"Who is it?" I asked from halfway up the upper stairs on the way to the bedroom.

"That Maori couple I've been working with. You know."

"Yes, sure, I know, that's why I asked. Which one?"

"That old couple. I've been trying to get them legally married for a long time. Of course they were married Maori fashion twenty years ago. They have eight children, you know." His mouth was full of half-chewed steak.

"Yes. Which one?"

"Daughter named Wairoa and little boy who quit school. Wonder where they are."

I couldn't pull my dress over my head because I had it on backwards and the arms wouldn't go in the sleeves. "What time is it?" I screeched from under the tent.

"Seven minutes to. Can't you hurry? What's taking you so long? They were to have been married Saturday, you know."

"No, I didn't know." My head was again under the dress, this time front side front and back side back.

"I told you," he said.

"Did you?"

"Huh?"

"I said, 'Did you.' I don't remember."

"Did I what? Here they are. Come quickly. Five minutes to go."

Never mind the comb, let your hair straggle. Five minutes. Five minutes and the dear *Tumuaki* is in a hurry. Five minutes and the couple must be married or they will lose their home and property. It's the law. Five minutes and the bride and groom have eight children and six *mokopunas*. Five crucial minutes. Get downstairs.

The bride was happy in a pink lace dress. Her husband-to-be beamed ecstatically.

"Take each other by the right hand," said *Tumuaki*. "Do you take this woman—"

A fumbling for the ring. A struggle with gloves, crocheted, that stuck to rough fingers.

"You may now kiss each other as man and wife."

The clock struck eight. Rain, driven by a south wind, drenched the carpet in the hall. The law had been fulfilled.

Man and wife giggled. Their daughter kissed them and wiped her tears on her mother's cheek. The fragile threads of the bridemother's dress stretched over her sturdy form and pulled at the seams. The groom smiled mischievously at his wife's I've-got-you-at-last look, and the daughter said, "Finally. I am so happy."

Tumuaki was pleased. To him the five-minute climax was worth a year and a half of work. "Now," he said, "while you sign the papers and I give you suggestions on how to have a successful married life, my wife will prepare the wedding breakfast. You must have a wedding breakfast."

Ah, the dear, dear *Tumuaki*.

I went into the kitchen, shut the door, leaned against the frame, and meditated on how to have a successful marriage and also a wedding breakfast.

The one piece of steak was hard. In watered soup it would not be a bite around. The pint bottle was half full of milk. And vegetables? In the garbage bucket, remember? The three potatoes and I were very sad.

"Hurry it up, dear. Anything will do. They have to catch a bus. Their boy is waiting for them." The voice of authority did not squeeze through the keyhole; it boomed through the wood panel of the door and shook me from the casing. "Fix anything, but hurry."

I bit off the end of one of the uncurled hairs that fell across my face.

Only last Sunday, *Tumuaki* had given a beautiful sermon about the loaves and fishes. "Jesus did not say to the disciples, 'How many people are there to feed?' He said, 'How many loaves and fishes are there?' and then proceeded with what He had, and so fed the multitude. Don't ever look at the size of the task," *Tumuaki* had applied the story and explained the meaning. "Count the resources and go immediately to do the job with what you have. Don't count the multitude, count the loaves and fishes." I had believed every word of the talk, and had fully intended to put it into practice from last Sunday on and forever after. If only I had five loaves and two fishes to count.

"Need some help in there?" called *Tumuaki.*

"Coming."

No fishes. Bread? One half loaf. Should always be prepared for wedding breakfasts. Three potatoes. Fry them. Butter? Yes. Cheese? Two ounces. Melted cheese on browned slices of potatoes on small pieces of toast, and— water milo drink. Good. "Coming right in."

Successful marriage and wedding breakfast on same trying evening? Yes.

"We haven't eaten a thing all day," said the fifty-two-year-old bride. "We were so excited." She finished the last cheese toast.

"Fill up the plate," said the dear *Tumuaki,* old Mr. Magnanimous himself. "Fill up the plate. They're hungry."

I closed the door between the kitchen and the dining room, opened the outside door, and stood there. Rain washed my face and cooled my temper. What to do? No cheese, no potatoes. Cinnamon and sugar on toast. Cut it thin. Inch squares. Ah-h. More water in milo. Icing sugar balls. Coconut? Yes. Roll them quickly.

The son-in-law with the bow tie dancing over his lumpy neck lifted the last lolly from the plate and laughed noisily. "No one afraid of being an old maid in this crowd," he said. "Cinnamon and sugar is it? An American idea. And beautiful."

"Don't be so stingy, my dear. These poor people haven't had a thing to eat all day."

I started for the kitchen door. At that instant I remembered the chapter in the *Odyssey* about black looks. I turned and faced the *Tumuaki.* He avoided my gaze. But I waited. When his eyes met mine, I gave him an exceedingly black look. He got the hint and jiggled his knee. Then in a placative tone he said, "We're not fussy, dear. Anything will do. Open a can of fruit."

And that is exactly what I did. I opened a can of fruit, cling peaches from Hawkes Bay. Let them finish them off in one swallow if they can. They couldn't. They tried, but could not cut the fruit from the stones. Chewing it off stopped all conversation.

They arose to go. We followed them to the door. *Tumuaki* smiled and called after them, "Now remember, you have to feed love to keep it alive. Be frank with each other. No secrets. Spend time with each other. Goodbye. We'll see you both in church." They were gone.

Tumuaki turned to me. "Have to go back to the office tonight. Must make up for the time lost at the wedding. Couple coming to see me. They have a real problem. I may be late getting home. Don't wait up for me." He kissed me and went out of the door.

Fifteen minutes to nine. One hour and fifteen minutes since he first called. So, they have a real problem, this couple coming to see him. He most certainly will be late getting home. I shall take a book, after washing the dishes, and he shall find me as usual, under the lamp reading, whether he comes at twelve midnight or two A.M. This was to have been our evening together, because thirty-three years ago this day, at high noon, we had been married.

And I would not, I would not have cleaned the living room. I would not have stood as witness. I would not have prepared the wedding breakfast, nor would I wait up for him, if he had not so many times before as he did that night, pushed the hair from my forehead with his big gentle hands when he kissed me goodbye, and afterward held my face for an extra shadow of a minute. ❧

SONNET 43

How do I love thee? Let me count the ways.
I love thee to the depth and breadth and height
My soul can reach, when feeling out of sight
For the ends of being and ideal grace.
I love thee to the level of every day's
Most quiet need, by sun and candle-light.
I love thee freely, as men strive for right;
I love thee purely, as they turn from praise;

I love thee with the passion put to use
In my old griefs, and with my childhood's faith.
I love thee with a love I seemed to lose
With my lost saints.—I love thee with the breath,
Smiles, tears, of all my life!—and if God choose,
I shall but love thee better after death.
(Elizabeth Barrett Browning.)

I know of no acquaintance over fifty who did not learn the following poem in grade school. My personal affection for Abou (and for his exotic name) was such that I was sure the angel mistreated him on the first visit. Our affection for the poem, however, should not cloud our judgment, for the poem's "doctrine" is flawed. We know that Abou, and all of us, are required to love both the Lord and our fellow mortals.

ABOU BEN ADHEM

Abou Ben Adhem (may his tribe increase!)
Awoke one night from a deep dream of peace,
And saw, within the moonlight in his room,
Making it rich, and like a lily in bloom,
An angel writing in a book of gold:—
Exceeding peace had made Ben Adhem bold,
And to the presence in the room he said,
"What writest thou?"—The vision rais'd its head,
And with a look made of all sweet accord,
Answer'd, "The names of those who love the Lord."
"And is mine one?" said Abou. "Nay, not so,"
Replied the angel. Abou spoke more low,
But cheerily still; and said, "I pray thee then,
Write me as one that loves his fellow men."
The angel wrote, and vanish'd. The next night
It came again with a great wakening light,
And show'd the names whom love of God had bless'd,
And lo! Ben Adhem's name led all the rest.
(Leigh Hunt.)

Louise Lake, a beacon of courage and faith to many of my parents' and suc-
ceeding generations, was stricken in her prime with a severe case of polio. It was in
the days of "iron lungs" and before the days of polio vaccines. She writes of one
night in particular. Fading in and out of consciousness, aching to turn in her hos-
pital bed, immobilized by a collapsed lung and paralyzed arms and legs, and
wracked with fever and consumed by thirst, she at last "cried out for help."

FROM *EACH DAY A BONUS*

A nurse who was not afraid of isolation opened the screened-off area. As she came swiftly to the foot of my bed, I noted the white cap and white gauze mask on her shining black face. Feebly I mumbled some distress, and as if she had heard exact instructions, she took my left heel in one hand and placed her other hand under my left knee. Slowly and gently she raised the leg from the frozen position it had been in for hours. There was some immediate relief. I hadn't known what to tell her to do for my comfort. Was she intuitive or knowledgeable? Anyway, she sensed my gratitude. She then quickly and silently passed to the opposite side of my bed, where she repeated this gesture of love with the other leg. I sighed warmly my appreciation to her. Then I said, "I feel so alone and in need of God's help. Will you pray with me?"

She at once stepped to the door and closed it tightly. Though she was risking her career, she came back to my side, dropped the isolation mask from her face, and took off her gloves. Taking my two helpless hands in her strong black hands, she lowered her head in reverence and said, "You'll have to pray—I can't."

Not the words, but only the feelings of my heart do I remember in that brief prayer when I sought for strength to endure. I thanked my Heavenly Father for the relief that had come in those moments of distress and for that nurse who had come like an angel to assist me. When I opened my eyes and looked up at her, tears were coursing down her face. Before she let go of my hands she looked into my face, also flooded with tears, and said, "I would give anything and have no fears if I knew God like that and could pray to him that way."

After that she slipped into my room many times to manipulate my legs and change their position. I never learned her name. Many times since I have wished that I could find her. Only God, that nurse, and I knew those cherished moments together that brought comfort and relief. ❦

Albert Schweitzer exhibited the kindness of "mourning with those who mourn":

On a stone on the river bank an old woman whose son had been taken sat weeping silently. I took hold of her hand and wanted to comfort her, but she went on crying as if she did not hear me. Suddenly I felt that I was crying with her, silently, towards the setting sun, as she was. ❦

In the following story, Pablo Neruda expands upon the connectedness created by kind acts.

FROM "CHILDHOOD AND POETRY"

One time, investigating in the backyard of our house in Temuco the tiny objects and miniscule beings of my world, I came upon a hole in one of the boards of the fence. I looked through the hole and saw a landscape like that behind our house, uncared for, and wild. I moved back a few steps, because I sensed vaguely that something was about to happen. All of a sudden a hand appeared—a tiny hand of a boy about my own age. By the time I came close again, the hand was gone, and in its place there was a marvelous white sheep.

The sheep's wool was faded. Its wheels had escaped. All of this only made it more authentic. I had never seen such a wonderful sheep. I looked back through the hole but the boy had disappeared. I went into the house and brought out a treasure of my own: a pinecone, opened, full of odor and resin, which I adored. I set it down in the same spot and went off with the sheep.

I never saw either the hand or the boy again. And I have never again seen a sheep like that either. The toy I lost finally in a fire. But even now, in 1954, almost fifty years old, whenever I pass a toy shop, I look furtively into the window, but it's no use. They don't make sheep like that any more.

I have been a lucky man. To feel the intimacy of brothers is a marvelous thing in life. To feel the love of people whom we love is a fire that feeds our life. But to feel the affection that comes from those whom we do not know, from those unknown to us, who are watching over our sleep and solitude, over our dangers and our weaknesses—that is something still greater and more beautiful because it widens out the boundaries of our being, and unites all living things.

That exchange brought home to me for the first time a precious idea: that all of humanity is somehow together. That experience came to me again much later; this time it stood out strikingly against a background of trouble and persecution.

It won't surprise you then that I attempted to give something resiny, earthlike, and fragrant in exchange for human brotherhood. Just as I once left the pinecone by the fence, I have since left my words on the door of so many people who were unknown to me, people in prison, or hunted, or alone.

That is the great lesson I learned in my childhood, in the backyard of a lonely house. Maybe it was nothing but a game two boys played who didn't know each other and wanted to pass to the other some good things of life. Yet maybe this small and mysterious exchange of gifts remained inside me also, deep and indestructible, giving my poetry light. ✦

According to Brigham Young:

A man or woman who has embraced, and who enjoys, the principles of this Church, ought to live like an angel. They ought never to be angry with each other, but live in the light of the truth continually, and every man be kind to his neighbor. (*Journal of Discourses* 1:245.) ✦

PSALM OF GRATITUDE AND SERVICE

With what coin shall I repay my eternal Father
for the gifts He hath bestowed upon me?
How shall my gratitude be made manifest and acceptable?
My payment shall not be in measure harsh and cold, the

clink and chill of mineral,
but in warmth and kindness shall I honor my Creator,
in loving-kindness, as did the Son of Man, to all
who stand in need of strength to heart and limb.
May I, as He, serve all who daily walk with heavy loads—
those who hunger and thirst for warm words and small
kindnesses.
So may my debt of mortal and immortal life be marked
in columns paid,
to serve His children.
Thus, daily succor to them doth bring eternal praise
to Him
and peace of soul to me.
(Janell R. Arrington.)

"I'VE COME TO CLEAN YOUR SHOES"

Still in shock, I stumbled about the house trying to decide what to put into the suitcases. Earlier that evening I'd received a call from my hometown in Missouri telling me that my brother and his wife, her sister and both the sister's children had been killed in a car crash. "Come as soon as you can," begged my mother.

That's what I wanted to do—to leave at once, to hurry to my parents. But my husband, Larry, and I were in the midst of packing all our belongings to move from Ohio to New Mexico. Our house was in total confusion. . . . Supper dishes still sat on the kitchen table. Toys were strewn everywhere.

While Larry made plane reservations for the following morning, I wandered about the house, aimlessly picking things up and putting them down. I couldn't focus. Again and again, the words I'd heard on the phone echoed through my head: "Bill is gone—Marilyn too. June—and both the children. . . ."

It was as though the message had mottled my brain with cotton.

Whenever Larry spoke, he sounded far away. As I moved through the house, I ran into doors and tripped over chairs.

Larry made arrangements for us to leave by seven o'clock the next morning. Then he phoned a few friends to tell them what had happened. Occasionally, someone asked to speak to me. "If there's anything I can do, let me know," that person would offer kindly.

"Thank you very much," I'd reply. But I didn't know what to ask for. I couldn't concentrate.

I sat in a chair, staring into space, while Larry called Donna King, the woman with whom I taught a nursery class at church each Sunday. Donna and I were casual friends, but we didn't see each other often. She and Emerson, her thin, quiet husband, were kept busy during the weekdays by their own "nursery"—six children ranging in age from two years to fifteen. I was glad Larry had thought to warn her that she'd have the nursery class alone the coming Sunday.

While I sat there, [my little daughter] Meghan darted by, clutching a ball. [Her brother] Eric chased after her. *They should be in bed,* I thought. I followed them into the living room. My legs dragged. My hands felt gloved with lead. I sank down on the couch in a stupor.

When the doorbell rang, I rose slowly and crept across the room. I opened the door to see Emerson King standing on the porch.

"I've come to clean your shoes," he said.

Confused, I asked him to repeat.

"Donna had to stay with the baby," he said, "but we want to help you. I remember when my father died, it took me hours to get the children's shoes cleaned and shined for the funeral. So that's what I've come to do for you. Give me all your shoes—not just your good shoes, but *all* your shoes."

I hadn't even thought about shoes until he mentioned them. . . .

While Emerson spread newspapers on the kitchen floor, I gathered . . . shoes. . . .

Emerson settled himself on the floor and got to work. Watching him concentrate intently on one task helped me pull my own thoughts into order. *Laundry first,* I told myself. While the washer chugged, Larry and I bathed the children and put them to bed.

While we cleared the supper dishes, Emerson continued to work, saying nothing. I thought of Jesus washing the feet of his disciples. Our Lord had knelt, serving his friends, even as this man now knelt, serving us. The love in that act released my tears at last, healing rain to wash the fog from my mind. I could move. I could think. I could get on with the business of living.

One by one, the jobs fell into place. I went into the laundry room to put a load of wash into the dryer, returning to the kitchen to find that Emerson had left. In a line against the wall stood all our shoes, gleaming, spotless. Later, when I started to pack, I saw that Emerson had even scrubbed the soles. I could put the shoes directly into the suitcases.

We got to bed late and rose very early, but by the time we left for the airport, all the jobs were done. Ahead lay grim, sad days, but the comfort of Christ's presence, symbolized by the image of a quiet man kneeling on my kitchen floor with a pan of water, would sustain me.

Now, whenever I hear of an acquaintance who has lost a loved one, I no longer call with the vague offer, "If there's anything I can do. . . ." Now I try to think of one specific task that suits that person's need—such as washing the family car, taking their dog to the boarding kennel, or house-sitting during the funeral. And if the person says to me, "How did you know I needed that done?" I reply, "It's because a man once cleaned my shoes." (Madge Harrah.) ❧

Elder Stayner Richards related the following story:

Our missionaries entered upon a program for six months of preaching love and kindness. Let me tell you how it worked with one of the missionaries. He was on a street meeting corner in Leeds and as he stood up, one of the hecklers gave him one of the worst lashings of invectives that any man could receive. He tore him down and tore the religion down.

What did this elder do? He lived what he had been preaching. He stepped down, walked over to the gentleman and said, "You have given me an awful calling down today. Possibly it is all right. I just want you to know that I hold nothing against you for it, that I love you, brother, and I would like to shake your hand." Then he went back to the stand.

A young woman was heard to comment to another, "I didn't know that anything like that could happen outside of the New Testament." ❧

From the teachings of Gautama Buddha, we read:

If a man foolishly does me wrong, I will return to him the protection of my ungrudging love; the more evil comes from him, the more good shall go from me; the fragrance of goodness always comes to me and the harmful air of evil goes to him. ❧

Everyday living can put a great strain on relationships unless we consciously cultivate gentleness in ourselves and exercise kindness toward others. One of love's dearest manifestations is friendship, for it is capable of bridging every barrier imaginable—chronological, geographical, racial, political, you name it. Many a tender expression of thoughtfulness in friendship has been and will yet be penned. The devotion of dear friends is mentioned in the Bible, especially in the story of Ruth and Naomi and that of Jonathan and David. Following is a similar tale of another famous friendship.

DAMON AND PYTHIAS

Dionysius was a tyrant who ruled the town of Syracuse, in Sicily. Whoever made him angry was put to death. The tyrant's wrath fell one day upon a youth named Damon, who had complained of the cruelty of Dionysius, and Damon was condemned to die. He begged first to be allowed to go to see his wife and children, but Dionysius laughed him to scorn. "Once you get out of my way," he thought, "you will never come back."

Damon said that he had a friend who would answer for his return, and his friend Pythias came forward to offer himself as surety in his friend's place.

The tyrant was astonished that a man should love his friend so dearly, and he gave Damon six hours to go to see his wife and children.

Damon expected to be back within four hours, but when four hours had gone he had not come. Five hours, then almost six hours passed, and still there was no sign of him. The happiest man in the prison was Pythias, who actually hoped that Damon would not return, because he was willing and anxious to suffer in his place and spare his friend for the sake of his wife and children. At last the death-day dawned, the very hour drew nigh, and Dionysius came to see his prisoner die.

Quietly and bravely, Pythias prepared for his execution. His friend, he said, had had an accident, or perhaps he was ill. At almost the very moment for the execution, however, Damon arrived and embraced his friend. He was tired and travel-stained. His horse had been killed, and he had had to get another, but by hard riding he returned just in time to save Pythias from suffering for him. But Pythias did not wish it so. He pleaded with Damon, he pleaded with Dionysius, to let him bear the punishment.

Dionysius had never seen such faithfulness before. Here was something beautiful that he did not think existed in the world—a friendship that welcomed death if death would help a friend. His heart was stirred within him; he wanted men like these to be his friends. He came up to Damon and Pythias as they were disputing, each eager to give up his life for the other. Dionysius took their hands, set them free, and begged to be allowed to share their friendship. ❦

Greater love hath no man than this, that a man lay down his life for his friends. (John 15:13.) ❦

THE BROTHERS

JUNE 24, 1844

Where are you riding,
 Joseph Smith?
The horse walks slowly
 Past the city,
Past the temple on the hill:
I ride toward Carthage town,
 To keep a rendezvous,
 A date with destiny.

And if I meet it well,
My people will not call
Me coward ever more.
And like a lamb I go—
The slaughter waits.

. . . .

I ride with Hyrum by my side.
He will not leave.
We've lived our lives,
Flesh of the same flesh,
Born of the same womb.
He has been unfaltering;
His love, no one can
Measure of its depth.
I would that he would
Stay and let me
Face this Gethsemane
Alone, stay and guide
The church on its next
Pilgrimage, for it has
Trials to face.
Its place
Is in the West.

. . . .

But Hyrum rides with me.
His loyalty transcends,
Exalts, the common blood
We share.
There is his heart,
A gentle heart. It beats
With great compassion
For the weak.
Remember Orson Hyde.

Hyrum pled his cause,
Reminded me of what
It means to be forgiven
After true repentance.
And there are others too,
Too many to remember now.
He truly lives the law of God:
I the Lord will forgive whom I will forgive,
But of you it is required to forgive all men.
He is not sure, not yet,
Of what we face, as I am sure,
And that is best.
Why don't I send him back?
Command in God's own name?
He might obey me and find rest,
Safe rest,
Among the saints.
But no, we're bound
Together now with bands
Like steel:
The bands of love,
The bands of blood,
The bands of waking and of
Sleeping,
The bands of sorrow and of
Weeping,
The bands of happiness and joy.
He stays with me, though he
Is free
To go,
And he will be with me
Eternally.
(S. Dilworth Young.)

Teach [your children] to love one another, and to serve one another. (Mosiah 4:15.) ❧

TO A FRIEND GOING ON A JOURNEY

Now you depart, and though your way may lead
Through airless forests thick with *hhagar* trees,
Places steeped in heat, stifling and dry,
Where breath comes hard, and no fresh breeze can reach—
Yet may God place a shield of coolest air
Between your body and the assailant sun.
And in a random scorching flame of wind
That parches the painful throat, and sears the flesh,
May God, in His compassion, let you find
The great-boughed tree that will protect and shade.
On every side of you, I now would place
Prayers from the Holy Koran, to bless your path,
That ills may not descend, nor evils harm,
And you may travel in the peace of faith.
To all the blessings I bestow on you,
Friend, yourself now say a last Amen.
(Mahammed Abdille Hassan.)

Martin Luther sums up the idea of Christian service:

Here is the truly Christian life, here is faith really working by love, when a man applies himself with joy and love to the works of that freest servitude in which he serves others voluntarily and for nought, himself abundantly satisfied in the fulness and riches of his own faith. ❧

3

CHARITY ENVIETH NOT

A sound heart is the life of the flesh:

but envy the rottenness of the bones.

PROVERBS 14:30

A grateful mind is not only the greatest of virtues,

but the parent of all the other virtues.

CICERO

There is not a single word or incident in the life of the Savior that even hints of envy. As the embodiment of divine love, he never gave the uncharitable emotion of envy place in his heart. And since envy usually accompanies worldly ambition and material cravings, it is no surprise that he was completely free of it. In our naivete, we might assume that we are safe from envy once we have acquired a great many so-called desirables, including power over others. At that point, indeed, there can hardly be many mortals left above us to provoke our envy.

But truly, one who "envieth not" is one who lives simply, appreciatively, and contentedly, without greed or covetousness, who does not spend precious life striving for superfluous material advantages, who gladly celebrates the successes of others, who takes pleasure in life's simple offerings and mercies, and who lives with an abiding sense of gratitude for having reaped where he or she has not sown. Albert Schweitzer reflects thoughtfully on the matter.

FROM *MEMOIRS OF CHILDHOOD AND YOUTH*

When I look back upon my early days I am stirred by the thought of the number of people whom I have to thank for what they gave me or for what they were to me. At the same time I am haunted by an oppressive consciousness of the little gratitude I really showed them while I was young. How many of them have said farewell to life without my having made clear to them what it meant to me to receive from them so much kindness or so much care! Many a time have I, with a feeling of shame, said quietly to myself over a grave the words which my mouth ought to have spoken to the departed, while he was still in the flesh. . . .

In the same way we ought all to make an effort to act on our first thoughts and let our unspoken gratitude find expression. Then there will be more sunshine in the world, and more power to work for what is good. But as concerns ourselves we must all of us take care not to adopt as part of our theory of life all people's bitter sayings about the ingratitude in the world. A great deal of water is flowing underground which never comes up as a spring. In that thought we may find comfort. But we ourselves must try to be the water which does find its way up; we must become a spring at which men can quench their thirst for gratitude. ✦

PSALM 100

Make a joyful noise unto the Lord, all ye lands.

Serve the Lord with gladness: come before his presence with singing.

Know ye that the Lord he is God: it is he that hath made us, and not we ourselves; we are his people, and the sheep of his pasture.

Enter into his gates with thanksgiving, and into his courts with praise: be thankful unto him, and bless his name.

For the Lord is good; his mercy is everlasting; and his truth endureth to all generations. ✦

Louise Lake, a Latter-day Saint mother confined to a wheelchair after recovering from polio, quietly teaches a powerful lesson about envying not, about being grateful for our own particular lives. She went with one friend to visit another in the hospital, but her mood was not happy. Nevertheless, she says, with a "tinge of self-pity and discouragement, I took the opportunity to visit the sick." The stark-ness of the hospital walls (it was 1947) depressed her, and she was glad the visit was brief.

FROM *EACH DAY A BONUS*

I was first to head for the exit door and find release. The spectacle was added to my already discouraged attitude.

With little enthusiasm I wheeled toward the door, and as I passed by a bed near the doorway I stopped short. My eyes were drawn to the sight of a young woman, lying on her back, peering up as if she saw beyond the white ceiling. Her hair, prematurely gray, was pulled straight back from her face. Her soft blue eyes did not turn to look at me when I stopped. It was her striking countenance, deep in thought, that pulled me to a halt. I said, "Hello."

For the first time she turned her gaze to me. "Hello," she answered.

I studied her expression as I inquired of her health. I thought, What an unusually beautiful face! She looked worn, but there was also a look of patience. Written in that countenance were peace and serenity. You don't see that look on the faces of people in the streets. I was impressed. I was in the presence of one who had gone that mile alone. And she had come through. How green I was. It was less than three years that I had known my handicap. There was not the slightest tension between us. It was close to the bone and touched a few nerves within me—more so when I learned that her name was Louise Johnson, the same as my maiden name.

She asked about my shiny new wheelchair. I inquired as to her knowl-edge of chairs. Did she know about chairs? "Yes," she said, "I used to be in one." I must have looked puzzled. Out from under the white sheets she brought her hands, folded together, and carefully placed them on top of the bed covers. The fingers of each hand, gnarled and twisted, looked as though they had been laced together. They were so distorted that it was a shock to me. "You see," she continued, "when my hands became so bent with arthritis, I could no longer wheel a chair. Before that only my feet and legs were involved."

I quietly gasped, "How long has that been?"

She replied, "Well, I have been confined here to the bed for eleven years."

I was stunned. I had really been off balance. I changed my despondent thinking fast. Instead, with all my heart I was silently praying for her. Over and over again I was silently saying, "God bless her and help her!" Before going there I had been too busy looking for the easy—and pleasing to me—way of life.

When I returned home, my own confusions had greatly lessened. I thought, "This has been a wonderful night. I must remember it through the years." So I have done. Far too often we compare ourselves with the wrong people—those who seem to possess everything. How good it is to compare ourselves with the right people. We will quickly count that which we have and build our houses of happiness. ❦

Sylvia Probst Young speaks of gratitude for gifts that have true value in life.

GIFTS FROM MY MOTHER

Yesterday, at the home of a friend, I admired a delicately beautiful figurine. "That," she said proudly, "is a gift from my mother. It was imported from Italy."

On my way home I thought about the gifts my mother had given me. Materially I don't have much from her—two patchwork quilts she made for me when I was married, an old-fashioned treadle sewing machine, a glass cakestand, a pair of embroidered pillowcases, and a knitting sampler that she made some eighty years ago in a little Swiss school. These things came to me when she died, and moneywise they aren't worth very much. But mother had left to me some priceless gifts that cannot be bought with money—a legacy for which I am deeply grateful.

Mother taught me to love God's great out-of-doors—the wonder of the seasons, the miracle of a seed, the song of a brook, the return of a bird. Morning after summer morning we worked together in the garden. Her neat rows of vegetables, bordered by sweet peas and delphinium were admired by friends and neighbors near and far. And how often in the opal twilight we climbed our hill to watch night come softly over the valley.

There was a cold winter morning when we walked across the crusted snow of the meadows to see how the frost had turned the creek and the willows into a regal fairyland.

To mother, books were as essential as bread and butter. She wanted us to know good literature, and we early came to know the works of such writers as Wordsworth and Shakespeare, Longfellow and Lowell.

When a traveling library came to our little town she would see that we borrowed some delightful books for our vacation reading.

The Church magazines—The Children's Friend, The Juvenile Instructor, The Young Ladies Journal, The Improvement Era, and The Relief Society Magazine were very carefully kept and at the end of the year we bound these precious volumes with the aid of a paper punch and some shoelaces. There was a special shelf in our clothes closet for these "bound volumes," and we read them over and over again.

Mother had a deep appreciation for good music, and she helped us to gain a love for it. Whenever I think of our front room I remember the corner where the organ stood, and the young people who gathered around it to sing together. Some of us children were always practicing on that old pump organ, and Mother willingly did washings to pay for music lessons.

My mother was deeply spiritual; her family and my father's had come to America for the gospel, and to them it was the most precious thing in the world. We learned about the Lord very early, and we were taught the value and importance of prayer and faith, repentance and baptism, the paying of tithing and the Word of Wisdom.

Our winter nights were spent around a wood-burning stove reading the gospel together. We took turns reading chapters from the Bible and The Book of Mormon. Together, we read the life of Christ from the New Testament, and *Joseph Smith's Story*. From the Old Testament, we read the stories of all the wonderful old prophets—Moses, Joseph, Samuel, Daniel, or sometimes, Mother told these stories. She loved to tell stories, and she was a wonderful storyteller. Through her teachings we learned the great value of spiritual blessings and gained a knowledge of the truth.

These are some of the gifts my mother gave to me. Time cannot efface them nor can thieves break in and take them from me. These gifts are far more precious than rubies, and for them I shall be eternally grateful to the wonderful woman who was my mother. ❦

Madeleine L'Engle reaffirms the importance of little things:

We lose that sense of wonder about each other as we lose it about God and all of creation. Little things. Wondrous things. When my grandmother got new sheets or towels, she embroidered her name on them, in red, and the date. Why is that wondrous? I'm not sure, but it is, and I still thrill when I see a sheet with the red embroidery and the date of a year long before I was born. ❦

George F. Richards tells a contrasting story of ingratitude:

A woman was left a widow with one child. She had a small home and meager income. She took in washing for her principal support. One morning she called Clarence earlier than usual, saying: "Come, now, son, you will have to get up. We have a larger wash than usual today. It will require a lot of wood." Clarence made no complaint but dressed and went to the woodshed where he cut a woodbox full of wood. Then he wrote a note to his mother and placed it under her plate at the table. When they came to breakfast the mother found Clarence's note which read as follows: "Mother owes Clarence fifty cents for cutting woodbox full of wood." The mother's countenance fell for a moment and then she went to her small earnings and found the half dollar which she gave to Clarence.

There wasn't much said at the table that morning, but the mother thought a great deal as she worked throughout the day. The next morning Clarence found a note on his own breakfast place: "Clarence debtor to mother for going down into the valley of the shadow of death to give him life—nothing. For board and lodgings nine years—nothing. For clothing, washing, and mending, nine years—nothing. Total—nothing." ❦

"I do not know of any, excepting the unpardonable sin, that is greater than the sin of ingratitude," said Brigham Young. (Journal of Discourses 14:277.) In the United States, and in other countries too, the idea of gratitude has been formalized by a national holiday. In the United States we typically observe the occasion by honoring the Pilgrim fathers and mothers who gratefully made a feast from simple fare.

FIRST THANKSGIVING OF ALL

Peace and Mercy and Jonathan,
And Patience (very small),
Stood by the table giving thanks
The first Thanksgiving of all.
There was very little for them to eat,
Nothing special and nothing sweet;
Only bread and a little broth,
And a bit of fruit (and no tablecloth);
But Peace and Mercy and Jonathan
And Patience, in a row,
Stood up and asked a blessing on
Thanksgiving, long ago.
Thankful they were their ship had come
Safely across the sea;
Thankful they were for hearth and home,
And kin and company;
They were glad of broth to go with their bread,
Glad their apples were round and red,
Glad of mayflowers they would bring
Out of the woods again next spring.
So Peace and Mercy and Jonathan,
And Patience (very small),
Stood up gratefully giving thanks
The first Thanksgiving of all.
(Nancy Byrd Turner.)

The meal Hannah Cornaby describes in the following account is not a Thanksgiving dinner, but certainly a meal of thanksgiving. A Mormon pioneer from England, she and her husband eventually settled in Spanish Fork.

FROM "AUTOBIOGRAPHY"

One morning having, as usual, attended to family prayer, in which, with greater significance than is often used, we asked, "give us this day our daily bread;" and having eaten a rather scanty breakfast—every morsel we had in the house—Edith was wondering what we should have for dinner and why 'Pa did not send us some fish.' I, too, was anxious, not having heard from Provo for some days; so telling my darlings I would go and see if Sister Ellen Jackson (whose husband was also one of the fishing party) had heard any news, I started off. Sister Jackson had not heard from the fishery; but was quite cheerful, and telling me how well her garden was growing, added that the radishes were fit for use, and insisted that I must have some.

It was good to see something to eat; and, quite pleased, I bade her good morning. Passing, on my way, the house of brother Charles Gray, sister Gray asked me where I had got such fine radishes. I told her, and offered to divide with her, to which she agreed, providing I would take in exchange some lettuce and cress, of which she had plenty. She filled a pan with these; and I hurried away thinking how pleased my children would be, if only we had bread to eat with them.

As I was passing brother Simon Baker's house, sister Baker saw me, and invited me in. I told her I had left my children, and could not stop. She then asked me where I had got such nice green stuff, and when I told her, and offered her some, she replied, "if I could exchange some for butter, [I] would be glad." She then gave me a piece of nice fresh butter, which had just come from their dairy on the Jordan; and also a large slice of cheese. If I only had bread, I thought, how good these would be! Just then my eyes rested upon a large vessel full of broken bread. Sister Baker, seeing I had noticed it, told me its history. It had been sent the day before, in a sack, to the canyon, where her husband had a number of men working. On the way it had fallen from the wagon and been crushed under the wheel. She did not know what to do with it, remarking that she would offer me some of it but feared I would feel insulted, although assuring me it was perfectly clean. I accepted her offer, when, filling a large pan, she sent her daughter home with me to carry it.

The children were watching for my return; and when they saw the bread, they clapped their hands with delight. Bread, butter, cheese, radishes, lettuce and cress! What a dinner we had that day! Elijah never enjoyed the dinner the ravens brought him more than I did that meal; nor more fully understood that a kind Providence had furnished it. ❦

Thanksgiving was not an official holiday in the United States until Abraham Lincoln proclaimed it so on October 3, 1863, with this published declaration— issued, incredibly, in the midst of heartbreaking civil war:

PROCLAMATION OF THANKSGIVING

The year that is drawing towards its close, has been filled with the blessings of fruitful fields and healthful skies. To these bounties, which are so constantly enjoyed that we are prone to forget the source from which they come, others have been added, which are of so extraordinary a nature, that they cannot fail to penetrate and soften even the heart which is habitually insensible to the ever watchful providence of Almighty God. In the midst of a civil war of unequalled magnitude and severity, which has sometimes seemed to foreign States to invite and provoke their aggression, peace has been preserved with all nations, order has been maintained, the laws have been respected and obeyed, and harmony has prevailed everywhere except in the theatre of military conflict; while that theatre has been greatly contracted by the advancing armies and navies of the Union.

Needful diversions of wealth and of strength from the fields of peaceful industry to the national defence, have not arrested the plow, the shuttle or the ship; the axe has enlarged the borders of our settlements, and the mines, as well of iron and coal as of the precious metals, have yielded even more abundantly than heretofore. Population has steadily increased, notwithstanding the waste that has been made in the camp, the siege and the battle-field; and the country, rejoicing in the consciousness of augmented strength and vigor, is permitted to expect continuance of years with large increase of freedom. No human counsel hath devised nor hath any mortal hand worked out these great things. They are the gracious gifts of the Most High God, who, while dealing with us in anger for our sins, hath nevertheless remembered mercy.

It has seemed to me fit and proper that they should be solemnly, reverently and gratefully acknowledged as with one heart and one voice by the whole American People. I do therefore invite my fellow citizens in every part of the United States, and also those who are at sea and those who are sojourning in foreign lands, to set apart and observe the last Thursday of November next, as a day of Thanksgiving and Praise to our beneficient Father who dwelleth in the Heavens. And I recommend to them that while offering up the ascriptions justly due to Him for such singular deliverances and blessings, they do also, with humble penitence for our national perverseness and disobedience, commend to His tender care all those who have become widows, orphans, mourners, or sufferers in the lamentable civil strife in which we are unavoidably engaged, and fervently implore the interposition of the Almighty Hand to heal the wounds of the nation and to restore it as soon as may be consistent with the Divine purposes to the full enjoyment of peace, harmony, tranquility, and Union. *

A life dedicated to the acquisition of material wealth for self-gratification is hardly a life of the gratitude, simplicity, and contentment that characterize true charity. We recognize, however, the great good accomplished through the generosity of people who have acquired and used wealth in the service of worthy causes. Brigham Young did also, at the same time offering "consolation" to the miserly "who wish to keep their riches." He promised them "leanness of soul, darkness of mind, narrow and contracted hearts." He warned them that "the bowels of your compassion will be shut up, and by and by you will be overcome with the spirit of apostasy and forsake your God and your brethren." (Journal of Discourses 12:127.) In attempting to dissuade the Saints from following the gold rush to California, Brigham Young reportedly said:

The worst fear that I have about this people is that they will get rich in this country, forget God and his people, wax fat, and kick themselves out of the church and go to hell. This people will stand mobbing, robbing, poverty, and all manner of persecution, and be true. But my greater fear for them is that they cannot stand wealth; and yet they have to be tried with riches, for they will become the richest people on this earth. (As told by James Brown.) ✦

The phrase "tried with riches" merits pondering. Delbert L. Stapley echoed President Young's warning:

Our modern scientific material world with its great achievements, conveniences, comforts, and tempting prosperity has diverted many a good man from his avowed plan to serve God faithfully. Opportunities for riches, and the power that goes with them, often impel men to pursue increased possessions, money, and the honors of men more than the love and favor of God. The faith of many such men often is destroyed and their spiritual opportunities and blessings sacrificed. They become cold and indifferent to religion and pierce themselves and families through with many sorrows.

. . . There is nothing against a person earning and enjoying material possessions provided he is not spiritually hurt in the process and fulfills completely his heavenly covenants and sacred obligations to his God. "For a man's life," says the Savior, "does not consist in the abundance of the things which he possesses." ✦

I made me great works; I builded me houses; I planted me vineyards:

I made me gardens and orchards, and I planted trees in them of all kind of fruits:

I made me pools of water, to water therewith the wood that bringeth forth trees:

I got me servants and maidens, and had servants born in my house; also I had great possessions of great and small cattle above all that were in Jerusalem before me:

I gathered me also silver and gold, and the peculiar treasure of kings and of the provinces: I gat me men singers and women singers, and the delights of the sons of men, as musical instruments, and that of all sorts.

So I was great, and increased more than all that were before me in Jerusalem: also my wisdom remained with me.

And whatsoever mine eyes desired I kept not from them, I withheld not my heart from any joy; for my heart rejoiced in all my labour: and this was my portion of all my labour.

Then I looked on all the works that my hands had wrought, and on the labour that I had laboured to do: and, behold, all was vanity and vexation of spirit, and there was no profit under the sun. (Ecclesiastes 2:4–11.) ✦

For Brigham Young, hoarding wisdom and talent was no different from hoarding money.

A man or woman who places the wealth of this world and the things of time in the scales against the things of God and the wisdom of eternity, has no eyes to see, no ears to hear, no heart to understand. What are riches for? For blessings, to do good. Then let us dispense that which the Lord gives us to the best possible use for the building up of his kingdom, for the promotion of the truth on the earth, that we may see and enjoy the blessings of the Zion of God here upon this earth. I look around among the world of mankind and see them grabbing, scrambling, contending, and every one seeking to aggrandize himself, and to accomplish his own individual purposes, passing the community by, walking upon the heads of his neighbors—all are seeking, planning, contriving in their wakeful hours, and when asleep dreaming, "How can I get the advantage of my neighbor? How can I spoil him, that I may ascend the ladder of fame?" That is entirely a mistaken idea. You see that nobleman seeking the benefit of all around him, . . . dispens[ing] his wisdom and talents among them and mak[ing] them equal with himself. . . . But the man who seeks honor and glory at the expense of his fellow-men is not worthy of the society of the intelligent. (*Journal of Discourses* 15:18.) ✦

The writer of Ecclesiastes likewise warns:

There is a sore evil which I have seen under the sun, namely, riches kept for the owners thereof to their hurt. (Ecclesiastes 5:13.)

In the fall of 1827, Parley P. Pratt married and moved his bride west, settling on his property near the mouth of the Black River in Ohio. On hearing Sidney Rigdon speak, he was converted to the restored gospel of Jesus Christ. In his autobiography, Parley tells of a compelling desire he felt in early 1830 to take the gospel to others. Just at this time, he was joyfully reunited with his brother William, who he supposed had drowned five years earlier in a steamer accident on the Hudson River. William exclaimed over Parley's material success and comfortable surroundings. Parley acknowledged his good fortune, but indicated that he and his wife would be giving it all up in order to spread the gospel. William was stunned.

FROM *AUTOBIOGRAPHY OF PARLEY P. PRATT*

[William said,] "This is your all; you have toiled years to obtain it, and why not now continue to enjoy it?" "William," said I, "I see plainly you know but little of my circumstances—of the changes which have taken place with me since we parted five years ago, nor how vastly wealthy I have become within that time. Why, sir, I have bank bills enough, on the very best institutions in the world, to sustain myself and family while we live."

"Indeed," said he, "well, I should like to see some of them; I hope they are genuine." "Certainly," I replied, "there is no doubt of that. They are true bills and founded on capital that will never fail, though heaven and earth should pass away. Of this I will convince you in a moment."

I then unlocked my treasury and drew from thence a large pocket book, full of promissory notes like the following: "*Whosoever shall forsake father or mother, brethren or sisters, houses or lands, wife or children, for my sake and the gospel's, shall receive an hundred fold in this life, and in the world to come life everlasting.*" . . .

"Now, William," said I, "are these the words of Jesus Christ, or are they not?" "They certainly are," said he, "I always believed the New Testament."

"Then you admit they are genuine bills?"

"I do."

"Is the signer able to meet his engagements?"

"He certainly is."

"Is he willing?"

"He is."

"Well, then, I am going to fulfil the conditions to the letter on my part. I feel called upon by the Holy Ghost to forsake my house and home for the gospel's sake; and I will do it, placing both feet firm on these promises with nothing else to rely upon.

"If I sink, they are false.

"If I am sustained, they are true. I will put them to the test. . . ."

"Well," said he, "try it, if you will; but for my part, although I always believed the Bible, I would not dare believe it *literally,* and really stand upon its promises, with no other prop."

We parted. He to his business, I to my preparations for a mission which should only end with my life. ❦

R. Eizel Harif would say, "What was the difference between the wilderness generation of those who left Egypt and subsequent generations? The wilderness generation that left Egypt disposed of its gold and silver to make for itself a god, while in our wilderness generation, people dispose of God in order to make gold and silver." (The Passover Haggadah: Legends and Customs.)

Leo Tolstoy related a story of a man hungry for property who traveled to a place where rich land was plentiful and sold for a pittance. The man was told that he might claim as much land as he could encircle on foot in one day, sunup to sundown. In his greed, he tried to acquire too much, and at day's end he died of exhaustion. Tolstoy's title raises the important question: "How Much Land Does a Man Need?" In the end, the servant who buried his unfortunate and greedy master discovered that "six feet from his head to his heels was all he needed." Another such story is the tale of King Midas, who wished that everything he touched would turn to gold.

Henry David Thoreau tried to teach us that striving for worldly success is the poorest of economies, that when we spend our lives for things, we do not own the things but are, rather, owned by them. He also insisted that simplifying our temporal lives would much improve our spiritual lives.

Our life is frittered away by detail. An honest man has hardly need to count more than his ten fingers, or in extreme cases he may add his ten toes, and lump the rest. Simplicity, simplicity, simplicity! I say, let your affairs be as two or three, and not a hundred or a thousand; instead of a million count half a dozen, and keep your accounts on your thumb-nail. . . . Instead of three meals a day, if it be necessary eat but one; instead of a hundred dishes, five; and reduce other things in proportion. ✦

Donald R. Marshall, a contemporary LDS writer whose style and methods are very different from Thoreau's, satirizes modernity's inordinate striving for professional "success." If we did not envy the accomplishments of others, would we drive ourselves so hard? Overscheduled and fragmented lives, whether we profess business or the humanities, can cost us our souls, Marshall warns.

THE PREPARATION

Unless he took a moment to revise his plans, everything, he reasoned, would be lost. The schedule had seemed feasible enough at 11:45 (no, he corrected himself, *11:40,* for he had been brushing his teeth by 11:45) the night before when he had completed it. But it was a traffic accident on 21st South that had started it. He had not counted on a delay there any more than he had foreseen the detour on Redwood Road the day before. He looked at his watch now—11:13—and fumbled in his pockets for the right papers. *Siddhartha, The Magic Mountain, Remembrance of Things Past* . . . Not that one. Here was another: TO LOOK UP: *antinomianism, Averroism, logical positivism, Dadaism* . . . The long list washed over his mind like a dark sea choked with debris. His stomach muscles tightened. Not that one. But he must get to it soon. He folded it carefully and put it in the left-hand inside pocket so that he would not forget. But his fingers there discovered still another scrap of paper: CHECK AGAIN AND MEM-ORIZE: *teleology, epistemology, eschatology.* He had looked for that one the other day. He would have to remember to combine it with the list he had made last Sunday while his mind wandered during the meeting. And with the partial list in his brown coat. Or was it the blue? Or had he put it instead with the papers in his wallet when he had sorted out his pockets? He felt a quick clenching inside as though his belt were being cinched tighter and tighter. His fingers felt nervously in all the pockets. He wanted to swear but caught himself when he happened to see the white corner of a paper protruding from the book he had placed between his knees during his search. Of course. Of course. He quickly snatched the paper—a scrap torn from an envelope—out of the book, held it in his teeth while he tore off a corner of still another piece of paper, this time an advertisement for a Pizza Special someone had stuck on his windshield, and hurriedly wrote: THINGS TO REMEMBER: Remember to check out a book on how to remember. His stomach signalled to him again when he stuffed the paper into a pocket and realized that he had forgotten to remember which one. But he would worry about that later. At least he had located today's schedule. His breath stopped and his insides somersaulted for an instant when he noticed the heading TO DO ON TUESDAY at the beginning of his penciled list. But he forced out a long breath of relief when he thought to turn it over and discovered another list, product of his labors between 11:30 and 11:45 the night before, preceded by the single word, thrice-underlined, THURSDAY.

Myron's eyes skimmed the penciled hours and parts of hours and their assigned duties. He glanced again at his watch. With a little shifting it was all still possible. He would simply go to the Public Library now, walking as fast as he could, of course, and then stop by the University library on his way to Kingsbury Hall at 3:20. If worse came to worst, he conceded reluctantly, he *could* omit sitting in on Dr. Nordby's lecture on Descartes and the Cartesian Formula since he had heard a related lecture on August 3, and had a note somewhere to remind him to check out some book by Campbell on a similar proposition. He would have to remember, however, not to miss the September 2 colloquium on Leibniz and Rationalism. And he should remember to ask Dr. Farnsworth if there was not somewhere in existence a list of suggested readings on monadology. He would have to make certain, in any event, that he would, finally, be prepared.

His eyes flitted once more over the day's schedule. Above all, he reminded himself, he must be careful that he did not run out of time, that the minutes between 2:45 and 3:20 allotted to sorting out and correlating lists was not sacrificed as it had been on Monday. Or had that been the previous Friday? In any case, this part of the preparation was most indispensable. He folded the schedule, stuffed it into a pocket, and became aware for the first time in five minutes—six minutes, he corrected himself, glancing at his watch—that he was still standing on the sidewalk beside the parking meter while the rest of the world, alive with activity, moved mindlessly down Main Street.

He was running out of time, he reminded himself. Hastily locating four pennies for the parking meter (and discovering in his pocket at the same time a crumpled list of THINGS TO STUDY SOON), Myron hurried along the sidewalk. He dodged traffic, stepped aside for a boisterous group of boy scouts cavorting haphazardly along the way, and avoided bumping against a bright-eyed woman, her arms loaded with gift-wrapped packages, who happened to step in his path. Only once did he stop, allowing himself three minutes, while he glanced uneasily at the record albums in the House of Music's window. Mahler's *8th Symphony,* John Field's *Nocturnes . . .* New recordings, he thought to himself, too many new records. Something seemed to expand inside his chest, even swell inside his throat. Is there time for it all, his voice strained to cry out above the strangling sensation, is there time? He would have to mark these down under THINGS TO HEAR, yet, because the three allotted minutes had already expired, he took no time for this now but hurried instead down the sidewalk until he found himself running at last up the steps of the Salt Lake City Public Library. No time now, he said to himself as he thought he recognized a face coming through the doorway and quickly turned aside to avoid a chance meeting, no time to talk when it was already so late in the day and there was so much left to do. He passed by the shelves marked New Acquisitions, felt the smothering feeling swell up again in his chest and throat, dropped the book he had been carrying into the slot marked RETURN, saw from a distance the cover of a *Life* magazine that he felt he must one day look into when there was time, hastened to the rows of cardfiles, pulled drawers and flipped cards and let his pen speed over the pieces of blank paper he had carried inside his coat. The meter was running out and he would be able to park no longer and all the rows of books and mark down that Latin phrase to be looked up when there was time and the new book by Wayment or was it Waysted and at 11:57 Myron Cludder dropped dead on the corner of 1st South and State Street and it was not even on his schedule. ❦

Marshall's story clearly predates day planners and personal computers, but the story is not a plea for organization, anyway. The satire is perhaps heaviest when we learn that Myron schedules time to make schedules, and that he has no time to look into Life, that is, life, which he observes only fleetingly from a distance. Contrast this with Thoreau, to whom the key is to reduce our wants, to appreciate what we have. The essence of his message is that less is more.

FROM "CONCLUSION"

However mean your life is, meet it and live it; do not shun it and call it hard names. It is not so bad as you are. It looks poorest when you are richest. The faultfinder will find faults even in paradise. Love your life, poor as it is. You may perhaps have some pleasant, thrilling, glorious hours, even in a poorhouse. The setting sun is reflected from the windows of the almshouse as brightly as from the rich man's abode; the snow melts before its door as early in the spring. I do not see but a quiet mind may live as contentedly there, and have as cheering thoughts, as in a palace. The town's poor seem to me often to live the most independent lives of any. Maybe they are simply great enough to receive without misgiving. ❦

It is instructive for us to consider the frugality practiced as a matter of course by our Mormon pioneer forebears. The following two examples are powerful lessons in thrift and gratitude.

In thinking over the economies of those days I remember seeing one lady rip up an old dress to make over for one of the children, and she picked out the stitches one by one and saved the thread to restitch it with. Another woman made a bed quilt out of . . . "Bull Durham" tobacco sacks. Another incident is old of a family who was at supper and the little brother called out, "Ma, Jake's wasty! He picked a fly out of the 'lasses and never licked its legs off!" "Wasty Jack Beecham" was a byword thru out the town for years, and still is in our home. We never did pass thru abject poverty, but we did have to observe strict economy. . . .

In the early days matches were 25¢ per box, and it was always considered an extravagance to strike one if there was a fire anywhere in the house. We used to make "squills" by rolling strips of newspaper or magazines between the thumb and finger into long pointed tapers. These were placed in vases or bottles at either end of the mantle piece, and on the kitchen shelf near the stove, where they were handy. They were always used to light the lamps, candles, etc. I often think of them [now] when I strike from 10 to 20 matches a day to light my little old gas stove, tho I am careful and use the stubs over and over so long as one burner is going. (Mary Elizabeth Woolley Chamberlain.) ◆

Thursday 15th [October, 1846] We have taken possession of our log house today. The first house my babe was ever in. I feel extremely thankful for the privilege of sitting by a fire where the wind cannot blow it in every direction, and where I can warm one side without freezing the other. Our house is minus floor and many other comforts but the walls protect us from the wind, if the sod roof does not from the rain. (Eliza Maria Partridge Lyman.) ◆

Frank Lloyd Wright urged simplicity in architecture, but defined it as something other than mere sparseness. If we apply to humanity—and to institutions such as the Church—his argument that simplicity leads to harmoniousness, we can see a fortuitous link to the doctrine of charity.

FROM "MODERN ARCHITECTURE:

THE CARDBOARD HOUSE"

Now *simplicity* being the point in question in this early constructive effort, organic simplicity I soon found to be a matter of true coordination. And beauty I soon felt to be a matter of the sympathy with which such coordination was effected. Plainness was not necessarily simplicity. Crude furniture of the Roycroft-Stickley-Mission Style, which came along later, was offensively plain, plain as a barn door—but never was simple in any true sense. Nor, I found, were merely machine-made things in themselves simple. To think "in simple," is to deal in simples, and that means with an eye single to the altogether. This, I believe, is the secret of simplicity.

Perhaps we may truly regard nothing at all as simple in itself. I believe that no one thing in itself is ever so, but must achieve simplicity (as an artist should use the term) as a perfectly realized part of some organic whole. Only as a feature or any part becomes an harmonious element in the harmonious whole does it arrive at the estate of simplicity. Any wild flower is truly simple, but double the same wild flower by cultivation, it ceases to be so. The *scheme* of the original is no longer clear. Clarity of design and perfect significance both are first essentials of the spontaneously born simplicity of the lilies of the field who neither toil nor spin, as contrasted with Solomon who had "toiled and spun"—that is to say, no doubt had put on himself and had put on his temple, properly "composed," everything in the category of good things but the cook-stove.

Five lines where three are enough is stupidity. Nine pounds where three are sufficient is stupidity. But to eliminate expressive words that intensify or vivify meaning in speaking or writing is not simplicity; nor is similar elimination in architecture simplicity—it, too, may be stupidity. In architecture, expressive changes of surface, emphasis of line and especially textures of material, may go to make facts eloquent, forms more significant. Elimination, therefore, may be just as meaningless as elaboration, perhaps more often is so. I offer any fool, for an example. ❦

Simplicity often seems equated with contentment.

A contented man is never disappointed. (Lao Tsu.) ❦

Those . . . who know the true use of money, and regulate the measure of wealth according to their needs, live contented with few things. (Baruch Spinoza.) ❦

By contrast, envy is sometimes expressed as discontent.

THE STORY OF GRUMBLE TONE

There was a boy named Grumble Tone, who ran away to sea.
"I'm sick of things on land," he said, "as sick as I can be,
A life upon the bounding wave is just the life for me!"
But the seething ocean billows failed to stimulate his mirth,
For he did not like the vessel or the dizzy rolling berth,
And he thought the sea was almost as unpleasant as the earth.

He wandered into foreign lands, he saw each wondrous sight,
But nothing that he heard or saw seemed just exactly right,
And so he journeyed on and on, still seeking for delight.
He talked with kings and ladies grand; he dined in courts, they say,
But always found the people dull and longed to get away
To search for that mysterious land where he should want to stay.

He wandered over all the world, his hair grew white as snow,
He reached that final bourne at last where all of us must go,
But never found the land he sought; the reason would you know?
The reason was that north or south, where'er his steps were bent,
On land or sea, in court or hall, he found but discontent,
For he took his disposition with him, everywhere he went.
(Ella Wheeler Wilcox.)

THE DISCONTENTED YEW-TREE

A dark-green prickly yew one night
Peeped round on the trees of the forest,
And said, "*Their* leaves are smooth and bright,
My lot is the worst and poorest:

"I wish I had golden leaves," said the yew;
And lo, when the morning came,
He found his wish had come suddenly true,
For his branches were all aflame.

Now, by came a man, with a bag on his back,
Who cried, "I'll be rich to-day!"
He stripped the boughs, and, filling his sack
With the yellow leaves, walked away!

The yew was as vexed as a tree could be,
And grieved as a yew-tree grieves,
And sighed, "If Heaven would but pity me,
And grant me crystal leaves!"

Then crystal leaves crept over the boughs;
Said the yew, "Now am I not gay?"
But a hailstorm hurricane soon arose
And broke every leaf away!

So he mended his wish yet once again,—
"Of my pride I do now repent;
Give me fresh green leaves, quite smooth and plain,
And I will be content."

In the morning he woke in smooth green leaf,
Saying, "This is a sensible plan;
The storm will not bring my beauty to grief,
Or the greediness of man."

But the world has goats as well as men,
And one came snuffing past,
Which ate of the green leaves a million and ten,
Not having broken his fast.

O then the yew-tree groaned aloud,
"What folly was mine, alack!
I was discontented, and I was proud—
O give me my old leaves back!"

So when daylight broke, he was dark, dark green,
And prickly as before!—

The other trees mocked, "Such a sight to be seen!
To be near him makes one sore!"
The south wind whispered his leaves between,
"Be thankful, and change no more!

"The thing you are is always the thing
That you had better be"—
But the north wind said, with a gallant fling,
"The foolish, weak yew-tree!

"What if he blundered twice or thrice?
There's a turn to the longest lane;
And everything must have its price—
Poor faulterer, try again!"
(William Brighty Rands.)

Envy is a littleness of soul, which cannot see beyond a certain point, and if it does not occupy the whole of space, feels itself excluded. (William Hazlitt.) ❧

Chieko Okazaki tells a Japanese folktale that illustrates, through both positive and negative example, the charity of contentment, of, as she says, "accepting what life offers."

THE OLD MAN WHO MADE

DEAD TREES BLOOM

In this ancient folktale, an old man and woman who were honest and kind-hearted lived next to a wicked and greedy old man.

The kindly couple had adopted a little dog as a pet. This dog led the old man to the garden one day and began barking and scratching at the ground in one certain spot. Perplexed, the old man dug there, and uncovered a treasure of jewels and *oban* and *koban*, coins minted during the feudal period of Japan. The greedy old man from next door happened by as the good couple were exclaiming over the find, and they cheerfully loaned him the dog.

As instructed, the greedy man followed the dog into his own garden and dug where the dog barked and scratched. But instead of riches, he dug up a disgusting nest of frogs, lizards, and reptiles. Angry and frustrated, he killed the little dog and buried it in the garden, marking the spot with a willow twig.

When their pet failed to return, the good old man went to his cruel neighbor and learned what he had done. The next day, he went to the spot where his dog was buried, to console his spirit. Imagine his surprise when he found a giant willow tree growing there! The man chopped down the tree and made a mortar and pestle out of the trunk. He and his wife put steamed rice in the mortar and were pounding it to make *mochi*, rice cakes, when *oban* and *koban* began pouring out.

The greedy neighbor just happened to be peeking in the window at the time, and asked to borrow the mortar and pestle. But as he began pounding the rice, filthy things tumbled out—discarded roof tiles, broken utensils, and the like, but not a glimpse of a gold coin. The infuriated old man threw the mortar and pestle into his kitchen brazier. When his kindly neighbor came to retrieve them, all that was left was a pile of ashes.

Resigned to his loss, the good man gathered up the ashes that had once been his mortar and pestle and started for home. On his way, he spilled some of the ashes onto a spot where green grass had long since withered. Instantly, the grass flowered into fresh green!

With joy, the old man hurried home, climbed a tree in his garden, and sprinkled the ashes all around. All the trees in the neighborhood, even the dead ones, burst out with beautiful blooms. The people all applauded the old man's feat and called him "Hanasaka jijii," which means "Old Man Who Makes Dead Trees Flower." ❦

Being contented with what we have was a favorite theme of ancient storytellers.

THE GOOSE WITH THE GOLDEN EGGS

A certain man had the good fortune to possess a Goose that laid him a Golden Egg every day. But dissatisfied with so slow an income, and thinking to seize the whole treasure at once, he killed the Goose; and, cutting her open, found her—just what any other goose would be!

Much wants more and loses all. (Aesop.) ✦

This fifteenth-century Persian adaptation of a moralistic story also teaches the perils of discontent.

POOR CAT, RICH CAT

In former times there was an old woman in a state of extreme debility. She possessed a cot more narrow than the heart of the ignorant, and darker than the miser's grave; and a cat was her companion, which had never seen even in the mirror of imagination, the face of a loaf, nor had heard from friend or stranger the name of meat. It was content if occasionally it smelt the odour of a mouse from its hole, or saw the print of the foot of one on the surface of a board, and if, on some rare occasion, by the aid of good-fortune and the assistance of happy destiny, one fell into its claws,

Like a poor wretch who finds out buried gold, its cheek lighted up with joy, and it consumed its past sorrow with the flame of its natural heat, and a whole week, more or less, it subsisted on that amount of food. . . . And inasmuch as the house of the old woman was the famine-year of that cat, it was always miserable and thin, and from a distance appeared like an idea.

One day, through excessive weakness, it had, with the utmost difficulty, mounted on the top of the roof; thence it beheld a cat which walked proudly on the wall of a neighbouring house, and after the fashion of a destroying lion, advanced with measured steps, and from excessive fat, lifted its feet slowly. When the cat of the old woman saw one of its own species in that state of freshness and fat, it was astonished, and cried out, saying:

"Truly with pride thou advancest, then wilt thou not tell me from whence?"

The neighbour-cat replied: "I am the crumb-eater of the tray of the sultan. Every morning I attend on the court of the king, and when they spread the tray of invitation, I display boldness and daring, and in general I snatch off some morsels of fat meats, and of loaves made of the finest flour; and I pass my time happy and satisfied till the next day."

The cat of the old woman inquired, "What sort of a thing may fat meat be? and what kind of relish has bread, made of fine flour? I, during my whole life, have never seen nor tasted aught save the old woman's broths, and mouse's flesh."

The neighbour-cat laughed, and said,

> "Cat, by thy tail and ears, one might thee deem,
> Yet, in all else, a spider thou wouldst seem."

The cat of the old woman said, most beseechingly, "O brother! thou art bound to me by the rights of neighbourship and the link of homogeneousness. Why not perform what is due to courtesy and fraternity, and this time, when thou goest, take me with thee; perchance by thy good fortune, I may obtain food, and by the blessing of thy society, I may acquire a place.

The heart of the neighbour-cat melted at his lamentable position, and he resolved that he would not attend the feast without him.

The cat of the old woman, from the happy tidings of this promise, felt new life and, descending from the roof, stated the case to her. The old dame began to advise the cat, saying, "O kind companion, be not deceived by the words of worldly people, and abandon not the corner of content, for the vessel of covetousness is not filled save with the dust of the grave; and the eye of lust is not stitched but with the needle of annihilation and the thread of death."

> Contentment makes man wealthy—Tell it then
> To the unsatisfied and world-o'er-wandering men,—
> They ne'er knew God, nor paid Him worship due,
> Since with their lot they no contentment knew.

The cat, however, had conceived such a longing for the table of the delicacies of the sultan, and to such an extent only that it was immune to the medicine of advice.

> 'Tis but to cage the wind advice to give
> To lovers, 'tis but water in a sieve.

In short, the next day, along with its neighbour, the old woman's cat

with tottering steps conveyed itself to the court of the sultan, and before
that helpless one could arrive there, ill-fortune had poured the water of disappointment on the fire of its crude wish, and the reason was as follows:—
The day before, the cats had made a general onslaught on the table, and
raised a clamour and uproar beyond bounds, and had annoyed to the last
degree, the guests and their host. Wherefore, on this day, the sultan had
commanded that a band of archers, standing in ambush, should watch, so
that for every cat who should enter the plain of audacity, the very first
morsel that it ate should be a liver-piercing shaft. The old woman's cat, ignorant of this circumstance, as soon as it smelt the odour of the viands, without the power of checking itself, turned its face like a falcon to the
hunting-ground of the table, and the scale of the balance of appetite had
not yet been weighted by heavy mouthfuls when the heart-piercing arrow
quivered in its breast.

> From the bone trickling flowed the sanguine tide.
> In terror of its life it fled and cried:
> "Could I escape this archer's hand, I'd dwell
> Content with mice and the old woman's cell.
> Dear friend! the honey pays not for the sting,
> Content with syrup is a better thing." ❦

THE MEANS TO ATTAIN A HAPPY LIFE

> Martiall, the means that do attain
> The happy life be these, I find:
> The riches left, not got with pain,
> The fruitful ground, the quiet mind;
>
> The equal friend, no grudge, no strife;
> No charge of rule, nor governance;
> Without disease, the healthful life;
> The household of continuance;
>
> The mean diét, no delicate fare;
> True wisdom, joined with simpleness;

The night dischargèd of all care;
Where wine the wit may not oppress;

The faithful wife, without debate;
Such sleeps as may beguile the night.
Contented with thine own estate,
Ne wish for death, ne fear his might.
(Henry Howard, Earl of Surrey.)

The words of Christ sum up for us the true antidote for envy and the key to living contentedly.

Lay not up for yourselves treasures upon earth, where moth and rust doth corrupt, and where thieves break through and steal:

But lay up for yourselves treasures in heaven, where neither moth nor rust doth corrupt, and where thieves do not break through nor steal:

For where your treasure is, there will your heart be also. . . .

No man can serve two masters: for either he will hate the one, and love the other; or else he will hold to the one, and despise the other. Ye cannot serve God and mammon.

Therefore I say unto you, Take no thought for your life, what ye shall eat, or what ye shall drink; nor yet for your body, what ye shall put on. Is not the life more than meat, and the body than raiment? (Matthew 6:19–21, 24–25.) ✦

4

CHARITY VAUNTETH
NOT ITSELF

*There is one kind of religion in which the more
devoted a man is, the fewer proselytes he
makes: the worship of himself.*

C. S. LEWIS

*Though I speak with the tongues of men and
of angels, and have not charity, I am become as
sounding brass, or a tinkling cymbal.*

1 CORINTHIANS 13:1

Paul's similes for self-vaunting—"sounding brass" and "tinkling cymbal"—
are superb, but it is Joseph Smith who describes that noisy and shallow
vaunting as self-righteousness. After reading 1 Corinthians 13:1 in a talk
to the Relief Society, April 18, 1842, Joseph Smith said, "Don't be limited in your
views with regard to your neighbor's virtue, but beware of self-righteousness, and
be limited in the estimate of your own virtues, and think not yourselves more righteous than others." (Teachings of the Prophet Joseph Smith, p. 228.)

LDS scholar Hugh Nibley declares that "next to covetousness it was self-
righteousness against which Joseph and Brigham most urgently warned the Saints.

83

'Let not any man publish his own righteousness,' said the Prophet Joseph (TPJS, 194)." Nibley then quotes several passages from Joseph Smith, including these:

"Christ was condemned by the self-righteous Jews because He took sinners into his society" (TPJS, 240).

"All the religious world is boasting of righteousness: it is the doctrine of the devil to retard the human mind, and hinder our progress, by filling us with self-righteousness. . . . We are full of selfishness; the devil flatters us that we are very righteous, when we are feeding on the faults of others" (TPJS, 241).

The "vaunting" of self particularly suggests boastfulness, conceit, self-promotion, and self-elevation. Such vaunting invades the spiritual realm in the form of self-righteousness, and it generally leads to criticism of others. A song that appeared for many years in the LDS hymnbook speaks to the subject.

>Let each man learn to know himself;
>To gain that knowledge let him labor,
>Improve those failings in himself
>Which he condemns so in his neighbor.
>How lenient our own faults we view,
>And conscience's voice adeptly smother,
>Yet, oh, how harshly we review
>The self-same failings in another!
>
>And if you meet an erring one
>Whose deeds are blamable and thoughtless,
>Consider, ere you cast the stone,
>If you yourself are pure and faultless.
>Oh, list to that small voice within,
>Whose whisperings oft make men confounded,
>And trumpet not another's sin;
>You'd blush deep if your own were sounded.
>
>And in self judgment if you find
>Your deeds to others are superior,

To you has Providence been kind,
As you should be to those inferior.
Example sheds a genial ray
Of light which men are apt to borrow,
So first improve yourself today
And then improve your friends tomorrow.

Joseph Smith was careful to avoid self-vaunting and quick to squelch any presumption of superior righteousness on his part. He said in a May 21, 1843, address: "I do not want you to think that I am very righteous, for I am not. God judges men according to the use they make of the light which He gives them." (Teachings of the Prophet Joseph Smith, p. 303.) In this, Joseph was following the pattern of the Savior.

And, behold, one came and said unto him, Good Master, what good thing shall I do, that I may have eternal life?

And he said unto him, Why callest thou me good? there is none good but one, that is, God. (Matthew 19:16–17.) ✦

Boastfulness and conceitedness are character flaws in any setting, and a number of items in this section caution against those negative traits. But there is a subtler form of self-vaunting, too: the tendency to regard some people or duties as beneath us, or to assume that we know better than God how we should serve. In the first example, George Albert Smith tells of gently assisting one man to recognize his inclination to vaunt himself.

THE STORY OF A GENEROUS MAN

One day on the street I met a friend whom I had known since boyhood. I had not visited with him for some time, and I was interested in being brought up to date concerning his life, his problems, and his faith, therefore, I invited him to go to a conference in Utah County with me. He drove his fine car (the make of car I was driving had not been received into society at that time). He took his wife, and I took mine.

At the conference, I called on him to speak. I did not know what it might do to him, but I thought I would take a chance. He made a fine talk.

He told of his trips to the East, how he explained the gospel to the people he met, and how grateful he was for his heritage. He stated that his opportunities in the world had been magnified and multiplied because his father and mother had joined the Church in the Old World.

As we drove home, he turned to me and said: "My, this has been a wonderful conference. I have enjoyed it."

I thought to myself he was like one of our sisters who came home from fast meeting and said to her family: "That is the best meeting I ever attended."

One of the daughters said: "Well, Mother, who spoke?" And then her mother replied, "I did."

I thought he had enjoyed it because he himself had participated. I was glad he had. Then, he said: "You know I have heard many things in this conference, but there is only one thing I do not understand the way you do."

I said: "What is it?"

"Well," he said, "it is about paying tithing."

He thought I would ask him how he paid his tithing, but I did not. I thought if he wanted to tell me, he would. He said: "Would you like me to tell you how I pay my tithing?"

I said, "If you want to, you may."

"Well," he said, "if I make ten thousand dollars in a year, I put a thousand dollars in the bank for tithing. I know why it's there. Then when the bishop comes and wants me to make a contribution for the chapel or give him a check for a missionary who is going away, if I think he needs the money, I give him a check. If a family in the ward is in distress and needs coal or food or clothing or anything else, I write out a check. If I find a boy or girl who is having difficulty getting through school in the East, I send a check. Little by little I exhaust the thousand dollars, and every dollar of it has gone where I know it has done good. Now, what do you think of that?"

"Well," I said, "do you want me to tell you what I think of it?"

He said, "Yes."

I said: "I think you are a very generous man with someone else's property." And he nearly tipped the car over.

He said, "What do you mean?"

I said, "You have an idea that you have paid your tithing?"

"Yes," he said.

I said: "You have not paid any tithing. You have told me what you have done with the Lord's money, but you have not told me that you have given anyone a penny of your own. . . . You have taken your best partner's money, and have given it away."

Well, I will tell you there was quiet in the car for some time. We rode on to Salt Lake City and talked about other things. . . .

About a month after that I met him on the street. He came up, put his arm in mine, and said: "Brother Smith, I am paying my tithing the same way you do." I was very happy to hear that.

Not long before he died, he came into my office to tell me what he was doing with his own money. ✦

In his autobiography, Lorenzo Snow wrote of having to submerge his ego and social pride in becoming a missionary.

A short time after my ordination and reception into the Elders' quorum, *i.e.*, early in the spring of 1837, I shouldered my valise and started out like the ancient missionaries, "without purse or scrip," on foot and alone, to proclaim the restoration of the fulness of the Gospel of the Son of God, and to bear witness of what I had seen and heard, and of the knowledge I had received by the inspiration of the Holy Ghost.

It was, however, a severe trial to my natural feelings of independence to go without purse or scrip—especially the purse; for, from the time I was old enough to work, the feeling that I "paid my way" always seemed a necessary adjunct to self respect, and nothing but a positive knowledge that God required it now, as He did anciently of His servants, the Disciples of Jesus, could induce me to go forth dependent on my fellow creatures for the common necessaries of life. But my duty in this respect was clearly made known to me, and I determined to do it. ✦

Lorenzo Snow also spoke of the "sore trial" it was for him to face his first "audience in the capacity of a preacher." But, he said, "I had humbled myself before the Lord," and "the Holy Ghost rested mightily upon me, filling my mind with light and communicating ideas and proper language by which to impart them."

Belle Spafford tells of the lesson she learned about just who needed whom when she was called to be general president of the Relief Society, a position she held for more than twenty-nine years.

FROM "THE QUALITIES NEEDED FOR GREATNESS"

I well remember my call as president of Relief Society. I had been serving as a counselor to Sister Amy Brown Lyman in the presidency. One day the First Presidency called me to their office. Just before I left for their office, Sister Lyman advised me that she was to be released at the forthcoming general conference and a new president was to be appointed, and she said offhand, "It is my understanding that from now on the auxiliary heads are to be called for a period of five years only."

I went to the office of the First Presidency and was told that the next morning in the opening session of the general conference my name would be presented for a sustaining vote of the Church membership as the new general president of Relief Society. All I could think of was *five years*, and I thought if I could stand it for five years maybe I could get by. So I said to the Brethren, "Am I to understand, Brethren, that this is to be a five-year calling?" Whereupon President Clark, who was inclined to lower his glasses and peer above them when he wanted to look through you, lowered his glasses and said, "Five years? Why, you may not last that long, Sister!" ✦

We recognize the great service Sidney Rigdon rendered to the early Church, but it is clear that at some point he began to see the Church as a means for elevating himself. Upon the martyrdom of the Prophet Joseph Smith, he actively sought to be Church president. Helen Mar Whitney describes her perception of events surrounding the appointment of a successor to Joseph.

As is well known, Sidney Rigdon, who had shirked his duties and moved with his family to Pittsburg some time previous to Joseph's death, took advantage of the absence of the majority of the Twelve, to hasten to Nauvoo to lay claim to the guardianship of the Church, claiming to have had a vision from the Lord concerning them, which he related at his first appearance before a congregation of the Saints, saying that he was the identical man whom the Prophets had sung about, wrote about, and rejoiced over in every preceding generation, etc.

Elder Parley P. Pratt remarked, "I am the identical man the Prophets never sung nor wrote a word about." I was one of the listeners, and I think that very few of the Saints felt that Sidney Rigdon, who had deserted his post when Joseph stood most in need of him, was "the man whom the Lord had called" for a shepherd to lead His sheep, in this the saddest and darkest hour of their experience.

A day was appointed by Marks, the president of the stake, for a special conference to choose a guardian. Bros. Willard Richards, Parley P. Pratt, John Taylor and George A. Smith were opposed to this hasty step, and the former counseled the Saints not to be in a hurry, but to wait till the Twelve Apostles returned, and "ask wisdom of God." Elder Rigdon evaded these men, as if unwilling to come in contact with them, until he was forced to meet them in council. ✦

As Helen Mar Whitney tells it, a very excitable Sidney Rigdon pressed for a quick choice of a leader, arguing that the anti-Mormon faction in Nauvoo would carry the civic election unless the Church acted immediately to install a "great leader." George A. Smith assured the people that there was no cause for alarm, that "the friends of law and order will be elected by a thousand majority," that "Brother Rigdon is inspiring fears there are no grounds for." Reason prevailed, as the Whitney account attests:

The second day after the Apostles' return to Nauvoo [August 6, 1844], President Brigham Young called a special conference, to give Elder Rigdon the opportunity to lay his claims before the Church. Meetings were then held in a grove some little distance east of the Temple, where a great multitude gathered together; for this day—was to decide who was to "lead Israel,"

Sidney Rigdon, or the Twelve Apostles. That was a day never to be forgotten. I was among the number that was obliged to stand, it being impossible for half of the congregation to be seated. Mr. Hatch, a young lawyer, whom I had formed acquaintance with at our theatre the Spring previous, stood by me. We had been on pleasant terms, but lately he had turned Rigdonite, and frequently, during that long harangue, he spoke in defence and praise of the speaker, and tried to convince me that he was the right man to lead the Church. He very quickly learned my feelings, and how offensive he had made himself. My father was seated there with Brigham and the rest of the Apostles, and I became very indignant, and quite a war of words ensued, neither of us (of course) yielding the point. Not long after this he married one of Rigdon's daughters, which proved to be the only lodestone that attracted him in that direction. ✦

Later that same day, the Church congregated again to hear from Brigham Young, who argued for the divine authority of the Twelve in directing the Church and choosing its leader. Brigham reportedly said, among other things, "Brother Rigdon has come 1,600 miles to tell you what he wants to do for you. If the people want Brother Rigdon to lead them, they may have him, but I say unto you, the Twelve have the keys of the kingdom of God in all the world." As Brigham Young spoke, not for his own ascendancy, but for the appointment of the Lord's choice, many witnessed a miraculous manifestation that convinced them Brigham was the man to lead the Church. He seemed to speak in the voice of Joseph. Fortunately, charitable humility triumphed over self-vaunting on that day.

Secular literature, especially that for children, suffers no shortage of verse about the hazards as well as the general unpleasantness of self-vaunting.

FROM "LITTLE DITTIES"

There was a man so very tall,
That when you spoke you had to bawl
Through both your hands, put like a cup,
His head was such a long way up!

But there was something even sadder,—
His wife had to go up a ladder
Whenever she desired a kiss—
And he, alas, was proud of this!

Said he, "I am the tallest man
That ever grew since time began,"
As down on a house-top he sat;
Well, he *was* tall; but what of that?

This monstrous man, as we shall see,
Was punished for his vanity:
He grew and grew,—the people placed
A telescope to see his waist!

He grew and grew—you could not see
Without a telescope his knee;
He grew till he was over-grown,
And seen by over-sight alone!
(William Brighty Rands.)

THE NEW DUCKLING

"I want to be new," said the duckling.
"O, ho!" said the wise old owl,
While the guinea-hen cluttered off chuckling
To tell all the rest of the fowl.

"I should like a more elegant figure,"
That child of a duck went on.
"I should like to grow bigger and bigger,
Until I could swallow a swan.

"I *won't* be the bond slave of habit,
I *won't* have these webs on my toes.
I want to run round like a rabbit,
A rabbit as red as a rose.

"I *don't* want to waddle like mother,
Or quack like my silly old dad.
I want to be utterly other,
And *frightfully* modern and mad."

"Do you know," said the turkey, "you're quacking!
There's a fox creeping up thro' the rye;
And, if you're not utterly lacking,
You'll make for that duck-pond. Good-bye!"

But the duckling was perky as perky.
"Take care of your stuffing!" he called.
(This was horribly rude to a turkey!)
"But you aren't a real turkey," he bawled.

"You're an Early-Victorian Sparrow!
A fox is more fun than a sheep!
I shall show that *my* mind is not narrow
And give him my feathers—to keep."

Now the curious end of this fable,
So far as the rest ascertained,
Though they searched from the barn to the stable,
Was that *only his feathers remained.*

So he *wasn't* the bond slave of habit,
And he *didn't* have webs on his toes;
And *perhaps* he runs round like a rabbit,
A rabbit as red as a rose.
(Alfred Noyes.)

A very short Zen story makes a good point: "Gettan used to say to his companions, 'When you have a talking mouth, you have no listening ears. When you have listening ears, you have no talking mouth. Think about this carefully.'" (Zen Antics.)

THE OWL-CRITIC

"Who stuffed that white owl?" No one spoke in the shop;
The barber was busy, and he couldn't stop;
The customers, waiting their turns, were all reading
The *Daily,* the *Herald,* the *Post,* little heeding
The young man who blurted out such a blunt question;
Not one raised a head, or even made a suggestion;
And the barber kept on shaving.

"Don't you see, Mr. Brown,"
Cried the youth with a frown,
"How wrong the whole thing is,
How preposterous each wing is,
How flattened the head, how jammed down the neck is—
In short, the whole owl, what an ignorant wreck 'tis!
I make no apology;
I've learned owl-eology.
I've passed days and nights in a hundred collections,
And cannot be blinded to any deflections
Arising from unskilful fingers that fail
To stuff a bird right, from his beak to his tail.
Mister Brown! Mr. Brown!
Do take that bird down,
Or you'll soon be the laughing-stock all over town!"
And the barber kept on shaving.

I've studied owls,
And other night-fowls,
And I tell you
What I know to be true!
An owl cannot roost
With his limbs so unloosed;
No owl in this world
Ever had his claws curled,

93

Ever had his legs slanted,
Ever had his bill canted,
Ever had his neck screwed
Into that attitude.
He can't do it, because
'Tis against all bird laws.
Anatomy teaches,
Ornithology preaches,
An owl has a toe
That can't turn out so!
I've made the white owl my study for years,
And to see such a job almost moves me to tears!

Mr. Brown, I'm amazed
You should be so gone crazed
As to put up a bird
In that posture absurd!
To *look* at that owl really brings on a dizziness.
The man who stuffed *him* don't half know his business!"
And the barber kept on shaving.
"Examine those eyes.
I'm filled with surprise
Taxidermists should pass
Off on you such poor glass;
So unnatural they seem
They'd make Audubon scream,
And John Burroughs laugh
To encounter such chaff.
Do take that bird down;
Have him stuffed again, Brown!"
And the barber kept on shaving.

"With some sawdust and bark
I could stuff in the dark
An owl better than that.

I could make an old bat
Look more like an owl
Than that horrid fowl,
Stuck up there so stiff like a side of coarse leather;
In fact, about him there's not one natural feather."

Just then with a wink and a sly normal lurch,
The owl, very gravely, got down from his perch,
Walked around, and regarded his fault-finding critic
(Who thought he was stuffed) with a glance analytic,
And then fairly hooted, as if he should say:
"Your learning's at fault, this time, anyway;
Don't waste it again on a live bird, I pray.
I'm an owl; you're another. Sir Critic, good-day!"
And the barber kept on shaving.
(James T. Fields.)

Emily Dickinson advocates with captivating charm the virtue of humility.

I'm Nobody! Who are you?
Are you—Nobody—Too?
Then there's a pair of us?
Don't tell! they'd advertise—you know!

How dreary—to be—Somebody!
How public—like a Frog—
To tell one's name—the livelong June—
To an admiring Bog!

Clement of Rome wrote to the church at Corinth:

Let any commendation of us proceed from God, and not from ourselves, for self-praise is hateful to God. Testimony to our good deeds is for others to give, as it was given to those righteous men who were our forefathers. Self-assertion, self-assurance, and a bold manner are the marks of men accursed of God; it is those who show consideration for others, and are unassuming and quiet, who win His blessing. ❧

The realization of debts and obligations older than oneself is part of the process of maturing past self-centeredness toward God-centeredness.

INDIAN GRANDMOTHER

Old One,
Forgive me for the long
Dark braids that do not
Fall down my back
And do not brush the arm
Of a fine strong husband,
As yours did.
Forgive me
For the pale words
And gray thoughts
That kept your
Good red blood
Out of my heart
For lo these long years,
These years of growing
Out of myself
And into God,
Out of despair
And into humility.
Old One,
When you find Him,
Tell Him of my love,
Tell Him I am finally
Receiving with upturned
Hands the gifts He has been
Drenching me with
Patiently,
Tenderly,
Constantly.

Tell Him how I love seeing
Your name every time I write
My own.
Tell Him I get up
Every morning
Joyous
With my heritage from Him
And my legacy from you.
Old One,
Think well of this,
Your daughter in flesh.
Speak kindly of me
When the moon begins
To bleed and He dons His
Wine-red robe.
Call me now, Old One;
Call my name
And whisper yours,
So that, hearing
Your voice, I may better
Be attuned for His.
(Charlotte Teresa Reynolds.)

As shown in the poem above, another aspect of "vaunting not oneself" is the turning from self-praise to praise of God and reverence for him and his magnificent works. Instead of broadcasting our own abilities and accomplishments, we should praise God, the source of all good gifts. Perhaps the most blatant form of boastfulness is the vaunting of self above the Creator—and by extension, above creation, prophets, and church. Reverence is a matter of outlook and attitude. It is an approach to life, an innate recognition of the sacred and valuable. It is a choice we make about the kinds of persons we will be and what we will value, revere, and sustain.

Irreverence is . . . a pretty sure sign of moral weakness. No man will rise high who jeers at sacred things. (David O. McKay.) ✦

Reverence is the chief joy and power of life. (John Ruskin.) ✦

Not one particle of all that comprises this vast creation of God is our own. Everything we have has been bestowed upon us for our action, to see what we would do with it—whether we would use it for eternal death and degradation, until we cease operating in this existence. (Brigham Young.) ✦

Albert Schweitzer, who spent much of his life in the thoughtful service of humankind, arrived at the conclusion that "the first spiritual act in man's experience is reverence for life." The phrase "reverence for life" became his guiding philosophy, his spiritual signature. In "The Ethics of Reverence for Life" he wrote:

What shall be my attitude toward other life? It can only be of a piece with my attitude towards my own life. If I am a thinking being, I must regard other life than my own with equal reverence. For I shall know that it longs for fullness and development as deeply as I do myself. Therefore, I see that evil is what annihilates, hampers, or hinders life. And this holds good whether I regard it physically or spiritually. Goodness, by the same token, is the saving or helping of life, the enabling of whatever life I can influence to attain its highest development. ✦

In the priesthood session of general conference, October 6, 1951, President David O. McKay addressed the subject of reverence, describing it as "one of the highest qualities of the soul," and declaring that "an irreverent man is not a believing man." Furthermore, he concluded, "Reverence indicates high culture, and true faith in deity and in his righteousness." President McKay's life exemplified that reverence. In an Ensign *article (January 1979, 69–70), Ferren L. Christensen tells of seeing President McKay give personal aid to an injured sea lion. Mr. Christensen's own first inclination, he says, had been to hurl a rock at the injured animal and scare it back to sea, perhaps too soon, before it had recovered strength. President McKay's gentle restraining arm conveyed a powerful message, as did his tender, comforting strokes on the animal's slick skin.*

A good many poets have echoed the angel who spoke to John the Revelator, saying, "Hurt not the earth, neither the sea, nor the trees." (Revelation 7:3.)

HURT NO LIVING THING

Hurt no living thing:
Ladybird, nor butterfly,
Nor moth with dusty wing,
Nor cricket chirping cheerily,
Nor grasshopper so light of leap,
Nor dancing gnat, nor beetle fat,
Nor harmless worms that creep.
(Christina Rossetti.)

Bertha S. Reeder, fifth general president of the Young Women's Mutual Improvement Association, greatly loved the outdoor world. She penned these words:

FROM "IF I WERE IN MY TEENS"

If I were in my teens, I would take time to come close to nature. I would learn to fish, to swim, to hike, and to find joy in God's great out-of-doors. I would learn to listen to the earth noises—to hear the birds, the crickets, the sighing of the wind in the trees, the lapping of the water against the shore. I would learn to see the differences in trees, in flowers, in grasses. I would realize again more fully the infinite variety in God's creation. I would learn to feel the difference in the seasons and to love each for what it gives to me. I would know that rain and sunshine are both important in God's plan. ❧

Like Henry David Thoreau in his time, our contemporary, Wendell Berry, has become something of a conscience for us, urging us to reverence rather than destroy life.

FROM "THE RISE"

Where the river was over the banks a stretch of comparatively quiet water lay between the trees on the bank top and the new shore line. After a while, weary of the currents, we turned into one of these. As we made our way past the treetops and approached the shore we flushed a bobwhite out of a brush pile near the water and saw it fly off downstream. It seemed strange to see only one. But we didn't have to wait long for an explanation, for presently we saw the dogs, and then the hunters coming over the horizon with their guns. We knew where their bird had gone, but we didn't wait to tell them.

These men come out from the cities now that the hunting season is open. They walk in these foreign places, unknown to them for most of the year, looking for something to kill. They wear and carry many dollars' worth of equipment, and go to a great deal of trouble, in order to kill some small creature that they would never trouble to know alive, and that means little to them once they have killed it. If those we saw had killed the bobwhite they would no doubt have felt all their expense and effort justified, and would have thought themselves more manly than before. . . . The diggers among our artifacts will find us to have been honorable lovers of death, having been willing to pay exorbitantly for it. How much better, we thought, to have come upon the *life* of the bird as we did, moving peaceably among the lives of the country that showed themselves to us because we were peaceable, than to have tramped fixedly, half oblivious, for miles in order to come at its death. ❖

In a memorable address in the priesthood session of general conference, October 1978, President Spencer W. Kimball spoke at length on the subject of reverence for created life. Early in that sermon, he quoted four verses from the first chapter of Genesis:

And God said, Let the waters bring forth abundantly the moving creature that hath life, and fowl that may fly above the earth in the open firmament of heaven. (Genesis 1:20.)

And God said, Behold, I have given you every herb bearing seed, which is upon the face of all the earth, and every tree, in the which is the fruit of a tree yielding seed; to you it shall be for meat.

And to every beast of the earth, and to every fowl of the air, and to every thing that creepeth upon the earth, wherein there is life, I have given every green herb for meat: and it was so.

And God saw every thing that he had made, and, behold, it was very good. And the evening and the morning were the sixth day. (Genesis 1:29–31.)

President Kimball then alluded to his talk in the priesthood session of conference six months earlier, and quoted again from a Primary song of his youth, "Don't Kill the Little Birds." On the later occasion he indicated that he had been impressed to "say something more along this line." He also referred to President Joseph Fielding Smith's great appreciation for birds and other forms of wildlife.

President Kimball then counseled the Saints against what he regarded as "the unnecessary shedding of blood and destruction of life" and urged them to follow the prophets' sentiments on the matter. He spoke, he said, not only of "the killing of innocent birds" but also of the killing of "the wildlife of our country that live upon the vermin that are indeed enemies to the farmer and to mankind. It is not only wicked to destroy them, it is a shame, in my opinion. I think that this principle should extend not only to the bird life but to the life of all animals. For that purpose I read the scripture where the Lord gave us all the animals. Seemingly, he thought it was important that all these animals be on the earth for our use and encouragement."

President Kimball also alluded to the following statement by Joseph F. Smith:

When I visited, a few years ago, the Yellowstone National Park, and saw in the streams and the beautiful lakes, birds swimming quite fearless of man, allowing passers-by to approach them as closely almost as tame birds, and apprehending no fear of them, and when I saw droves of beautiful deer [feeding] along the side of the road, as fearless of the presence of men as any domestic animal, it filled my heart with a degree of peace and joy that seemed to be almost a foretaste of that period hoped for when there shall be none to hurt and none to molest in all the land, especially among all the inhabitants of Zion. These same birds, if they were to visit other regions, inhabited by man, would, on account of their tameness, doubtless become more easily a prey to the gunner. The same may be said of those beautiful creatures—the deer and the antelope. If they should wander out of the park, beyond the protection that is established there for these animals, they would become, of course, an easy prey to those who were seeking their lives. I never could see why a man should be imbued with a blood-thirsty desire to kill and destroy animal life. I have known men—and they still exist among us—who enjoy what is, to them, the 'sport' of hunting birds and slaying them by the hundreds, and who will come in after a day's sport, boasting of how many harmless birds they have had the skill to slaughter, and day after day, during the season when it is lawful for men to hunt and kill (the birds having had a season of protection and not apprehending danger) go out by scores or hundreds, and you may hear their guns early in the morning on the day of the opening, as if great armies had met in battle; and the terrible work of slaughtering the innocent birds goes on.

I do not believe any man should kill animals or birds unless he needs them for food, and then he should not kill innocent little birds that are not intended for food for man. I think it is wicked for men to thirst in their souls to kill almost everything which possesses animal life. It is wrong, and I have been surprised at prominent men whom I have seen whose very souls seemed to be athirst for the shedding of animal blood.

As he continued his address, President Kimball said:

It is quite a different matter when a pioneer crossing the plains would kill a buffalo to bring food to his children and his family. There were also those vicious men who would kill buffalo only for their tongues and skins, permitting the life to be sacrificed and the food also to be wasted.

He then recounted the following story by the Prophet Joseph Smith:

We crossed the Embarras river and encamped on a small branch of the same about one mile west. In pitching my tent we found three massasaugas or prairie rattlesnakes, which the brethren were about to kill, but I said, 'Let them alone—don't hurt them! How will the serpent ever lose his venom, while the servants of God possess the same disposition and continue to make war upon it? Men must become harmless, before the brute creation; and when men lose their vicious dispositions and cease to destroy the animal race, the lion and the lamb can dwell together, and the sucking child can play with the serpent in safety.' The brethren took the serpents carefully on sticks and carried them across the creek. I exhorted the brethren not to

102

kill a serpent, bird, or an animal of any kind during our journey unless it became necessary in order to preserve ourselves from hunger. ❧

From The Journal of John Woolman, *we read:*

He whose tender mercies are over all his works hath placed a principle in the human mind which incites to exercise goodness toward every living creature; and this being singly attended to, people become tender-hearted and sympathizing, but being frequently and totally rejected, the mind shuts itself up in a contrary disposition. ❧

Again, I believe that to turn our minds from self-praise to praise of God is to exercise the charity Paul speaks of when he says it vaunts not itself. Splendid, worshipful expressions of praise for the Lord of Creation are plentiful, in sacred and secular literature alike. The Psalms (see Psalm 19, for example) are especially eloquent, but the following passage from modern scripture is probably unequaled on the subject:

He comprehendeth all things, and all things are before him, and all things are round about him; and he is above all things, and in all things, and is through all things, and is round about all things; and all things are by him, and of him, even God, forever and ever.

And again, verily I say unto you, he hath given a law unto all things, by which they move in their times and their seasons;

And their courses are fixed, even the courses of the heavens and the earth, which comprehend the earth and all the planets.

And they give light to each other in their times and in their seasons, in their minutes, in their hours, in their days, in their weeks, in their months, in their years—all these are one year with God, but not with man.

The earth rolls upon her wings, and the sun giveth his light by day, and the moon giveth her light by night, and the stars also give their light, as they roll upon their wings in their glory, in the midst of the power of God. (Doctrine and Covenants 88:41–45.) ❧

Religious writers whose works appear in the Apocrypha are inspiring in their reverent praise of God.

FROM "THE WISDOM OF SIRACH"

I will call to mind the doings of the Lord,
And recount the things that I have seen.
By the commands of the Lord his works are done;
The light-giving sun looks down on everything,
And his work is full of the glory of the Lord.
He has not permitted the saints of the Lord
To recount all his wonders,
Which the Lord, the Almighty, has firmly established,
So that the universe might stand fast through his glory.
He searches out the great deep and the human mind,
And he understands their designs;
For the Most High possesses all knowledge,
And looks upon the portent of eternity,
And declares the things that are past and the things that are to come,
And uncovers the tracks of hidden things.
No thought escapes him,
Not one word is hidden from him.
He has ordained the majesty of his wisdom,
For he is from everlasting to everlasting.
It cannot be increased or diminished,
And he has no need of any counselor.
How much to be desired are all his works,
And how sparkling they are to see.
All these things live and last forever,
With all their functions, and they are all obedient.
They are all in pairs, one facing another,
Not one of them is missing.
One confirms the good of the other,
And who can have too much of beholding his glory?

*And these joyous, poetic expressions of glory to God celebrate the diversity
and beauty of creation:*

PIED BEAUTY

Glory be to God for dappled things—
For skies of couple-colour as a brinded cow;
For rose-moles all in stipple upon trout that swim;
Fresh-firecoal chestnut-falls; finches' wings;
Landscape plotted and pieced—fold, fallow, and plough;
And all trades, their gear and tackle trim.

All things counter, original, spare, strange;
Whatever is fickle, freckled (who knows how?)
With swift, slow; sweet, sour; adazzle, dim;
He fathers-forth whose beauty is past change:
Praise him.
(Gerard Manley Hopkins.)

HIGH FLIGHT

Oh, I have slipped the surly bonds of earth,
And danced the skies on laughter-silvered wings;
Sunward I've climbed and joined the tumbling mirth
Of sun-split clouds—and done a hundred things
You have not dreamed of—wheeled and soared and swung
High in the sunlit silence. Hov'ring there
I've chased the shouting wind along and flung
My eager craft through footless halls of air.
Up, up the long delirious, burning blue
I've topped the wind-swept heights with easy grace,
Where never lark, or even eagle, flew;
And, while with silent, lifting mind I've trod
The high untrespassed sanctity of space,
Put out my hand, and touched the face of God.
(John Gillespie Magee, Jr.)

*In 1906, John G. McQuarrie, then president of the LDS Church's eastern
states mission, published a little book titled* Talks to the Saints. *Its purpose was to*

sustain Church members who lived outside the central valleys of Zion. One of the talks in the book establishes the connection between character and reverence for God.

WORSHIP

First then, the members are required to worship God. Is this requirement to gratify His vanity? Evidently not, but rather to develop our character. Worship is extreme admiration. Taken in this sense you will see what a potent power it really is. There is to be seen all around us the effects of a law which tend to conform the individual to that which he habitually admires. Have you not noticed how the dress, the habits and even the physical form of the individual change as his ideals are changed by fashion, association or education?

Is it not evident then that if you worship the good, the beautiful, and the true, the impress of such qualities will be seen on your character; and on the other hand, if you admire that which is bad, uncomely, and false, will not the effect be just the opposite? Then how thankful we should be that the Lord has revealed a character worthy of our worship. How careful we should be to call this image up in our minds at least in the morning and evening of each day. How anxious we should be to meet with our brothers and sisters on the Sabbath day to talk over the goodness, the mercy, and the love of God. ✦

Bishop Robert L. Simpson tells the following story about reverence for temples:

Two teen-age youngsters stood at the base of the stairs leading to the glistening New Zealand Temple on the eve before its dedication in 1958. Being after dark, the temple appeared to be suspended in space as large floodlights bathed it in a fluorescent, bluish glow. It was beautiful to behold.

The youngsters had just completed a long tedious journey in an open truck, and as they arrived, they ran directly from the truck to the temple steps. This was a dream come true. They were looking at a temple of the Lord for the first time in their young lives. After a moment of silence, one of them finally spoke and said, "Let us go up where we can touch it."

After a few short moments the other one said, "Do you really think we should?"

Then following a short discussion, both agreed that it would be better to wait until morning after they had had a chance to clean up and put on their finest Sunday clothes before going up to touch the House of the Lord.

As Sister Simpson and I stood there unnoticed by these two young people, our hearts were overjoyed at the thought of parental teaching that had given this spiritual dimension to the youth of Zion, way down in the South Pacific. ❦

One of our finest discourses on worship, and therefore on reverence in the religious sense, comes from Elder James E. Talmage. He implores us to reverence only that which is worthy of reverence, and he reminds us that ritual alone does not constitute worship. Worship, he says, is a reflection of love—charity.

"WHAT IS WORSHIP?"

What is Worship?—The derivation of the term suggests an answer. It comes to us as the lineal descendant of a pair of Anglo-Saxon words, *weorth,* meaning worthy, and *scipe,* the old form of *ship,* signifying condition or state, and connotes the thought of *worthy-ship.* The worship of which one is capable depends upon his comprehension of the worthiness characterizing the object of his reverence. Man's capacity for worship is a measure of his comprehension of God. The fuller the acquaintance and the closer the communion between the worshiper and Deity, the more thorough and sincere will be his homage. When we say of one that he is a worshiper of the good, the beautiful, the true, we mean that he possesses a deeper conception of worth in the object of his adoration, than does another whose perception does not lead him to reverence those ennobling qualities.

Man, then, will worship according to his conception of the divine attributes and powers, and this conception approaches the correct one in proportion to the spiritual light that has come to him. True worship cannot exist where there is no reverence or love for the object. This reverence may be ill-founded; the adoration may be a species of idolatry; the object may be in fact unworthy; yet of the devotee it must be said that he worships if his conscience clothe the idol with the attribute of worthy-ship. . . . Worship is not a matter of form any more than is prayer. It consists not in posture, in gesture, in ritual or in creed. Worship most profound may be rendered with none of the artificial accessories of ritualistic service; for altar, the stone in the desert may serve; the peaks of the everlasting hills are as temple spires; the vault of heaven is of all the grandest cathedral dome.

Man is at heart an expression in part of that which he worships. . . . The revolting practises of idolatry are traceable to perverted conceptions of human excellence, and these are reflected in the hideous creations of man-made, devil-inspired deities. On the other hand, the man whose enlightened soul has received the impress of love, pure and undefiled, will ascribe to his God the attributes of gentleness and affection, and will say in his heart "God is love." Knowledge, therefore, is essential to worship; man cannot adequately serve God in ignorance; and the greater his knowledge of the divine personality, the fuller and truer will be his adoration. He may learn to know the Father, and the Son who was sent; and such knowledge is man's guaranty to eternal life.

Worship is the voluntary homage of the soul. Under compulsion, or for purposes of display, one may insincerely perform all the outward ceremonies of an established style of adoration; he may voice words of prescribed prayers; his lips may profess a creed; yet his effort is but a mockery of worship and its indulgence a sin. God asks no reluctant homage nor unwilling praise. Formalism in worship is acceptable only so far as it is accompanied by an intelligent devoutness; and it is genuine only as it is an aid to the spiritual devotion that leads to communion with Deity. The spoken prayer is but empty sound if it be anything less than an index to the volume of the soul's righteous desire. Communications addressed to the Throne of Grace must bear the stamp of sincerity if they are to reach their high destination. The most acceptable form of worship is that which rests on an unreserved compliance with the laws of God as the worshiper has learned their purport. ❧

Elder Bruce R. McConkie delivered a powerful sermon on worship at general conference in October 1971. Much of the sermon makes an implicit, yet clear, connection between charity as Paul describes it and worship of God:

[The Eternal Father] has planted in our hearts an instinctive desire to worship, to seek salvation, to love and serve a power or being greater than ourselves. Worship is implicit in existence itself. . . .

. . . our purpose is to worship the true and living God and to do it by the power of the Spirit and in the way he has ordained. The approved worship of the true God leads to salvation; devotions rendered to false gods and which are not founded on eternal truth carry no such assurance.

A knowledge of the truth is essential to true worship. We must learn that God is our Father; that he is an exalted and perfected personage in whose image we are created; that he sent his Beloved Son into the world to redeem mankind; that salvation is in Christ, who is the revelation of God to the world; and that Christ and his gospel laws are known only by revelation given to those apostles and prophets who represent him on earth.

There is no salvation in worshiping a false god. It does not matter one particle how sincerely someone may believe God is a golden calf, or that he is an immaterial, uncreated power that is in all things; the worship of such a being or concept has no saving power. Men may believe with all their souls that images or powers or laws are God, but no amount of devotion to these concepts will ever give the power that leads to immortality and eternal life.

If a man worships a cow or a crocodile, he can gain any reward that cows and crocodiles happen to be passing out this season.

If he worships the laws of the universe or the forces of nature, no doubt the earth will continue to spin, the sun to shine, and the rains to fall on the just and on the unjust.

But if he worships the true and living God, in spirit and in truth, then God Almighty will pour out his Spirit upon him, and he will have power to raise the dead, move mountains, entertain angels, and walk in celestial streets. . . .

To worship the Lord is to follow after him, to seek his face, to believe his doctrine, and to think his thoughts.

It is to walk in his paths, to be baptized as Christ was, to preach that gospel of the kingdom which fell from his lips, and to heal the sick and raise the dead as he did.

To worship the Lord is to put first in our lives the things of his kingdom, to live by every word that proceedeth forth from the mouth of God, to center our whole hearts upon Christ and that salvation which comes because of him.

It is to walk in the light as he is in the light, to do the things that he wants done, to do what he would do under similar circumstances, to be as he is.

To worship the Lord is to walk in the Spirit, to rise above carnal things, to bridle our passions, and to overcome the world.

It is to pay our tithes and offerings, to act as wise stewards in caring for those things which have been entrusted to our care, and to use our talents and means for the spreading of truth and the building up of his kingdom.

To worship the Lord is to be married in the temple, to have children, to teach them the gospel, and to bring them up in light and truth.

It is to perfect the family unit, to honor our father and our mother; it is for a man to love his wife with all his heart and to cleave unto her and none else.

To worship the Lord is to visit the fatherless and the widows in their affliction and to keep ourselves unspotted from the world.

It is to work on a welfare project, to administer to the sick, to go on a mission, to go home teaching, and to hold family home evening.

To worship the Lord is to study the gospel, to treasure up light and truth, to ponder in our hearts the things of his kingdom, and to make them part of our lives.

It is to pray with all the energy of our souls, to preach by the power of the Spirit, to sing songs of praise and thanksgiving.

To worship is to work, to be actively engaged in a good cause, to be about our Father's business, to love and serve our fellowmen.

It is to feed the hungry, to clothe the naked, to comfort those that mourn, and to hold up the hands that hang down and to strengthen the feeble knees.

To worship the Lord is to stand valiantly in the cause of truth and righteousness, to let our influence for good be felt in civic, cultural, educational, and governmental fields, and to support those laws and principles which further the Lord's interests on earth.

To worship the Lord is to be of good cheer, to be courageous, to be valiant, to have the courage of our God-given convictions, and to keep the faith.

It is ten thousand times ten thousand things. It is keeping the commandments of God. It is living the whole law of the whole gospel.

To worship the Lord is to be like Christ until we receive from him the blessed assurance: "Ye shall be even as I am." . . .

True and perfect worship is in fact the supreme labor and purpose of man. God grant that we may write in our souls with a pen of fire the command of the Lord Jesus: "Thou shalt worship the Lord thy God, and him only shalt thou serve" (Luke 4:8); and may we in fact and with living reality worship the Father in spirit and in truth, thereby gaining peace in this life and eternal life in the world to come. ❧

Those who love prophecy and doctrine are disposed to reverence sacred text as the discourse of a divine author. John even suggests the sanctity of language in his celebration of Christ as the Word. Writing in the first half of the eighteenth century, distinguished theologian Philip Doddridge is full of praise for the New Testament because Christ is at its center.

FROM "ON THE POWER AND BEAUTY

OF THE NEW TESTAMENT"

We have here the authentic records of that Gospel which was intended as the great medicine for our souls! of that character which is our pattern; of that death which is our ransom; of him, in short, whose name we bear, as we are professed Christians; and before whose tribunal we are all shortly to appear, that our eternal existence may be determined, blissful or miserable, according to our regard for what he has taught and done and endured. Let not the greatest, therefore, think it beneath their notice; nor the meanest imagine that amidst all the most necessary cares and labors they can find any excuse for neglecting or for even postponing it. . . .

The account which the New Testament gives us of the temper and character of our Divine Redeemer is a topic of argument by no means to be forgotten. We do not, indeed, there meet with any studied encomiums [formal expressions of high praise] upon the subject. The authors deal not in such sort of productions; but, which is a thousand times better, they show us the character itself. The sight of what is great and beautiful has another kind of effect than the most eloquent description of it. And here we behold the actions of Christ; we attend his discourses, and have a plain and open view of his behavior. In consequence of this we see in him everything venerable, everything amiable. We see a perfection of goodness nowhere in the world to be seen or to be heard; and numberless arguments plead at once to persuade the heart that it is absolutely impossible such a person should be engaged in a design founded in known falsehood, and tending only to mislead and ruin his followers.

And though it is true the character of his Apostles does not fully come up to the standard of their Master, nor is entirely free from some small blemishes; yet we see so little of that kind in them, and, on the contrary, such an assemblage of the human, divine, and social virtues, that we cannot, if we thoroughly know them, if we form an intimate acquaintance with them, entertain with patience the least suspicion that they were capable of a part so detestable as theirs must have been, if they knew Jesus to have been an imposter, and the Gospel a fable; with which they must be chargeable, if Christianity were not indeed authentic and divine. . . .

To conclude this head, the history before us represents, in the most clear and convincing light, the genius of that doctrine which Christ taught, and of the religion which he came to settle in the world. When we view it as exhibited in human writings we may mistake; for it is too often tinctured with the channel through which it has passed. . . . But here we drink this water of life at its fountain head, untainted and unmixed, and with that peculiar spirit, which, at a distance from it, is so apt to evaporate. Here we plainly perceive there is nothing in the scheme but what is most worthy of God to reveal, and of his Son to publish—to publish to the world.

Here we see, not, as in the heathen writers, some detached sentiment, finely heightened with the beauty of expression and pomp of words, like a scattered fragment, with the partial traces of impaired elegance and magnificence; but the elevation of a complete temple, worthy of the Deity to whom it is consecrated: so harmonious a system of unmingled truth, so complete a plan of universal duty, so amiable a representation of true morality in all its parts, without redundancy, and without defect, that the more capable we are of judging of real excellence, the more we shall be prepossessed in its favor.

And if we have a capacity and opportunity of examining together with it the books which the followers of other religions have esteemed sacred, and the system of doctrines and manners which their respective founders have published to the world, we shall find how much the Gospel is credited by the comparison—shall indeed find the difference much like that of a coarse picture of sunshine, from the original beams of that celestial luminary. This I have so deeply felt in mine own heart, while reading these books, and especially while commenting upon them, that it has been a matter of astonishment, as well as grief, to me, that there should be any mind capable of resisting evidence so various, so powerful, and so sweet. ❧

A radio address by Hugh B. Brown provides a useful summation.

FROM "PRAYER"

We need the growth that comes to all who praise and worship the Creator. It is not implied that he needs our praise or seeks our adoration. He is our ideal of all the good we know and to praise and adore him is to hold before us all the virtues which in him have reached perfection. Contemplation of the life of Christ, and adoration of the Deity, will tend to lift us above the petty, selfish, and superficial thoughts and experiences of our daily existence and to make us more like that which we adore. ✦

5

CHARITY IS NOT PUFFED UP

Be clothed with humility: for God resisteth

the proud, and giveth grace to the humble.

1 PETER 5:5

T he subject of the present chapter is closely related to that of the preceding one, but the figure Paul chooses here to describe the absence of charity is distinctive. *"Puffed up"* suggests pride, first and last—the pride Jesus condemned, the pride the prophets have decried, the pride that closes our hearts to both the perception and the exercise of Christ's love. The Book of Mormon repeatedly and emphatically links pride in Nephite society with a loss of charity, Christ's pure love. Jacob speaks keenly to the subject:

And the hand of providence hath smiled upon you most pleasingly, that you have obtained many riches; and because some of you have obtained more abundantly than that of your brethren ye are lifted up in the pride of your hearts, and wear stiff necks and high heads because of the costliness of your apparel, and persecute your brethren because ye suppose that ye are better than they.

And now, my brethren, do ye suppose that God justifieth you in this thing? Behold, I say unto you, Nay. But he condemneth you, and if ye persist in these things his judgments must speedily come unto you.

O that he would show you that he can pierce you, and with one glance of his eye he can smite you to the dust!

O that he would rid you from this iniquity and abomination. And, O that ye would listen unto the word of his commands, and let not this pride of your hearts destroy your souls!

Think of your brethren like unto yourselves, and be familiar with all and free with your substance, that they may be rich like unto you. (Jacob 2:13–17.) ✦

To be "puffed up" is to be haughty and then some. It is pursuing stubbornly one's own path or point of view, needing to prove one's superiority over others, being "above counsel." Conversely, a person who is not puffed up does not have to be right all the time or to turn every situation into a competitive event. The charitable person is willing to be obedient, to submit to a higher and wiser authority than his or her own.

Jesus taught that "whosoever shall exalt himself shall be abased" (Matthew 23:12), and he several times targeted the spiritual dangers of intellectual pride. Eliza R. Snow playfully mocks that particular folly with a "puffed up" metaphor:

MENTAL GAS

Charles to his teacher—Sir, you say
That nature's laws admit decay—
That changes never cease;
And yet you say, no void or space;
'Tis only change of shape or place—
No loss, and no increase.

That space or vacuum, sir, explain—
When solid sense forsakes the brain,
Pray what supplies its place?
O, sir, I think I see it now—
When substance fails, you will allow
Air occupies the space.

Not so, my child, that rule must fail;
For, by my philosophic scale,
The substitute for sense
Is lighter far than common air;

And with the most consummate care,
No chemic skill can dense.

But when misfortune turns the screw,
'Tis oft compress'd from outward view—
By outward force confin'd:
But with expansive power 'twill rise,
Destroy the man, increase his size,
And swell his optics blind.

Of various hues, yet still the same;
Though *mental gas* its chemic name,
Some Poets call it *pride:*
Th' important aid this gas imparts
Among the various *human arts*
Can never be denied.

This gas, entire, may be obtain'd
From skulls whence sense is mostly drain'd,
Or never had supplies:
But were the noblest heads disclos'd,
From acts and motives decompos'd,
This mental gas would rise.

The parson's lecture, lawyer's plea,
Devoted sums of charity,
The sage with book profound;
The Muse's pen, the churchman's creed,
The mill-boy on his pacing steed,
Are more or less compound.

And whoso knocketh, to him will he open; and the wise, and the
learned, and they that are rich, who are puffed up because of their learning,
and their wisdom, and their riches—yea, they are they whom he despiseth;
and save they shall cast these things away, and consider themselves fools

before God, and come down in the depths of humility, he will not open unto them. (2 Nephi 9:42.) ❧

Karl G. Maeser's account of his conversion to the restored gospel demonstrates the ultimate wisdom of humility over intellectual pride.

As "Oberlahrer" at the Budich Institute, Neustadt, Dresden, I, like most of my fellow teachers, had become imbued with the scepticism that characterizes, to a large extent, the tendency of modern higher education; but I was realizing at the same time the unsatisfactory condition of the mind that has nothing to rely upon but the ever-changing propositions of speculative philosophy.

Although filled with admiration for the indomitable courage, sincere devotion, and indefatigable energy of the great German reformer, Martin Luther, I could not fail to see that his work had been merely an initiatory one, and that the various Protestant sects . . . had entirely failed to comprehend the mission of the Reformation. The only strength of Protestantism seemed to be its negative position to the Catholic Church; while in most of these multifarious Protestant sects, their antagonism to one another culminated only too often in uncompromising zealotry. These ideas illustrate, in the main, my views on religious subjects at this time, and are explanatory of the fact that scepticism had undermined the religious impressions of my childhood days, and why infidelity, now known by its modern name as agnosticism, was exercising its disintegrating influence on me.

In this dark period of my life, when I was searching for a foothold among the political, social, philosophic, and religious opinions of the world, my attention was called to a pamphlet on the Mormons, written by a man named Busch. The author wrote in a spirit of opposition to that strange people, but his very illogical deductions and sarcastic invectives aroused my curiosity, and an irresistible desire to know more about the subject of the author's animadversions, caused me to make persistent inquiries concerning it. [Karl Maeser then describes how, through a series of sometimes aborted efforts, he managed to obtain pamphlets and books from LDS mission authorities in Europe. He tells of his response to the writings, noting that the very humility of their presentation impressed him.]

. . . I had some conceited notions in those days about literacy, and I had no faith in the Bible and religious doctrines; therefore, the inaccuracies and the poverty of language I found in those publications were, at first, sources of some ironical amusement; but as I read on I came to be convinced that "Mormonism" was a bigger thing than I had anticipated it to be. The humble but straightforward statements of testimony, the mistakes and meagreness of the language used in the exposition of the wonderful truths that I could see back of it all, brought such uneasiness to me that I could not rest, my soul was on fire, as it were, and I therefore expressed a desire to have an elder sent to me. ❦

In the biography just cited, Karl Maeser's son, Reinhard, comments on the surprising appeal of the unsophisticated doctrines of the gospel to learned men such as his father.

But these simple doctrines of faith, repentance, and baptism, and reception of the Holy Ghost, made deeper impressions on the minds of these young professors than had all the religious teachings and philosophies of their profoundest study before; and if they had thought that the superiority of their education, or the knowledge they had gained through the study of the old philosophers would give them weapons of defense and assault against the teachings of "Mormonism" as now presented to them, in humiliation and chagrin they found their mistake, for they were completely vanquished. The "still small voice" bore witness to them that the truth of heaven was being spoken to them in the broken and disjointed sentences of this man of God, who had come to them with his wonderful message. ❦

When the French philosopher Voltaire was told that a certain professor had an answer for everything, he reportedly exclaimed, "Heavens! is he as ignorant as all that?" In a similar vein, Carl Sandburg relates this incident:

A foreign diplomat demurred at Lincoln's condemning a certain Greek history as tedious. "The author of that history, Mr. President, is one of the profoundest scholars of the age. Indeed, it may be doubted whether any man of our generation has plunged more deeply in the sacred fount of learning." "Yes," said Lincoln, "or come up dryer." ❦

GLOWWORM

Never talk down to a glowworm—
Such as *What do you knowworm?*
How's it down belowworm?
Guess you're quite a slowworm.
No. Just say
Helloworm!
(David McCord.)

Desiring to meet Joseph Smith and to find out more about the religion he taught, in late 1837 a somewhat skeptical Edwin D. Woolley set out for Kirtland on horseback. As it turned out, Joseph had left Kirtland, so Edwin Woolley hastened to New Portage to catch the Prophet's father. Joseph Smith, Sr., went home with Woolley and stayed there part of the winter. According to historian Leonard Arrington, "This personal relationship with Joseph Smith, Sr., along with what he heard from [Lorenzo] Barnes, must have cleared some of the tantalizing confusion in Edwin's mind. A few words from Erastus Snow, a visiting elder, helped too. After hearing Snow preach, Edwin reportedly told him, 'If you show me some sign like the Apostle Paul had, I will believe in your doctrine.'" Snow was quick to deliver a lesson in humility, as Woolley's daughter tells it, and Woolley was quick to learn it.

Erastus Snow, being a small stocky-built man, the same size as father, and he being about such a man as I am myself, Mr. Snow, raising upon his tip toes to appear looking down upon father, replied, "and who are you, Mr. Woolley, that you should demand a sign like the Apostle Paul? If you came into our Church you could do us very little good, and if you remain out, you certainly can do us no harm." ❦

Edwin Woolley asked for baptism on the spot.

The following excerpt from Albert Schweitzer's writings reminds us that humility is an attribute of the truly great. Note his genuine, unassuming charitableness toward his old schoolmates.

FROM "MEMOIRS OF

CHILDHOOD AND YOUTH"

All my life I have been glad that I began in the village school. It was a good thing for me that in the process of learning I had to measure myself with the village boys, and thus make it quite clear to myself that they had at least as much in their heads as I had in mine. I was never a victim of that ignorance which afflicts so many of the boys who go straight to a Gymnasium [a classical preparatory school], and there tell each other that the children of the educated classes have more in them than the lads who go to school in darned stockings and wooden clogs. Even to-day if I meet any of my old schoolfellows in the village or on a farm, I at once remember vividly the points in which I did not reach their level. One was better at mental arithmetic; another made fewer mistakes in his dictation; a third never forgot a date; another was always top in geography; another—I mean you, Fritz Schöppeler—wrote almost better than the school-master. Even to-day they stand in my mind for the subjects in which they were at that time superior to me. ✦

The story is told of one of Martin Luther's teachers, John Trebonius, that he would not wear the traditional scholar's cap and gown when he taught. Asked why, Trebonius replied that he "always bared his head in the presence of so many future burgomasters, chancellors, doctors, and regents." (Roland H. Bainton, Here I Stand: A Life of Martin Luther *[Nashville: Abingdon Press, 1950], p. 25.)*

In a long poem Orson F. Whitney draws an inspiring portrait of the noble teacher, the "mind-uplifting, soul-expanding, master educator." The stanza quoted below has particular application to the subject of pride.

FROM "THE EDUCATOR"

Tolerant of all opinion,
Modest, temperate of expression;
Given not to contradiction,
E'en though clearest fact confirm him;
Wielding an advantage mildly,

Generous to a fallen foeman;
Angered not by loss or losing,
Nor in triumph's hour exulting;
Willing, eager for correction,
Welcoming from truth instruction;
Humbled by his weight of knowledge,
Ne'er too lofty to be learning.

Florida Scott-Maxwell reminds us that gifts as well as material wealth can be shared, but only if those gifts are allowed to blossom in the persons blessed with them. Humility does not imply a leveling of gifts to the lowest common denominator—rather, the truly humble actually value the inequality of gifts among human beings. Furthermore, Scott-Maxwell asks, "If we could be equal, what would happen to reverence and compassion?" In truth, she says, the wish for equality can be heard "as the cry of unlived pride."

Who would be equal to whom? Do we all go as low as we can to prove we are above no one? Must all the gifts of those greater than we disappear from the world? No triumphs of accomplishment? No drive to discover the rare in ourselves and others? Never to be bemused by beauties we lack? No sudden insight of what might be? No respect or loyalty or humility stirred by what you had not known was possible? But these are our ennobling moments. It is at these times we outgrow ourselves. ❖

In a comment about the spelling of his wife's family name, Abraham Lincoln is said to have remarked, "I guess one 'd' is good enough for God, but the Todds need two." (Carl Sandburg, The Prairie Years *2:289.) Lincoln was known well, of course, for his ready wit, but he was also known for his humility. He was one who could admit it when he was wrong. In a letter to General Ulysses S. Grant, dated July 13, 1863, he praised the general for his service and then confessed that at one point in the military operations he feared Grant was making a serious mistake. He concluded his letter with this generous statement: "I now wish to make the personal acknowledgment that you were right and I was wrong." (Selections from the Letters, Speeches, and State Papers of Abraham Lincoln, edited by Ida M. Tarbell [Boston: Ginn, 1911], p. 97.)*

Lincoln's best known official proclamation is the "Emancipation Proclamation" (January 1, 1863). Three months after that famous proclamation, March 30, 1863, he issued another, remarkable in its own right though lesser known—for a national day of fasting. In fact, it was the second such proclamation, the first having been issued August 12, 1861, after a joint request from both houses of Congress, and the latter in response to a Senate resolution. In the 1863 proclamation, Lincoln asked the people of the nation, as a body, to humble themselves before their God.

"PROCLAMATION FOR A NATIONAL FAST DAY"

Whereas, the Senate of the United States, devoutly recognizing the supreme authority and just government of Almighty God in all the affairs of men and of nations, has by a resolution requested the President to designate and set apart a day for national prayer and humiliation:

And whereas, it is the duty of nations as well as of men to own their dependence upon the overruling power of God; to confess their sins and transgressions in humble sorrow, yet with assured hope that genuine repentance will lead to mercy and pardon; and to recognize the sublime truth, announced in the Holy Scriptures and proven by all history, that those nations only are blessed whose God is the Lord:

And insomuch as we know that by his divine law nations, like individuals, are subjected to punishments and chastisements in this world, may we not justly fear that the awful calamity of civil war which now desolates the land may be but a punishment inflicted upon us for our presumptuous sins, to the needful end of our national reformation as a whole people? We have been the recipients of the choicest bounties of Heaven. We have been preserved, these many years, in peace and prosperity. We have grown in numbers, wealth, and power as no other nation has ever grown; but we have forgotten God. We have forgotten the gracious hand which preserved us in peace, and multiplied and enriched and strengthened us; and we have vainly imagined, in the deceitfulness of our hearts, that all these blessings were produced by some superior wisdom and virtue of our own. Intoxicated with unbroken success, we have become too self-sufficient to feel the necessity of redeeming and preserving grace, too proud to pray to the God that made us:

It behooves us, then, to humble ourselves before the offended Power, to confess our national sins, and to pray for clemency and forgiveness:

Now, therefore, in compliance with the request, and fully concurring in the views, of the Senate, I do by this my proclamation designate and set apart Thursday, the 30th day of April, 1863, as a day of national humiliation, fasting, and prayer. And I do hereby request all the people to abstain on that day from their ordinary secular pursuits, and to unite at their several places of public worship and their respective homes in keeping the day holy to the Lord, and devoted to the humble discharge of the religious duties proper to that solemn occasion. All this being done in sincerity and truth, let us then rest humbly in the hope authorized by the divine teachings, that the united cry of the nation will be heard on high, and answered with blessings no less than the pardon of our national sins, and the restoration of our now divided and suffering country to its former happy condition of unity and peace. ❦

Consider this point made in the apocryphal book of the Wisdom of Solomon, chapter 5, verses 8–9:

What good did our arrogance do us?
And what have wealth and ostentation done for us?
They have all passed away like a shadow. ❦

Few fallen heroes are better known to Americans than the infamous "Casey at the Bat," a victim of overblown pride. Following is the Casey poem as it was printed the first time, in the San Francisco Examiner, June 3, 1888. Other versions of the poem have appeared over the years.

A BALLAD OF THE REPUBLIC,

SUNG IN THE YEAR 1888

The outlook wasn't brilliant for the Mudville nine that day;
The score stood four to two with but one inning more to play.

And then when Cooney died at first, and Barrows did the same,
    A sickly silence fell upon the patrons of the game.

    A straggling few got up to go in deep despair. The rest
Clung to that hope which springs eternal in the human breast;
    They thought if only Casey could but get a whack at that—
    We'd put up even money now with Casey at the bat.

    But Flynn preceded Casey, as did also Jimmy Blake,
    And the former was a lulu and the latter was a cake;
So upon that stricken multitude grim melancholy sat,
For there seemed but little chance of Casey's getting to the bat.

    But Flynn let drive a single, to the wonderment of all,
    And Blake, the much despis-ed, tore the cover off the ball;
And when the dust had lifted, and the men saw what had occurred,
    There was [Jimmy] safe at second and Flynn a-hugging third.

    Then from 5,000 throats and more there rose a lusty yell;
    It rumbled through the valley, it rattled in the dell;
    It knocked upon the mountain and recoiled upon the flat,
    For Casey, mighty Casey, was advancing to the bat.

There was ease in Casey's manner as he stepped into his place;
There was pride in Casey's bearing and a smile on Casey's face.
    And when, responding to the cheers, he lightly doffed his hat,
    No stranger in the crowd could doubt 'twas Casey at the bat.

Ten thousand eyes were on him as he rubbed his hands with dirt;
Five thousand tongues applauded when he wiped them on his shirt.
    Then while the writhing pitcher ground the ball into his hip,
    Defiance gleamed in Casey's eye, a sneer curled Casey's lip.

And now the leather-covered sphere came hurtling through the air,
    And Casey stood a-watching it in haughty grandeur there.
    Close by the sturdy batsman the ball unheeded sped—
    "That ain't my style," said Casey. "Strike one," the umpire said.

From the benches, black with people, there went up a muffled roar,
Like the beating of the storm-waves on a stern and distant shore.
"Kill him! Kill the umpire!" shouted some one on the stand;
And it's likely they'd have killed him had not Casey raised his hand.

With a smile of Christian charity great Casey's visage shone;
He stilled the rising tumult; he bade the game go on;
He signaled to the pitcher, and once more the spheroid flew;
But Casey still ignored it, and the umpire said, "Strike two."

"Fraud!" cried the maddened thousands, and echo answered fraud;
But one scornful look from Casey and the audience was awed.
They saw his face grow stern and cold, they saw his muscles strain,
And they knew that Casey wouldn't let that ball go by again.

The sneer is gone from Casey's lip, his teeth are clenched in hate;
He pounds with cruel violence his bat upon the plate.
And now the pitcher holds the ball, and now he lets it go,
And now the air is shattered by the force of Casey's blow.

Oh, somewhere in this favored land the sun is shining bright;
The band is playing somewhere, and somewhere hearts are light,
And somewhere men are laughing, and somewhere children shout;
But there is no joy in Mudville—mighty Casey has struck out.
(Ernest L. Thayer.)

Heber J. Grant tells a humbling experience of his own.

Do we not often take the credit when we excel instead of giving it to
God? We are not yet humble enough, and therefore, when we offer a fine
prayer or speech, or whatever it may be, we allow Satan to flatter us, and
say, "How beautiful." To the Lord alone is due the praise.

I shall make a confession. When I was made the president of the Tooele
Stake of Zion and made my maiden speech, I ran out of ideas in seven and
one-half minutes by the watch. That night I heard in a very contemptuous
voice in the dark, "Well, it is a pity [that] if the General Authorities of the
Church had to import a boy from the city to come out here to preside over

us, they could not have found one with sense enough to talk ten minutes." So you see, he held his stop watch on me, he knew I did not take ten minutes. I knew I did not, because I timed myself—seven and one-half minutes was the limit. The next speech, and the next, and the next were the same. One of them was only five minutes. The next speech was at a little town called Vernon, sometimes called Stringtown, as it spread over twelve miles as I remember it. . . .

I had taken a couple of brethren with me that day to do the preaching. I got up expecting to take five or six minutes and talked forty-five minutes with as much ease, if not more, than I have ever enjoyed since. I shed tears of gratitude that night to the Lord for the inspiration of his Spirit.

The next Sunday I went to Grantsville, the largest town in Tooele County. [I] got up with all the assurance in the world and told the Lord I would like to talk forty-five minutes, and ran out of ideas in five. I not only ran out of ideas in five minutes, but I was perspiring, and [I] walked fully two and one-half, if not three, miles, after that meeting, to the farthest haystack in Grantsville, and kneeled behind that haystack and asked the Lord to forgive me for my egotism in that meeting. And [I] made a pledge to the Lord that never again in my life would I stand before an audience without asking for his Spirit to help me, nor would I take personally the credit for anything I said; and I have kept this pledge. ❖

Several of Aesop's fables teach humility, including this one:

THE TREE AND THE REED

A great tree would never bow him for none wind. And a reed which was at his foot bowed himself as much as the wind would. And the tree said to him: "Why dost thou not abide still as I do?" And the reed answered: "I have not the might which thou hast." And the tree said to the reed proudly: "Then have I more strength than thou." And anon after came a great wind, which threw down to the ground the said great tree, and the reed abode in his own being. For the proud shall be always humbled, and the meek and humble shall be enhanced, for the root of all virtue is obedience and humility. ❖

In the words of King Benjamin:

Are we not all beggars? Do we not all depend upon the same Being, even God, for all the substance which we have, for both food and raiment, and for gold, and for silver, and for all the riches which we have of every kind? (Mosiah 4:19.) ✦

Following are excerpts from another personal story about humility from Heber J. Grant, this one with a different twist. It is about his humbly coming to accept the fact of his call to the apostleship, despite misgivings and feelings of inadequacy. We realize, with him, that humility did not lie in his sense of inadequacy, but rather in his recognition that a prophet had called him, and that he must serve and could serve.

FROM "A REMARKABLE MANIFESTATION"

From October, 1882, when I was called to be one of the council of the Twelve, until the following February, I had but little joy and happiness in my labors. There was a spirit following me that told me that I lacked the experience, that I lacked the inspiration, that I lacked the testimony to be worthy of the position of an apostle of the Lord Jesus Christ. My dear mother had inspired me with such a love of the gospel and with such a reverence and admiration for the men who stood at the head of this Church, that when I was called to be one of them I was overpowered; I felt my unworthiness and the adversary taking advantage of that feeling in my heart. . . .

[He then tells of diverting alone to a cut-off trail while traveling among the Navajos and the Moquis with a party of Church leaders. He wanted solitude and a chance to meditate on this matter.]

I had perhaps gone one mile when in the kind providences of the Lord it was manifested to me perfectly so far as my intelligence is concerned—I did not see heaven, I did not see a council held there, but like Lehi of old, I seemed to see, and my very being was so saturated with the information that I received, as I stopped my animal and sat there and communed with heaven, that I am as absolutely convinced of the information that came to me upon that occasion as though the voice of God had spoken the words to me.

It was manifested to me there and then as I sat there and wept for joy that it was not because of any particular intelligence that I possessed more than a testimony of the gospel, that it was not because of my wisdom, that I had been called to be one of the apostles of the Lord Jesus Christ in this last dispensation, but it was because the prophet of God, the man who was the chosen instrument in the hands of the living God of establishing again upon the earth the plan of life and salvation, Joseph Smith, desired that I be called, and that my father, Jedediah M. Grant, who gave his life for the gospel, while one of the presidency of the Church, a counselor to President Brigham Young, and who had been dead for nearly twenty-six years, desired that his son should be a member of the council of the Twelve. It was manifested to me that the prophet and my father were able to bestow upon me the apostleship because of their faithfulness, inasmuch as I had lived a clean life, that now it remained for me to make a success or failure of that calling. I can bear witness to you here today that I do not believe that any man on earth from that day, February 1883, until now, thirty-five years ago, has had sweeter joy, more perfect and exquisite happiness than I have had in lifting up my voice and testifying of the gospel at home and abroad in every land and in every clime where it has fallen my lot to go. ❦

Writer Madeleine L'Engle also tells of learning a valuable lesson in humility. Almost uncannily, her opening sentences echo the perceptions of Heber J. Grant.

Each year as I read the great stories of Scripture, it becomes more and more apparent to me that the people God chooses to do the work of the Kingdom are not chosen because they are worthy or virtuous or qualified or because they deserve to be chosen.

Joseph with his coat of many colors was a spoiled younger son of an indulgent father, justly infuriating his elder brothers with his bragging. But there was no question of whether or not Joseph was *worthy;* Joseph was *called.*

Jesus was not very tolerant with the smugly qualified. He didn't think much of the Pharisee who knew how well he kept the law and how good and charitable he was.

I don't have much trouble in separating myself from that Pharisee. Or do I? . . .

[L'engle talks of running for president of the student council in high school, of wanting the position terribly. She was certain, she says, that her opponent would not make nearly so good a president as she herself. She prayed for God to let her win. But she lost the election and was miserable.]

Maybe I lost the election because I was being like the Pharisee. I went home and took a fresh look at myself, and my head, which had been rather swollen, went down to normal size.

When I got back to school in September, the girl who had won the election had not returned. There was another election, and I was elected. And I was a far better president of student government than I would have been had I won the election the year before, when I thought it was a matter of winning, and qualification, and popularity. It was a responsibility, and a heavy one. ❧

> Humble we must be, if to heaven we go;
> High is the roof there, but the gate is low.
> (Robert Herrick.)

Elray L. Christiansen links humility and its implicit submissive obedience to the Lord with the other virtues of saintliness and charity.

Humility, submissiveness, willingness to abide by the teachings of the Lord bring out the best that is in men because they become teachable and can be molded into agents usable to him. . . .

Now, humility is not an abject, groveling, self-despising spirit. It seems to me that it is rather a right and proper estimate of what one is in the sight of God. When we have that estimate of ourselves, we become as children, and we realize that he controls the universe. We learn then, to appreciate even the very air that we breathe, and our ability to go and come and to see and to do, and to accept and to reject. But until he can submit himself to this status, man is an "enemy to God."

True humility, in my opinion, implies acknowledgment, thanksgiving, prayerfulness, all those virtues which become a Latter-day Saint. It is becoming to an individual no matter what his status in life, to acknowledge the Lord for his goodness and for his mercy, to be humble and prayerful and submissive to his will. True humility is uplifting, ennobling. . . .

Humility, in my opinion, implies a grateful heart. . . .

. . . The person with true humility will not seek to aggrandize himself. He will serve for the sake of service. He will give his gifts in secret and let it be found out by accident. He will realize that all knowledge comes from God—for he knows all. He will not be contentious, unruly, or critical. He will not profane the name of Deity. As a literal child of God, he will feel it a privilege to do his will and keep his commandments.

Finally, the Lord has left us this: In order to shape ourselves to be fit candidates for his kingdom by leading lives of meekness and humility before him, he admonishes us to "let every man esteem his brother as himself, and practise virtue and holiness before me" (Doctrine and Covenants 38:24–25). ✦

Elder Christiansen also touched on the matter of pride and enmity when he counseled against contentiousness. But in our time, no one has spoken more urgently and more insightfully about pride and its danger to the soul than President Ezra Taft Benson. He has taught us to look at the concept of pride, and thus at pride's opposites, too, with new understanding. In a landmark sermon delivered at the LDS Church's general conference, April 1, 1989, President Benson declared enmity to be the principal component of pride, enmity toward both God and fellow beings, enmity the destroyer of charity. He spoke of pride as "a very misunderstood sin" and declared that "many are sinning in ignorance."

FROM "BEWARE OF PRIDE"

Most of us think of pride as self-centeredness, conceit, boastfulness, arrogance, or haughtiness. All of these are elements of the sin, but the heart, or core, is still missing.

The central feature of pride is enmity—enmity toward God and enmity toward our fellowmen. *Enmity* means "hatred toward, hostility to, or a state of opposition." It is the power by which Satan wishes to reign over us.

Pride is essentially competitive in nature. . . .

The proud cannot accept the authority of God giving direction to their lives. (See Hel. 12:6.) They pit their perceptions of truth against God's great knowledge, their abilities versus God's priesthood power, their accomplishments against His mighty works. . . .

The proud wish God would agree with them. They aren't interested in changing their opinions to agree with God's.

President Benson also counseled against the temptation "to elevate ourselves above others and diminish them. "The proud," he said, "make every man their adversary by pitting their intellects, opinions, works, wealth, talents, or any other worldly measuring device against others." Then he quoted C. S. Lewis: "Pride gets no pleasure out of having something, only out of having more of it than the next man. . . . It is the comparison that makes you proud: the pleasure of being above the rest. Once the element of competition has gone, pride has gone." (Mere Christianity.) Following are a few isolated excerpts from the remainder of President Benson's address:

The proud stand more in fear of men's judgment than of God's judgment. (See D&C 3:6–7; 30:1–2; 60:2.) "What will men think of me?" weighs heavier than "What will God think of me?" . . .

Some prideful people are not so concerned as to whether their wages meet their needs as they are that their wages are more than someone else's. Their reward is being a cut above the rest. This is the enmity of pride. . . .

Most of us consider pride to be a sin of those on the top, such as the rich and the learned, looking down at the rest of us. (See 2 Ne. 9:42.) There is, however, a far more common ailment among us—and that is pride from the bottom looking up. It is manifest in so many ways, such as faultfinding, gossiping, backbiting, murmuring, living beyond our means, envying, coveting, withholding gratitude and praise that might lift another, and being unforgiving and jealous. . . .

Selfishness is one of the more common faces of pride. "How everything affects me" is the center of all that matters—self-conceit, self-pity, worldly self-fulfillment, self-gratification, and self-seeking. . . .

Another face of pride is contention. Arguments, fights, unrighteous dominion, generation gaps, divorces, spouse abuse, riots, and disturbances all fall into this category of pride. . . .

The proud depend upon the world to tell them whether they have value or not. Their self-esteem is determined by where they are judged to be on the ladders of worldly success. They feel worthwhile as individuals if the numbers beneath them in achievement, talent, beauty, or intellect are large enough. Pride is ugly. It says, "If you succeed, I am a failure."

If we love God, do His will, and fear His judgment more than men's, we will have self-esteem. . . .

Pride is the universal sin, the great vice. Yes, pride *is* the universal sin, the great vice. . . .

God will have a humble people. Either we can choose to be humble or we can be compelled to be humble. . . .

Let us choose to be humble. We can do it. I know we can. . . .

Pride is the great stumbling block to Zion. I repeat: Pride *is* the great stumbling block to Zion. ✦

The fear of the Lord is the instruction of wisdom; and before honour is humility. (Proverbs 15:33.) ✦

Orson F. Whitney consciously linked obedience to humility. Asserting that George Q. Cannon was correct in identifying obedience (rather than order, as Alexander Pope had maintained) as "heaven's first law," Elder Whitney insists that "the proper attitude" of those who seek citizenship in the kingdom of heaven is "humility, not self-righteousness." He points to the example of Abraham.

FROM "THE LAW OF OBEDIENCE"

What if Abraham, when commanded to offer up his son, had refused, citing in support of his position the divine law against homicide, a law dating from the time of Cain and Abel—would that have justified him? No; God's word is his law, and the word last spoken by him must have precedence over any earlier revelation on the same subject. If Abraham, after being forbidden to slay his son, had fanatically persisted in slaying him, he would have been a transgressor, just as much as if he had refused to obey in the first instance. After receiving the second command, he could not consistently plead that he was under obligation to carry out the first. Had he done so, he would have placed himself in a false position, that of honoring the dead letter above the living oracle. ✦

The story of Abraham's anguish and humble obedience in taking his beloved son to the altar of sacrifice has captured the imagination of writers and students of scripture. In medieval dramatic literature alone, seven different versions of the story have survived. My favorite of these is a fourteenth- or fifteenth-century miracle (or "mystery") play preserved and found at Brome Manor in Suffolk. Most miracle plays were part of a lengthy cycle of plays, sponsored by trade guilds and performed in processions of horse-drawn floats, but this one apparently was an isolated piece. Here are a few lines from near the end of the play:

FROM "ABRAHAM AND ISAAC"

ABRAHAM: In sooth, son, unless I kill thee, I should grieve God right sore, I fear. It is His commandment and His will that I should do this deed. He commanded me, son, certainly to make my sacrifice with thy blood.

ISAAC: And is it God's will that I should be slain?

ABRAHAM: Yea, truly, Isaac, my good son; therefore my hands I wring.

ISAAC: Now, father, I will never complain, aloud or silently, against my Lord's will. But he might have sent me a better destiny if it had been His pleasure. . . .

ABRAHAM: [*Aside.*] Lo, now the time is surely come that my sword must bite into his neck. Ah, Lord, my heart rebels against it; I may not find it in my heart to strike; my heart will not consent thereto. Yet I would fain do my Lord's will. But this young innocent lies so quietly, I may not find it in my heart to kill him. O, Father of Heaven, what shall I do?

ISAAC: Ah, mercy, father, why tarry ye so, and let me lie thus long on this heath? I would to God the stroke were done! Father, I pray you heartily, shorten my woe and let me not wait for my death!

ABRAHAM: Now, heart, why wouldst thou not break in three? Yet thou shalt not make me disobedient to my God. I will no longer delay for thy sake, for my God would be wroth. Now receive the stroke, my own dear child!

Here Abraham struck, and the angel took the sword in his hand suddenly.

ANGEL: I am an angel, thou mayst gladly see, who is sent to thee from heaven. Our Lord thanks thee a hundred times for keeping his commandment. He knows thy will and also thy heart, that thou fearest Him above all things. And to dispel some of thy sorrow I have brought a fair ram yonder; lo, he stands tied among the briars. Now, Abraham, mend thy cheer, for Isaac, thy young son, shall not shed his blood this day. Go, make thy sacrifice with yonder ram. Farewell, blessed Abraham, for now I go home to heaven; right short is the way. Take up thy noble son. [*Exit.*] ❧

On a lighter note, following is a scrap of rhymed wisdom, the deliciously frightening version of which I knew only as edited by my mother's and my grandmother's memories. Here it appears as its originator published it, a lesson on the perils of uncharitable disobedience and pride.

LITTLE ORPHANT ANNIE

Inscribed
With All Faith and Affection
To all the little children:—The happy ones; and sad ones;
The sober and the silent ones; the boisterous and glad ones;
The good ones—Yes, the good ones, too; and all the lovely bad ones.

Little Orphant Annie's come to our house to stay,
An' wash the cups an' saucers up, an' brush the crumbs away,
An' shoo the chickens off the porch, an' dust the hearth, an' sweep,
An' make the fire, an' bake the bread, an' earn her board-an-keep;
An' all us other childern, when the supper-things is done,
We set around the kitchen fire an' has the mostest fun
A-list'nin' to the witch-tales 'at Annie tells about,
An' the Gobble-uns 'at gits you
Ef you
Don't
Watch
Out!

Wunst they was a little boy wouldn't say his prayers,—
An' when he went to bed at night, away up-stairs,
His Mammy heerd him holler, an' his Daddy heerd him bawl,
An' when they turn't the kivvers down, he wuzn't there at all!
An' they seeked him in the rafter-room, an' cubby-hole, an' press,
An' seeked him up the chimbly-flue, an' ever'-wheres, I guess;
But all they ever found wuz thist his pants an' roundabout:—
An' the Gobble-uns 'll git you
Ef you
Don't
Watch
Out!

An' one time a little girl 'ud allus laugh an' grin,
An' make fun of ever' one, an' all her blood-an'-kin;
An' wunst, when they was "company," an' ole folks wuz there,
She mocked 'em an' shocked 'em, an' said she didn't care!
An' thist as she kicked her heels, an' turn't to run an' hide,
They wuz two great big Black Things a-standin' by her side,
An' they snatched her through the ceilin' 'fore she knowed
what she's about!
An' the Gobble-uns 'll git you
Ef you
Don't
Watch
Out!

An' little Orphant Annie says, when the blaze is blue,
An' the lamp-wick sputters, an' the wind goes woo-oo!
An' you hear the crickets quit, an' the moon is gray,
An' the lightnin'-bugs in dew is all squenched away,—
You better mind yer parunts, an' yer teachurs fond an' dear,
An' churish them 'at loves you, an' dry the orphant's tear,
An' he'p the pore an' needy ones 'at clusters all about,
Er the Gobble-uns 'll git you

Ef you

Don't

Watch

Out!

(James Whitcomb Riley.)

It is generally accepted that children should render obedience to adults who are responsible for their care and training. Nevertheless, there is much discussion as to the interplay of obedience and individual agency. When the source is clearly the Lord, a faithful servant obeys, as did Lorenzo Snow after being directed by the Spirit to go to St. George, for reasons he did not understand at the time. The Church was struggling financially, and President Snow was wrestling with possible solutions. Nevertheless, as his son tells it, though he did not know the purpose of the journey, he "answered the call to go, and then wondered and worried until further light was given."

And it was given, during a general conference in the St. George tabernacle. Suddenly President Snow paused at the pulpit.

FROM "THE LORD'S WAY OUT OF BONDAGE"

Complete stillness filled the room. I shall never forget the thrill as long as I live. When he commenced to speak again his voice strengthened and the inspiration of God seemed to come over him, as well as over the entire assembly. His eyes seemed to brighten and his countenance to shine. He was filled with unusual power. Then he revealed to the Latter-day Saints the vision that was before him.

God manifested to him there and then not only the purpose of the call to visit the Saints in the South, but also Lorenzo Snow's special mission, the great work for which God had prepared and preserved him, and he unveiled the vision to the people. He told them that he could see, as he had never realized before, how the law of tithing had been neglected by the people, also that the Saints, themselves, were heavily in debt, as well as the Church, and now through strict obedience to this law—the paying of a full and honest tithing—not only would the Church be relieved of its great indebtedness, but through the blessings of the Lord this would also be the means of freeing the Latter-day Saints from their individual obligations, and they would become a prosperous people. ❦

In the article just quoted, LeRoi Snow points out that the Dixie Saints were just then in the grips of a severe drought, and President Snow promised them that if they would faithfully obey the law of tithing, they could plow and plant and the rains would come. President Snow had the answer to the Church's financial problems and to those of the Saints in the parched southland. As it turned out, those Saints did not receive rain immediately, but eventually it did come.

In an April 1900 general conference address, Elder George Teasdale said: "We encourage the rising generation to trust in the Lord and individually seek His counsel. The Lord does not require a blind obedience, but an intelligent obedience, and the Savior has exhorted us to ask and it shall be given us, to seek and we shall find, to knock and it shall be opened unto us."

Matthew Cowley makes a thoughtful distinction between true obedience and blind obedience, and links disobedience to pride.

OBEDIENCE

"To obey is better than sacrifice, and to hearken than the fat of rams." (I. Samuel xv:22.) In an age of the world when independence is the proud boast of the nations, obedience is, by mistaken ideas of freedom, considered a mark of humiliation. To the reader I will say, in reality, true obedience to the Lord's commands is an indication of moral courage, union and power. It is not blind obedience that is referred to and maintained, but that type which characterized the ancient seers and saints, who, like the Messiah, were ready to say by word and deed, "I came not to do mine own will, but the will of my Father who sent me."

The Latter-day Saints are credited with being obedient and submissive to authority, this fact being often used by their opponents as the occasion of reproach. Those who so use it surely must forget that God requires obedience; that the best embodiment of this principle, the most humble and yielding to the divine will, was the best and purest Being who ever dwelt in mortality, viz., the Lord Jesus Christ; He in whose mouth there was found no guile; who was perfect and without blemish in all the walks of life. While

He was obedient to His Father's will and humble to the extreme, He was independent of the influence and persuasions of wicked men.

The status of Latter-day Saints is conformable to this example. They are obedient to conscience, to convictions of right, to divine authority and to God, in whom they trust. . . .

The obedience rendered by Latter-day Saints to the authority of the priesthood is not secured by virtue of any solemn obligation entered into by the adherent to obey the dictum of his superiors in office; but upon the nature of the Gospel, which guarantees to every adherent the companionship of the Holy Spirit, and this Spirit secures to every faithful individual a living testimony concerning the truth or falsity of every proposition presented for his consideration. . . .

The statement of the Savior, recorded in St. John vii:17, covers the ground in the broadest light: "If any man will do His will, he shall know of the doctrine, whether it be of God or whether I speak of myself." This secures to every true Saint, if he is faithful, protection against imposture, the abuse of power and the false decisions of man-made councils. In this particular the Church of Christ is distinguished from all other systems and institutions. He has promised to guide and direct, and that He "doeth nothing, but He revealeth His secrets unto His servants, the prophets." (Amos iii:7.) This does not imply the infallibility of man, but it does imply the promise that no man or council of men who stand at the head of the church shall have power to lead the Saints astray. . . .

. . . Obedience to [God's] appointed authority upon the earth is obedience to Him, and is so taught by the Savior. "He that receiveth you receiveth me, and he that receiveth me receiveth Him that sent me." (Matthew x:40.) "He that heareth you heareth me; and he that despiseth you despiseth me; and he that despiseth me despiseth Him that sent me. (Luke x:16.) "Verily, verily, I say unto you, He that receiveth whomsoever I send, receiveth me; and he that receiveth me, receiveth Him that sent me." (St. John xiii:20.)

It is not the attractive qualities of the individual, however great, that renders submission to his administration valid, but the authority of God which he fears. . . .

Obedience is essential to salvation, essential to success in every avenue of human enterprise. Whether rendered to the laws of God direct, in their moral and spiritual phases, or to His authority vested in man, obedience must be implicit. The haughty man boasts of independence. He scorns the humble followers of the Lord, but while he prates of freedom, he is himself slavishly obedient to his own whims and mistaken ideas or to the spirit of evil, to popular sentiment or to some other influence always dangerous to the welfare of mankind. ✦

Those who know D. H. Lawrence only as a writer of rather frank fiction might be surprised to read what he says about freedom and commitment:

FROM "THE SPIRIT OF PLACE"

[The early immigrants who left Europe and sailed to America] didn't come for freedom. Or if they did, they sadly went back on themselves. . . .

They came largely to get *away*—that most simple of motives. To get away. Away from what? In the long run, away from themselves. Away from everything. That's why most people have come to America, and still do come. To get away from everything they are and have been. . . .

Which is all very well, but it isn't freedom. Rather the reverse. A hopeless sort of constraint. It is never freedom till you find something you really *positively want to be.* And people in America have always been shouting about the things they are *not.* Unless, of course, they are millionaires, made or in the making. . . .

Liberty is all very well, but men cannot live without masters. There is always a master. And men either live in glad obedience to the master they believe in, or they live in a frictional opposition to the master they wish to undermine. . . .

Every continent has its own great spirit of place. Every people is polarized in some particular locality, which is home, the homeland. . . .

Men are free when they are in a living homeland, not when they are straying and breaking away. Men are free when they are obeying some deep, inward voice of religious belief. Obeying from within. Men are free when they belong to a living, organic, *believing* community, active in fulfilling some unfulfilled, perhaps unrealized purpose. Not when they are escaping to some wild west. The most unfree souls go west, and shout of freedom. Men are freest when they are most unconscious of freedom. The shout is a rattling of chains, always was.

Men are not free when they are doing just what they like. The moment you can do just what you like, there is nothing you care about doing. ❧

The key to true humility is submissiveness to the will of God, as expressed in these thoughts by Orson F. Whitney:

"THY WILL BE DONE"

Words that should be written in letters of fire on the mind of every son and daughter of God. A motto that should be engraven on every heart, a motive that should guide and govern every impulse, a spirit that should inspire every prayer wafted on wings of faith through the open portals of eternity.

The fiat of the Gods in the councils of the beginning, the chorus of the stars in the glad morning of creation; the prayer of the suffering Savior at Life's weary noon; the song of Saints on earth, the anthem of the angels in heaven; it yet shall be the closing hymn, the benediction over the burial of human history, the solemn epitaph inscribed on the tombstone of Time.

"Thy will be done!" A river of power and of purity, flowing from the throne of God, making heavenly melody as it surges along the shores of life, bearing like bubbles on its breast the mightiest of human aims and achievements, it glides down the channel of the ages, glittering in the sunbeams of eternal truth, and rolling the music of its bright waves into the boundless ocean of the Evermore. ❧

6

CHARITY DOTH NOT
BEHAVE ITSELF UNSEEMLY

Finally, be ye all of one mind,

having compassion one of another,

love as brethren, be pitiful, be courteous:

Not rendering evil for evil, or railing

for railing: but contrariwise blessing.

1 PETER 3:8-9

Be "of one mind," have "compassion," "love as brethren," "be pitiful," or full of pity, "be courteous," and "bless." It is significant that Peter joins courtesy with other traits that we readily associate with charity. He also reaffirms the Savior's commandment to turn the other cheek rather than return wrong for wrong. In these two concepts, courtesy and self-control, Peter encapsulates the essence of Paul's injunction against unseemly behavior.

By extension, "unseemly behavior" shows lack of character and discipline, especially self-discipline, in all its manifestations: bad manners, discourtesy, heedless surrender to whim and appetite, unruly temper and tongue, and disregard for honorable decorum and for the feelings and rights of others. Part of any youngster's training and any adult's practice should be the habit of respect for others—the consideration and polite manners we exercise in the name of community and decency. When we remember the quiet sensitivity and thoughtfulness of the Savior, we recognize still another manifestation of the charity he embodies.

142

In a letter prepared as special counsel to his children, Heber C. Kimball addressed the subject of courteous behavior.

FROM "ADDRESS TO MY CHILDREN"

I want my children to show proper respect to all men, and be gentle to them, as you wish they should be gentle to you. Be subject to all the officers, both civil and religious, and reverence them in their offices. When you speak of the Prophet and the Apostles, speak well of them and not reproachfully. Reverence all men in their respective places, and never speak disrespectfully of them, nor of any person on the earth. If you cannot speak well, keep your mouth shut. If you do this you shall be respected as your father has been, for this has always been my course. ❦

On at least one occasion, Wilford Woodruff spoke on the subject of discourtesy.

I want to preach a short sermon to this congregation. To begin with, I have heard President Young and President Taylor a great many times from this stand ask the people to keep quiet until the meeting was dismissed; but as soon as the sermon ends there are a hundred of them rush for the doors. I do not like it. It pains me to see the President of the Church make this request, and the people pay no attention to it.

Now, in this fast age we are passing from a polite age to a very rude one in many respects. When I was a boy sixty-five years ago, and went to school, I never thought of passing a man whom I knew in the street, or a woman, without taking off my hat and making a bow. I never thought of saying "yes" or "no" to those that were placed over me. I was taught to say "yes, sir," and "no, sir"; but today it is "yes" and "no," "I will," "I won't," "I shall" and "I shan't." Now, when I see this rudeness amongst us, I sometimes wish that the spirit of the New England fathers was more among the people. But I do hope, brethren, sisters and friends, when a man stops talking and the choir rises to sing, that you will keep your seats. You can afford to do this as well as the President of the Church, the Twelve Apostles, or others who are sitting on this stand. You don't see us jump and run for the door the moment a speaker is done. The Lord is displeased with any such thing. I hope you will pardon me for so speaking. I felt to say that much. ❦

The problem seems to dog every age. Belle Spafford wrote on the subject nearly a hundred years later.

GOOD MANNERS

Interesting, challenging, demanding, life today moves forward with speed and aggressiveness. Its driving force is so pronounced that individuals cannot relax and keep pace. All are constantly faced with struggle—struggle in the home, in business, and in social pursuits. The spirit of present-day living is making people self-assertive, thoughtless of the rights of one another, and often genuinely selfish. More or less unconscious of this trend, most of us if accused would deny it. However, conditions all about us bear testimony of its existence. The high accident rate on the highway, the lack of reverence in our churches, crowding and jostling for positions of vantage in public gatherings, handling of merchandise in shops, care of books in libraries, and the general disrespect for the rights and possessions of others cry out for control of our selfish impulses and increased courtesy and good manners.

Using good manners after all is the suiting of our behavior to the greatest benefit, comfort, and ease of others. Human felicity is produced not so much by great pieces of good fortune as by little considerations every day. Genuine courtesy comes from the heart and is based on morality, decency, and consideration. Good manners involve the art of adjusting our behavior to all. They transcend the habits of clique, caste, or period of time.

Too often we think of good manners in rather a restricted sense, interpreting them as a knowledge of what constitutes "good form." Time, place, and situation dictate correct form. There are continual revolutions in social forms according to prevailing fashion. What is "the right thing to do" today may not be so tomorrow. What is right in one situation may not be so in another. "Good form" changes with more or less frequency and must be learned, while good manners come from within and never go out of fashion.

Emerson it was who said, "A beautiful behavior is better than a beautiful form; it gives higher pleasure than statues or pictures; it is the finest of fine arts."

Every one of us should consciously endeavor to develop perception of the best interests of one another. We should avail ourselves of every opportunity to learn what constitutes acceptable behavior. We should constantly teach and exercise good manners until they become fixed habits.

There are few other things that will tend to unite people more or pay higher dividends on time and attention invested. ✦

Respect for others was the order of the day among the apostles who served the first missions to England, as this excerpt from a letter written by Orson Hyde to his wife Marinda indicates.

We have not said a hard word against priests since we came here, neither have we spoken against any sect, yet they say all manner of evil against us. The people have discovered this difference between us, and they are most agreeably surprised, and it gives us unbounded influence. ✦

President John Taylor speaks important words on the subject of mutual respect and courtesy.

We Latter-day Saints, we elders of Israel and we sisters of Israel, we ought to be ladies and gentlemen, we ought to treat one another with courtesy and kindness, and true politeness. . . . I will tell you, in a few words, what it is to be polite: try to make everybody as comfortable and happy as you can, in all your words and in all your acts, and then you will be polite. Study the feelings of those with whom you are associated and those with whom you come in contact. And when a man meets an elder, why, says he, that is an honorable man, that man is anointed of the Lord, I will respect him, I expect to be associated with him in time and in eternity, and shall I degrade myself by speaking harshly or acting harshly towards him? No, but we will treat one another with kindness and courtesy.

And we will treat our sisters in the same way, and act the part of gentlemen towards them, and protect them in all their rights and in all their privileges, and never be afraid that they are going to run away with some of our rights. When I hear people talk that way I think they are a little in doubt of themselves. . . . And then let the sisters turn round and treat their husbands and brothers and fathers in the same way; and let us all cultivate those principles that are calculated to promote one another's happiness and peace, that it may reign in our own bosoms, and dwell in our habitations, and prevail throughout the land, that the peace of God and the blessings of God may rest upon us. ✦

By all accounts, Joseph Smith was a man of immense civility—courteous, thoughtful, and disciplined, though never stuffy and self-righteous. Emmeline B. Wells sensed that quality in him the first time she saw him, and at every meeting thereafter.

In the Prophet Joseph Smith, I believed I recognized the great spiritual power that brought joy and comfort to the Saints; and withal he had that strong comradeship that made such a bond of brotherliness with those who were his companions in civil and military life, and in which he reached men's souls, and appealed most forcibly to their friendship and loyalty. He possessed too the innate refinement that one finds in the born poet, or in the most highly cultivated intellectual and poetical nature; this extraordinary temperament and force combined is something of a miracle and can scarcely be accounted for except as a "heavenly mystery" of the "higher sort." To quote Tennyson (with a slight alteration),

> "Whereof the man who with us trod
> This planet was a noble type
> Appearing when the times were ripe
> That friend of men who lives with God." ✦

There are countless stories and poems about good and bad manners, all designed for the delight and instruction of the young. One such story that I remember from my own childhood, like many of the genre, has a number of versions. For purely subjective reasons, I prefer the oral version told countless times by my mother, Rhoda C. Arnold, passed down to her by her mother. Of course, without the drama and inflections provided by my mother, a born storyteller, the story loses some of its appeal, but the imaginative reader can bring it to life with an oral telling.

146

THE PIG BROTHER

"John," John's mother said, "come wash your hands and face and comb your hair, then come out and eat your dinner." But John was sick and tired of washing his hands and face and combing his hair, so he said, "I think I'll go for a walk." He started out.

He hadn't gone far when he met a kitty. He said, "Hello, kitty, are you my brother?" The kitty looked at John's dirty hands and face, and he said, "No, I'm not your brother. You don't wash your hands and face and you don't comb your hair. I'm not your brother."

John walked along farther, and pretty soon he met a dog. He said, "Hello, dog, are you my brother?" The dog looked at John's dirty hands and face and said, "No, I'm not your brother. You don't wash your hands and face and you don't comb your hair. I'm not your brother."

John walked along farther, and pretty soon he met a cow. He said, "Hello, cow, are you my brother?" The cow said, "No, I'm not your brother. You don't wash your hands and face, and you don't comb your hair. I'm not your brother."

John wasn't feeling very well now, but he walked on farther and he met a horse. He said, "Hello, horse, are you my brother?" The horse looked at John's dirty hands and face, and he said, "No, I'm not your brother. You don't wash your hands and face, and you don't comb your hair. I'm not your brother."

John really felt sad now. But he walked along with his head down, and pretty soon he heard a voice say, "Hello, John, you're my brother!" John looked, and he saw a pig wallowing around in dirty, black mud. And John said, "I'm not your brother!" And the pig said, "Oh, yes you are my brother. You don't wash your hands and face, and you don't comb your hair, and neither do I! So you must be my brother. C'mon, John, wallow around in this dirty black mud with me." And John said, "No!"

He turned around and ran home as fast as he could. He ran up the back stairs, into the kitchen, into the bathroom. He washed his hands and face and combed his hair, and went out and ate his dinner. ❧

THE GOOPS

The Goops they lick their fingers,
And the Goops they lick their knives;
They spill their broth on the tablecloth—
Oh, they lead disgusting lives!
The Goops they talk while eating,
And loud and fast they chew;
And that is why I'm glad that I
Am not a Goop—are you?
(Gelett Burgess.)

Adults may be less likely than children to "lick their knives" in company, but they are known to exercise "selective hearing," a discourtesy this English nursery rhyme satirizes delightfully.

Old woman, old woman,
Shall we go a-shearing?
Speak a little louder, sir,
I'm very thick of hearing.
Old woman, old woman,
Shall I love you dearly?
Thank you very kindly, sir,
Now I hear you clearly.

Most of us are familiar with the first stanza of the following little verse, some-times attributed to Henry Wadsworth Longfellow, but we probably have never heard the stanzas that detail Jemima's unseemly behavior and its consequences. This is one of several versions.

JEMIMA

There was a little girl who had a little curl,
Right in the middle of her forehead,
And when she was good, she was very, very good,
But when she was bad she was horrid.

One day she went upstairs, while her parents, unawares,
In the kitchen down below were at their meals,
And she stood upon her head, on her little truckle bed,
And she then began hurraying with her heels.

Her mother heard the noise, and thought it was the boys,
A-playing at a combat in the attic,
But when she climbed the stair and saw Jemima there,
She took and she did spank her most emphatic!

One can't help wondering if the boys would have been similarly spanked if they had been the source of the ruckus.

"CHARACTER BUILDING"

Spanking is something that must go,
Say some psychologists, although
Character building is a feat
Sometimes accomplished through the seat.
(Edward Anthony.)

On March 17, 1843, Eliza R. Snow took her departure from schoolteaching in Nauvoo. Her farewell address to her students highly recommends seemly behavior, and practices it too, in what she calls the "City of the Saints." She also neatly links spiritual counsel with practical advice, advocating in all a Christian charitableness.

FROM AN ADDRESS "TO MY DEAR PUPILS"

I take the liberty on this occasion to express my satisfaction and approbation of your conduct in general, while under my charge, and you will please accept my thanks for the respectful attention which, with very few exceptions, you have paid to my instructions.

The progress you have made in your several studies while under my tuition, is very gratifying to me, and does honor to yourselves. Before relinquishing my care, I wish again to impress your minds with the importance of scholastic pursuits. Altho' they may appear of little consequence in themselves; they form the laws of civilization, literature and refinement; therefore let them occupy a due share of your youthful attention—let not your time run to waste—let not your early life be trifled away on nonsensical objects; but in all your pursuits, have a wise reference to the future, ever bearing in mind that the manner in which you improve the present period, will have a bearing upon your conditions and character hereafter, and let the attention and the improvement of your minds and manners engage much of your present attention in order to prepare you for the relations you will be call'd to sustain in the busy scenes of life which are lying before you.

You live in a very important age, an age teeming with events, and if your lives are spared, you will each have a part to act in the grand scenery which precedes and is to prepare the way for the second [coming] of the Messiah. You should endeavor to realize the consequence of the period, and to act accordingly. Let your thoughts be elevated—let them rise superior to the superficial glare—the pompous nothingness of the fashion of this world which ever passes away, and study to make yourselves useful. By early habit you will accustom yourselves to blend the useful with the agreeable in such a manner as that the every-day duties of life will be pleasurable; and that course of life which proposes the most usefulness, will conduce most to your individual happiness by contributing most to the happiness of others. How much better—how much nobler the principle of habituating yourselves to derive pleasure by contributing to the happiness of those around you, than to seek it in the indulgence of that little selfishness of feeling which extends no farther, and has no other object than mere personal gratification?

Endeavor to cultivate sufficient independence of mind, that you will *dare to do right*—that will inspire you with moral courage enough to stem the tide of evil example, realizing that the eyes of the great God are continually upon you, and let his approbation be esteemed the richest reward, regardless of the frowns and the smiles of the vain & unprincipled, who would fain lead you from the paths of rectitude. . . .

Do not overestimate the merit of your own actions, and console your feelings with the idea that the eyes of Him who judgeth righteously are upon you—that the time will come when all will be rewarded according to their works—when the secrets of all hearts will be made known; and endeavor to hold sufficient command over your feelings to be satisfied with the approval of the great God, and patiently await the decision of his tribunal, regardless of the praise and censure, smiles and frowns of those persons who are guided by the preconceived notions of contracted, silly, and selfish minds.

The human mind possesses an adhesive quality—it is apt to adhere to, and contract a likeness to that with which it comes most in contact, or with which it is most conversant; therefore it is all important that you should be wise in the choice of your particular associates—Let the good—the honest and the upright constitute the society in which you familiarize your thoughts and feelings, [and] at the same time, be courteous and affable to all. That kind of haughtiness of manner which many mistake for dignity, which by its repulsiveness is calculated to hold every body at a distance, is a stranger to the amiability which flows from a philanthropic disposition, and genuine goodness of heart.

Court the society of the aged who have trod the path of life before you—those who have accumulated wisdom by length of years and practical experience. Listen respectfully to their instructions, and profit by their counsels. Never treat them with that arrogance and insolence which too much characterizes the manners of the present age. Honor them as they honor God—look up to them with reverence and treat them with kindness and affection; reflecting that, should you arrive to their years, how gratifying it will be to yourselves to see the children and youth, look up to you with respectful attention, and leaning upon you as the guardians of their virtues, and the protectors and supporters of their morals, like the tender twig sheltering itself beneath the spreading umbrage of the sturdy and inflexible oak.

Many of you now are in that season of life when fascinating charms of the world seem most attractive to the human heart, and when its ten-thousand snares are most liable to attract the unsuspecting and inexperienced feet aside from the paths of virtue, religion and piety; and as many if not all of you are members of the Church of Jesus Christ, let me say to you, remember now your Creator in the days of your youth and serve him with a perfect heart and a willing mind—set your faces as flint to keep the commandments of God, and to live by every word that proceedeth out of his mouth. Turn your backs upon the vanities and follies of the world, and hold them in comparative contempt. Be steadfast without bigotry. If you are faithful and true to the profession you have made, you are to become the companions of angels. ✦

Ardeth Greene Kapp tells the story of a little boy acting in a Christmas pageant whose natural instincts rejected the unseemly behavior of an innkeeper in Bethlehem.

Perhaps you are familiar with the school pageant where the little innkeeper forgot his lines and responded from his heart instead. When Joseph asked if there was room in the inn, the young innkeeper hesitated and the prompter whispered his lines from the wings: "There is no room. Be gone." The young innkeeper repeated the words. The young actor, Joseph, sadly placed his arm around Mary, and the two little people who had rehearsed their lines so well started to move away according to the script and the rehearsal. Suddenly this Christmas pageant became different from any other. "Don't go, Joseph," the innkeeper cried out. "Bring Mary back. She can have my room." ✦

Quoting her sister Sharon's version of a modern parable, Ardeth Kapp describes yet another kind of unseemly behavior.

A certain sister went down from her home to the supermarket and fell among thieves who stripped her of her confidence and self-esteem when she overheard them talking about her and her children, and they walked away, leaving her alone.

And by chance there came down the aisle a certain lady dressed in fine clothes, and when she saw her, she passed down another grocery aisle.

And likewise a lady who was a leader in the community, when she was at the place, came and looked on her and passed down another aisle without speaking.

But a certain sister came down the aisle where she was, and when she saw her, she had compassion and went to her and bound up her wounds as she said, "Let's go talk."

And at a time of doubt and discouragement, one sister ministered to another as she spoke of faith and hope and extended unconditional love—charity. ✦

In some instances, especially when someone is discourteous to us, our first inclination is to respond in kind. How many times do we use the automobile horn as a device for editorial comment instead of merely for safety? There is no indication in the "parable" above that either the mistreated woman or her friend thought to strike back against their ill-mannered, uncharitable neighbors. Rather, they chose not to be uncharitable themselves. They exercised self-mastery, which is often the key to avoiding thoughtless, unseemly behavior. To be master of oneself is to resist stooping to the behavior of uncharitable persons. Belle Spafford writes of the power of such composure:

Too often when we face a grave situation, when our accustomed way of life is interrupted, when some unexpected calamity sweeps down upon us, or even when we are overworked or face tasks for which we feel inadequate, a sort of hysteria takes possession of us; our normal poise is upset and we "go to pieces." We exhibit imperfect self-control and indulge in destructive emotional outbursts. Thus, we lose mastery of both self and the situation.

Though we recognize the power of composure, we argue, "Anyone would be upset facing what I face." We genuinely believe it would be more than human to remain calm and serene. But the emotions need education as well as the mind. We should strive constantly for emotional stability. We should form habits which utilize our emotional energy in constructive ways. When we are not able to change a situation, we should try changing our attitude. While it is probably true that some people naturally possess a greater degree of emotional stability than others, an honest effort to be less sensitive to disturbing stimuli and to remain self-possessed under trying circumstances usually results in improved behavior. . . .

The Church is proud of its record of composed leadership; it is equally proud of its numerous examples of outstanding group composure. Recall with me the terrible experience of the saints at the time of the martyrdom. It was expected that the outraged and grief-stricken people would burn the town. The people of Carthage fled in all directions. Even the governor and his posse took flight. But there was no uprising or violence on the part of the Saints. Elder Willard Richards stood before eight or ten thousand Saints at Nauvoo and advised them "to keep the peace." He stated that he had pledged his honor and his life for their peaceful conduct. When the multitude heard that, notwithstanding the scene of outraged justice under which they labored and the cruel invasion of the rights of liberty and life—in the very midst of their grief and excitement, with the means at their hands to wreak a terrible vengeance, they voted to a man to follow the counsel of their leader. Such composure is scarcely paralleled in the history of our country—if in the world. ❖

In the words of Plato, "The first and best victory is to conquer self; to be conquered by self is, of all things, the most shameful and vile." The sentiment is echoed by Pythagoras, who said, "No man is free who cannot command himself," and by Brigham Young:

To gain the spiritual ascendancy over ourselves, and the influences with which we are surrounded, through a rigid course of self-discipline, is our first consideration, it is our first labor, before we can pave the way for our children to grow up without sin unto salvation. (*Journal of Discourses* 2:131.) ❖

Brigham Young had a good deal to say about the unseemliness and foolishness of subjecting others, enemies included, to our uncontrolled tempers and tongues. Under the heading "Fighting Fire with Non-fire," Hugh Nibley introduces a number of Brigham Young's statements on the subject, at the same time providing interlacing commentary. Nibley opens the section with his own observation: "In dealing with this particular enemy, the enemy of all righteousness, the first rule is never to use his methods, for if we do he has already won. He does not care which 'side' we are on as long as we act like devils, just as God does not care which side we are on if we keep the great commandments." Nibley then proceeds to quote President Young, who ties the idea to charity.

"We are never going to destroy the enemies of God by the evil passions that are in us—never, no never. When those who profess to be Saints contend against the enemies of God through passion or selfwill, it is then man against man, evil against evil, the powers of darkness against the powers of darkness" [*Journal of Discourses* 8:325]. We do *not* fight fire with fire or match hate with hate. "No man or people possessing wisdom will give vent to wrath, for that is calculated to weaken, to destroy, to blot out of existence. When the Supreme Ruler of the universe wishes to destroy a nation, he takes away their wisdom . . . and they are filled with wrath: they give way to their anger, and thus lay the foundation of their own destruction" [*Millennial Star* 16:724]. "If we are permitted to rule, govern, and control, in the first place we must control our passions until they are in perfect subjection to us" [*Journal of Discourses* 8:324]. As a stimulant, anger has no long-term value: "The Lord said, 'Hold on.' He can fight our battles far better than we can. Anger towards them [the enemy] is a poor, miserable feeling; and I am trying to get rid of it" [*Journal of Discourses* 8:357].

Brigham Young was a forceful and formidable man who was often provoked and knew what anger was—but he also knew it was wrong: "I will say, there is not a man in this house who has a more indomitable and unyielding temper than myself. But there is not a man in the world who cannot overcome his passion, if he will struggle earnestly to do so. If you find passion coming on you, go off to some place where you cannot be heard; . . . struggle till it leaves you; and pray for strength to overcome" [*Journal of Discourses* 11:290]. "When evil arises within me let me throw a cloak over it, subdue it instead of acting it out upon the false presumption that I am honest and no hypocrite. Let not thy tongue give utterance to the evil that is in thine heart. . . . So far I believe in being a hypocrite" [*Journal of Discourses* 11:255]. The trouble with feeding and yielding to anger is that it is altogether too easy: "Cast all bitterness out of your own hearts—all anger, wrath, strife, covetousness, and lust, and sanctify the Lord God in your hearts, that you may enjoy the Holy Ghost" [*Journal of Discourses* 8:33].

That is the real victory, as the Prophet Joseph put it: "We shall go on from victory to victory, and from conquest to conquest; our evil passions will be subdued, our prejudices depart; we shall find no room in our bosoms for hatred" [*Teachings of the Prophet Joseph Smith*, 179]. In this it is ourself we fight all the time, and no one else: "It is natural for me to contend, and if I am opposed to oppose in return, and if a sharp word is spoken to me to give a sharp word back, I have done so but rarely. It is wrong, and we must subdue the inclination" [*Journal of Discourses* 14:149]. As one of the great leaders of all time, Brigham Young understood why this was so: "No man ever did, or ever will rule judiciously on this earth, with honor to himself and glory to his God, unless he first learn to rule and control himself" [*Journal of Discourses* 3:256].

If you want to meet the enemy head-on, here he is. "This is what I call resisting the devil, and he flees from me. I strive to not speak evil, to not feel evil, and if I do, to keep it to myself until it is gone from me, and not let it pass my lips. . . . 'Had I not better let it out than to keep it rankling within me?' No. I will keep bad feelings under and actually smother them to death, then they are gone" [*Journal of Discourses* 3:195]. They do not fester in the subconscious, because they simply vanish: hatred is vanquished only when it turns to love. Must the battle always be within ourselves? Where else? "With all the power I possess, I cannot prevent a man from cursing and swearing if he is disposed to do so" [*Journal of Discourses* 10:191]. Whom can he command? Himself. "If I did not feel like praying, . . . I should say, 'Brigham, get down here, on your knees, bow your body down before the throne of Him who rules in the heavens, and stay there until you can feel to supplicate at that throne of grace erected for sinners" [*Journal of Discourses* 16:28]. ❦

Nibley concludes the section with this quotation from Brigham Young: "Do not say a word to grieve the Spirit of God." (Journal of Discourses 12:218.)

A story told by Oscar A. Kirkham indicates that Brigham Young indeed practiced what he preached.

Lucy B. Young, one of President Brigham Young's wives, said one day in Germany to me, "I went up the hall in the Lion House. President Young had just crossed the road on South Temple and hurried into his office. With the curiosity of a good woman, I walked up to the end of the hall and listened at the door. I heard President Brigham Young say: 'Down on your knees, Brigham? Down on your knees!' He had had some difficulty with the men across the street. In a few moments he opened the door calmly, with perfect control, and went about his work." ✦

Some of the most unseemly behavior mortals permit themselves is uncouth, disrespectful language. Lack of manners and self-control, not to mention charitable love, are readily apparent in an unbridled tongue. Truly, as an anonymous writer has said, "Of thine unspoken word thou art master; thy spoken word is master of thee." In the words of Henry David Thoreau, "Speech never made man master of men, but the eloquent refraining from it." And thirteenth-century Persian sage Sa'di offers this thought, in language vaguely reminiscent of Paul: "A wise man is, like a vase in a druggist's shop, silent but full of virtues; and the ignorant man resembles the drum of the warrior, being full of noise, and an empty babbler." (The Gulistan, translated by James Ross.)

A wise old owl sat in an oak,
The more he heard the less he spoke;
The less he spoke the more he heard.
Why aren't we all like that wise old bird?
(English nursery rhyme.)

THE PEPPERY MAN

The Peppery Man was cross and thin;
He scolded out and scolded in;
He shook his fist, his hair he tore;
He stamped his feet and slammed the door.

Heigh ho, the Peppery Man,
The rabid, crabbed Peppery Man!
Oh, never since the world began
Was anyone like the Peppery Man.

His ugly temper was so sour
He often scolded for an hour;
He gnashed his teeth and stormed and scowled,
He snapped and snarled and yelled and howled.

He wore a fierce and savage frown;
He scolded up and scolded down;
He scolded over field and glen,
And then he scolded back again.

His neighbors, when they heard his roars,
Closed their blinds and locked their doors,
Shut their windows, sought their beds,
Stopped their ears and covered their heads.

He fretted, chafed, and boiled and fumed;
With fiery rage he was consumed,
And no one knew, when he was vexed,
What in the world would happen next.

Heigh ho, the Peppery Man,
The rabid, crabbed Peppery Man!
Oh, never since the world began
Was anyone like the Peppery Man.
(Arthur Macy.)

I know a starling
Who does so much snarling
That only his mother believes he's a darling.
(Edward Anthony.)

In a 1973 address, Elder Gordon B. Hinckley greatly enlarged our understanding of the principle of discipline.

Any system dealing with the eternal consequences of human behavior must set guidelines and adhere to them, and no system can long command the loyalties of men that does not expect of them certain measures of discipline, and particularly of self-discipline. The cost in comfort may be great. The sacrifice may be real. But this very demanding reality is the substance of which come character and strength and nobility.

Permissiveness never produced greatness. Integrity, loyalty, and strength are virtues whose sinews are developed through the struggles that go on within a man as he practices self-discipline under the demands of divinely spoken truth.

But there is another side of the coin, without which this self-discipline is little more than an exercise. Discipline imposed for the sake of discipline is repressive. It is not in the spirit of the gospel of Jesus Christ. It is usually enforced by fear, and its results are negative.

But that which is positive, which comes of personal conviction, builds and lifts and strengthens in a marvelous manner. In matters of religion, when a man is motivated by great and powerful convictions of truth, then he disciplines himself, not because of demands made upon him by the Church but because of the knowledge within his heart that God lives; that he is a child of God with an eternal and limitless potential. ✦

The following is an excerpt from the first of six "nonlectures" by poet e e cummings, cited earlier. Here cummings describes his mother, whose self-control, sense of decorum, and "seemly" behavior in the midst of tragedy were a beacon of sure light to her children.

FROM "I AND MY PARENTS"

It isn't often you meet a true heroine. I have the honour to be a true heroine's son. My father and mother were coming up from Cambridge to New Hampshire, one day, in their newly purchased automobile—an air-cooled Franklin, with an ash frame. As they neared the Ossippees, snow fell. My mother was driving; and, left to herself, would never have paused for such a trifle as snow. But as the snow increased, my father made her stop while he got out and wiped the windshield. Then he got in; and she drove on. Some minutes later, a locomotive cut the car in half, killing my father instantly. When two brakemen jumped from the halted train, they saw a woman standing—dazed but erect—beside a mangled machine; with blood "spouting" (as the older said to me) out of her head. One of her hands (the younger added) kept feeling of her dress, as if trying to discover why it was wet. These men took my sixty-six year old mother by the arms and tried to lead her toward a nearby farmhouse; but she threw them off, strode straight to my father's body, and directed a group of scared spectators to cover him. When this had been done (and only then) she let them lead her away.

A day later, my sister and I entered a small darkened room in a country hospital. She was alive—why, the headdoctor couldn't imagine. She wanted only one thing: to join the person she loved most. He was very near her, but she could not quite reach him. We spoke, and she recognized our voices. Gradually her own voice began to understand what its death would mean to these living children of hers; and very gradually a miracle happened. She decided to live. "There's something wrong with my head" she kept telling us faintly; and she didn't mean the fracture of her skull. As days and nights passed, we accidentally discovered that this ghastly wound had been sewn up by candlelight when all the town lights went out at once.

But the headdoctor had no intention of losing his patient—"move her?" he cried "impossible! It would kill her just to sit up" and several centuries wandered away before we found a method of overruling him. When the ambulance arrived, ready to transfer my mother to a big Boston hospital, she was sitting up (fully dressed and smiling) by the entrance-door. She admired the ambulance, conversed cheerfully with its chauffeur, and refused to lie down because by so doing she'd miss the scenery en route. We shot through towns and tore through cities. "I like going fast" she told us; beaming. At last came the goal. After an interminable time in an operatingroom— where (we learned later) she insisted on watching in a handmirror whatever was happening, while a great brain-surgeon removed a piece of bone and carefully cleansed the wound—up came my mother in a wheelchair; very erect, and waving triumphantly a small bottle in which (at her urgent request) he'd placed the dirt and grime and splinters of whose existence his predecessor had been blissfully unaware. "You see?" she cried to us, smiling "I was right!"

And though the wound had later to be reopened, she came out of that hospital in record time; recovered completely at home in a few months— attending, now and then, a nearby meeting of The Society of Friends—then boarded a train alone for New York, and began working as a volunteer for the Travellers' Aid in the Grand Central Station. "I'm tough!" was her daunt-less comment when we tried to express our amazement and our joy. ✦

The world's enduring literature offers many texts that speak to the principle of self-mastery and self-discipline. One of Shakespeare's frequent themes is the tragedy of goodness and nobility that succumbs to uncontrolled passion and thus to behavior unworthy of itself. Othello comes immediately to mind. The honorable Moor surrenders his will to the evil Iago and ends up wronging his friend Cassio and killing his faithful wife, Desdemona. When he finally awakens to what has happened, he recognizes that he has lost self-control, that he has served the evil whim of another. He has betrayed pure love.

Just as heartbreaking is Mark Antony's recognition that "I have fled myself" in surrendering volition to his unchecked desire for Cleopatra. In the midst of battle, the once magnificent Antony turns his ships in retreat to follow those of Cleopatra—to his everlasting shame. Filled with remorse at this costly lapse of character, he cries:

> O, whither hast thou led me, Egypt? See,
> How I convey my shame out of thine eyes
> By looking back what I have left behind
> 'Stroy'd in dishonour. (iii.7.)

In his essay on "The Golden Mean," Aristotle argues that "by doing the actions of self-mastery we come to be perfected in self-mastery," for "the habits are produced from the acts of working like to them." The same is true, he says, of courage and other virtues. Further, he states, "He is perfected in Self-Mastery who not only abstains from the bodily pleasures but is glad to do so; whereas he who abstains but is sorry to do it has not Self-Mastery."

Seventeenth-century British essayist John Earle has written delightfully on human foibles, including the inconstancy and lack of self-discipline in the adolescent.

A YOUNG MAN

He is now out of nature's protection, though not yet able to guide himself; but left loose to the world and fortune, from which the weakness of his childhood preserved him; and now his strength exposes him. He is indeed just of age to be miserable, yet in his own conceit first begins to be happy; and he is happier in this imagination, and his misery not felt is less. He sees yet but the outside of the world and men, and conceives them according to their appearing glister, and out of this ignorance believes them. He pursues all vanities for happiness, and enjoys them best in this fancy. His reason serves not to curb, but understand his appetite, and prosecute the motions thereof with a more eager earnestness. Himself is his own temptation, and needs not Satan, and the World will come hereafter. He leaves repentance for gray hairs, and performs it in being covetous. He is mingled with the vices of the age as the fashion and custom, with which he longs to be acquainted, and sins to better his understanding.

He conceives his youth as the season of his lust and the hour wherein he ought to be bad; and because he would not lose his time, spends it. He distastes religion as a sad thing, and is six years elder for a thought of heaven. He scorns and fears, and yet hopes for old age, but dare not imagine it with wrinkles. He loves and hates with the same inflammation, and when the heat is over is cool alike to friends and enemies. His friendship is seldom so steadfast but that lust, drink or anger may overturn it. He offers you his blood to-day in kindness, and is ready to take yours to-morrow. He does seldom anything which he wishes not to do again, and is only wise after a misfortune. He suffers much for his knowledge, and a great deal of folly it is makes him a wise man. He is free from many vices, by being not grown to the performance, and is only more virtuous out of weakness. Every action is his danger, and every man his ambush. He is a ship without pilot or tackling, and only good fortune may steer him. If he scape this age, he has scaped a tempest, and may live to be a man. ❧

Similarly, Mark Twain used to refer to the time when he was a young man "studying for the gallows." Jonathan Swift, however, recognized that the young are not alone in needing to exercise self-mastery in order to avoid unseemly behavior.

[RESOLUTIONS] WHEN I COME TO BE OLD

Not to marry a young woman.

Not to keep young company unless they really desire it.

Not to be peevish, or morose, or suspicious.

Not to scorn present ways, or wits, or fashions, or men, or war, &c.

Not to be fond of children, or let them come near me hardly.

Not to tell the same story over and over to the same people.

Not to be covetous.

Not to neglect decency, or cleanliness, for fear of falling into nastiness.

Not to be over severe with young people, but give allowances for their youthful follies and weaknesses.

Not to be influenced by, or give ear to knavish tattling servants, or others.

Not to be too free of advice, nor trouble any but those that desire it.

To conjure some good friends to inform me which of these resolutions I break, or neglect, and wherein; and reform accordingly.

Not to talk much, nor of myself.

Not to boast of my former beauty, or strength, or favour with ladies, &c.

Not to hearken to flatteries, nor conceive I can be beloved by a young woman. *Et eos qui haereditatem captant, odisse ac vitare.*

Not to be positive or opinionatre.

Not to set up for observing all these rules, for fear I should observe none. ❧

And Lewis Carroll also suggests, humorously, that unseemly behavior is not the exclusive province of the young.

FROM "ADVICE TO A CATERPILLAR"

"You are old, Father William," the young man said
    "And your hair has become very white;
And yet you incessantly stand on your head—
    Do you think, at your age, it is right?"

"In my youth," Father William replied to his son,
    "I feared it might injure the brain;

But, now that I'm perfectly sure I have none,
Why, I do it again and again."

"You are old," said the youth, "as I mentioned before.
And have grown most uncommonly fat;
Yet you turned a back-somersault in at the door—
Pray, what is the reason of that?"

"In my youth," said the sage, as he shook his grey locks,
"I kept all my limbs very supple
By the use of this ointment—one shilling the box—
Allow me to sell you a couple?"

"You are old," said the youth, "and your jaws are too weak
For anything tougher than suet;
Yet you finished the goose, with the bones and the beak—
Pray, how did you manage to do it?"

"In my youth," said his father, "I took to the law,
And argued each case with my wife;
And the muscular strength, which it gave to my jaw
Has lasted the rest of my life."

"You are old," said the youth, "one would hardly suppose
That your eye was as steady as ever;
Yet you balanced an eel on the end of your nose—
What made you so awfully clever?"

"I have answered three questions, and that is enough,"
Said his father. "Don't give yourself airs!
Do you think I can listen all day to such stuff?
Be off, or I'll kick you down-stairs!"

But perhaps it is easier to behave appropriately as we advance in years.
Winston Churchill observed, "We are all happier in many ways when we are old
than when we were young. The young sow wild oats. The old grow sage." In her

eighties, Florida Scott-Maxwell wrote of the self-mastery that is a quiet expression of love.

One cannot be honest even at the end of one's life, for no one is wholly alone. We are bound to those we love, or to those who love us, and to those who need us to be brave, or content, or even happy enough to allow them not to worry about us. So we must refrain from giving pain, as our last gift to our fellows. For love of humanity consume as much of your travail as you can. Not all, never that terrible muteness that drains away human warmth. But when we are almost free of life we must retain guile that those still caught in life may not suffer more. The old must often try to be silent, if it is within their power, since silence may be like space, the intensely alive something that contains all. The clear echo of what we refrained from saying, everything, from the first pause of understanding, to the quiet of comprehension. ❧

On another note, Nathaniel Hawthorne writes fictionally of the discipline of the artist. The story, here retold and condensed, also portrays the impoliteness and lack of charity in those who neither appreciate nor understand the artist's search and his achievement.

THE ARTIST OF THE BEAUTIFUL

An elderly man, with his pretty daughter on his arm, was passing along the street, and emerged from the gloom of the cloudy evening into the light that fell across the pavement from the window of a small watchmaker's shop. Seated within the shop, sidelong to the window, with his pale face bent earnestly over some delicate piece of mechanism on which was thrown the concentrated lustre of a shade lamp, appeared a young man.

"What can Owen Warland be about?" muttered old Peter Hovenden, himself a retired watchmaker, and the former master of this same young man whose occupation he was now wondering at. "These six months past I have never come by his shop without seeing him just as steadily at work as now. It would be a flight beyond his usual foolery to seek for the perpetual motion; and yet I know enough of my old business to be certain that what he is now so busy with is no part of the machinery of a watch."

"Perhaps, father," said Annie, without showing much interest in the question, "Owen is inventing a new kind of timekeeper. I am sure he has ingenuity enough."

"Poh, child! He has not the sort of ingenuity to invent anything better than a Dutch toy," answered her father, who had formerly been put to much vexation by Owen Warland's irregular genius.

Moving on, Peter Hovenden and his daughter Annie passed the open door of a blacksmith shop. Moving about in the shop's red glare and alternate dusk was the muscular figure of the blacksmith. "Now, that is a pleasant sight," said the old watchmaker. "I know what it is to work in gold; but give me the worker in iron after all is said and done. He spends his labor upon a reality, earning his bread with a bare and brawny arm. Such work takes the nonsense out of a man! Did you ever hear of a blacksmith being such a fool as Owen Warland yonder?"

The blacksmith, Robert Danforth, was Owen's old school-fellow, but the two had little in common, except for their affection for Annie Hovenden. Those who discovered Owen's peculiar gift for searching out the hidden mysteries of mechanism sometimes saw reason to suppose that he was attempting to imitate the beautiful movements of Nature as exemplified in the flight of birds or the activity of little animals. It seemed, in fact, a new development of the love of the beautiful, such as might have made him a poet, a painter, or a sculptor.

A few fanciful liberties taken with clocks brought to him for repair quite destroyed the young watchmaker's credit with that steady and matter-of-fact class of people who hold the opinion that time is not to be trifled with.

After the old watchmaker and his pretty daughter had passed, Owen Warland was seized with a fluttering of the nerves, which made his hand tremble too violently to proceed with such delicate labor as he was now engaged upon. "Annie! dearest Annie! thou shouldst give firmness to my heart and hand, and not shake them thus; for if I strive to put the very spirit of beauty into form and give it motion, it is for thy sake alone."

Owen Warland had another visitor that night, Robert Danforth, who had fashioned a small anvil for Owen and delivered it to him. "How strange it is," whispered Owen Warland after Robert left, "that all my musings, my purposes, my passion for the beautiful, my consciousness of power to create it—a finer, more ethereal power, not perpetual motion as the world understands it—all, all, look so vain and idle whenever my path is crossed by Robert Danforth! He would drive me mad were I to meet him often. His hard, brute force darkens and confuses the spiritual element within me; but I, too, will be strong in my own way. I will not yield to him."

He took from beneath a glass a piece of minute machinery, which he set in the condensed light of his lamp, and, looking intently at it through a magnifying glass, proceeded to operate with a delicate instrument of steel. In an instant, however, he fell back in his chair and clasped his hands, with a look of horror on his face.

"What have I done?" exclaimed he. "The vapor, the influence of that brute force—it has bewildered me and obscured my perception. I have made the very stroke—the fatal stroke—that I have dreaded from the first. It is all over—the toil of months, the object of my life. I am ruined!"

And there he sat, in strange despair, until his lamp flickered in the socket and left the Artist of the Beautiful in darkness.

Thus it is that ideas, which grow up within the imagination and appear so lovely to it and of a value beyond whatever men call valuable, are exposed to be shattered and annihilated by contact with the practical. It is requisite for the ideal artist to possess a force of character that seems hardly compatible with its delicacy; he must keep his faith in himself while the incredulous world assails him with its utter disbelief; he must stand up against mankind and be his own sole disciple, both as respects his genius and the objects to which it is directed.

For some time after this crushing event, Owen became unusually responsible. He applied himself to business with dogged industry, for the heavy weight upon his spirits kept everything in order. Old Peter Hovenden was pleased with his former apprentice, and advised Owen to rid himself permanently of his "nonsensical trash about the beautiful."

Finally, Owen partially emerged from his torpid state and began wasting the sunshine, as people said, in wandering through the woods and fields and along the banks of streams. There, like a child, he found amusement in chasing butterflies or watching the motions of water insects. There was something truly mysterious in the intentness with which he contemplated these living playthings as they sported on the breeze or examined the structure of an imperial insect whom he had imprisoned. The chase of butterflies was an apt emblem of the ideal pursuit in which he had spent so many golden hours; but would the beautiful idea ever be yielded to his hand like the butterfly that symbolized it?

When Annie came one day to Owen's shop with a small bit of business, he fancied, though mistakenly, that this young girl possessed the gift to comprehend him better than all the world besides. And what a help and strength it would be to him, he thought, if he could gain the sympathy of the only being whom he loved! She was fascinated by the delicate mechanism of his labor, but one slight touch undid it all again. And again, Owen abandoned his life's work, this time giving himself up to dismal habits, including quaffing from the cup of supposed enchantment, the golden wine.

From this perilous state he was redeemed by a very simple incident. On a warm afternoon of spring, as the artist sat among his riotous companions with a glass of wine before him, a splendid butterfly flew in at the open window and fluttered about his head.

"Ah," exclaimed Owen, "are you alive again, child of the sun and playmate of the summer breeze, after your dismal winter's nap? Then it is time for me to be at work." Perhaps the bright butterfly, which had come so spirit-like into the window as Owen sat with the rude revellers, was indeed a spirit commissioned to recall him to the pure, ideal life that had so etherealized him among men. Again, Owen took up the work, and again—upon learning of Annie's forthcoming marriage to Robert Danforth—he gave it up. In favor of common sense, he thought.

But in Owen Warland the spirit was not dead nor passed away; it only slept. How it awoke again is not recorded. Whether it were pain or happiness that thrilled through his veins, his first impulse was to thank Heaven for rendering him again the being of thought, imagination, and keenest sensibility that he had long ceased to be.

It was his fortune, good or ill, to achieve the purpose of his life. Pass we over a long space of intense thought, yearning, effort, minute toil, and wasting anxiety, succeeded by an instant of solitary triumph: let all this be imagined; and then behold the artist, on a winter evening, seeking admittance to Robert Danforth's fireside circle. There was Annie, with her child.

Owen produced a small, carved box, which he opened to release a magnificent butterfly. It is impossible to express by words the glory, the splendor, the delicate gorgeousness which were softened into the beauty of this object. Nature's ideal butterfly was here realized in all its perfections; not in the pattern of such faded insects as flit among earthly flowers, but of those which hover across the meads of paradise for child-angels and the spirits of departed infants to disport themselves with. The rich down was visible upon its wings; the lustre of its eyes seemed instinct with spirit. In its perfect beauty, the consideration of size was entirely lost. Had its wings overreached the firmament, the mind could not have been more filled or satisfied.

As Owen's butterfly flew from one outstretched hand to another, it glowed or faded, depending on the credulity of the observer. Close to Peter Hovenden, it drooped its wings and seemed on the point of falling to the floor. Its exquisite susceptibility to doubt and mockery could mean destruction within minutes. The butterfly struggled, but regained its brilliance as it approached the infant. As if sensing something not entirely congenial in the child's nature, however, it moved toward the artist, only to be turned away. "Not so! not so!" murmured Owen Warland. "Thou has gone forth out of thy master's heart. There is no return for thee."

As the butterfly returned to the little child, a child innately imbued with his father's strength and his grandfather's shrewdness, the infant made a snatch at the marvelous insect and compressed it in his hand. Annie screamed. Old Peter Hovenden burst into a cold and scornful laugh. The blacksmith, by main force, unclosed the infant's hand, and found within the palm a small heap of glittering fragments, whence the mystery of beauty had fled forever. And as for Owen Warland, he looked placidly at what seemed the ruin of his life's labor, and which was yet no ruin. He had caught a far other butterfly than this. When the artist rose high enough to achieve the beautiful, the symbol by which he made it perceptible to mortal senses became of little value in his eyes while his spirit possessed itself in the enjoyment of the reality. ❧

In a famous essay, Francis Bacon speaks of the discipline required in the wise application of learning.

FROM "OF STUDIES"

Studies serve for delight, for ornament, and for ability. Their chief use for delight is in privateness and retiring; for ornament, is in discourse; and for ability, is in the judgement and disposition of business. For expert men can execute, and perhaps judge of particulars, one by one; but the general counsels, and the plots and marshalling of affairs, come best from those that are learned. To spend too much time in studies is sloth; to use them too much for ornament is affectation; to make judgement wholly by their rules is the humour [temperamental folly] of a scholar. They perfect nature, and are perfected by experience; for natural abilities are like natural plants, that need proyning [pruning] by study; and studies themselves do give forth directions too much at large, except they be bounded in by experience. Crafty men contemn studies; simple men admire them; and wise men use them: for they teach not their own use; but that is a wisdom without them and above them, won by observation. Read not to contradict and confute; nor to believe and take for granted; nor to find talk and discourse; but to weigh and consider.

Some books are to be tasted, others to be swallowed, and some few to be chewed and digested: that is, some books are to be read only in parts; others to be read, but not curiously; and some few to be read wholly, and with diligence and attention. Some books also may be read by deputy, and extracts made of them by others; but that would be only in the less important arguments, and the meaner sort of books; else distilled books are like common distilled waters, flashy things. Reading maketh a full man; conference a ready man; and writing an exact man. And therefore, if a man write little, he had need have a great memory; if he confer little, he had need have a present wit; and if he read little, he had need have much cunning, to seem to know that [i.e., what] he doth not. ❦

John A. Widtsoe enlarges the point.

God has told us that we should secure to the best of our ability all knowledge. . . . So we can lay aside the doctrine that we have too much knowledge. We do need, however, to secure mastery over ourselves. This lies at the foundation of life in the gospel of the Lord Jesus Christ. It has been talked about here time and time again. To conquer an army, it was said in olden days, is a very great achievement, but to conquer oneself is greater still. It is the duty of Latter-day Saints to learn little by little to be conquerors of themselves. Self-conquest is the great desire of all Latter-day Saints who understand the gospel of the Lord Jesus Christ. Under the power of self-conquest knowledge becomes precious to man. ❦

Orson F. Whitney was an eloquent defender of learning, but he was perhaps even more fervent in his plea for self-mastery.

Oh, reader, the redemption of Zion is more than the purchase or recovery of lands, the building of cities, or even the founding of nations. It is the conquest of the heart, the subjugation of the soul, the purifying of the flesh, the sanctifying and ennobling of the passions. Greater is he who subdues himself, who captures and maintains the citadel of his own soul, than he who, misnamed conqueror, fills the world with the roar of drums, the thunder of cannon, the lightning of swords and bayonets, overturns and sets up kingdoms, lives and reigns a king, yet wears to the grave the fetters of unbridled lust, and dies the slave of sin. ❦

And finally, from Leonardo da Vinci:

You can have neither a greater nor a less dominion than that over yourself.

It is easier to resist at the beginning than at the end. ❦

7

Charity Seeketh Not Her Own

He that findeth his life shall lose it: and he

that loseth his life for my sake shall find it.

MATTHEW 6:25

In observing cultures ancient and modern throughout the world, mythologist
Joseph Campbell arrived at this definition of the hero: one who lives for some-
thing other than himself or herself. It seems that Campbell's hero is, in real-
ity, the person of charity, and that his definition is a good gloss on the phrase
"seeketh not her own." Other terms come to mind, too: selflessness, sacrifice, gen-
erosity. Charity is not so much a premeditated act of goodness as it is a basic func-
tion of our deeper, spiritual natures. It describes what we are or can become.
Oddly enough, it is in seeking not our own that we truly find our own.

Orson F. Whitney writes of a comment made by a friend, an Episcopal bishop,
charging Mormons with "narrowness" and "illiberality."

"You people," he said, "are not interested in anything going on outside
of your own social and religious system. Insulated, wrapped up in yourselves, you take no note of what other peoples are doing, and give them no
credit for the good they accomplish."

The Bishop's remark surprised me. I was astonished that one so well
informed in other ways could entertain such an opinion of the Latter-day
Saints. There may be such a thing as a narrow notion in the mind of some

"Mormon"; but there never has been and never will be such a thing as narrow "Mormonism." To those who know it best, it is a synonym for largeness and liberality, another name for all that is generous, charitable and sublime. ❧

One of our richest legacies is the principle and practice of personal sacrifice, charity pure and sweet, in the name of faith. Joseph Smith is eloquent on the subject.

Let us here observe, that a religion that does not require the sacrifice of all things never has power sufficient to produce the faith necessary unto life and salvation; for, from the first existence of man, the faith necessary unto the enjoyment of life and salvation never could be obtained without the sacrifice of all earthly things. It was through this sacrifice, and this only, that God has ordained that men should enjoy eternal life; and it is through the medium of the sacrifice of all earthly things that men do actually know that they are doing the things that are well pleasing in the sight of God. When a man has offered in sacrifice all that he has for the truth's sake, not even withholding his life, and believing before God that he has been called to make this sacrifice because he seeks to do his will, he does know, most assuredly, that God does and will accept his sacrifice and offering, and that he has not, nor will not seek his face in vain. Under these circumstances, then, he can obtain the faith necessary for him to lay hold on eternal life. ❧

There are many inspiring stories of selflessness and sacrifice from the lives and experiences of early members of the fledgling Church of Jesus Christ of Latter-day Saints. Women's diaries, journals, autobiographies, and poems chronicle a self-forgetful courage that is aptly characterized by western writer Wallace Stegner: "That I do not accept the faith that possessed them [the Mormons] does not mean I doubt their frequent devotion and heroism in its service. Especially their women. Their women were incredible." (The Gathering of Zion [Lincoln: University of Nebraska Press, 1964], p. 13.) The numerous published narratives are just the tip of the iceberg; countless others are known only to scholars, archivists, and families. And they confirm that the men and children, as well as the women, were incredible. Among the personal accounts edited and published in a book first issued in 1877 is the following firsthand report of Amanda Smith, whose family were victims of the Haun's Mill massacre:

We sold our beautiful home in Kirtland for a song, and traveled all summer to Missouri—our teams poor, and with hardly enough to keep body and soul together.

We arrived in Caldwell county, near Haun's Mill, nine wagons of us in company. Two days before we arrived we were taken prisoners by an armed mob that had demanded every bit of ammunition and every weapon we had. We surrendered all. They knew it, for they searched our wagons.

A few miles more brought us to Haun's Mill, where that awful scene of murder was enacted. My husband pitched his tent by a blacksmith's shop.

Brother David Evans made a treaty with the mob that they would not molest us. He came just before the massacre and called the company together and they knelt in prayer.

I sat in my tent. Looking up I suddenly saw the mob coming—the same that took away our weapons. They came like so many demons or wild Indians.

Before I could get to the blacksmith's shop door to alarm the brethren, who were at prayers, the bullets were whistling amongst them.

I seized my two little girls and escaped across the mill-pond on a slab-walk. Another sister fled with me. Yet though we were women, with tender children, in flight for our lives, the demons poured volley after volley to kill us.

A number of bullets entered my clothes, but I was not wounded. The sister, however, who was with me, cried out that she was hit. We had just reached the trunk of a fallen tree, over which I urged her, bidding her to shelter there where the bullets could not reach her, while I continued my flight to some bottom land.

When the firing had ceased I went back to the scene of the massacre, for there were my husband and three sons, of whose fate I as yet knew nothing.

As I returned I found the sister in a pool of blood where she had fainted, but she was only shot through the hand. Farther on was lying dead

Brother McBride, an aged white-haired revolutionary soldier. His murderer had literally cut him to pieces with an old corn-cutter. His hands had been split down when he raised them in supplication for mercy. Then the monster cleft open his head with the same weapon, and the veteran who had fought for his country, in the glorious days of the past, was numbered with the martyrs.

Passing on I came to a scene more terrible still to the mother and wife. Emerging from the blacksmith shop was my eldest son, bearing on his shoulders his little brother Alma.

"Oh! my Alma is dead!" I cried in anguish.

"No, mother; I think Alma is not dead. But father and brother Sardius are killed!"

What an answer was this to apal[l] me! My husband and son murdered; another little son seemingly mortally wounded; and perhaps before the dreadful night should pass the murderers would return and complete their work!

But I could not weep then. The fountain of tears was dry; the heart overburdened with its calamity, and all the mother's sense absorbed in its anxiety for the precious boy which God alone could save by his miraculous aid. ✦

What resonates in the modern mind is the willingness with which sacrifices were made, once the gospel was embraced. Elizabeth Ann Whitney, wife of Bishop Newel K. Whitney, echoed a good many of her sister Saints when she wrote the following:

During all these absences and separations from my husband I never felt to murmur or complain in the least, and although heretofore my husband's time had been devoted to the business he was engaged in, and his hours of leisure to his family in private yet I was more than satisfied to have him give all, time, talents and ability into the service of the Kingdom of God; and the change in our circumstances and associations which were consequent upon our embracing the Gospel, never caused me a moment's sorrow. I looked upon it as a real pleasure to give all for the sake of my faith in the religion of

Jesus, considering all as nought in comparison with the example of our blessed Savior. ❧

Emmeline B. Wells later paid rhymed tribute to that same "Mrs. Elizabeth Ann Whitney, on her 74th birthday, Dec. 26, 1874." These few lines from that tribute emphasize selflessness and compassion.

FROM "A TRIBUTE OF RESPECT"

Honored forever be thy name, for truest worth;
And hallowed, the propitious day that gave thee birth.
Where'er thy name is known, they speak thy praise;
All womankind should strive to emulate thy ways.
A Christian true thou art, in thought, in word, in deed,
Yet for the weak and erring thy soul would pitying plead;
Forgetful of thyself, thou feel'st another's woe,
And with a bounteous hand doth charity bestow;
Thy virtues bright shall shine in an immortal wreath,
Crowning thee victor, even at the gates of death.

With no fanfare, much less complaint, over her husband's sacrifice, Zina Diantha Huntington Jacobs simply noted the following in her journal for December 20, 1844:

Henry sold his Cote [coat], vest and hat to Br Lewes to answer up on his tithing for $19.50. O may he be enabled to pay his tithing that he or we may receive the promised blessings of the Lord. ❧

The following snatches from a personal account, the autobiography of Mary Goble Pay, illustrate the sacrifices that were almost commonplace to many early Saints.

We traveled on till we got to the Platt River. That was the last walk I ever had with my mother. [Mary's baby sister had died in Iowa of illness and exposure. Mary was barely thirteen when the family left for Council Bluffs and the long journey west.] We caught up with the Handcart companies that day. We watched them cross the river. There were great lumps of ice floating down the river. It was bitter cold. The next morning there were fourteen dead in camp through the cold. We went back to camp and went to prayers. We sang the song "Come, Come, Ye Saints. No Toil Nor Labor Fear." I wondered what made my mother cry. That night my mother took sick and the next morning my little sister was born. It was the 23rd of September. We named her Edith and she lived six weeks and died for want of nourishment. . . .

When we arrived at Devil's Gate it was bitter cold. We left lots of our things there. There were two or three log houses there. We left our wagons and joined teams with a man named James Barman. He had a sister Mary who froze to death. We stayed there two or three days. While there an ox fell on the ice and the brethren killed it and the beef was given out to the camp. My brother James ate a hearty supper was as well as he ever was when he went to bed. In the morning he was dead.

My feet were frozen also my brother Edwin and my sister Caroline had their feet frozen. It was nothing but snow. We could not drive the pegs in the ground for our tents. . . .

We arrived in Salt Lake City nine o'clock at night the 11th of Dec. 1856. Three out of four that were living were frozen. My mother was dead in the wagon.

. . . When Bro. Young came in he shook hands with us all. When he saw our condition—our feet frozen and our mother dead—tears rolled down his cheeks. ❧

A WIDOW'S LULLABY

AT WINTER QUARTERS, 1846

Sleep, my little one—
Sleep while Mother dreams
Of your comely smile
And your small hands cupping my heart;
Of my completeness, holding you;
The happy burden of your trust;
My pride in your unfolding;

The wonders wished for you
Since our first touch.

Even here—
Here in this wind-whipped place,
This savage wilderness,
You have been my courage
And my star.
Sleep, my little one—
Sleep in your narrow bed
Under your coverlet of prairie sod
And stones gently piled . . .
Sleep, while your Mother dreams
And weeps—
Walking the long, lonely miles ahead.
(Edna S. Browne.)

In early Utah, Church members, including children, were asked to sacrifice toward the building of temples. Mary E. Woolley Chamberlain writes:

In my very early childhood . . . we were taught to save every cent we got and donate it to the St. George Temple which was being built at that time.

Father made Minnie and me a little bank by taking a small pasteboard box, covering it, lid and all, with wrapping paper and sealing the edges so we could not possibly get into it. [He] then cut a slit in the top for us to drop the coins in. Pennies were not in circulation at that date, so it was nickels and dimes. I do not remember ever spending one for candy or useless toys, and it tries me even today to see children run to the store as soon as they get hold of a penny. ❧

Members of the Church are not the only ones who have contributed to the building of LDS temples, as this story told by Oscar A. Kirkham attests.

I walked down the street of a small village in Maui one day with a Hawaiian woman, one of the presidency of the Relief Society. As we walked along, she said, "You see that building over there? Well, I have a very dear friend, a Chinese woman, who lives there. I went to visit her when we were building the temple at Laie. I asked her if she would like to contribute to the building of the temple. And although not a member of the Church, she said, 'Oh, yes, I believe in temples; I'd love to assist.' We chatted for a few minutes and then [I] left her. Eight months later I was coming down this way again, and I thought, 'Why, I haven't been to see my Chinese friend.' So I went over and said, 'Have you forgotten our conversation?'

"She said, 'No, I've been waiting for you to come. Have you a purse or something to put the money in?' I took out of my bag a small black purse, and she said, 'Oh, I'm afraid that will not hold what I have saved for you.' She went into another room and brought back a bowl containing coins and other money. She said, 'If you'll kindly open your apron.' I opened it, and the Chinese woman poured the money into my lap. I said to her, 'Is this all for the temple? Do you mean for me to take it all?' 'Oh, yes,' she said, 'you may have the money. I have the blessing.'" ✦

Matthew Cowley told a similar story of an old woman he had known in New Zealand, "on my first mission when I was just a young boy."

In those days she called me her son. When I went back to preside she called me her father. . . .

Now, on one occasion I called in as I always did when I visited that vicinity, to see this grand little woman, then in her eighties, and blind. She did not live in an organized branch, had no contact with the priesthood except as the missionaries visited there. We had no missionaries in those days. They were away at war.

I went in and greeted her in the Maori fashion. She was in her back yard by her little fire. I reached forth my hand to shake hands with her, and I was going to rub noses with her and she said, "Do not shake hands with me, Father."

I said: "Oh, that is clean dirt on your hands. I am willing to shake hands with you. I am glad to. I want to."

She said: "Not yet." Then she got on her hands and knees and crawled over to her little house. At the corner of the house there was a spade. She lifted up that spade and crawled off in another direction measuring the distance as she went. She finally arrived at a spot and started digging down into the soil with that spade. It finally struck something hard. She took out the soil with her hands and lifted out a fruit jar. She opened that fruit jar and reached down in it, took something out and handed it to me, and it turned out to be New Zealand money. In American money it would have been equivalent to one hundred dollars.

She said: "There is my tithing. Now I can shake hands with the priesthood of God."

I said: "You do not owe that much tithing."

She said: "I know it. I do not owe it now, but I am paying some in advance, for I do not know when the Priesthood of God will get around this way again."

And then I leaned over and pressed my nose and forehead against hers, and the tears from my eyes ran down her cheeks, and as I left her, I asked God in my heart to bring down upon me a curse if from that day henceforth and forever I did not return to God his . . . one-tenth of all that should ever come into my hands. ◆

There are many stories of the selflessness of early Saints who left their loved ones, or were left, in almost desperate circumstances when mission calls came. Often these calls meant separations of several years. Nor did the Saints who suffered persecution, deprivation, and loss of home and loved ones for the sake of their faith find ease and comfort when they reached the Salt Lake Valley. Many were asked to move yet again and build Zion elsewhere. Antoine R. Ivins tells the following story.

I think of the good old brother who lived in Washington a few miles from St. George. When the time came to put the glass into the tabernacle, I believe it was, there was no money with which to buy it. It had to be procured in California. Men with their teams were ready to go and get it, but there was no money available, and this good brother had recently received from England a thousand dollars, and a thousand dollars in those days was a fortune. He slept on that a night or two and thought it over, then one morning he arose and walked the distance from Washington City to St.

George and put that thousand dollars into the hands of the brethren. The teams went off to California and brought back the glass and other supplies that were necessary. Thus the building was completed.

. . . It was a noble gesture, a wonderful thing. And why do you think he did it? Do you think he had any idea that in making that contribution the brethren would look at him and maybe make him a bishop or something of that sort? Not in the world. It was sheer devotion to the work of the Lord that prompted him to do it. ✦

In recognizing the immense sacrifices made by those who have preceded us, we sometimes forget that there are also those among us today who have made significant, even incredible, sacrifices for their faith. Several years ago, President Gordon B. Hinckley alluded to such sacrifices.

Someone occasionally says that there was so much of sacrifice in the early days of the Church, but there is no sacrifice today. The observer goes on to say that in pioneer days people were willing to lay their fortunes and even their lives on the altar. "What has happened to the spirit of consecration?" some of these ask. I should like to say with great emphasis that this spirit is still very much among us. I have discovered that no sacrifice is too great for faithful Latter-day Saints. ✦

Certainly, it would be difficult to overestimate the selflessness and sacrifice of the thousands who monthly embark on missionary service, and the thousands more who bid them good-bye. A gifted LDS mother has written poignantly about the experience.

TO A DAUGHTER ABOUT TO

BECOME A MISSIONARY

FOR DINNY

Twenty-two, she sleeps upstairs
between the windows of my life,
in the sleigh bed that has housed
the comings of four generations

like exotic plants chosen
to color bedrooms with blossoming.
Two high birdseye dressers contain her,
drawers closed on pink turtlenecks

and Speedos; walls of rackets and mustachioed
smiles. Mirrors swing her reflection
of medicated soap and squashed rollers
dropping away from night to issue

a daytime Pieta laughing and grieving,
beautifully turned out, surprising as
a crocus in snow. Other rights postponed,
the child that God intended will wear

the sanctity of the blue blazer,
skirted and frocked, innocent in her
expectation. Of course we have known
she would leave, the covers

opened and closed. It is time.
The horizon whitens. Water runs.
This is morning. She will see. France
will tell. She is changing to

the garments of The Word, will take on
the terrors of the verb To Be,
not knowing yet why departure
spells return. Five hundred forty-seven

and a half-days. She will open wide
her arms sweatered for the long cold.
The darkness will lighten and she will become
the waiting room for the willing stranger.

Kisses blow like blizzards through my empty
spaces saying, God, please. I go up to sit on

her suitcase that will not close,
press messages into her shoes,

the smell of kitchen under the leather
of her scriptures. Snow has made feathers
of the trees. She lifts the sleepy shadow
of her face, steps into the air. She is gone.

I do not dare breathe in the bedroom.
Or move. Only to listen to the runners
of the sleigh bed following her.
And me unable to touch it for fear

of blanketing the sweet shiny smell
of Dr. Pepper lip gloss beneath the down,
above the furrows of knees along the floor.
(Emma Lou Thayne.)

One woman whose everyday life illustrated the charity that seeks not its own was early American Martha Ballard. Her diaries have been made accessible in an award-winning book by LDS scholar Laurel Thatcher Ulrich. We need take only a few pages from the diarist's own matter-of-fact record to see selflessness personified. As Ulrich says of Martha Ballard, "Her values had been formed in an older world, in which a woman's worth was measured by her service to God and her neighbors rather than to a nebulous and distant state." The record, which reads like an abbreviated, self-forgetful log of charitable acts, begins in August 1787, in a river settlement off the north Atlantic coast. (Note: The first number indicates the day of the month, the second number the day of the week. Letters indicate Sundays.)

3 6 Clear & very hot. I have been pulling flax. Mr Ballard Been to Savages about some hay.

4 7 Clear morn. I pulld flax till noon. A very severe shower of hail with thunder and Litning began at half after one continued near 1 hour. I hear it broke 130 pains of glass in fort western. Colonel Howard made me a

present of 1 gallon white Rhum & 2 lb sugar on acount of my atendance of his family in sickness. Peter Kenny has wounded his Legg & Bled Excesivily.

5 g Clear morn. Mr Hamlin Breakfastd here. Had some pills. I was calld at 7 O Clok to Mrs Howards to see James he being very sick with the canker Rash. Tarried all night.

6 2 I am at Mrs Howards watching with her son. Went out about day, discovered our saw mill in flames. The men at the fort went over. . . . I tarried till Evinng. Left James Exceeding Dangerously ill. My daughter Hannah is 18 years old this day. Mrs Williams here when I came home. . . . Mr Ballard complains of a soar throat this night. He has been to take Mr gardners hors home.

7 3 Clear. I was Calld to Mrs Howards this morning for to see her son. Find him very low. Went from Mrs Howards to see Mrs Williams. Find her very unwell. Hannah Cool is there. From thence to Joseph Fosters to see her sick Children. Find Saray & Daniel very ill. Came home went to the field & got some Cold water root. Then Calld to Mr Kenydays to see Polly. Very ill with the Canker. Gave her some of the root. I gargled her throat which gave her great Ease. Returned home after dark. Mr Ballard been to Cabesy. His throat is very soar. He gargled it with my tincture. Find relief & went to bed comfortably.

8 4 Clear. I have been to see Mary Kenida. Find her much as shee was yesterday. Was at Mr McMasters. Their children two of them very ill. The other 2 recovering. At Mr Williams also. Shee is some better. Hear James Howard is mending. Hannah Cool came home.

9 5 Clear. I workd about house forenoon. Was Calld to Mrs Howards to see James. Found him seemingly Expireing. Mrs Pollard there. We sett up. He revivd.

10 6 At Mrs Howards. Her son very sick. Capt Sewall & Lady sett up till half after 4. Then I rose. The Child seems revivd.

11 7 Calld from Mrs Howard to Mr McMasters to see their son William who is very low. Tarried there this night.

12 g Loury. At Mr McMasters. Their son very sick. I sett up all night. Mrs Patin with me. The Child very ill indeed.

13 2 William McMaster Expird at 3 O Clock this morn. Mrs Patin & I laid out the Child. Poor mother, how Distressing her Case, near the hour of Labour and three Children more very sick. I sett out for home. Calld at Mrs Howards. I find her son very Low. At Mr Williams. Shee very ill indeed. Now at home. It is nin O Clok morn. I feel as if I must take some rest. . . . Ephraim & I went to see Mrs Williams at Evining. I find her some Better. ❧

The diary continues in this fashion, year in and year out, for more than two decades. One wonders when its author slept. As Ulrich points out, "Martha Ballard was a midwife—and more. Between August 3 and 24, 1787, she performed four deliveries, answered one obstetrical false alarm, made sixteen medical calls, prepared three bodies for burial, dispensed pills to one neighbor, harvested and prepared herbs for another, and doctored her own husband's sore throat. In twentieth-century terms, she was simultaneously a midwife, nurse, physician, mortician, pharmacist, and attentive wife."

Mae R. Winters, daughter of pioneer parents, writes of fond memories associated with her mother's apron, a piece of cloth that came to stand for love's generosity and selflessness.

FROM "THE APRON"

She always wore one. It was a large straight affair gathered at the waist, with strings that fastened in the back and tied in a bow. . . . There was always at least one pocket, but usually two large ones.

The white apron was for very special occasions: Relief Society homemaking activities, special quiltings, and parties for the sisters. Sunday afternoon it enhanced Mother's best black dress.

The everyday one, slow to show dirt, was edged all around with bias tape of contrasting color. I was most impressed with this apron. Its uses were limitless. It made a basket for eggs gathered from the chicken coop, or from a nest found in the tall weeds or grass. Many times Mother would bring in a brood of fluffy yellow chickens in the apron, the bottom edge being brought up to form a temporary nest. The mother hen, squawking and stirring up a fuss, would follow behind. Mother transferred the chickens from a stolen nest to the protection of the stable. The same apron was used, by giving it a swish, to frighten chickens from the flower bed or back porch.

To dry a tear from a child's face, wipe away the dirt, and comfort the children, the apron seemed to be made for this purpose. For a game of hide-and-seek there was never a better place to hide than under the apron, for, with our heads under, and our feet sticking out, we were completely hidden. Kindling and firewood, vegetables and fruit found their way into the kitchen by way of the apron route. When company came unexpectedly, the apron was hastily used as a duster on the dining room table or buffet. . . .

Almost everything could be found in the apron pockets: a spool of thread, lost buttons, peppermint candy, cookies, handkerchiefs, bits of paper, a pencil, a piece of string, safety pins, and a coin or two.

For me, there is a never-to-be-forgotten memory of the little ones curled up on Mother's lap as she rocked them and pulled a corner of the big apron over their feet and legs, not alone for warmth, but as a sort of drawing them closer into her wonderful ways.

She was a pioneer mother, with love to go around and around, and her wonderful apron was just one way of showing it.

Tucked away in my chest of memories is one of her ever-useful aprons. In these days of sometimes forgotten aprons, it suggests to me that perhaps my own children and grandchildren have missed some very valuable lessons of life for the lack of a big apron. A very special accessory! ❦

Sometimes selflessness is as simple as doing what brings pleasure to someone else. And when two people are thinking first of the other's enjoyment, the doing usually turns out to be pleasurable for both parties.

AFTERNOON WITH GRANDMOTHER

I always shout when Grandma comes,
But Mother says, "Now please be still
And good and do what *Grandma* wants."
And I say, "Yes, I will."

So off we go in Grandma's car.
"There's a brand new movie quite near by,"
She says, "that I'd rather like to see."
And I say, "So would I."

The show has horses and chases and battles;
We gasp and hold hands the whole way through.
She smiles and says, "I liked that lots."
And I say, "I did, too."

"It's made me hungry, though," she says,
"I'd like a malt with tarts and jam.
By any chance are you hungry, too?"
And I say, "Yes, I am."

Later at home my Mother says,
"I hope you were careful to do as bid.
Did you and Grandma have a good time?"
And I say, "YES, WE DID!!!"
(Barbara A. Huff.)

There is a lovely moment in a story by Willa Cather in which a slow-witted servant girl selflessly eases the burden of the elderly grandmother who is expected to live almost "invisibly" while sharing a small home with her daughter's large family.

FROM "OLD MRS. HARRIS"

Mandy, the bound girl, appeared at the kitchen door.

"Miz' Harris," she said in a guarded tone, ducking her head, "you want me to rub your feet for you?"

For the first time in the long day the old woman's low composure broke a little. "Oh, Mandy, I would take it kindly of you!" she breathed gratefully.

That had to be done in the kitchen; Victoria didn't like anybody slopping about. Mrs. Harris put an old checked shawl round her shoulders and followed Mandy. Beside the kitchen stove Mandy had a little wooden tub full of warm water. She knelt down and untied Mrs. Harris's garter strings and took off her flat cloth slippers and stockings.

"Oh, Miz' Harris, your feet an' legs is swelled turrible tonight!"

"I expect they air, Mandy. They feel like it."

"Pore soul!" murmured Mandy. She put Grandma's feet in the tub and, crouching beside it, slowly, slowly rubbed her swollen legs. Mandy was tired, too. Mrs. Harris sat in her nightcap and shawl, her hands crossed in her lap. She never asked for this greatest solace of the day; it was something that Mandy gave, who had nothing else to give. If there could be a comparison in absolutes, Mandy was the needier of the two,—but she was younger. The kitchen was quiet and full of shadow, with only the light from an old lantern. Neither spoke. Mrs. Harris dozed from comfort, and Mandy herself was half asleep as she performed one of the oldest rites of compassion. ✦

This scriptural scene reverberates behind the fictional passage just quoted, quietly hallowing it:

He riseth from supper, and laid aside his garments; and took a towel, and girded himself.

After that he poureth water into a bason, and began to wash the disciples' feet, and to wipe them with the towel wherewith he was girded. . . .

So after he had washed their feet, and had taken his garments, and was set down again, he said unto them, Know ye what I have done to you?

Ye call me Master and Lord: and ye say well; for so I am.

If I then, your Lord and Master, have washed your feet; ye also ought to wash one another's feet.

For I have given unto you an example, that ye should do as I have done to you. (John 13:4–5, 12–15.) ✦

There are many ways to give gifts, and many kinds of gifts.

WHY THE CHIMES RANG

There was once, in a far-away country where few people have ever traveled, a wonderful church. It stood on a high hill in the midst of a great city;

and every Sunday, as well as on sacred days like Christmas, thousands of people climbed the hill to its great archways.

When you came to the building itself, you found stone columns and dark passages, and a grand entrance leading to the main room of the church. This room was so long that one standing at the doorway could scarcely see to the other end, where the choir stood by the marble altar.

But the strangest thing about the whole building was the wonderful chime of bells. At one corner of the church was a great gray tower, with ivy growing over it as far up as one could see. It was only in very fair weather that anyone claimed to be able to see the top. Even then one could not be certain that it was in sight.

Now, all the people knew that at the top of the tower was a chime of Christmas bells. They had hung there ever since the church had been built, and were the most beautiful bells in the world. Some described them as sounding like angels far up in the sky; others, as sounding like strange winds singing through the trees.

But the fact was that no one had heard them for years and years. There was an old man living not far from the church who said that his mother had spoken of hearing them when she was a little girl, and he was the only one who was sure of as much as that. They were Christmas chimes, you see, and were not meant to be played by men or on common days. It was the custom on Christmas Eve for all the people to bring to the church their offerings to the Christ child; and when the greatest and best offering was laid on the altar, there used to come sounding through the music of the choir the Christmas chimes far up in the tower. Some said that the wind rang them, and others that they were so high the angels could set them swinging. But for many long years they had never been heard.

It was said that the people had been growing less careful of their gifts for the Christ child, and that no offering was brought great enough to deserve the music of the chimes. Every Christmas Eve the rich people still crowded to the altar, each one trying to bring some gift better than any other, without giving anything that he wanted for himself, and the church was crowded with those who thought that perhaps the wonderful bells might be heard again. But although the service was splendid and the offerings plenty, only the roar of the wind could be heard, far up in the stone tower.

Now a number of miles from the city, in a little country village where nothing could be seen of the great church but glimpses of the tower when the weather was fine, lived a boy named Pedro and his little brother. They knew very little about the Christmas chimes, but they had heard of the service in the church on Christmas Eve, and had a secret plan to go see the beautiful celebration.

"Nobody can guess, Little Brother," Pedro would say, "all the fine things there are to see and hear; and I have even heard it said that the Christ child sometimes comes down to bless the service. What if we could see Him?"

The day before Christmas was bitterly cold, with a few lonely snowflakes flying in the air and a hard white crust on the ground. Sure enough, Pedro and Little Brother were able to slip quietly away early in the afternoon; and although the walking was hard in the frosty air, before nightfall they had trudged so far, hand in hand, that they saw the lights of the big city just ahead of them. Indeed, they were about to enter one of the great gates in the wall that surrounded it when they saw something dark on the snow near their path, and stepped aside to look at it.

It was a poor woman who had fallen just outside the city, too sick and tired to get in where she might have found shelter. The soft snow made of a drift a sort of pillow for her, and she would soon be so sound asleep that no one could ever waken her again. All this Pedro saw in a moment, and he knelt down beside her and tried to rouse her, even tugging at her arm a little, as though he would have tried to carry her away.

"It's no use, Little Brother," Pedro said. "You will have to go on alone."

"Alone?" cried Little Brother. "And you not see the Christmas festival?"

"No," said Pedro, and he could not keep back a bit of a choking sound in his throat. "See this poor woman. Her face looks like the Madonna in the chapel window, and she will freeze to death if nobody cares for her. Everyone has gone to the church now, but when you come back you can bring someone to help her. I will rub her to keep her from freezing, and perhaps get her to eat the bun that is left in my pocket."

He added, "I am sure the Christ child must know how I should love to come with you and worship Him; and oh! if you get a chance, Little Brother, to slip up to the altar without getting in anyone's way, take this little silver piece of mine, and lay it down for my offering when no one is looking. Do not forget where you have left me, and forgive me for not going with you."

In this way he hurried Little Brother off to the city, and winked hard to keep back the tears as he heard the crunching footsteps sounding farther and farther away in the twilight. It was pretty hard to lose the music and splendor of the Christmas celebration that he had been planning for so long, and spend the time instead in that lonely place in the snow.

The great church was a wonderful place that night. Everyone said that it had never looked so bright and beautiful before. When the organ played and the thousands of people sang, the walls shook with the sound, and little Pedro, away outside the city wall, felt the earth tremble around him.

At the close of the service came the procession with the offerings to be laid on the altar. Rich men and great men marched proudly up to lay down their gifts to the Christ child. Some brought wonderful jewels, some baskets of gold so heavy that they could scarcely carry them down the aisle. A great writer laid down a book that he had been making for years and years. And last of all walked the king of the country, hoping with all the rest to win for himself the chime of the Christmas bells. There went a great murmur through the church, as the people saw the king take from his head the royal crown, all set with precious stones, and lay it gleaming on the altar, as his offering to the holy Child. "Surely," everyone said, "we shall hear the bells now, for nothing like this has ever happened before."

But still only the cold old wind was heard in the tower, and the people shook their heads; and some of them said, as they had before, that they never really believed the story of the chimes, and doubted if they ever rang at all.

The procession was over, and the choir began the closing hymn. Suddenly the organist stopped playing as though he had been shot, and everyone looked at the old minister, who was standing by the altar holding up his hand for silence. Not a sound could be heard from anyone in the church, but as all the people strained their ears to listen, there came softly, but distinctly, swinging through the air, the sound of the chimes in the tower. So far away and yet so clear the music seemed—so much sweeter were the notes than anything that had been heard before, rising and falling away up there in the sky, that the people in the church sat for a moment as still as though something held each of them by the shoulders. Then they all stood up together and stared straight at the altar, to see what great gift had awakened the long-silent bells.

But all that the nearest of them saw was the childish figure of Little Brother, who had crept softly down the aisle when no one was looking, and had laid Pedro's little piece of silver on the altar. ❧

The following story of two men who "sought not their own" appeared in the June 1880 issue of the Contributor, *the official publication of the young men's organization in the Church, and the precursor to the* Improvement Era. *It was written as a class assignment by an unnamed Deseret University student.*

ABRAM AND ZIMRI

Abram and Zimri were brothers and tilled their lands in a happy vale together. The same plow turned the sod of both their farms in the Spring, and when the Autumn came with its fruitful harvest, they shared equally the bounteous product of their common labor, and each stored away his portion in his barn.

Now Abram had a wife and seven sons, but Zimri lived alone. One evening, as Zimri lay upon his lonely bed, he thought of Abram and his family, and said within himself: "There is my brother Abram. He has a wife and seven sons, for whom he must provide, while I have neither wife nor child, and yet we share our crops alike. Surely this is injustice to my brother. I will arise and gird myself, and go down to the fields to add unto my brother's store." So he girded up his loins and went softly to the field. The moon looked out from between the murky clouds, and threw a shimmering light upon the stubbled field, but newly reaped. He took a generous third of sheaves from his own abundant store, and carried them unto his brother Abram's pile, and returned with a light heart to his home, and soundly slept.

As Abram lay upon his bed that night, he thought of his brother and said within himself: "There is my brother Zimri. He is alone. He has no sons to help him. He does his work without assistance, while I have seven lusty sons who bind my sheaves, and yet we equally divide our gains. Surely this is not pleasing in the sight of God. I will arise and go down to the field and add unto my brother's store. The trees stood up straight in the light of the cold, round moon, and their yellow leaves were shown, then hidden, as the playful moon sported with the clouds. Abram arose and girded up his loins, and, guided by the doubtful light, stole softly to the fertile field. From his ample store he took a generous third, and carried it to add unto his brother Zimri's pile, and then returned with a good heart to his home and slept, for his soul was untormented.

When morning came, and each surveyed his store of sheaves, he wondered how it was his own store had not decreased, although the night before he had given away a third; but neither of the brothers spoke in explanation. At length their day's toil was ended, the sun reclined upon its bed covered by the western hills, and the brothers returned to their homes.

Before the generous Zimri slept that night, he arose and girded up his loins, and led by the beneficent thought that Abram's share should be greater than his own, again visited the scene of his exploit the night before. The tall cedars stood up black against the sky, and the moon silvered their high tops with a mellow, slanting light. Again he carried from his sheaves a third, and stored them with his brother Abram's lot, and then retired behind his pile to watch. It was not long before the noble Abram came stealing softly down the silent field. He turned now right, now left, as if he wished not be to seen, and took from his sheaves again the third, to Zimri's store.

And now the brothers met. Zimri saw it all, but could not speak, for his heart was full, and he leaned upon his brother's breast and wept. ❧

In a lighter vein is this fanciful story of a princess faced with a wrenching decision: whether to make a selfish or a selfless choice for the young man she loves.

THE LADY, OR THE TIGER?

In the very olden time, there lived a semi-barbaric king, whose ideas, though somewhat polished and sharpened by the progressiveness of distant Latin neighbors, were still large, florid, and untrammelled, as became the half of him which was barbaric. He was a man of exuberant fancy, and, withal, of an authority so irresistible that, at his will, he turned his varied fancies into facts. He was greatly given to self-communing; and, when he and himself agreed upon anything, the thing was done. When every member of his domestic and political systems moved smoothly in its appointed course, his nature was bland and genial; but whenever there was a little hitch, and some of his orbs got out of their orbits, he was blander and more genial still, for nothing pleased him so much as to make the crooked straight, and crush down the uneven places.

Among the borrowed notions by which his barbarism had become semified was that of the public arena, a vast amphitheater in which, by exhibitions of manly and beastly valor, the minds of his subjects were refined and cultured, albeit in an unusual way. When a subject was accused of a crime of sufficient importance to interest the king, public notice was given that on an appointed day the fate of the accused person would be decided in the king's arena. But the amphitheater was so constructed as to be itself the agent of poetic justice; crime was punished, or virtue rewarded not by determination of a juried hearing, but by impartial and incorruptible chance. The accused person, therefore, was instantly punished if he found himself guilty; and, if innocent, he was rewarded on the spot, whether he liked it or not. There was no escape from the judgments of the king's arena.

When all the people had assembled in the galleries, and the king, surrounded by his court, sat high up on his throne of royal state on one side of the arena, he gave a signal, a door beneath him opened, and the accused subject stepped out into the amphitheater. Directly opposite him, on the other side of the enclosed space, were two doors, exactly alike and side by side. It was the duty and privilege of the person on trial to walk directly to these doors and open one of them. He could open either door he pleased: he was subject to no guidance or influence but that of the aforementioned

194

impartial and incorruptible chance. If he opened the one, there came out of it a hungry tiger, the fiercest and most cruel that could be procured, which immediately sprang upon him, and tore him to pieces, as a punishment for his guilt.

But, if the accused person opened the other door, there came forth from it a lady, the most suitable to his years and station that his majesty could select among his fair subjects; and to this lady he was immediately married, as a reward of his innocence. It mattered not that he might already possess a wife and family, or that his affections might be engaged upon an object of his own selection: the king allowed no such subordinate arrangements to interfere with his great scheme of retribution and reward.

The institution was a very popular one. When the people gathered together on one of the great trial days, they never knew whether they were to witness a bloody slaughter or a hilarious wedding. This element of uncertainty lent an interest to the occasion which it could not otherwise have attained.

This semi-barbaric king had a daughter as blooming as his most florid fancies, and with a soul as fervent and imperious as his own. As is usual in such cases, she was the apple of his eye, and was loved by him above all humanity. Among his courtiers was a young man of that fineness of blood and lowness of station common to the conventional heroes of romance who love royal maidens. This royal maiden was well-satisfied with her lover, for he was handsome and brave to a degree unsurpassed in all this kingdom. This ardent love affair moved on happily for many months, until the king chanced to discover it. The youth was immediately cast into prison, and a day was appointed for his trial in the king's arena.

There was great interest in this trial, as might be expected. From far and near the people gathered, and thronged the great galleries of the arena. The king and his court were in their places, opposite the twin doors,—those fateful portals, so terrible in their similarity. All was ready. The signal was given. A door beneath the royal party opened, and the lover of the princess walked into the arena. Tall, beautiful, fair, his appearance was greeted with a low hum of admiration and anxiety. Half the audience had not known so grand a youth had lived among them. No wonder the princess loved him!

As the youth advanced into the arena, he turned, as the custom was, to bow to the king: but he did not think at all of that royal personage; his eyes were fixed upon the princess, who sat to the right of her father. From the moment that the decree had gone forth calling her lover to trial, she had thought of nothing, night or day, but this great event and the various subjects connected with it. Possessed of more power, influence, and force of character than anyone who had ever before been interested in such a case, she had done what no other person had done,—she had possessed herself of the secret of the doors. She knew in which of the two rooms, that lay behind those doors, stood the cage of the tiger, and in which waited the lady.

And not only did she know in which room stood the lady ready to emerge, all blushing and radiant, should her door be opened, but she knew who the lady was. It was one of the fairest and loveliest of the damsels of the court. Often had she seen, or imagined that she had seen, this fair creature throwing glances of admiration upon the person of her lover, and sometimes she thought these glances were received and even returned. The girl was lovely, but she had dared to raise her eyes to the loved one of the princess; and, with all the intensity of the savage blood transmitted to her through long lines of wholly barbaric ancestors, she hated the woman who blushed and trembled behind that silent door.

When her lover turned and looked at her, and his eye met hers, he saw, by that power of quick perception which is given to those whose souls are one, that she knew behind which door crouched the tiger, and behind which stood the lady. Then it was that his quick and anxious glance asked the question: "Which?" It was as plain to her as if he shouted it from where he stood. There was not an instant to be lost. The question was asked in a flash; it must be answered in another.

Her right arm lay on the cushioned parapet before her. She raised her hand, and made a slight, quick movement toward the right. No one but her lover saw her. Every eye but his was fixed on the man in the arena.

He turned, and with a firm and rapid step he walked across the empty space. Every heart stopped beating, every breath was held, every eye was fixed immovably upon that man. Without the slightest hesitation, he went to the door on the right, and opened it.

Now, the point of the story is this: Did the tiger come out of that door, or did the lady?

The more we reflect upon this question, the harder it is to answer. It involves a study of the human heart which leads us through devious mazes of passion. Think of it, fair reader, not as if the decision of the question depended on yourself, but upon that hot-blooded, semi-barbaric princess, her soul at a white heat beneath the combined fires of despair and jealousy. She had lost him, but who should have him?

How often, in her waking hours and in her dreams, had she started in wild horror, and covered her face with her hands as she thought of her lover opening the door on the other side of which waited the cruel fangs of the tiger!

But how much oftener had she seen him at the other door! How in her grievous reveries had she gnashed her teeth, and torn her hair, when she saw his start of rapturous delight as he opened the door of the lady! How her soul had burned in agony when she had seen him rush to meet that woman, with her flushing cheek and sparkling eye of triumph; when she had seen him lead her forth, his whole frame kindled with the joy of recovered life; when she had heard the glad shouts from the multitude, and the wild ringing of the happy bells.

Would it not be better for him to die at once, and go to wait for her in the blessed regions of semi-barbaric futurity?

And yet, that awful tiger, those shrieks, that blood!

Her decision had been indicated in an instant, but it had been made after days and nights of anguished deliberation. She had known she would be asked, she had decided what she would answer, and, without the slightest hesitation, she had moved her hand to the right.

The question of her decision is one not to be lightly considered, and it is not for me to presume to set myself up as the one person able to answer

it. And so I leave it with all of you: Which came out of the opened door,—
the lady, or the tiger? (Frank R. Stockton.) ❦

*A famous fable decries the selfishness that hoards and refuses to share even
what it has no use for.*

THE   ENVIOUS   DOG

None ought not to have envy of the good of the other
As it appeareth by this fable
Of a dog which was envious
and that sometime was within a stable of oxen
the which was full of hay.
This dog kept the oxen that they should not enter in to their stable
and that they should not eat of the said hay.
And then the oxen said to him
Thou art well perverse and evil to have envy of the good
the which is to us needful and profitable
And thou hast of it nought to do
for thy kind is not to eat hay. (Aesop.)

*Bruce Barton summarizes the relative fruits of selfishness and unselfishness
in a moral drawn from the natural world.*

THERE   ARE   TWO   SEAS

There are two seas in Palestine.

One is fresh, and fish are in it. Splashes of green adorn its banks. Trees
spread their branches over it, and stretch out their thirsty roots to sip of its
healing waters.

Along its shores the children play, as children played when He was
there. He loved it. He could look across its silver surface when He spoke
His parables. And on a rolling plain not far away He fed five thousand
people.

The river Jordan makes this sea with sparkling water from the hills. So it laughs in the sunshine. And men build their houses near to it, and birds their nests; and every kind of life is happier because it is there.

The river Jordan flows on south into another sea.

Here is no splash of fish, no fluttering leaf, no song of birds, no children's laughter. Travellers choose another route, unless on urgent business. The air hangs heavy above its waters, and neither man nor beast nor fowl will drink.

What makes this mighty difference in these neighbor seas?

Not the river Jordan. It empties the same good water into both. Not the soil in which they lie; not the country round about.

This is the difference. The Sea of Galilee receives but does not keep the Jordan. For every drop that flows into it another drop flows out. The giving and receiving go on in equal measure.

The other sea is shrewder, hoarding its income jealously.

It will not be tempted into any generous impulse. Every drop it gets, it keeps.

The Sea of Galilee gives and lives. This other sea gives nothing. It is named The Dead.

There are two kinds of people in the world.

There are two seas in Palestine. ❦

8

CHARITY IS NOT
EASILY PROVOKED

And above all things, clothe yourselves with

the bond of charity, as with a mantle, which

is the bond of perfectness and peace.

DOCTRINE AND COVENANTS 88:125

When Paul says the charitable person "is not easily provoked," he *equates the charity of pure love with peaceableness, with slowness to anger, with a disinclination to contend with our fellow beings. Modern revelation suggests that charity embraces the whole concept of peace with its attendant "perfection" of calmness and tranquillity.*

The word peace and its derivatives appear numerous times in scripture, most often in connection with the Savior. He is spoken of as the Prince of Peace, the publisher of peace, the source of peace, and our haven in a world of turmoil. Isaiah foretold splendidly the first and second comings of the Prince of Peace, and his description of millennial peace is pure poetry.

And there shall come forth a rod out of the stem of Jesse, and a Branch shall grow out of his roots. . . .

And righteousness shall be the girdle of his loins, and faithfulness the girdle of his reins.

The wolf also shall dwell with the lamb, and the leopard shall lie down with the kid; and the calf and the young lion and the fatling together; and a little child shall lead them.

And the cow and the bear shall feed; their young ones shall lie down together: and the lion shall eat straw like the ox.

And the sucking child shall play on the hole of the asp, and the weaned child shall put his hand on the cockatrice' den.

They shall not hurt nor destroy in all my holy mountain: for the earth shall be full of the knowledge of the Lord, as the waters cover the sea. (Isaiah 11:1, 5–9.) ❖

Jesus taught peace by word and by example. Time after time, those who sought to discredit him tried to provoke him, to draw him into their snare of contention, but he refused to be caught. He sidestepped their arguments and defeated them with thoughtful repose or a quiet comment. He did not allow himself to be provoked even when questioned before Pilate.

And Jesus stood before the governor: and the governor asked him, saying, Art thou the King of the Jews? And Jesus said unto him, Thou sayest.

And when he was accused of the chief priests and elders, he answered nothing.

Then said Pilate unto him, Hearest thou not how many things they witness against thee?

And he answered him to never a word; insomuch that the governor marvelled greatly. (Matthew 27:11–14.) ❖

By John's account, Jesus had a lengthier conversation with Pilate, but it was not a contentious one in any sense. Similarly, Alma and Amulek quietly suffered the buffetings of the chief judge and his cohorts in the wicked city of Ammonihah. They had been forced to watch the burning of faithful women and children, and then to suffer the tauntings and blows of their captors, yet they had refrained from invoking divine retaliation. Later, the judge "smote them with his hand upon their cheeks" and asked, "What say ye for yourselves?" But "Alma and Amulek answered him nothing." Angered, "he smote them again, and delivered them to the officers to be cast into prison."

And when they had been cast into prison three days, there came many lawyers, and judges, and priests, and teachers, who were of the profession of Nehor; and they came in unto the prison to see them, and they questioned them about many words; but they answered them nothing.

And it came to pass that the judge stood before them, and said: Why do ye not answer the words of this people? Know ye not that I have power to deliver you up unto the flames? And he commanded them to speak; but they answered nothing. (Alma 14:14–19.) ✦

The torment continued for many days, and included gnashing of teeth, spitting, mocking, withholding of food and water, stripping of clothing, and binding with strong cords. All this they endured, knowing that if they asked, the Lord would deliver them. Finally, they asked, and they were delivered.

Alma and Amulek certainly were the personification of Eliza R. Snow's injunction:

It is better to suffer than do wrong, and it is sometimes better to submit to injustice rather than contend; it is certainly better to wait the retribution of Jehovah than to contend where effort will be unavailable [avail nothing]. ✦

Being slow to provocation is a trait of character that reflects charity and internal peace. It is incomprehensible to the vexatious nature.

For verily, verily I say unto you, he that hath the spirit of contention is not of me, but is of the devil, who is the father of contention, and he stirreth up the hearts of men to contend with anger, one with another. (3 Nephi 11:29.) ✦

Persons of charity consciously promote unity and harmony, as opposed to divisiveness and discord, in themselves and in others. There are people who calm the waters, as Jesus did, and there are people who unnecessarily stir them up. In intellectual pursuits, of course, and in artistic or athletic performance, a certain amount of friendly stirring is healthy; it challenges us and keeps us on our toes. Opposition that provides choice between good and evil is important, but mean-spirited contentiousness is damaging to the soul.

"Do you think it would be wrong for me to learn the art of self-defense?" a young [man] asked the bishop.

"Certainly not," answered the bishop. "I learned it in youth myself, and I have found it of great value during my life."

"Did you learn boxing or something like karate?"

"Neither. I learned the Biblical system."

"The Biblical system?"

"Yes; you will find it laid down in the first verse of the fifteenth chapter of Proverbs: 'A soft answer turneth away wrath.' It is the best system of self-defense of which I know." ✦

Traditional Chinese philosophy, represented in these lines from Lao Tsu, advises noncombativeness as the surest means to ascendancy.

A man is born gentle and weak.
At his death is he is hard and stiff.
Green plants are tender and filled with sap.
At their death they are withered and dry.
Therefore the stiff and unbending is the disciple of death.
The gentle and yielding is the disciple of life.

Brigham Young stated, "It is our duty to live in peace with one another." (Journal of Discourses 15:63.) *Those who contend may be telling more about themselves than they realize.*

A man pushed forward into a crowd to see what was causing the commotion.

"What's happening?" he asked of a bystander.

"Can't you see? Those Chinese laborers are fighting."

"Those two men talking heatedly there? Why, they are just arguing—not fighting."

"Yes, they are fighting. The man who strikes the first blow admits that his ideas have given out." ✦

Joseph Smith clearly saw himself as a person of peace, despite circumstances that were frequently trying in the extreme. He closed the King Follett sermon with these words:

You don't know me; you never knew my heart. No man knows my history; I cannot tell it. I shall never undertake it. I don't blame any one for not believing my history. If I had not experienced what I have, I would not have believed it myself. I never did harm any man since I have been born in the world. My voice is always for peace.

I cannot lie down until all my work is finished. I never think any evil, nor do anything to the harm of my fellow-man. When I am called by the trump of the archangel and weighed in the balance, you will all know me then. ✦

Brigham Young echoed his sentiments:

I used to say to the ministers, when I was travelling and preaching, "I will not dispute. If you want the truth I will give it to you; and if you have a truth that I have not, I want all you have; but contention is not my calling; it is no part of the gospel of Christ; that is peace, life, light, and salvation. The Lord has given that to me and you, and you are welcome to it." (*Journal of Discourses* 14:121.) ✦

Wilford Woodruff's account of his missionary experiences in England demonstrates that his slowness to be provoked contributed to his success at teaching and baptizing.

When I arose in the evening to speak at Brother Benbow's house, a man entered the door and informed me that he was a constable, and had been sent by the rector of the parish with a warrant to arrest me.

I asked him, "For what crime?"

He said, "For preaching to the people."

I told him that I, as well as the rector, had a license for preaching the gospel to the people, and that if he would take a chair I would wait upon him after the meeting.

He took my chair and sat beside me. I preached the first principles of the everlasting gospel for an hour and a quarter. The power of God rested upon me, the Spirit filled the house, and the people were convinced.

At the close of the meeting I opened a door for baptism, and seven offered themselves. Among the number were four preachers and the constable.

The latter arose and said, "Mr. Woodruff, I would like to be baptized."

I told him I would like to baptize him. I went down to the pool and baptized the seven. We then met together and I confirmed thirteen, and broke bread unto the Saints and we all rejoiced together.

The constable went to the rector and told him if he wanted Mr. Woodruff taken up for preaching the gospel, he must go himself and serve the writ, for he had heard him preach the only true gospel sermon he had ever listened to in his life.

The rector did not know what to make of it, so he sent two clerks of the Church of England as spies, to attend our meeting, and find out what we did preach.

But they were both pricked in their hearts and received the word of the Lord gladly, and were baptized and confirmed members of the Church of Jesus Christ of Latter-day Saints.

The rector became alarmed and did not dare to send anybody else. ✦

A much later incident, in Salt Lake City, indicates that Wilford Woodruff did not change his views about the best way to deal with opposition.

When our Methodist friends came to this city, erected their tent and held their big camp meeting, what was the course pursued by the Latter-day Saints? The President of the Church, the Twelve Apostles and citizens with their wives and children gave them a congregation of many thousands, and we sat in their tent and listened to them while they abused us just as much as they pleased. We believe in giving every man the privilege of saying what he pleases, we have always been willing to let every man express his sentiments here among us. We are not afraid of them. If we have not the truth, that is what we are after, we want it. ✦

This little verse from an unknown author suggests that quarreling can be hazardous to one's health, especially if one is a cat:

There were once two cats of Kilkenny,
Each thought there was one cat too many;
So they fought and they fit,
And they scratched and they bit,
Till, excepting their nails
And the tips of their tails,
Instead of two cats, there weren't any.

I don't know that cats are particularly susceptible to the squabble bug, but this little verse from my childhood is also about infelicitous felines. It has traveled verbally from my grandmother to my mother, and from my mother to her children and grandchildren:

Two little kittens one stormy night
Began to quarrel and then to fight.
One had a mouse and the other had none,
And that was how the quarrel'd begun.
"I'll have that mouse," said the larger cat.
"You won't have that mouse, we'll see about that!"
So the angry old woman took her sweeping broom,
And she swept those two kittens right out of the room.
The ground was covered with ice and snow,
And the poor little kittens had nowhere to go.
So they laid themselves down on the mat by the door
Until the angry old woman finished sweeping her floor.
Then they crept in, as quiet as mice,
All wet with snow and as cold as ice.
They thought it was better that stormy night
To lie down and sleep than to quarrel and fight.
(As told by Rhoda C. Arnold; author unknown.)

Lullabies such as the following seem literally to breathe peace from a divine source.

ALL THROUGH THE NIGHT

Sleep, my child and peace attend thee,
All through the night;
Guardian angels God will send thee,
All through the night;
Soft the drowsy hours are creeping,
Hill and vale in slumber sleeping,
Mother dear her watch is keeping,
All through the night.

God is here, thou'lt not be lonely,
All through the night;
'Tis not I who guards thee only,
All through the night.
Night's dark shades will soon be over,
Still my watchful care shall hover,
God his loving vigil keeping,
All through the night.

Poets speak of peaceableness as a quality that can be cultivated. They often suggest that stepping outside the hustle and bustle of life for a moment or a season brings serenity and renewal. The Savior himself taught that principle when he sought the solitude of the wilderness at the beginning of his ministry and the quiet of the Garden at its conclusion.

Henry David Thoreau found peace at the edge of a New England lake and wrote about it in Walden. In all, although Thoreau was a man concerned, he was not a man easily provoked. E. B. White confirmed as much when he took the occasion of Walden's one-hundredth anniversary to pay tribute to its unique brand of wisdom. When the essay first appeared in Yale Review, White called it "Walden— 1954." In White's The Points of My Compass, *it is titled "A Slight Sound at Evening," in recognition of Walden's capacity to engender the spiritual renewal that flowers into peace.*

In his journal for July 10–12, 1841, Thoreau wrote: "A slight sound at evening lifts me up by the ears, and makes life seem inexpressibly serene and grand. It may be in Uranus, or it may be in the shutter." The book into which he managed to pack both Uranus and the shutter was published in 1854, and now, a hundred years having gone by, "Walden," its serenity and grandeur unimpaired, still lifts us up by the ears, still translates for us that language we are in danger of forgetting. . . .

On this its hundredth birthday, Thoreau's "Walden" is pertinent and timely. In our uneasy season, when all men unconsciously seek a retreat from a world that has got almost completely out of hand, his house in the Concord woods is a haven. In our culture of gadgetry and the multiplicity of convenience, his cry "Simplicity, simplicity, simplicity!" has the insistence of a fire alarm. In the brooding atmosphere of war and the gathering radioactive storm, the innocence and serenity of his summer afternoons are enough to burst the remembering heart, and one gazes back upon that pleasing interlude—its confidence, its purity, its deliberateness—with awe and wonder, as one would look upon the face of a child asleep. ❦

FROM "HIGHER LAWS"

If the day and the night are such that you greet them with joy, and life emits a fragrance like flowers and sweet-scented herbs, is more elastic, more starry, more immortal,—that is your success. . . . The true harvest of my daily life is somewhat as intangible and indescribable as the tints of morning or evening. It is a little star-dust caught, a segment of the rainbow which I have clutched. (Henry David Thoreau.) ❦

Irish poet William Butler Yeats also yearned for his cabin and his "Walden Pond."

THE LAKE ISLE OF INNISFREE

I will arise and go now, and go to Innisfree,
And a small cabin build there, of clay and wattles made;
Nine bean-rows will I have there, a hive for the honeybee,
And live alone in the bee-loud glade.

And I shall have some peace there, for peace comes dropping slow,
Dropping from the veils of the morning to where the cricket sings;
There midnight's all a-glimmer, and noon a purple glow,
And evening full of the linnet's wings.

I will arise and go now, for always night and day
I hear lake water lapping with low sounds by the shore;
While I stand on the roadway, or on the pavements grey,
I hear it in the deep heart's core.

VELVET SHOES

Let us walk in the white snow
In a soundless space;
With footsteps quiet and slow.
At a tranquil pace,
Under veils of white lace.

I shall go shod in silk,
And you in wool,
White as a white cow's milk,
More beautiful
Than the breast of a gull.

We shall walk through the still town
In a windless peace;
We shall step upon white down,
Upon silver fleece,
Upon softer than these.

We shall walk in velvet shoes:
Wherever we go
Silence will fall like dews
On white silence below.
We shall walk in the snow.
(Elinor Wylie.)

Thoreau, Yeats, and Wylie celebrate both external and internal peace. The two seem to complement each other; setting contributes to personal serenity. One who might disagree with those who seek peace in nature and solitude is Seneca the Younger (circa A.D. 3–65), who left his birthplace in Spain to study philosophy and rhetoric in Rome. His philosophical Stoicism is evident in the engaging essay below as he argues the necessity of creating an unprovokable climate within, regardless of a clangorous climate without. His conclusion, however, suggests that even a Stoic has limits.

FROM "ON NOISE"

I cannot for the life of me see that quiet is as necessary to a person who has shut himself away to do some studying as it is usually thought to be. Here am I with a babel of noise going on all about me. I have lodgings right over a public bathhouse. Now imagine to yourself every kind of sound that can make one weary of one's years.

[The writer goes on at some length, detailing the specific kinds of "racket" that daily assault his ears—noises from the gymnasium and street alike. He claims, however, to "no more notice all this roar of noise than I do the sound of waves or falling water," noting that "voices . . . are more inclined to distract one than general noise; noise merely fills one's ears, battering away at them while voices actually catch one's attention." Seneca proceeds to catalogue another batch of noises, from a carpenter's sawing to a "fellow tuning horns and flutes." He then grows philosophical.]

. . . I force my mind to become self-absorbed and not let outside things distract it. There can be absolute bedlam without so long as there is no commotion within, so long as fear and desire are not at loggerheads, so long as meanness and extravagance are not at odds and harassing each other. For what is the good of having silence throughout the neighbourhood if one's emotions are in turmoil?

The peaceful stillness of the night had lulled
The world to rest. [From Apollonius' *Argonautica*.]

This is incorrect. There is no such thing as "peaceful stillness" except where reason has lulled it to rest. Night does not remove our worries; it brings them to the surface. All it gives us is a change of anxieties. For even when people are asleep they have dreams as troubled as their days. The only true serenity is the one which represents the free development of a sound mind. . . .

The temperament that starts at the sound of a voice or chance noises in general is an unstable one and one that has yet to attain inward detachment. It has an element of uneasiness in it, and an element of the rooted fear that makes a man a prey to anxiety, as in the description given by our Virgil:

And I, who formerly would never flinch
At flying spears or serried ranks of Greeks,
Am now alarmed by every breeze and roused
By every sound to nervousness, in fear
For this companion and this load alike.
[*Aeneid* II:726–29. Aeneas speaks as he carries his father and guides his son from a Troy under siege.]

The earlier character here is the wise man, who knows no fear at the hurtling of missiles, or the clash of weapons against weapons in the close-packed ranks, or the thunderous noise of a city in destruction. The other, later one has everything to learn; fearing for his belongings he pales at every noise; a single cry, whatever it is, prostrates him, being immediately taken for the yelling of the enemy; the slightest movement frightens him out of his life; his baggage makes him a coward. Pick out any one of your "successful" men, with all they trail or carry about with them, and you will have a picture of the man "in fear for this companion and this load." You may be sure, then, that you are at last "lulled to rest" when noise never reaches you and when voices never shake you out of yourself, whether they be menacing or inviting or just a meaningless hubbub of empty sound all round you.

"This is all very well," you may say, "but isn't it sometimes a lot simpler just to keep away from the din?" I concede that, and in fact it is the reason why I shall shortly be moving elsewhere. What I wanted was to give myself a test and some practice. Why should I need to suffer the torture any longer than I want to when Ulysses found so easy a remedy for his companions

211

even against the Sirens? [In the *Odyssey,* Ulysses put beeswax in the ears of his crew until they were safely past the lure of the Sirens.] ❧

Several LDS women have written about the routes they have taken to peace.

MY SACRED PLACE

I have my own
Sacred Place.

I've found it
While kneeling here,
Alone,
In the basement.

I would have liked
Lush green grass
Beneath my knees,
And
I would have loved
To have heard
Birds singing
Instead
Of the constant
Rumblings of
The old freezer.

But
Somehow the Spirit
Didn't seem to care
Whether I was kneeling
Near cement walls or
Quaking aspen trees.

I needed
Spiritual guidance.
I needed answers . . .

And I received them,
Right here,
Across the room from
The canned fruit,
Near the washing machine.
(Ranae Pearson.)

FROM "THY WILL BE DONE"

My proving ground came in learning to be obedient to a frightening command—that of accepting the imminent death of my husband after only eleven years of marriage and accepting the challenge of being a mother and woman alone in the world.

I had watched Lloyd become weaker and lose ground from day to day. This happened in spite of the blessings (which I interpreted as promises) that he should yet perform a great work upon the earth and that thousands would be given their sight through his skillful hands. How could he die when his fellow high councilors in the Twin Falls Stake, and later in the Denver Stake, had gathered about his bed in fasting, prayer, and administration, blessing him with recovery of health? An apostle of the Lord had blessed him to rise in health and continue his professional work and family responsibility. The spirit of peace was reassuring in the presence of these brethren of the priesthood. I felt that I must not let him die from any lack of faith on my part. Did his blessing not say that he had not chosen his profession alone—that God had imposed it upon him? Surely seven brief years of medical practice could not fulfill such an assignment.

But new complications continued to arise, and after reassuring myself with these thoughts, I would then be cast into utter despair and an even deeper gloom. I interpreted all this to mean that I was the one holding up the fulfillment of his blessings because I lacked faith. I censured myself and searched my soul. I learned to fast and pray on a level I had not previously known was possible. I am sure now that my determination and love kept him alive months longer than need have been.

One June night I knelt alone in prayer, utterly spent, wondering at that midnight hour how humble one had to be to receive an answer to one's pleading. It was just at that moment that I felt an envelopment of the spirit of peace, a profound assurance that God is over all and that it was his will that was in command and not mine. I could finally say, "Thy will be done," and feel peace instead of guilt. I relaxed in my faith and discovered that I had a new trust in the Lord.

But even though this sweet peace enveloped me I still could not sleep, and once more I turned on the light. As I reached for the Doctrine and Covenants, it seemed to be actually propelled off the table into my hands; it fell open to a section where black velvet, raised letters indicated where I was to begin and end. I then experienced an expanded power of perception. In a flash I knew some specific things! I knew that the Lord was calling Lloyd to a great mission where all the promised blessings would be fulfilled in greater measure than I could at present perceive. I was given to know that the Lord loved me and that I would be made equal to my mission. I felt an encircling love that has sustained me ever since that great moment of change in my life. I have had continual hardships and challenges but always the sure knowledge that Jesus is the Christ, our Redeemer, and that he sustains us through the opposition that must arise in all things. (Stella Oaks.) ✤

In the poem below, Eliza R. Snow extols peace of mind and advises Mary Woolley that subduing one's desires to prevail can bring inner peace.

LINES FOR MRS. WOOLLEY'S ALBUM

Lady were it mine to bless you
With the purest, noblest joys
Nought on earth should dispossess you
One gift that never cloys.

Be thou blest, and blest forever
With what few perchance to find;
From your brest, let nothing sever
Heav'n's best jewel, *peace of mind.*

Hold your *feelings* in subjection
To your judgment's better sway:
Proud to yield to the direction
Of the lord whom you obey.

Noble are the condescensions
Which superior spirits make:
Thus they widen their dimensions,
And of purer joys partake.

If we're prompt to do whatever
Duty claims our service here;
We may calmly rest, and never
Need indulge an idle fear.

For this holy approbation
God our Father will bestow;
And the streams of consolation
Sweetly to our bosoms flow.

May your infl'ence wise & cheering
Wider and more widely spread;
Till ten thousand hearts endearing
Pour their blessings on your head.

Be thou blest and blest forever
With that gem the upright find;
Guard it well—let nothing sever
From your bosom, *peace of mind.*

Essential to peace is a sense of harmony and brotherhood among mortal beings—within the body of Christ's church, as Jesus and Paul taught, but also outside that body. Peacemakers, those slow to be provoked, are a blessing to humanity and to themselves. "Blessed are the peacemakers: for they shall be called the children of God." (Matthew 5:9; 3 Nephi 12:9.)

Daryl V. Hoole and Donette V. Ockey retell a story of a naturally gifted peacemaker.

My grandmother had eleven children, and it seemed as if there was always harmony in her family. I asked my mother one day if she could remember anything specific that might help me to be like her. She said that the incident she remembered best was one time her brothers, who were supposed to be sawing wood, were quarreling. She recalled that her mother was hurrying to prepare a dinner for Church officials, but she stopped and went out and sat on a block of wood near where the boys were sawing, and said the magic words, "Let me tell you a story." My mother said she didn't hear the story, but soon saw her brothers and mother laughing. Later when she went inside, the boys resumed their work without any thought of what they had been quarreling about.

The thought I gleaned from this incident was that my grandmother and mother, too, always took the time to create the harmony which was in our homes. They always had the time to listen to our thoughts, to tell us a story, always to be conscious of our needs. ❧

Jacob Hamblin relates events that changed him from being a hunter of then-troublesome Indians to a peacemaker among them. The Hamblins settled in Tooele Valley where, with other settlers, they became the frequent targets of Indians who stole their livestock and sometimes threatened their lives. The provocations led the settlers to form a military company that occasionally launched expeditions against their Native American antagonists. Following are excerpts from Jacob Hamblin's own account.

[One] winter I asked for a company of men to make another effort to hunt up the Indians. On this scout we traveled at night and watched during the day, until we discovered the location of a band of them.

One morning at daybreak, we surrounded their camp before they were aware of our presence. The chief among them sprang to his feet, and stepping towards me, said, "I never hurt you, and I do not want to. If you shoot, I will; if you do not, I will not." I was not familiar with their language, but I knew what he said. Such an influence came over me that I would not have killed one of them for all the cattle in Tooele Valley.

The running of the women and the crying of the children aroused my sympathies, and I felt inspired to do my best to prevent the company from shooting any of them. . . .

I wished some of the men to go with us to the settlement. They were somewhat afraid, but confided in my assurance that they should not be injured.

On my arrival home, my superior officer ignored the promise of safety I had given the Indians, and decided to have them shot.

I told him I did not care to live after I had seen the Indians whose safety I had guaranteed, murdered, and as it made but little difference with me, if there were any shot I should be the first. At the same time I placed myself in front of the Indians. This ended the matter and they were set at liberty.

[Nevertheless, later on Jacob was again sent with a company under orders to shoot on sight all Indians they could find. As it turned out, every member of that company who tried to shoot an Indian was thwarted by a rifle that misfired.]

In my subsequent reflections [on that curious set of circumstances], it appeared evident to me that a special providence had been over us, in this and the two previous expeditions, to prevent us from shedding the blood of the Indians. The Holy Spirit forcibly impressed me that it was not my calling to shed the blood of the scattered remnant of Israel, but to be a messenger of peace to them. It was also made manifest to me that if I would not thirst for their blood, I should never fall by their hands. The most of the men who went on this last expedition, also received an impression that it was wrong to kill these Indians. ✦

The message of the preceding selections is that peace begins inside an individual's heart and works its way out to others—families, friends, and neighbors; then town and countrymen; then all members of the human family. In three famous addresses to the nation, three presidents of the United States have pleaded for unity—George Washington and Abraham Lincoln within the nation, John Kennedy throughout a shrinking world. These observations by Brigham Young and Mormon serve as an apt preface to the formal presidential statements:

It has been told me from my youth up that opposition is the life of business, especially in the political arena. It is opposition that has ruined our nation, and has been, is and will be the ruin of all nations. (*Journal of Discourses* 10:190.)

When the people's affections are interwoven with a republican government administered in all its purity, if the administrators act not in virtue and truth it is but natural that the people become disaffected with maladministration, and divide and sub-divide into parties, until the body politic is shivered to pieces. (*Journal of Discourses* 10:108.)

Parties in our Government have no better idea than to think the Republic stands all the firmer upon opposition; but I say that it is not so. A republican Government consists in letting the people rule by their united voice, without a dissension,—in learning what is for the best, and unitedly doing it. That is true republicanism. (*Journal of Discourses* 5:229.) ❦

And it came to pass that there was no contention in the land, because of the love of God which did dwell in the hearts of the people.

And there were no envyings, nor strifes, nor tumults, nor whoredoms, nor lyings, nor murders, nor any manner of lasciviousness; and surely there could not be a happier people among all the people who had been created by the hand of God.

There were no robbers, nor murderers, neither were there Lamanites, nor any manner of -ites; but they were in one, the children of Christ, and heirs to the kingdom of God. (4 Nephi 1:15–17.) ❦

At the heart of George Washington's final words to the people of the United States, delivered in September 1796, is a plea to avoid factionalism:

Let me now . . . warn you in the most solemn manner against the baneful effects of the spirit of party generally.

This spirit, unfortunately, is inseparable from our nature, having its root in the strongest passions of the human mind. It exists under different shapes in all governments, more or less stifled, controlled, or repressed; but in those of the popular form it is seen in its greatest rankness and is truly their worst enemy.

The alternate domination of one faction over another, sharpened by the spirit of revenge natural to party dissension, which in different ages and countries, has perpetrated the most horrid enormities, is itself a frightful despotism. But this leads at length to a more formal and permanent despotism. The disorders and miseries which result gradually incline the minds of men to seek security and repose in the absolute power of an individual, and sooner or later the chief of some prevailing faction, more able or more fortunate than his competitors, turns this disposition to the purpose of his own elevation, on the ruins of public liberty.

Without looking forward to an extremity of this kind (which nevertheless ought not to be entirely out of sight), the common and continual mischiefs of the spirit of party are sufficient to make it the interest and duty of a wise people to discourage and restrain it.

It serves always to distract the public councils and enfeeble the public administration. It agitates the community with ill-founded jealousies and false alarms; kindles the animosity of one part against another; foments occasionally riot and insurrection. It opens the door to foreign influence and corruption, which find a facilitated access to the government itself through the channels of party passion. Thus the policy and will of one country are subjected to the policy and will of another.

There is an opinion that parties in free countries are useful checks upon the administration of the government, and serve to keep alive the spirit of liberty. This within certain limits is probably true; and in governments of a monarchical cast patriotism may look with indulgence, if not with favor, upon the spirit of party. But in those of the popular character, in governments purely elective, it is a spirit not to be encouraged. From their natural tendency it is certain there will always be enough of that spirit for every salutary purpose; and there being constant danger of excess, the effort ought to be by force of public opinion to mitigate and assuage it. A fire not to be quenched, it demands a uniform vigilance to prevent its bursting into a flame, lest, instead of warming, it should consume. ✦

Abraham Lincoln inherited the reins of a nation literally torn in two over the issue of slavery. His first inaugural address confronts a divided populace head-on and asserts his intention to mend the division and reestablish unity in the land. Lincoln's concluding words urge a return to brotherly love:

In *your* hands, my dissatisfied fellow country-men, and not in *mine,* is the momentous issue of civil war. The Government will not assail *you.* You can have no conflict without being yourselves the aggressors. *You* have no oath registered in Heaven to destroy the Government, while *I* shall have the most solemn one to "preserve, protect, and defend it."

I am loath to close. We are not enemies, but friends. We must not be enemies. Though passion may have strained it must not break our bonds of affection. The mystic chords of memory, stretching from every battlefield and patriot grave, to every living heart and hearthstone all over this broad land, will yet swell the chorus of the Union, when again touched, as surely they will be, by the better angels of our nature. ❧

On the occasion of his first inaugural address, John F. Kennedy spoke in the spirit of his predecessors, though the times called for a world as well as a national view. That address was, in effect, a plea for charity, for hearts not easily provoked.

To those old allies whose cultural and spiritual origins we share, we pledge the loyalty of faithful friends. United, there is little we cannot do in a host of cooperative ventures. Divided, there is little we can do—for we dare not meet a powerful challenge at odds and split asunder. . . .

Finally, to those nations who would make themselves our adversary, we offer not a pledge but a request: that both sides begin anew the quest for peace, before the dark powers of destruction unleashed by science engulf all humanity in planned or accidental self-destruction. . . .

Let both sides explore what problems unite us instead of laboring those problems which divide us. . . .

Let both sides seek to invoke the wonders of science instead of its terrors. Together let us explore the stars, conquer the deserts, eradicate disease, tap the ocean depths, and encourage the arts and commerce.

Let both sides unite to heed in all corners of the earth the command of Isaiah—to "undo the heavy burdens . . . [and] let the oppressed go free." . . .

Can we forge against these enemies [tyranny, poverty, disease, and war] a grand and global alliance, North and South, East and West, that can assure a more fruitful life for all mankind? Will you join in that historic effort? . . .

And so, my fellow Americans, ask not what your country can do for you: Ask what you can do for your country.

My fellow citizens of the world: Ask not what America will do for you, but what together we can do for the freedom of man.

Finally, whether you are citizens of America or citizens of the world, ask of us the same high standards of strength and sacrifice which we ask of you. With a good conscience our only sure reward, with history the final judge of our deeds, let us go forth to lead the land we love, asking His blessing and His help, but knowing that here on earth God's work must truly be our own. ❧

One of the tenderest moments in scripture is Jesus' intercessory prayer on behalf of his beloved disciples, given during his final hours with them. It is a plea for loving unity among the faithful—the same kind of unity that the Son and Father enjoy.

Neither pray I for these alone, but for them also which shall believe on me through their word;

That they all may be one; as thou, Father, art in me, and I in thee, that they also may be one in us: that the world may believe that thou has sent me.

And the glory which thou gavest me I have given them; that they may be one, even as we are one:

I in them, and thou in me, that they may be made perfect in one; and that the world may know that thou hast sent me, and hast loved them, as thou hast loved me. . . .

And I have declared unto them thy name, and will declare it: that the love wherewith thou has loved me may be in them, and I in them. (John 17:20–23, 26.) ❧

I think it no coincidence that, prior to offering the intercessory prayer, Jesus promised his disciples that when he left he would send them another Comforter. Therein would lie their peace. Unity and peace, his peace, are inextricably bound.

Peace I leave with you, my peace I give unto you: not as the world giveth, give I unto you. Let not your heart be troubled, neither let it be afraid. (John 14:27.) ❦

The central text for this entire collection is 1 Corinthians 13, and it must be by design that Paul leads into his discussion of charity by discoursing on spiritual gifts in chapter 12. His concern is not simply to name the gifts and celebrate their variety and value, but rather to insist that all gifts and persons have worth in a unified scheme. All derive from the same divine source, and all are necessary. In an important sense, mortals, like spiritual gifts, cannot be considered autonomous. Paul uses these gifts as metaphors for individual parts of the human body, and those parts again as metaphors for the individual members of the Church. On each level, distinct entities are essential parts of a larger whole. "For," he says, "as the body is one, and hath many members, and all the members of that one body, being many, are one body: so also is Christ." (1 Corinthians 12:12.) There is much to ponder in 1 Corinthians 12:11–27, not the least of which is the relationship of harmony to the principle of charity, to which Paul gives major and immediate attention.

Dame Julian of Norwich, a fourteenth-century anchoress, expresses confidence in the Lord's ability to transform a nature disposed to be easily provoked.

FROM "REVELATIONS OF DIVINE LOVE"

For He that wasteth and destroyeth our wrath and maketh us meek and mild,—it behoveth needs to be that He [Himself] be ever one in love, meek and mild: which is contrary to wrath.

For I saw full surely that where our Lord appeareth, peace is taken and wrath hath no place. For I saw no manner of wrath in God, neither for short time nor for long;—for in sooth, as to my sight, if God might be wroth for an instant, we should never have life nor place nor being. For as verily as we have our being in the endless Might of God and of the endless Wisdom and of the endless Goodness, so verily we have our being in the endless Might of God, in the endless Wisdom, and in the endless Goodness. For though we feel in ourselves, [frail] wretches, debates and strifes, yet are we in all-mannerful enclosed in the mildness of God and in His meekness, in

His benignity and in His graciousness. For I saw full surely that all our end-less friendship, our place, our life and our being, is in God.

For that same endless Goodness that keepeth us when we sin, that we perish not, the same endless Goodness continually treateth in us a peace against our wrath and our contrarious falling, and maketh us to see our need with a true dread, and mightily to seek unto God to have forgiveness, with a gracious desire of our salvation. And though we, by the wrath and the contrariness that is in us, be now in tribulation, distress, and woe, as falleth to our blindness and frailty, yet are we *securely* safe by the merciful keeping of God, that we perish not. But we are not *blissfully* safe, in having of our endless joy, till we be all in peace and in love: that is to say, full pleased with God and with all His works, and with all His judgments, and loving and peaceable with our self and with our even-Christians and with all that God loveth, as love beseemeth. And this doeth God's Goodness in us.

Thus saw I that God is our very Peace, and He is our sure Keeper when we are ourselves in unpeace, and He continually worketh to bring us into endless peace. And thus when we, by the working of mercy and grace, be made meek and mild, we are fully safe; suddenly is the soul oned [united] to God when it is truly peaced in itself: for in Him is found no wrath. And thus I saw when we are all in peace and in love, we find no contrariness, nor no manner of letting [hindrance] through that contrariness which is now in us; [nay], our Lord of His Goodness maketh it to us full profitable. For that contrariness is cause of our tribulations and all our woe, and our Lord Jesus taketh them and sendeth them up to Heaven, and there are they made more sweet and delectable than heart may think or tongue may tell. And when we come thither we shall find them ready, all turned into very fair and endless worships. Thus is God our steadfast Ground: and He shall be our full bliss and make us unchangeable, as He is, when we are there. ❧

Clement of Rome, one of the early Apostolic fathers, concurs that our peace lies in the Creator of a harmoniously ordered universe:

Let us then make haste and get back to the state of tranquillity which was set before us in the beginning as the mark for us to aim at. Let us turn our eyes to the Father and Creator of the universe, and when we consider how precious and peerless are His gifts of peace, let us embrace them eagerly for ourselves. Let us contemplate Him with understanding, noting with the eyes of the spirit the patient forbearance that is everywhere willed by Him, and the total absence of any friction that marks the ordering of His whole creation. ❧

The words of a now beloved modern hymn harmonize with the sentiments of all the selections in this chapter.

WHERE CAN I TURN FOR PEACE?

Where can I turn for peace? Where is my solace
When other sources cease to make me whole?
When with a wounded heart, anger, or malice,
I draw myself apart, Searching my soul?

Where, when my aching grows, Where, when I languish,
Where, in my need to know, where can I run?
Where is the quiet hand to calm my anguish?
Who, who can understand? He, only One.

He answers privately, Reaches my reaching
In my Gethsemane, Savior and Friend.
Gentle the peace he finds for my beseeching.
Constant he is and kind, Love without end.
(Emma Lou Thayne.)

9

CHARITY THINKETH NO EVIL

For as he thinketh in his heart, so is he.

PROVERBS 23:7

L ike Paul, the author of Proverbs makes a persuasive link between thought
and the pure love that is charity, for he locates at least some cognitions in
the heart. In a baccalaureate sermon, Stephen L Richards also connects
heart and feeling with thought, tying all three to questions of right and wrong.

FROM "TRIED AND NOT FOUND WANTING"

I suppose I would get into much difficulty if I attempted to distinguish
psychologically between thinking and feeling, between the emotions of the
heart, to use an old and commonplace expression, and the rationalizing of
the brain. I only get confused myself when I attempt such an analysis, so I
assure you I won't try it on you. But for my purposes here today I must ask
you to accept, at least tentatively, the conclusion that there are innate within
most of us deep-seated feelings and inner convictions about the unseen and
supernatural which constitute the basis for religion and the spiritual life.
This thinking and feeling of the heart is a very old concept set forth innu-
merable times in the literature of the past and epitomized most impressively
in that great scriptural passage: "As a man thinketh *in his heart* so is he." (See
Prov. 23:7.) I cannot believe that the phrase "in his heart" was there used
indifferently. Too many far-reaching implications flow from it.

So it is that this thinking "in the heart," however metaphorical such an
expression may be, commands my attention as I ponder the conditions of

225

these young men and women who today go out to meet the realities of a strangely perturbed world. It is important, of course, that we appraise the equipment, mental and otherwise, which we have secured to meet the exigencies which life shall put upon us. I don't mean by such equipment to include only that secured in vocational training to help us make a living. I would also encompass in our equipment that invaluable training which has enlarged our tolerances, our appreciations, and our general outlook on life and which has likewise increased our curiosity and quest for truth. After you have made these appraisals and gratitude has welled up within your heart for the opportunities you enjoy living in a free country with education and comparative abundance in all things surrounding us, will you pause for a moment and soberly ask yourselves a few questions all beginning, "How do I feel?

"How do I feel about honor and integrity? What is my reaction to polite lying to facilitate easy social intercourse? How much tolerance have I for either suppression or misrepresentation of facts to promote business advantage? Do I accept without compunction the old adage, that all's fair in love and war and politics and college athletics?" It isn't very difficult to test ourselves in this matter of honesty. We need only probe our feelings about it. ❦

In the words of J. Golden Kimball:

A man must be honest, and he must be true, and he must be chaste and benevolent, virtuous, and continue doing good to all men. What can God do for a man who is not honest? You may baptize him every fifteen minutes, but if he does not repent, he will come up out of the water just as dishonest as ever. What can God do for a liar who refuses to repent? Can the Lord save him? He can't claim salvation. Baptizing him in water will not settle the trouble, unless you keep him under. ❦

Hugh B. Brown expressed some thoughts on the source of true greatness.

FROM "YOU ARE AN ORIGINAL"

The education of the heart is important. I have met some very highly educated men, as the world views education, who have been thought to be successful and have thought themselves successful. I have met them at the peak of their so-called success and have met them after they have gone over the top and were about ready to leave and evaluate their own lives. And I've been amused at the unanimity of these so-called great men on one point. Their success—real, genuine, lasting success—has been dependent upon the education of the heart. Faith in God, faith in themselves, faith in their fellowmen and willingness to serve—these have been fundamental in the lives of many great men whom I have had the pleasure of meeting. ✦

Thinking evil not only precludes charity, it shapes character in the mold of evil. In April 1900, at a general meeting of the Deseret Sunday School Union, Dr. J. M. Tanner spoke of the importance of teaching youngsters in the Church both to think and to feel in ways consistent with the gospel. "For both" thinking and feeling, he says, "are necessary in a complete life." He cautions against making "this work in the Sunday schools purely an argumentative work," and urges teachers instead to "make the lessons correspond with the spirit of faith which we have."

The purpose of religion, the purpose of teaching religion, is that our children may be taught to feel as well as to think; for religion is not a system of philosophy. . . . Religion is the Gospel of correct living, thinking and feeling, of correct lives, if you please, including all that we are, including our feelings as well as our thoughts, and for that reason we ought to be instructed how to think correctly and how to feel correctly. ✦

Thinking no evil, and feeling no evil, therefore, are tantamount to living no evil. George Albert Smith evidently learned this truth at a young age.

THE PRODUCT OF MY THOUGHTS

As a child thirteen years of age, I went to school at the Brigham Young Academy. It was fortunate that part of my instruction came under Dr. Karl G. Maeser, that outstanding educator who was the first builder of our great Church schools. . . . I cannot remember much of what was said during the year that I was there, but there is one thing that I will probably never forget. Dr. Maeser one day stood up and said:

"Not only will you be held accountable for things that you do, but you will be held responsible for the very thoughts you think."

Being a boy, not in the habit of controlling my thoughts very much, it was quite a puzzle to me what I was to do, and it worried me. In fact, it stuck to me just like a burr. About a week or ten days after that it suddenly came to me what he meant. I could see the philosophy of it then. All at once there came to me this interpretation of what he had said: "Why, of course, you will be held accountable for your thoughts because when your life is complete in mortality, it will be the sum of your thoughts." That one suggestion has been a great blessing to me all my life, and it has enabled me upon many occasions to avoid thinking improperly because I realize that I will be, when my life's labor is complete, the product of my thoughts. ❧

A fanciful story is told about a man whose countenance—and whose life—changed with the content of his thoughts.

THE MAGIC MASK

In a far off country across the seas lived a great and powerful prince. He had hundreds of fine trained soldiers in his army. With banners flying, he would set out to battle against his foes. With the help of his soldiers, he was often victorious and ruled with an iron hand over vast strips of country.

His enemies as well as his friends feared him because of his strong determination to have his own way in all things, and unlucky was the man who brought upon himself the thunder and lightning of his wrath.

Yet he won the respect of all by his bravery. The prince was always found in the foremost ranks or in the thickest of the fray. But no one loved him, and as he grew older, he became lonely and unhappy which made him more stern and severe. His face became seamed with hard, cruel lines, and a deep frown was furrowed on his forehead, and no one ever saw him smile or heard him laugh.

Now it happened that in one of the cities which he had taken from his enemies, lived a beautiful princess whom he wished to marry. He had watched her for many months as she went about among those in need administering to their wants, and he knew she was as good and kind as she was beautiful. Because he always wore his heavy helmet when he rode through the city, the princess had never seen his face.

One day he put on his royal robes and golden crown and set forth to ask the lovely princess to marry him and live in his beautiful castle.

As he entered the hall of the home of the fair Lenore, he caught a glimpse of his reflection in a great mirror that stood against the wall. He sprang back startled, for in his face he saw nothing but what would cause fear and dislike. He tried to smile, but so set were the frowns that it made him look worse than ever. So he quickly gave it up and fled back to his own castle without seeing the princess. Then to him came a happy thought. Sending for the great magician of his court he said to him: "Make for me a mask of thinnest wax so that it will follow every line of my features, but paint it with your magic paints so that it will look kind and pleasant. Fasten it upon my face so that I shall never take it off, and I will pay you any price you ask."

"This I can do," said the magician, "on one condition only. You must keep your face in the same lines that I shall paint, or the mask will be ruined. One angry frown, one cruel smile will crack the mask and ruin it forever; nor can I replace it. Will you agree to this?"

"Yes," replied the prince, "I agree, but tell me how may I keep the mask from breaking?"

"You must train yourself to think kindly thoughts," said the magician, "and to do this, you must do kindly deeds. You must try to make your kingdom happy rather than great. Whenever you are angry, keep absolutely still until the feeling has gone away. Be gracious and courteous to all men."

So the wonderful mask was made, and when it was put on, no one would have guessed it was not the prince's true face.

The lovely princess willingly became his bride, for she could see no fault in his smiling countenance.

As time went on the magic mask was often in danger of being destroyed, but the prince made a tremendous struggle to overcome his terrible temper and ugly frowns. His subjects marveled at his gentleness and said: "It is the princess who has made him like herself."

The prince, however, was very unhappy. He knew he was deceiving the princess with the magic mask. At last he could bear it no longer, and, sending for the magician, he commanded him to remove it.

"Remember," protested the magician, "I can never make another."

"So be it," cried the prince. "Anything would be better than to continue to deceive one whose love and trust I value so greatly."

The mask was removed and in fear and anguish the prince sought his reflection in the mirror. To his joy and surprise, the ugly lines were gone, the frowns had disappeared, and his face was moulded in the exact lines of the magic mask!

And when he came into the presence of his wife and his subjects, they saw only the kindly features of the prince they had learned to honor and love. (Author unknown.) ❧

If we think evil thoughts—if we think ill of others, of life itself, or of Deity—that process of thought defines us, as the following childhood story teaches. The story also teaches, as do King Benjamin and Alma, of the beauty and charity of a changed heart.

The following story is indebted to Thornton W. Burgess, who created several volumes of "Mother West Wind" stories, most of them about animals and not about Mother West Wind at all. This particular story does not appear in the Burgess volumes, not even in Mother West Wind's Children *(1911). My guess is that the first oral teller combined Burgess's characters with a storyline from an unknown author.*

MOTHER WEST WIND

AND THE SEVEN LITTLE BREEZES

Mother West Wind had quite a problem. She had to go to work every day so that she could earn a living for her seven little breezes. She did not like to leave them home alone all the time, but she would always caution them when she would leave to go to work in the morning not to open the door and let any strangers in. It was her job to blow the fishermen's boats out to sea in the morning so that they could catch fish. Then she would have to wait and blow their boats back home at night, so they could sell their fish and make a living for their families. So she cautioned her little breezes: "Goodbye, little breezes, don't let anyone in the house. Don't let any strangers in."

One day while Mother West Wind was away at work, there was a knock at the door. The little breezes said, "Who is it? Who is it?" A gruff voice at the door said, "I'm your friend, let me come in." And the little breezes laughed and laughed. They said, "We know you're not our friend. You sound like the Green Goblin. We can't let you in." So the Green Goblin went away, and he went to a voice specialist, and he said, "I have such a coarse, ugly voice. It makes people afraid of me. Can't you do something to help me?" The voice specialist said, "Yes, I can help you, but you have to really want to, and work really hard at it." "I really want to, and I'll work really hard."

So the voice specialist worked with him, and pretty soon he didn't have a coarse ugly voice; so he went back and knocked at the little breezes' house. They said, "Who is it? Who is it?" He said in a sweet voice, "I'm your friend, let me come in." They said, "Oh, you sound like our friend. Open the door, open the door!" But the cautious little breeze said, "You sound like our friend. Let's see your hands." The Goblin put his hands up to the window, and the breezes laughed and laughed. "Ah, we know you're not our friend. You're the Green Goblin. We can tell by your ugly green hands."

So the Green Goblin went to a flour mill, and he said, "Look at my ugly, green hands. Can't you do something to help me so my hands won't look like this?" They said, "Yes, we can help you, but you have to really want to, and you have to work really hard." He said, "I really want to, and I'll work really hard." After a time, he looked at his hands, and they weren't ugly and green any more. So he went back to the little breezes' house and knocked on the door. "Who is it, who is it?" they cried, and the Green Goblin said, "I'm your friend, let me come in." They said, "You sound like our friend, let's see your hands." He put his hands up to the window and they said, "Oh, that looks like our friend. Open the door, open the door and let him come in!" But the cautious little breeze said, "You sound like our friend, your hands look like our friend. Let's see your face." He put his ugly green face up to the window, and they laughed and laughed. "We know that you're not our friend. We can tell by your ugly green face."

So the Green Goblin went to a beauty parlor, and he said, "Look at my ugly green face. Isn't there something you can do to help me so that I won't have an ugly green face any more?" They said, "Yes, we can help you change, but you have to really want to, and you have to work really hard." He said, "I really want to change, and I'll work really hard." And he did, and finally he didn't have an ugly green face any more. So he went back to the little breezes' house and knocked on the door. "Who is it, who is it?" they cried, and the Green Goblin said, "I'm your friend, let me come in." They said, "You sound like our friend, let's see your hands." He put his hands up to the window and they said, "You look like our friend, let's see your face." He put his face to the window and they said, "Oh, that looks like our friend. Open the door, open the door! Let him come in!" But the cautious little breeze said, "No, don't open the door yet. You sound like our friend, you look like our friend, but what do you want us to do?"

"Oh ho," chuckled the Green Goblin, "if you'll just open the door, I'll let you come outside. We'll have the most fun. We'll blow down the street. We'll blow trees down. We'll blow the roof off Farmer Brown's barn. We'll blow chicken coops over. We'll take the roofs off from houses. Oh, we'll have a lot of fun!" Then the little breezes said, "Now we know you're not our friend. Our friend wouldn't have ugly, mean thoughts like that." So the Green Goblin went away. He decided that he would go to Sunday School. So he went to Sunday School, and he talked to a teacher. He said, "What can I do? I have such ugly, mean thoughts, and people don't like me because of it. Can't you help me change?" The teacher said, "Yes, I can help you change, but you have to really want to, and you have to try really hard." "I really want to change, and I'll try really hard." And he did. And pretty soon he didn't have ugly, mean thoughts any more.

So he went back to the little breezes' house and knocked on the door. "Who is it, who is it?" they cried. "I used to be the Green Goblin, but I don't look like the Green Goblin, I don't feel like the Green Goblin, and I don't sound like the Green Goblin. And I don't want you to open the door to let me come in when your mother isn't home. I'll just wait here in the yard until she gets home tonight." So that night, as Mother West Wind came blowing up the sidewalk, she stopped because she saw a beautiful creature standing there. It looked like a fairy, and she said, "Who are you?" He said, "I used to be the Green Goblin. I don't sound like the Green Goblin, I don't look like the Green Goblin, I don't feel like the Green Goblin any more. Mother West Wind, I know that you have a lot to do when you get home at night. If you'd like, I'll come and take care of the little breezes during the day while you're at work. I'll see to it that they don't get into any mischief, but they can play outside and have fun."

Mother West Wind was so happy because she could go to work after that and not have to worry about the little breezes. (As told by Rhoda C. Arnold; author unknown.) ✦

If we were to assign a moral to that story, one possibility might be: As a Green Goblin thinketh, so is he. All changes prior to change of thought (and therefore heart) were merely cosmetic.

There is another lesson, too. Although six of the little breezes were unwisely trusting of a stranger, it seems clear that Mother West Wind had not trained her children to be unduly suspicious, either. She would not have wanted them to think evil of everyone they met. Oscar A. Kirkham tells of how trust extended—thinking good rather than ill of someone—actually changed a heart full of evil intent. The risk might often be too great for such an action in today's world, but the incident illustrates a valuable point nonetheless.

On the way from Carson City to Ely, Nevada, a friend of mine said he picked up a man one day; and when he looked in the mirror, he saw he was hard looking. He said, "Come around here and sit in the front seat. Open that box. My wife put up a lunch. Let's enjoy it together."

And the fellow opened that box—white napkin, lovely sandwiches inside. They ate together. They chatted freely. That's what friendship does.

When they got nearly to Ely the man who had been invited into the automobile reached into his pocket and pulled out a gun and said, "I want to leave this with you. Three months ago I got out of the state penitentiary in Nevada. I resolved that the first man I met—I hadn't been able to get a job—I'd stick him up."

But the lunch box did something to him.

"When I saw the white napkin, when I felt your hospitality—something happened."

Then my courageous friend said, "Well, something's happened to me. Come to my office in the morning, and I'll have a job for you. I employ about three hundred men."

When I saw my friend just recently down in Ely, I said, "What about that fellow?"

"Oh, he's still working for me. We got along gloriously." ⬅

From our pioneer past comes another story illustrating the fruits of thinking good rather than evil of another, and behaving on that impulse.

A FRIGHTENING EXPERIENCE

The first sawmill in Escalante, Utah, was situated in North Creek Canyon, about fourteen miles from town. This mill was built and managed by Henry J. White.

One Sunday it became necessary for Mr. White to leave his young wife, Susannah, alone at the sawmill until the next day. He disliked to do this because Indians were camped close by, and one of [them] was known to be the meanest Indian in the country.

About two hours after Mr. White left, this very Indian came to the mill. He rode up to the cabin and said, "Where is your Mormon?" Susannah pretended that she wasn't frightened, and told the Indian that Mr. White was in town. He said he wanted to hunt above the mill, so Susannah told him to go. He rode away, but reappeared in the late afternoon with two deer tied on his horse, and again asked, "Where is your Mormon?" She told him he was still in town. The Indian then asked to stay all night. She told him he could stay and for him to put his horse in the corral and feed it.

The deer were hung in a nearby tree, and the horse cared for before the Indian came to the cabin. Susannah had supper ready when he came in, and after eating, they sat by the fire place. He tried to tell her the town news and passed her a little dirty sack of pine nuts.

While sitting there the Indian asked, "You 'fraid?"

"No, I'm not afraid," replied Susannah. "I can shoot as good as any Indian."

The reply amused the Indian and laughingly he replied, "You no shoot Indian."

When the time came to retire, Susannah gave him some matches and said, "My Mormon always makes the fire in the morning." She then gave him a quilt and some rugs to make himself a bed by the fire.

Susannah, thinking she would have to remain awake all night and watch him, just slipped off her shoes and went to bed. When she looked around, she was amazed to see the Indian kneeling in prayer by the side of his bed.

Susannah had been terribly frightened all evening, but seeing the Indian now she said to herself, "I don't need to be afraid of a praying Indian." Soon after, she went to sleep and slept until next morning when she was awakened by the Indian who was building the fire. He insisted on helping milk the cows, but she explained that the cows would be afraid of him; but she told him he could cut her an armload of wood, which he gladly did. He cut a large pile instead of an armful.

After they had eaten breakfast, the Indian left. But before going, he cut two hind quarters off one of the deer and left them hanging in the tree for her. ✦

Paul said that "the end of the commandment is charity out of a pure heart." (1 Timothy 1:5.) Most surely, if thought comes from the heart, purity of heart and purity of thought are virtually synonymous. The person possessed of a pure heart "thinketh no evil." More than once the Old Testament speaks of thought in relation to the heart's purity (see Genesis 6:5 and Deuteronomy 15:9 in addition to Proverbs 23:7). The twenty-fourth Psalm enlarges the subject:

The earth is the Lord's, and the fulness thereof; the world, and they that dwell therein.

For he hath founded it upon the seas, and established it upon the floods.

Who shall ascend into the hill of the Lord? or who shall stand in his holy place?

He that hath clean hands, and a pure heart; who hath not lifted up his soul unto vanity, nor sworn deceitfully.

He shall receive the blessing from the Lord, and righteousness from the God of his salvation. (Psalm 24:1–5.) ❧

In that psalm, David makes a distinct allusion to speech, as did Jesus when he taught in person as well as through Moses (see Moses 8:22) that the heart is the residence of thought, and that

Not that which goeth into the mouth defileth a man; but that which cometh out of the mouth, this defileth a man.

. . . those things which proceed out of the mouth come forth from the heart; and they defile the man.

For out of the heart proceed evil thoughts, murders, adulteries, fornications, thefts, false witness, blasphemies:

These are the things which defile a man. (Matthew 15:11, 18–20.) ❧

Much has been said across the pulpit about the uncharitable practice of judging others, of thinking—and speaking—ill of them. Stephen L Richards observed:

Someone has said that the supreme charity of the world consists in obeying the divine injunction, "Judge not." How do you feel about this? How sacredly do you regard the good name of another? Is my conviction about this sufficiently strong to restrain me, even under the urgent temptation of adding spicy bits to entertaining conversation, from repeating rumors and stories which have not been submitted to the test that evidence and hearing may produce? In this respect it is not difficult to test the sincerity of our friendship. I know of no finer demonstration of loyalty than for one to come to the defense of the good name of a friend in his absence.

Elder Richards alluded to the subject on another occasion.

Mankind are all one great brotherhood, some weaker than others, and it would seem some are vicious and malicious, and intentionally do great harm. Thank God I am not the judge of my brother and sister. I am persuaded sometimes to believe with him who says that the supreme charity in all this world is to judge not, but to leave the judgment of our fellow men in the hands of Him who is the great and just Judge of all. As I desire mercy for myself, I plead for mercy for all mankind. ❖

Often we judge others out of the narrow self-righteousness that constricts our own hearts and thoughts. Harold B. Lee tells this story:

FROM "DOING THE RIGHT THING

FOR THE RIGHT REASONS"

I remember sitting with a group of men after a 24th of July parade in Salt Lake City and hearing someone say to President David O. McKay, "President McKay, didn't that shock you—the immodesty of those girls who rode the floats? My, wasn't that a spectacle?"

President McKay listened patiently and then said, "Well, you know, I never noticed it. I thought it was beautiful. I never noticed any such immodesty."

After the election of John F. Kennedy as President of the United States, someone said, "President McKay, doesn't it worry you that a Catholic has been elected President?" And do you know what he replied? "You know, all I thought about on election day was how wonderful it is that in this great country everybody can go to the polls and vote for a Catholic or a Quaker just as they please and not have to worry about it." You see how we can think higher about the many things about which we are so ready to judge. He was not seeking to dig out the little sliver or the little tiny speck in a neighbor's eye. He was not concerned about that. He was only concerned about his own reaction to these things. ❖

The person eager to think evil of others, and to judge them, may well be guilty of hypocrisy, as J. Reuben Clark suggests in his last address to a general conference of the Church.

Very early in his ministry, the Savior, in that great conversation between him and Nicodemus, said that the Father sent the Savior to redeem the world, not to condemn it. The Lord never condemns the individual, except on rare occasions. He condemns the sin. And I can never forget that the most scathing denunciation that I know of in our literature, scriptural or otherwise, is that denunciation which the Savior made, and which is recorded in the latter chapters of Matthew, against hypocrisy. He leaves one almost with the persuasion that nothing is so bad as that.

. . . Personally, I have felt that nobody need keep much of a record about me, except what I keep myself in my mind, which is part of my spirit. I often question in my mind, whether it is going to require very many witnesses in addition to my own as to my wrongdoing. ◄

Joseph F. Smith cautioned against the evil thinking that is manifest in gossip.

How idle to go about whispering mysterious words here and there—words often without foundation in fact, but uttered with injurious intent, and perhaps with the idea of creating for the whisperer some imaginary respect, because of his supposed possession of special knowledge! But such action seldom bodes good, or sets upon the round of human lips sentiments of appreciation for the excellent, the beautiful, and the true, in a brother, neighbor, or friend. Such gossip and meddling constantly hold to view the defects of its subjects, and the scandals that are born fly as upon the wings of eagles. To be thus engaged is a positive injury, also, to the person so employed, because, by constantly holding the defects of others in his own mind, he ruins his own ability to see and appreciate the virtues of his fellows, thus stifling his nobler self.

It is so very much better for a person to strive to develop himself by observing all the good points he can find in others, than to strangle the growth of his better self by cherishing a fault-finding, sullen, and inter-meddling spirit. . . .

The meddler, the gossip, the fault-finder . . . soon ruin their own capacity for observing the better side of human nature; and, not finding it in others, search in vain for its influence in their own souls. ◄

President Smith later reemphasized his injunction to look for good rather than evil in others.

Change the focus of your view, and of your eye, from watching for evil to watching for that which is good, that which is pure, and leading and prompting those who err into that path which has no error in it, and that will not admit of mistakes. Look for good in men, and where they fail to possess it, try to build it up in them; try to increase the good in them; look for the good; build up the good; sustain the good; and speak as little about the evil as you possibly can. It does not do any good to magnify evil, to publish evil, or to promulgate it by tongue or pen. There is no good to be obtained by it. It is better to bury the evil and magnify the good, and prompt all men to forsake evil and learn to do good; and let our mission be to save mankind and to teach and guide in the path of righteousness, and not to sit as judges and pass judgment upon evil-doers, but rather to be saviors of men. ◆

The danger of thinking evil of others is illustrated in a story told by S. Dilworth Young.

FROM "COURAGE TO BE RIGHTEOUS"

One time I was conducting a conference in Salt Lake City and President George F. Richards of the Council of the Twelve was there. I invited him to speak and he said, no, he didn't care to speak but to go ahead. So I began to speak and I told them that if they ever told a story about anybody, that story would stick to that person no matter how long he lived, and it would be believed by most people, and therefore they must not bear false witness.

While I was speaking, I felt a tap on my shoulder, and there stood Brother Richards right behind me, and he said, "I've changed my mind. I want to speak."

He said words about like this: "Once upon a time I was a high council member in a stake and somebody made a serious accusation against a man. We debated whether to have him in and try him. Finally, the stake president decided he would talk to the man privately, and apparently he did, and the man *proved* to the satisfaction of all of us that not only was he *not* guilty of the accusation, but he hadn't even been in the country when it was sup-posed to have taken place. He was away somewhere, and he couldn't pos-sibly have done it."

He said, "Forty years went by, and that man's name came up for a very high appointment in the Church." He said, "In spite of myself, I caught myself wondering if the story told about the man was true, even though it had been proven false. I had to get hold of myself to keep from voting negatively against that man on a false story, told forty years before, which was proved false." ❦

Leonard Arrington writes of the "Female Indian Relief Society" that was established by the women of the Salt Lake City Thirteenth Ward, seemingly in 1854. Interest in the organization dwindled, but the covenant to which they pledged annually bears repeating.

We [covenant that we will] speak no evil of each other nor of the authorities of the Church, but endeavor by means in our power to cultivate a spirit of unison, humanity and love and that this shall be the covenant into which all shall enter who become members of this society. ❦

The words of Sirach refute the old adage about the relative harm of sticks, stones, and names. He declares that names hurt more than sticks and stones.

Curse the whisperer and the deceitful man;
For he has destroyed many who were at peace.
A third person's tongue has stirred many up,
And removed them from one nation to another;
It has torn down strongly fortified cities,
And overthrown the houses of the great.
A third person's tongue has driven out noble women,
And robbed them of the fruit of their labors.
The man who listens to it will find no rest,
And will not live in peace.
The blow of a whip leaves a bruise,
But the blow of a tongue breaks the bones.
Many have fallen by the edge of the sword,
But not so many as have fallen by the tongue.

An unknown author suggests:

There are ten things for which no one has ever yet been sorry. They are: for doing good to all; for speaking evil of none; for hearing before judging; for thinking before speaking; for holding an angry tongue; for being kind to the distressed; for asking pardon for all wrongs; for being patient toward everybody; for stopping the ears to a tale-bearer; for disbelieving most of the ill reports. ❖

I note that several of the ten virtues just named have to do with speaking, and three more with discernment in listening to the speech of others. Most of the ten, then, address the principle that charity thinketh no evil. The following segment from a well-loved poem is whimsical and delightful, but it also has a serious undertone in its play on evil thinking and tongues that deceive.

FROM "THE WALRUS AND THE CARPENTER"

. . . .
"O Oysters, come and walk with us!"
The Walrus did beseech.
"A pleasant walk, a pleasant talk,
Along the briny beach:
We cannot do with more than four,
To give a hand to each."

The eldest Oyster looked at him,
But never a word he said:
The eldest Oyster winked his eye,
And shook his heavy head—
Meaning to say he did not choose
To leave the oyster-bed.

But four young Oysters hurried up,
All eager for the treat:
Their coats were brushed, their faces washed,
Their shoes were clean and neat—

And this was odd, because, you know,
    They hadn't any feet.

Four other Oysters followed them,
    And yet another four;
And thick and fast they came at last,
    And more, and more, and more—
All hopping through the frothy waves,
    And scrambling to the shore.

The Walrus and the Carpenter
    Walked on a mile or so,
And then they rested on a rock
    Conveniently low:
And all the little Oysters stood
    And waited in a row.

"The time has come," the Walrus said,
    "To talk of many things:
Of shoes—and ships—and sealing-wax—
    Of cabbages—and kings—
And why the sea is boiling hot—
    And whether pigs have wings."

"But wait a bit," the Oysters cried,
    "Before we have our chat;
For some of us are out of breath,
    And all of us are fat!"
"No hurry!" said the Carpenter.
    They thanked him much for that.

"A loaf of bread," the Walrus said,
    Is what we chiefly need:
Pepper and vinegar besides
    Are very good indeed—
Now if you're ready, Oysters dear,
    We can begin to feed."

"But not on us!" the Oysters cried,
Turning a little blue.
"After such kindness, that would be
A dismal thing to do!"
"The night is fine," the Walrus said.
"Do you admire the view?

"It was so kind of you to come!
And you are very nice!"
The Carpenter said nothing but
"Cut us another slice:
I wish you were not quite so deaf—
I've had to ask you twice!"

"It seems a shame," the Walrus said,
"To play them such a trick,
After we've brought them out so far,
And made them trot so quick!"
The Carpenter said nothing but
"The butter's spread too thick!"

"I weep for you," the Walrus said:
"I deeply sympathize."
With sobs and tears he sorted out
Those of the largest size,
Holding his pocket-handkerchief
Before his streaming eyes.

"O Oysters," said the Carpenter,
"You've had a pleasant run!
Shall we be trotting home again?"
But answer came there none—
And this was scarcely odd, because
They'd eaten every one.
(Lewis Carroll.)

Although evil thoughts lock virtue out—as we saw with the Green Goblin—absence of thought is no virtue either. Parley P. Pratt implies as much in an imaginative piece titled "A Dialogue between Joseph Smith and the Devil." Since a blank mind is not a pure mind any more than blank paper is great literature, Parley's devil is unhappy with a church that values thinking minds.

Devil: . . . Thus, you see, I have full influence and control of the multitude by a means far more effectual than argument or reason, and I even teach them that it is a sin to reason, think or investigate, as it would disturb the even tenor of their pious breathings and devout groans and responses. Smith, you must be extremely ignorant of human nature, as well as of the history of the past to presume that reason and truth would have much effect with the multitude.

. . . .

Devil: . . . you are in spite of all my efforts, and that of my fellows, daily thinning our ranks by adding to the number of those who think, and such a thinking is kept up that we are often exposed in some of our most prominent places, and are placed in an awkward predicament. ❦

Joseph F. Smith stated:

To be Latter-day Saints men and women must be thinkers and workers; they must be men and women who weigh matters in their minds; men and women who consider carefully their course of life and the principles that they have espoused. Men cannot be faithful Latter-day Saints unless they study and understand, to some extent at least, the principles of the gospel that they have received. ❦

Henry David Thoreau made the following journal entry about the blessing and power of wholesome thought.

Great thoughts hallow any labor—To day I earned seventy five cents heaving manure out of a pen, and made a good bargain of it. If the ditcher muses the while how he may live uprightly, the ditching spade and turf knife may be engrav[e]d on the coat of arms of his posterity. ❦

French philosopher Blaise Pascal made the following observations:

Man is but a reed, the most feeble thing in nature; but he is a thinking reed. The entire universe need not arm itself to crush him. A vapour, a drop of water suffices to kill him. But, if the universe were to crush him, man would still be more noble than that which killed him, because he knows that he dies and the advantage which the universe has over him; the universe knows nothing of this.

All our dignity consists, then, in thought. By it we must elevate ourselves, and not by space and time which we cannot fill. Let us endeavor, then, to think well; this is the principle of morality. ✦

Lest we assume that Pascal framed his whole philosophy when he wrote that "thought constitutes the greatness of man," it is well to remember that he believed in two sources of knowing, reason and faith, and he insisted that only through the latter, through the heart, can one experience God. "Faith is a gift of God; do not believe that we said it was a gift of reasoning."

We know truth, not only by the reason, but also by the heart, and it is in this last way that we know first principles; and reason, which has no part in it, tries in vain to impugn them. The sceptics, who have only this for their object, labour to no purpose. We know that we do not dream, and however impossible it is for us to prove it by reason, this inability demonstrates only the weakness of our reason, but not, as they affirm, the uncertainty of all our knowledge. . . .

Therefore, those to whom God has imparted religion by intuition are very fortunate, and justly convinced. But to those who do not have it, we can give it only by reasoning, waiting for God to give them spiritual insight, without which faith is only human, and useless for salvation. ✦

In Doctrine and Covenants 121:45, the Lord speaks of both charity and the content of our thoughts, indirectly establishing the link between them, as Paul taught in his first epistle to the Corinthians. What the Lord says to priesthood holders undoubtedly applies to all of us: "Let thy bowels also be full of charity towards all men, and to the household of faith, and let virtue garnish thy thoughts unceasingly."

The word unceasingly *does not leave much allowance for either empty thoughts or impure thoughts. And we should not be misled into assuming that the word* garnish *as used here alludes to the ornamental. We seldom contemplate the abstraction of virtue itself, even though we are instructed to make certain that all our thoughts are characterized, and thus enhanced—enlivened, improved, and purified—by virtue.*

In a passage that is clearly Joseph Smith's source for the thirteenth Article of Faith, Paul offers a number of specific things which are to occupy thought. And note, his emphasis is on thought: "Whatsoever things are true, whatsoever things are honest, whatsoever things are just, whatsoever things are pure, whatsoever things are lovely, whatsoever things are of good report; if there be any virtue, and if there be any praise, think on these things." (Philippians 4:8; emphasis added.)

VIRTUE

Sweet day, so cool, so calm, so bright,
The bridal of the earth and sky,
The dew shall weep thy fall tonight;
For thou must die.

Sweet rose, whose hue, angry and brave,
Bids the rash gazer wipe his eye,
Thy root is ever in its grave,
And thou must die.

Sweet spring, full of sweet days and roses,
A box where sweets compacted lie,
My music shows ye have your closes,
And all must die.

Only a sweet and virtuous soul,
Like seasoned timber, never gives;
But though the whole world turn to coal,
Then chiefly lives.
(George Herbert.)

SHE WALKS IN BEAUTY

She walks in Beauty, like the night
Of cloudless climes and starry skies;
And all that's best of dark and bright
  Meet in her aspect and her eyes:
Thus mellowed to that tender light
Which Heaven to gaudy day denies.

One shade the more, one ray the less,
Had half impaired the nameless grace
  Which waves in every raven tress,
    Or softly lightens o'er her face;
Where thoughts serenely sweet express,
How pure, how dear their dwelling-place.

And on that cheek, and o'er that brow,
    So soft, so calm, yet eloquent,
The smiles that win, the tints that glow,
    But tell of days in goodness spent,
    A mind at peace with all below,
    A heart whose love is innocent!
    (George Gordon, Lord Byron)

WINTER DAY AND NIGHT

It's been snow since
early morning,
both the easily seen
and the hardly there kinds,
swelling the air except where
in the heat of dark ground
it is not to be found;
Nothing,
not even your hand,
can contain it:

Oh,
that virtue
is so fine a thing,
and
all the night
and all the night
I marveled at the fragile white of it.
(Maryann Olsen MacMurray.)

*In close harmony with Christian teachings on the subject of one's thoughts,
and the virtuous life generally, is a collection of wise sayings attributed to Buddha.
They predate Christ by five centuries.*

THE TWIN-VERSES

All that we are is the result of what we have thought: it is founded on
our thoughts, it is made up of our thoughts. If a man speaks or acts with
an evil thought, pain follows him, as the wheel follows the foot of the ox
that draws the carriage.

All that we are is the result of what we have thought: it is founded on
our thoughts, it is made up of our thoughts. If a man speaks or acts with a
pure thought, happiness follows him, like a shadow that never leaves him.

"He abused me, he beat me, he defeated he, he robbed me"—in those
who harbour such thoughts hatred will never cease.

"He abused me, he beat me, he defeated me, he robbed me"—in those
who do not harbour such thoughts hatred will cease.

For hatred does not cease by hatred at any time: hatred ceases by love,
this is an old rule. . . .

They who know truth in truth, and untruth in untruth, arrive at truth,
and follow true desires.

As rain breaks through an ill-thatched house, passion will break
through an unreflecting mind.

As rain does not break through a well-thatched house, passion will not
break through a well-reflecting mind. . . .

The thoughtless man, even if he can recite a large portion of the law, but is not a doer of it, has no share in the priesthood, but is like a cowherd counting the cows of others. ✦

With minds and hearts attuned to the promptings of the Holy Spirit rather than those of the adversary, modern-day prophets of The Church of Jesus Christ of Latter-day Saints have on many occasions been spared physical injury or loss. Below are several stories, part of the classic LDS tradition, detailing such events. These faithful, pure-minded men experienced, in a very direct way, the pure love of Christ for them, his matchless charity.

David O. McKay, following a meeting at Hilo in the Hawaiian Islands in 1921, mentioned in his World-Tour Diary a night visit to the active Kilauea volcano. He did not, however, record the event described below. Clare Middlemiss presents this firsthand account written by Virginia Budd Jacobsen, then a missionary in Hawaii and a member of the party that accompanied President McKay on that occasion.

We stood on the rim of that fiery pit watching Pele in her satanic antics, our backs chilled by the cold winds sweeping down from snowcapped Mauna Loa, and our faces almost blistered by the heat of the molten lava. Tiring of the cold, one of the elders discovered a volcanic balcony about four feet down inside the crater where observers could watch the display without being chilled by the wind. It seemed perfectly sound, and the "railing" on the open side of it formed a fine protection from intense heat, making it an excellent place to view the spectacular display.

After first testing its safety, Brother McKay and three of the elders climbed down into the hanging balcony. As they stood there warm and comfortable, they teased the others of us more timid ones who had hesitated to take advantage of the protection they had found. For quite some time we all watched the ever-changing sight as we alternately chilled and roasted.

After being down there in their protected spot for some time, suddenly Brother McKay said to those with him, "Brethren, I feel impressed that we should get out of here."

With that he assisted the elders to climb out, and then they in turn helped him up to the wind-swept rim. It seems incredible, but almost immediately the whole balcony crumbled and fell with a roar into the molten lava a hundred feet or so below. . . .

None of us, who were witnesses to this experience could ever doubt the reality of "revelation in our day!" Some might say it was merely inspiration, but to us, it was a direct revelation given to a worthy man. ❧

Wilford Woodruff has told a number of such experiences, which in Leaves from My Journal he prefaces with this statement: "The teachings of the Prophet Joseph Smith to President Taylor and the rest of us was to obtain the Holy Spirit, get acquainted with it and its operations, and listen to the whisperings of that Spirit and obey its voice, and it soon will become a principle of revelation unto us."

SAVING THE FARM

After one conference, when we had set apart a good many missionaries, I went home quite weary, and I said to myself, I will go and have a rest. Before I got in my house, the Spirit told me to take my team and go to my farm. My wife said, "Where are you going?"

"I am going down to the farm."

"What for?"

"I don't know," said I.

I went down to the farm. I found that the river had broken over and had surrounded my house. The water was two feet deep around my house. My hogs were drowning, and my stables were full. By going there I saved my house and surroundings and stopped up the break. These may be considered small things; still they show the working of the Spirit. ❧

THE PITTSBURGH

STEAMBOAT EXPERIENCE

When I got back to Winter Quarters from the pioneer journey [1847], President Young said to me, "Brother Woodruff, I want you to take your wife and children and go to Boston and stay there until you can gather every Saint of God in New England and Canada and send them up to Zion."

I did as he told me. It took me two years to gather up everybody, and I brought up the rear with a company (there were about one hundred of them). We arrived at Pittsburgh one day at sundown. We did not want to stay there, so I went to the first steamboat that was going to leave. I saw the captain and engaged passage for us on that steamer. I had only just done so when the Spirit said to me, and that, too, very strongly, "Don't go aboard that steamer, nor your company." Of course, I went and spoke to the captain, and told him I had made up my mind to wait.

Well, that ship started, and had only got five miles down the river when it took fire, and three hundred persons were burned to death or drowned. If I had not obeyed that Spirit, and had gone on that steamer with the rest of the company, you can see what the result would have been. ✦

MOVING THE CARRIAGE

After I came to these valleys and returned to Winter Quarters, I was sent to Boston by President Young. He wanted me to take my family there and gather all the Saints of God in New England, in Canada, and in the surrounding regions, and stay there until I gathered them all. I was there about two years. While on the road there, I drove my carriage one evening into the yard of Brother Williams. Brother Orson Hyde drove a wagon by the side of mine. I had my wife and children in the carriage. I had not been there but a few minutes when the Spirit said to me, "Get up and move that carriage." I told my wife I had to get up and move the carriage.

She said, "What for?"

I said, "I don't know."

That is all she asked me on such occasions. When I told her I did not know, that was enough. I got up and moved my carriage four or five rods, and put the off fore wheel against the corner of the house. I then looked around me and went to bed. The same Spirit said, "Go and move your animals from that oak tree." They were two hundred yards from where my carriage was. I went and moved my horses, and put them in a little hickory grove. I again went to bed.

In thirty minutes a whirlwind came up and broke that oak tree off within two feet from the ground. It swept over three or four fences and fell square in that dooryard, near Brother Orson Hyde's wagon, and right where mine had stood. What would have been the consequences if I had not listened to that Spirit? Why, myself and wife and children doubtless would have been killed. That was the still, small voice to me—no earthquake, no thunder, no lightning—but the still, small voice of the Spirit of God. It saved my life. It was the Spirit of revelation to me. ✦

Peter summarizes our duty with regards to our thoughts, words, and actions:

Wherefore gird up the loins of your mind, be sober, and hope to the end for the grace that is to be brought unto you at the revelation of Jesus Christ. . . .

But as he which hath called you is holy, so be ye holy in all manner of conversation. . . .

Seeing ye have purified your souls in obeying the truth through the Spirit unto unfeigned love of the brethren, see that ye love one another with a pure heart fervently. (1 Peter 1:13, 15, 22.) ✦

10

CHARITY REJOICETH NOT IN INIQUITY

Ye have sought for happiness in doing iniquity,

which thing is contrary to the nature of that

righteousness which is in our great and Eternal Head.

HELAMAN 13:38

These words of Samuel, the Lamanite prophet, pinpoint the motivation behind much of the individual iniquity in this world: the search for personal happiness. A worthy enough goal, but in the search we often forget to distinguish between shallow pleasures and true joy. And we fail to associate happiness with its source, Jesus Christ. Some think to find thrills in certain kinds of iniquity—drugs, pornography, sex, violence, disobedience, vanity, greed, and the like. They "call evil good, and good evil." Self-deluded, they "put darkness for light, and light for darkness," and they "put bitter for sweet, and sweet for bitter," as Isaiah says (5:20). But ultimately, there can be no rejoicing in iniquity because lasting joy resides only in righteous living.

Iniquity is a destructive force in society, harming perpetrators and victims alike. Iniquity harms the whole of humanity by tearing at its moral fabric as well as its civic and social structures. Those who seek iniquity—who enjoy it, relish it, celebrate it, patronize it, purchase it—are persons without charity, without love for Christ or their fellow beings. Passages in Proverbs (22:8) and Isaiah (5:18) link iniquity with vanity, with self-centeredness; and the Lord links it explicitly with the loss of love: "And because iniquity shall abound, the love of many shall wax cold." (Matthew 24:12; see also D&C 45:27 and Joseph Smith—Matthew 1:10, 30.)

It is not difficult to find synonyms for iniquity, or antonyms for it. The charitable life that Paul advocates is a life of goodness, virtue, integrity, honor, and righteousness—a life that shuns both iniquity and taking pleasure in iniquity.

Most of us are familiar with Henry David Thoreau's statement in the conclusion to Walden about marching to a different drummer. We may even have wrested its meaning on occasion to rationalize our own bad behavior. The statement's precursor in Thoreau's journal offers a useful backdrop to the familiar saying and to our subject:

A man's life should be a stately march to a sweet but unheard music, and when to his fellows it shall seem irregular and inharmonious, he will only be stepping to a livelier measure; or his nicer ear hurry him into a thousand symphonies and concordant variations. There will be no halt ever but at most a marching on his post, or such a pause as is richer than any sound, when the melody runs into such depth and wildness, as to be no longer heard, but implicitly consented to with the whole life and being. He will take a false step never, even in the most arduous times; for then the music will not fail to swell into greater sweetness and volume, and itself rule the movement it inspired. ❧

Thoreau was one who did not rejoice in iniquity; he abhorred it. His writing is an undeviating endorsement of the virtuous life, the commitment to right living rather than to iniquity.

Thoreau's language is its own revelation of intent. One's life, he says, "should be a stately march." It is not to be an uncontrolled romp into every alluring rhythm and byway. Moreover, that disciplined march is to be to "sweet" music, not raucous, tempestuous, evil, or bitter music—"music" being what guides or tempts us—and the march is to be to "music," not to noise. One's less finely tuned companions might not perceive the inherent beauty in order and sweetness, but the "nicer ear" of integrity will lead the virtuous person into a life of harmony ("a thousand symphonies") and peace ("concordant variations"). That person will not interrupt his righteous course ("there will be no halt ever"), though he will perform his duty ("marching on his post"), pausing when prompted by spiritual tuitions.

Moreover, the virtuous person will follow only that course "consented to with the whole life and being." That person is not self-divided in matters of ethics and morality but is what he or she appears to be. The inner and the outer selves are in agreement, are not in conflict with each other. That person has integrity. Furthermore, Thoreau says, the person who hears and marches to this sweet music "will take a false step never, even in the most arduous times." In times of trial, the music issues forth with "greater sweetness and volume" so as to be heard more clearly. This is not to turn Thoreau into a Mormon, but to suggest that he understood and described, though in a different set of words, what Mormons style "living by the Spirit."

Thoreau used the metaphor of music to delineate the virtuous life, the life that refuses to entertain iniquity. In a letter to the Ephesians, Paul used the metaphor of armor:

Be strong in the Lord, and in the power of his might.

Put on the whole armour of God, that ye may be able to stand against the wiles of the devil.

For we wrestle not against flesh and blood, but against principalities, against powers, against the rulers of the darkness of this world, against spiritual wickedness in high places.

Wherefore take unto you the whole armour of God, that ye may be able to withstand in the evil day, and having done all, to stand.

Stand therefore, having your loins girt about with truth, and having on the breastplate of righteousness;

And your feet shod with the preparation of the gospel of peace;

Above all, taking the shield of faith, wherewith ye shall be able to quench all the fiery darts of the wicked.

And take the helmet of salvation, and the sword of the Spirit, which is the word of God:

Praying always with all prayer and supplication in the Spirit, and watching thereunto with all perseverance and supplication for all saints. (Ephesians 6:10–18.) ❧

Paul's specific warning against "spiritual wickedness in high places" is echoed in Brigham Young's words in a General Conference address. In his reference to heeding "the counsels of the Spirit of God," we see a parallel with Thoreau's sweet and orderly music.

Will I serve God, or will I serve Mammon? is the question that arises in my breast, and I feel it in my soul. . . .

. . . Then if I have elected to follow Him, what will I do as one who has taken upon him this responsibility? I tell you one thing that I will do: I will support good men in every position. I care not what proposition may be submitted to me, I will sustain good men. For it is written, "When the wicked rule, the people mourn." When the righteous rule, the people rejoice. In every condition, spiritual and temporal, moral, political, religious, and in every sense of the word, I stand before God as a man who has covenanted before Him and before His people, solemnly in sacred places, that I will sustain Him and His kingdom and people. I am not a covenant-breaker, unless I depart from the counsels of the Spirit of God within me. I seek to have that spirit constantly with me; and when there is any doubt I seek light from the source that He has appointed to direct me in the things of life, here and hereafter.

. . . You know as well as I do, that the perpetuity of this people, the perpetuity of the nation, depends upon the virtue that is developed in the midst of the people. It is a reproach to any nation, or to any individual, to be unvirtuous. I feel for one that the day is come when the voice of this people shall be raised for good men to rule over us. What do I care about party feeling! A lot of men meet together and get up names, among them some shyster that has foisted himself into notice through some means or other of his own making, and they rush that upon me, and because I would not vote for such men two or three years ago, they said, "You are a mugwump." Well, I would rather be a know-nothing than to subscribe to conditions which will make me responsible for the actions of the wicked. I will not do it, I do not care who it cuts, nor what the consequences may be. I say it to the nation, I say it to the world: As God lives, I will never support a man that I know is a wicked man, for any office. The word of the Prophet of God has been given to me, as it has to you, and we have got to take cognizance of these things. ❧

Obert C. Tanner writes of the need for honesty and integrity:

We do need men who have no price; who, for any glory or pleasure or wealth, are not for sale. It is a terrible commentary on human nature and our culture today, to say or believe that every man has his price. There is nothing finer in history than a soul that is not for sale, of impeccable honesty—within—to himself, as well as without in his dealings with men. Few men care to probe around for a clear look at their own true motives. They bring out reasons to justify themselves, better than they deserve. In business they talk of service when the real situation is greed for excessive profits; in politics men speak of humility when the insatiable drive for more glory prods them on. It is a great day in a man's life when he examines himself and decides to guide his life as truly as possible by the best motives he can find—gospel standards that now go deep and purify us before God and man. ❧

And Brigham Young notes:

It is the fashion in the world to embrace men in their faith, or a fine meeting house, or a genteel congregation, thinking, "O, what perfect order, and how pretty they look; how straight they walk to meeting, and how long their faces are during the service; how pretty that deacon looks under the pulpit; the people are so pretty, the meeting house is so nice, that we want to join such pretty people." Such feelings will take a people to hell. Embrace a doctrine that will purge sin and iniquity from your hearts, and sanctify you before God, and you are right, no matter how others act. (*Journal of Discourses* 4:78.) ❧

The writer (an Egyptian monk or monks) of the following segment from The Bestiary, *a series of thirteen medieval verses, designed it, like the others, to draw lessons from the natural world. Composed sometime before* A.D. *500,* The Bestiary *was immensely influential on art and literature for many centuries. This particu-*

257

lar piece uses the whale to exemplify the devil's devious iniquity, then explains the "signification" of the example.

THE WHALE'S NATURE

The great whale is a fish,
The greatest that in the water is;
Thou wouldest say, indeed,
If thou were to see it when it floated,
That it was an island
Stationed on the sea-sand.
This fish, which is enormous,
When he is hungry, gapeth wide;
Out of his throat there rusheth a breath,
The sweetest thing that is on land;
For this, other fishes draw to him;
When they smell it, they are delighted;
They come and hover in his mouth;
Of his trap they are unwary.
The whale his jaws then locketh,
All these fishes in he sucketh;
The small he will thus entrap;
The great he may in no wise catch.
This fish dwelleth on the sea bottom,
And liveth ever hale and sound,
Till there cometh the time
When the storm stirreth all the sea,
When summer and winter contend.
He cannot dwell therein,
So troubled is the sea's bottom
That he cannot remain there that time,
But he cometh up and floateth still,
Whilst that weather is so ill.
The ships that are storm-driven on the sea,—

Death is loath to them, to live is dear,—
They look about them, and see this fish;
An island they suppose it is.
For that they are deeply grateful,
And with all their might thereto they draw
The ships to anchor,
And they all go ashore.
From stone and steel in the tinder
They kindle a fire on this monster;
They warm them well and eat and drink.
The fire he feeleth and maketh them sink;
At once he diveth to the ground,
And destroyeth them all without a wound.

Signification
The devil is great in will and might,
As witches are in their craft;
He causeth men hunger and thirst,
And many another sinful lust;
He draweth men to him with his savor;
Who followeth him, findeth shame.
Those are the little ones in the faith's law,
The great to him he cannot draw;
By the great I mean the steadfast,
In true belief, in flesh and spirit.
Who listeneth to the devil's lore,
At length he shall rue it sore;
Whoso fasteneth hope on him
Shall follow him to hell so dim.

*Mischievous youngsters have been known to rejoice in each other's misery—
to a point. In poetry, as in life, retribution for such iniquitous rejoicing can sometimes be swift, as in this poem by Elizabeth Madox Roberts.*

MUMPS

I had a feeling in my neck,
And on the sides were two big bumps;
I couldn't swallow anything
At all because I had the mumps.

And Mother tied it with a piece,
And then she tied up Will and John,
And no one else but Dick was left
That didn't have a mump rag on.

He teased at us and laughed at us,
And said, whenever he went by,
"It's vinegar and lemon drops
And pickles!" just to make us cry.

But Tuesday Dick was very sad
And cried because his neck was sore,
And not a one said sour things
To anybody any more.

The story of Thomas Marsh's lapse into serious iniquity over a small incident is well known in the annals of the Church. It is related here by Kay Briggs.

When the Saints were living in Far West, Missouri, Thomas Marsh's wife and Sister Harris agreed to exchange milk, in order to enable each of them to make more cheese than they could do separately. It was agreed that they should not save the "strippings" (the last milk drawn at milking), that milk and strippings should all go together. Mrs. Harris performed her part of the agreement, but Mrs. Marsh kept a pint of strippings from each cow so as to make some really good cheese.

When this matter became known an appeal was taken to the bishop. He sustained Mrs. Harris. If Brother Marsh had obeyed the revelation (D&C 31) and governed his house in humility and with steadfastness, he would have righted the wrong done, but instead of doing so he appealed to the high council. Brother Marsh, who at the time was president of the Twelve,

260

possibly thought that the council would favor him, but that body confirmed the bishop's decision.

He was not yet satisfied. He appealed to Joseph Smith and the First Presidency, who consented to review the case. Joseph and his two counselors considered the case, then approved the high council's decision. Was Brother Marsh satisfied then? No. With stubborn persistency he declared that he would uphold the character of his wife "even if he had to go to hell for it."

Elder George A. Smith observed that Brother Marsh, who as president of the Twelve should have been the first to repent and do justice by returning the few "pints of milk strippings," became so angry that "he went before a magistrate and swore that the 'Mormons' were hostile towards the State of Missouri. That affidavit brought from [Governor Lilburn W. Boggs and] the government of Missouri an extermination order, which drove some 15,000 Saints from their homes . . . and some thousands perished through suffering the exposure consequent on this state of affairs." (*Journal of Discourses* 3:283–84.) ❦

A favorite subject of John Henry Smith in his General Conference talks was the nature of the entertainments pursued by the early Saints during their leisure hours. He was especially concerned about Sabbath Day activities.

The spirit of the times leads us in the way of amusement. I am not one of those that have serious objections to amusement; on the contrary, I am in sympathy with a reasonable amount of recreation and pleasure. But when we note the fact that the weekdays are devoted largely to pleasure, and the Sabbath day is also taken for that purpose, we cannot help but feel that there is an overstepping of legitimate bounds in this direction. . . . When we see our young people engaged in a variety of amusements nearly every evening in the week, with scarcely an evening spent at home, and indulging in companionships that are not in keeping with the right, going to places of amusement where men and women of all classes [i.e., types] are permitted to congregate, and mingling with influences that tend to demoralization, it would seem to be time to call a halt. . . .

Where places are open continuously for those classes of amusement that bring the immoral and impure into contact with the innocent and the pure, and the door is opened for the introduction of immorality and crime into every village, town and city throughout the land, the Latter-day Saints should be much more thoroughly upon their guard in regard to this than they have been perchance. As I remarked before, I am a believer in legitimate and proper amusements. The boys and girls, the fathers and mothers, should mingle together and have proper recreation and pleasure, but free from the possibility of vicious and impure association.

The children entrusted to our watchcare should not be turned loose thoughtlessly, without guardians or chaperones, into the companionship of men who scheme and devise for the injury and overthrow of their kind, who boast of their conquests, and who rejoice in the opportunities offered them to lead from the path of rectitude any young or thoughtless girl that may be brought into their company. The same is true in regard to the other sex, where there are abandoned and impure women, whose companionship is a menace to thoughtless and imprudent boys. Thrown into that species of company, they are apt to be led from the path of rectitude and the mark of shame written upon their brows by some overt act of an impure character. ❧

In a letter of counsel to his children, Heber C. Kimball wrote:

Don't give way to evil, my children, lay aside all wickedness, and never suffer yourselves to go into wicked company or corrupt places. If we give way to sin even a little, it will conceive in our bosoms and grow. I know if I am faithful no good things will be withheld from me, but if I make a misstep it may all be taken away. We are acting in view of eternity; we are laying a foundation for eternity. ❧

Today, young people are perhaps as likely to be led into iniquity by those who claim to be their friends as by scheming adults. People we look to as friends can exert immense influence on us, for good or ill.

Cicero defined friendship as "complete sympathy in all matters of importance, plus goodwill and affection." But he echoed Scipio's conviction that friendships were "quite properly broken up when men demanded of their friends something that was morally reprehensible." "Wrongdoing," Cicero added, "is not excused if it is committed for the sake of a friend; after all, the thing that brings friends together is their conviction of each other's virtue; it is hard to keep up a friendship, if one has deserted virtue's camp."

Samuel Johnson would agree: "That friendship may be at once fond and lasting, there must not only be equal virtue on each part, but virtue of the same kind; not only the same end must be proposed, but the same means must be approved by both."

A pupil asked about friendship. Confucius said, "Speak truthfully and guide them in good ways. If they do not agree, then stop and do not disgrace yourself for them." ❧

BIRDS OF A FEATHER

A man who was intending to buy a donkey took one on trial and placed it along with his own donkeys at the manger. It turned its back on all of them save one, the laziest and greediest of the lot; it stood close beside this one and just did nothing. So the man put a halter on it and took it back to its owner, who asked if he thought that was giving it a fair trial. "I don't want any further trial," he answered. "I am quite sure it is like the one that it singled out as a companion."

A man's character is judged by that of the friends whose society he takes pleasure in. (Aesop.) ❧

Belle Spafford, long-time General Relief Society president, often spoke to youth groups as well as to adults. Here, she offers suggestions to young Latter-day Saints.

FROM "THE LATTER-DAY SAINT PRICE TAG"

And what is the image of the young Latter-day Saint that one has an obligation to protect? He or she will be modest in dress and refined in speech and manner. He will seek after those things that are virtuous, of good report, and praiseworthy. He will honor his father and his mother. He will be sensitive to the best interests of the Church. He will seek learning.

He will respect the right of others to their own viewpoints, but in no wise adopt them as his own if they run counter to revealed truth. He will be tolerant, but he will not be self-righteous. He will be a person of integrity.

In regard to maintaining good relationships with associates who may differ in behavioral standards, may I suggest that the problem usually is not that one does not know the way; rather, it rests in mustering the courage and the stamina to stay on the right track when others whose good will we would court might invite or entice us to follow a path of their choosing.

Elder Sterling W. Sill, Assistant to the Council of the Twelve, tells the story of a schoolboy who once wrote a lesson about a backbone. Among other things he said, "Your head sits on one end and you sit on the other." Backbone as commonly used in reference to character implies courage and staying power. In dealing with the permissiveness and false philosophies that are abroad today, we need backbone. ❧

On another occasion President Spafford told a story on herself, an occasion when she behaved out of character.

I have an eleven-year-old grandson who comes on Saturday to do a few chores for me. Each Sunday I am invited to the home of his parents for Sunday dinner. One week I decided that I would not accept their invitation and would give them one Sunday to themselves; so I said to my son, "I won't be with you for dinner tomorrow because I am going to have dinner with some friends. I have accepted an invitation." He said, "Who are your friends?" I promptly told him. Then on Sunday he came to me and said, "You know, Mother, I don't believe you went out with friends to dinner today." He said, "I think you were lying to me." I had to confess that I had been. I said to the little boy the next Saturday, "How do you suppose your father knew I was telling a lie?" And the little fellow looked up at me in surprise and smiled and said, "Oh, Grandma, anybody can tell when you're telling a lie. You don't keep in practice." ❧

I recall hearing a brief segment of a post-game interview with Utah Jazz basketball star John Stockton. Apparently, in an incident extremely rare for Stockton, an opposing player riled him to the point that he yelled something that resulted in a technical foul call. The interviewer said, "Well, it must have felt good, anyway, to let off a little verbal steam." Stockton's quiet response was, "That isn't my style, and it never feels good to act out of character."

In our day, especially, artistic talent has sometimes been corrupted to serve spiritually debased greed. Two important discourses by writers, past and present, speak of the positive influence that art can and must have on human thought and behavior. The first, by Leo Tolstoy, addresses the charity of such endeavor.

FROM "WHAT IS ART?"

If art has been able to convey the sentiment of reverence for images, for the Eucharist, and for the king's person; of shame at betraying a comrade, devotion to a flag, the necessity of revenge for an insult, the need to sacrifice one's labour for the erection and adornment of churches, the duty of defending one's honour, or the glory of one's native land,—then that same art can also evoke reverence for the dignity of every man and for the life of every animal; can make men ashamed of luxury, of violence, of revenge, or of using for their own pleasure that of which others are in need; can compel people freely, gladly, and spontaneously, to sacrifice themselves in the service of man. ❧

Before his untimely death, modern American novelist John Gardner argued passionately for what he called "moral fiction," art that affirms rather than destroys the life of the soul, art that reveres the good. He said, "To worship the unique, the unaccountable and freaky, is—if we're consistent—to give up the right to say to our children, 'Be good.'" Art instructs, he claimed, whether toward reverence for the good or acceptance of that which is killing to the spirit; and he insisted that "moral art in its highest form holds up models of virtue. . . . The artist so debilitated by guilt and self-doubt that he cannot be certain real virtues exist is an artist doomed to second-rate art." (On Moral Fiction [New York: Basic Books, 1978], pp. 22, 82.) We can extend Gardner's point to include all forms of art and the media of mass communications.

James S. Brown remembers that Brigham Young instructed members of the Mormon Battalion in principles of honor and right living in his final counsel to them before they left the body of Saints.

FROM *LIFE OF A PIONEER*

Just before our last farewell to friends at the Missouri River, and preparatory to taking up our line of march, we were formed into a hollow square, and President Brigham Young, with Heber C. Kimball and others of the Apostles, came to our camp, rode into the square, and gave us parting blessings and instructions. The words of President Young, as they fastened themselves upon my memory, were in substance as follows: "Now, brethren, you are going as soldiers at your country's call. You will travel in a foreign land, in an enemy's country; and if you will live your religion, obey your officers, attend to your prayers, and as you travel in enemy's land, hold sacred the property of the people, never taking anything that does not belong to you only in case of starvation; though you may be traveling in an enemy's country, do not disturb fruit orchards or chicken coops or beehives, do not take anything but what you pay for—although it is customary for soldiers to plunder their enemies in time of war, it is wrong—always spare life when possible; if you obey this counsel, attending to your prayers to the Lord, I promise you in the name of the Lord God of Israel that not one soul of you shall fall by the hands of the enemy. You will pass over battlefields; battles will be fought in your front and in your rear, on your right hand and on your left, and your enemies shall flee before you. Your names shall be held in honorable remembrance to the latest generation." ✦

Later on, James Brown confirms the fulfillment of that remarkable promise to the men who followed Brigham Young's injunction when he put them on their honor.

Asked to define the phrase word of honor, *Karl G. Maeser is reported to have replied:*

My young friends, I have been asked what I mean by word of honor. I will tell you. Place me behind prison walls—walls of stone ever so high, ever so thick, reaching ever so far into the ground—there is a possibility that in some way or another I may be able to escape, but stand me on that floor and draw a chalk line around me and have me give my word of honor never to cross it. Can I get out of that circle? No, never! I'd die first! ✦

Following are portraits of three women, all uniquely individual but all pertinent to the subject of individual virtue. The first is a playful one, intended to delight rather than instruct.

AN ELEGY ON THAT GLORY OF HER SEX,

MRS. MARY BLAIZE

Good people all, with one accord,
    Lament for Madam Blaize,
Who never wanted [ie., lacked] a good word—
    From those who spoke her praise.

The needy seldom pass'd her door,
    And always found her kind;
She freely lent to all the poor,—
    Who left a pledge behind.

She strove the neighbourhood to please,
    With manners wond'rous winning,
And never followed wicked ways,—
    Unless when she was sinning.

At church, in silks and satins new,
    With hoop of monstrous size,
She never slumber'd in her pew,—
    But when she shut her eyes.

Her love was sought, I do aver,
    By twenty beaux and more;
The king himself has follow'd her,—
    When she has walked before.

But now, her wealth and finery fled,
    Her hangers-on cut short all;
Her doctors found, when she was dead,—
    Her last disorder mortal.

Let us lament, in sorrow sore,
For Kent-street well may say,
That, had she lived a twelve-month more,—
She had not died to-day.
(Oliver Goldsmith.)

The following story is told of Ruth May Fox, third general president of the Young Women's organization.

When Ruth consulted a doctor about what she described as an "occasional feeling of faintness," he suggested that she drink a cup of coffee every morning. That advice did not set well with her. "I was ninety-two years of age," she commented, "and had by precept and example taught the importance of the 'Word of Wisdom' to my children and grandchildren, and in public addresses to thousands of Church members. I decided that living a few more years was not nearly as important as my example to posterity, and I have not followed the doctor's prescription." ✦

The biblical portrait from Proverbs 31:10–31 is a classic. I cite here just the first and the last several verses.

Who can find a virtuous woman? for her price is far above rubies. . . .

Strength and honour are her clothing; and she shall rejoice in time to come.

She openeth her mouth with wisdom; and in her tongue is the law of kindness.

She looketh well to the ways of her household, and eateth not the bread of idleness.

Her children arise up, and call her blessed; her husband also, and he praiseth her.

Many daughters have done virtuously, but thou excellest them all.

Favour is deceitful, and beauty is vain: but a woman that feareth the Lord, she shall be praised.

Give her of the fruit of her hands; and let her own works praise her in the gates.

Juanita Brooks paints a portrait of another forthright mortal who is wholly committed to a righteous cause and who is a stranger to iniquity.

FROM *QUICKSAND & CACTUS*

Grandpa had come with the first Mormon missionaries to the southern Indians in 1854, living first on the Santa Clara Creek, and moving down onto the Virgin River to live the United Order. But he considered all his life a mission, so eager was he to further the work of the Lord. As a boy in Illinois he had known Joseph Smith, the Mormon prophet, and had become wholly converted to his teachings; he had known Brigham Young, and had the same implicit faith in him as the mouthpiece of God. Now, looking back over his life, he often talked of the Prophet Joseph and of the grief of the people when he was martyred by the mob at Carthage jail; he told of the hard days at Nauvoo when his family were driven from their farm across a frozen river; he told of experiences crossing the plains to Utah, his Zion.

. . . .

Grandpa's religion was really a living thing. When he prayed, he talked man-to-man with God; when he sang the hymns, they took on a special meaning; and when he quoted Scripture, rolling the sentences and speaking in a voice that was groomed to fill all outdoors, I was filled with awe: "Hear, O ye Heavens, and give ear O earth, and rejoice ye inhabitants thereof! For the Lord is God, and beside Him there is no other. Great is His wisdom, marvelous are His ways, and the extent of His doings no man can find out. . . ." It has never sounded quite the same since.

Grandpa considered himself important in the general scheme of things. As he figured it, God had work that He wanted done in this part of His Vineyard, and it took men like Grandpa to do it. If the Kingdom were ever to be established on the earth, he must help to establish it. He needed God—but quite as importantly, God needed him.

A visiting brother once looked over a field of wheat on newly cleared land.

"That is a good crop that you have been able to raise, Brother Leavitt," he said. "You have had the help of the Lord. Between you and the Lord, you have done all right."

"Brother," Grandpa said gently, "you should have seen that piece of land when the Lord was trying to run it without me."

. . . .

Grandpa thought of all his life as a mission. Whether he was preaching to Indians or chasing them, whether stampeding cattle or building a dam, he thought he was laboring in the Lord's Vineyard. Sometimes it looked like he was trying to establish a vineyard where the Lord never intended one to be. He broke the ground, cleared off the brush and rocks, struggled with the river, killed the rattlesnakes, and left his part of the Lord's Vineyard better than he found it.

He knew that try as they would, his children could never become wealthy here; they could hardly become situated comfortably. For him, wealth had no value except as it might aid in promoting God's work, the establishment of the Kingdom. If his children could raise families who were honest, who walked uprightly, who paid their debts and helped their neighbors, who kept the Word of Wisdom and were prayerful, they would have succeeded. And only in this way could Grandpa succeed in his labors in the vineyard of the Lord. ◆

Wilford Woodruff writes of his own faithfulness to what he knew was a God-given gift, journal-keeping.

I have had this spirit and calling upon me since I first entered this Church. I made a record from the first sermon I heard, and from that day until now I have kept a daily journal. Whenever I heard Joseph Smith preach, teach, or prophesy, I always felt it my duty to write it; I felt uneasy and could not eat, drink, or sleep until I did write; and my mind has been so exercised upon this subject that when I heard Joseph Smith teach and had no pencil or paper, I would go home and sit down and write the whole sermon, almost word for word and sentence by sentence as it was delivered, and when I had written it it was taken from me, I remembered it no more. This was the gift of God to me.

The devil has sought to take away my life from the day I was born until now, more so even than the lives of other men. I seem to be a marked victim of the adversary. I can find but one reason for this: the devil knew if I got into the Church of Jesus Christ of Latter-day Saints, I would write the history of that Church and leave on record the works and teachings of the prophets, of the apostles and elders. ✦

An unknown writer has illustrated the importance of individual integrity.

A little boy had disturbed to the breaking point his student father's study for an examination. In exasperation, at the thousandth question, the father said:

"Here's a picture of a world map. I'm tearing it to bits. You take the jig-saw-puzzle pieces and put it together. That ought to keep you occupied for quite some time."

But in a surprisingly short time, the boy was at his father's elbow again. "See, I got it all put back together again."

"Why, Son, that's marvelous. How did you ever do it so quickly?" the father looked up.

"That's easy, Daddy," the boy explained, "there was a man's picture on the other side of the map. I just put the man back together and the world took care of itself." ✦

Some men seem to think that as long as they keep out of jail they have a sure chance of getting into heaven. (Abraham Lincoln.) ✦

I find that a man can act good and talk good and look good and not do any good. (J. Golden Kimball.) ✦

The stoic philosophers had a somewhat unusual approach to the matter of personal integrity and right living. Marcus Aurelius, in the second century A.D., describes iniquity in terms of violence done to one's own soul.

The soul of man does violence to itself, first of all, when it becomes an abscess, and, as it were, a tumour on the universe, so far as it can. For to be vexed at anything which happens is a separation of ourselves from nature, in some part of which the natures of all other things are contained. In the next place, the soul does violence to itself when it turns away from any man, or even moves towards him with the intention of injuring, such as are the souls of those who are angry. In the third place, the soul does violence to itself when it is overpowered by pleasure or by pain. Fourthly, when it plays a part, and does or says anything insincerely and untruly. Fifthly, when it allows any act of its own and any movement to be without an aim, and does anything thoughtlessly and without considering what it is, it being right that even the smallest things be done with reference to an end. ✦

In one form or another, we reap the consequences of our own iniquity, our failed integrity, as indicated in this little story told by President Hugh B. Brown.

FROM "BUILDING MANSIONS"

The story is told of a rich man who, before leaving on a long journey, instructed a contractor to build a house for him. He left with him a large sum of money and said, "Because I trust you, I shall give you full charge of the selection of the building materials and the construction of the house. I want it built of the best materials, deep and broad foundations, heavy joists, strong beams, hardwood floors, substantial walls, enduring roof—build it only of the best, and have it ready for me upon my return."

As the rich man went away, the builder, being tempted by the money entrusted to him, began to think of ways by which he could cheat his employer and thereby have for himself part of the building fund. He there-upon purchased poorer materials for those parts of the house which would not be seen. The foundation was narrow and shallow, the joists and beams inferior, the inner walls of poor materials, the supports for the roof inadequate in size and quality. He employed second and third class laborers, and thus he saved a large percentage of the money and boasted of his "business ability."

The builder was careful to see that there was proper veneer wherever the eye of the owner might appraise the worth of the building from outer appearance. While the building was according to plan it would not have stood a careful inspection, but the painting and the camouflage were so expertly done that upon his return the owner expressed great delight at the excellence of the work of his trusted friend.

The owner, during his absence, had decided to take up his residence in a foreign land. Therefore, after commending the builder for his honesty and the quality of his work, he said to him, "As a reward for your faithful service, I give this house to you, on condition that you live in it. It shall be a faithful reminder that honesty pays, that integrity is a real asset, that a trust faithfully discharged brings satisfaction and peace of mind."

When the rich man had gone away, the builder said to himself, "Oh, fool that I am! If I had only known that I was building for myself, that I must inhabit this house, how different it would have been! The foundation, joists, and beams must soon give way; the walls will crumble and the roof cave in; the gift is a liability rather than an asset—I have cheated myself. My house built upon the sand must fall."

Our Heavenly Father has entrusted to each of us the building of a house and has advised . . . that it should be built of the best materials and by honest and efficient craftsmen. He furthermore requires that the unseen parts shall be even better than the seen, for upon them the superstructure must rest. The outward appearance is of minor importance. He leaves the job to us, but someday we must report to Him upon our stewardship. ⤛

Similarly, poet Oliver Wendell Holmes saw in the pearly nautilus a metaphor for our lives. The nautilus is a mollusk that builds its shell spirally by adding a new, larger section each year and then living in that new chamber. His poem "The Chambered Nautilus" ends with these lines:

> Year after year beheld the silent toil
> That spread his lustrous coil;
> Still, as the spiral grew,
> He left the past year's dwelling for the new,
> Stole with soft step its shining archway through,
> Built up its idle door,
> Stretched in his last-found home, and knew the old no more.
>
> Thanks for the heavenly message brought by thee,
> Child of the wandering sea,
> Cast from her lap, forlorn!
> From thy dead lips a clearer note is born

Than ever Triton blew from wreathed horn!
While on mine ear it rings,
Through the deep caves of thought I hear a voice that sings:—

Build thee more stately mansions, O my soul,
As the swift seasons roll!
Leave thy low-vaulted past!
Let each new temple, nobler than the last,
Shut thee from heaven with a dome more vast,
Till thou at length art free,
Leaving thine outgrown shell by life's unresting sea!

Thomas à Kempis explained the importance of the "inner life" in this way:

The life of a good religious [man] ought to abound in every virtue: that he may be such inwardly as he seemeth to men outwardly to be.

And with good reason ought he to be much more within than he appears outwardly; for it is God that overseeth us, and we should exceedingly stand in awe of Him, and walk in His sight wherever we may be, as the Angels do, in purity. ❧

Below is an early Spanish version of a story most of us know as "The Emperor's New Clothes," by Hans Christian Andersen. It was adapted from an unknown source by Don Juan Manuel (1282–c. 1349) and translated by James York in 1868. Both the story, which is used as an exemplum, and its framing narrative relate to the deception of appearances. Portrayed here is the elaborate trickery of some who rejoice in iniquity.

A KING AND THREE IMPOSTERS

Count Lucanor, conversing at another time with Patronio, his adviser, said:

"Patronio, a man came to me and told me something, giving me to understand it would be of great advantage to me if I followed his suggestions; but he said no man must be informed of the secret, that I must trust in him, and, more than this, affirmed that if I should confide it to any man in the world I should place not only my property but my life in danger. And as I know no man able to detect a fraud so quickly as yourself I pray you give me your opinion in this case."

"My lord," said Patronio, "in order that you may know how to act under these circumstances, it would please me to be permitted to inform you what happened to a King and three imposters."

The Count requested to know what that was.

"My lord," said Patronio, "three imposters came to a King, and told him they were cloth-weavers, and could fabricate a cloth of so peculiar a nature that a legitimate son of his father could see the cloth; but if he were illegitimate, though believed to be legitimate, he could not see it.

"Now the King was much pleased at this, thinking that by this means he would be able to distinguish the men in his kingdom who were legitimate sons of their supposed fathers from those who were not, and so be enabled to increase his treasures, for among the Moors only legitimate children inherit their father's property; and for this end he ordered a palace to be appropriated to the manufacture of this cloth. And these men, in order to convince him that they had no intention of deceiving him, agreed to be shut up in this palace until the cloth was manufactured, which satisfied the King.

"When they were supplied with a large quantity of gold, silver, silk, and many other things, they entered the palace, and, putting their looms in order, gave it to be understood that they were working all day at the cloth.

"After some days, one of them came to the King and told him the cloth was commenced, that it was the most curious thing in the world, describing the design and construction; he then prayed the King to favour them with a visit, but begged he would come alone. The King was much pleased, but, wishing to have the opinion of some one first, sent the Lord Chamberlain to see it, in order to know if they were deceiving him. When the Lord Chamberlain saw the workmen, and heard all they had to say, he dared not admit he could not see the cloth, and when he returned to the King he stated that he had seen it; the King sent yet another, who gave the same report. Since they whom he had sent declared that they had seen the cloth, he determined to go himself.

"On entering the palace he saw the men at work, and they began to describe the texture and relate the origin of the invention as also the design and colour, in which they all appeared to agree, although in reality they were not working. When the King saw how they appeared to work, and heard the character of the cloth so minutely described, and yet could not see it, although those he had sent had seen it, he began to feel very uneasy, fearing he might not be the son of the King who was supposed to be his father, and that if he acknowledged he could not see the cloth he might lose his kingdom; under this impression he began praising the fabric, describing its peculiarities after the manner of the workmen.

"On the return to his palace he related to his people how good and marvellous was the cloth, yet at the same time suspected something wrong.

"At the end of two or three days the King requested his Alguacil (or officer of justice) to go and see the cloth. When the Alguacil entered and saw the workmen, who, as before, described the figures and pattern of the cloth, knowing that the King had been to see it, and yet could not see it himself, he thought he certainly could not be the legitimate son of his father, and therefore could not see it. He, however, feared if he was to declare that he could not see it he would lose his honourable position; to avoid this mischance he began praising the cloth even more vehemently than the others.

"When the Alguacil returned to the King and told him that he had seen the cloth, and that it was the most extraordinary production in the world, the King was much disconcerted; for he thought that if the Alguagcil had seen the cloth, which he was unable to see, there could no longer be a doubt that he was not the legitimate son of the King, as was generally supposed; he therefore did not hesitate to praise the excellence of the cloth and the skill of the workmen who were able to make it.

"On another day he sent one of his Councillors, and it happened to him as to the King and the others of whom I have spoken; and in this manner and for this reason they deceived the King and many others, for no one dared to say he could not see the cloth.

"Things went on thus until there came a great feast, when all requested the King to be dressed in some of the cloth; so the workmen, being ordered, brought some rolled up in a very fine linen and inquired of the King how much of it he wished them to cut off; so the King gave orders how much and how to make it up.

"Now when the clothes were made and the feast day had arrived, the weavers brought them to the King, informing his Majesty that his dress was made of the cloth as he had directed; the King all this time not daring to say he could not see it.

"When the King had professed to dress himself in this suit he mounted on horseback and rode into the city; but fortunately for him it was summer time. The people seeing his Majesty come in this manner were much surprised; but, knowing that those who could not see this cloth would be considered illegitimate sons of their fathers, kept their surprise to themselves, fearing the dishonour consequent upon such a declaration. Not so, however, with one commoner, who happened to notice the King thus equipped; for he, having nothing to lose, came to him and said: 'Sire, to me it matters not whose son I am, therefore I tell you that you are riding without any clothes." On this the King began beating him, saying that he was not the legitimate son of his supposed father, and therefore it was that he could not see the cloth. But no sooner had the peasant said this than others were convinced of its truth, and said the same; until at last, the King and all with him lost their fear of declaring the truth, and saw through the trick of which these imposters had made them the victims. When the weavers were sought for they were found to have fled, taking with them all they had received from the King by their imposition.

"Now you, Count Lucanor, since that man of whom you speak forbids your trusting to any one, and demands your entire confidence, be careful you are not deceived; for, you ought to know very well that he can have no reason for seeking your advantage more than his own; nor has he more reason to serve you than have those who are indebted to you and are already in your service."

Count Lucanor found this to be good advice, so adopted it. And Don Juan, also seeing that it was a good example, wrote it in this book, and made these lines, which say as follows:

Who counsels thee to secrecy with friends
Seeks to entrap thee for his own base ends. ❦

I believe it is universally understood and acknowledged that all men will act correctly unless they have a motive to do otherwise. (Abraham Lincoln.) ❦

The fear of punishment may be necessary to the suppression of vice; but it also suspends the finer motives to virtue. (William Hazlitt.) ❦

There are many thoughtful essays about personal morality and about people who rejoice not in iniquity—and about people who do. Only a few such essays can be represented here, but mention should be made of two exceptional pieces whose length and complexity of style and argument prohibit their full inclusion in this collection. One of those is by nineteenth-century British novelist George Eliot (Mary Ann Evans), and the other is by C. S. Lewis. In the essay excerpted below, Eliot uses the example of an unethical businessman to argue that morality means more than observable surface behavior, more, that is, than apparent sexual fidelity, temperance with regard to drink, and public religious dutifulness. It also means charity.

FROM "MORAL SWINDLERS"

Until we have altered our dictionaries and have found some other word than *morality* to stand in popular use for the duties of man to man, let us refuse to accept as moral the contractor who enriches himself by using large machinery to make pasteboard soles pass as leather for the feet of unhappy conscripts fighting at miserable odds against invaders: let us rather call him a miscreant, though he were the tenderest, most faithful of husbands, and contend that his own experience of home happiness makes his reckless infliction of suffering on others all the more atrocious. Let us refuse to accept as moral any political leader who should allow his conduct in relation to great issues to be determined by egoistic passion, and boldly say that he would be less immoral, even though he were as lax in his personal habits as Sir Robert Walpole, if at the same time his sense of the public welfare were supreme in his mind. . . .

And though we were to find among that class of journalists who live by recklessly reporting injurious rumors, insinuating the blackest motives in opponents, descanting at large and with an air of infallibility on dreams which they both find and interpret, and stimulating bad feeling between nations by abusive writing, which is as empty of real conviction as the rage of a pantomime king, and would be ludicrous if its effects did not make it appear diabolical—though we were to find among these a man who was benignancy itself in his own circle, a healer of private differences, a soother in private calamities, let us pronounce him nevertheless flagrantly immoral—a root of hideous cancer in the commonwealth, turning the channels of instruction into feeders of social and political disease.

In opposite ways one sees bad effects likely to be encouraged by this narrow use of the word *morals*, shutting out from its meaning half those actions of a man's life which tell momentously on the well-being of his fellow-citizens, and on the preparation of a future for the children growing up around him. . . . But this duty of doing one's proper work well, and taking care that every product of one's labor shall be genuinely what it pretends to be, is not only left out of morals in popular speech, it is very little insisted on by public teachers, at least in the only effective way—by tracing the continuous effects of ill-done work. ❧

C. S. Lewis, a gifted essayist, delivered the Memorial Oration at King's College, the University of London, in 1944. In that important address to male college students, he argues the basic immorality, and uncharitableness, of what he calls exclusive "inner rings" of people. These rings have no formal membership lists and requirements, but everyone in a given society knows who belongs and who does not. Lewis urges his listeners to avoid them.

FROM "THE INNER RING"

In the whole of your life as you now remember it, has the desire to be on the right side of that invisible line [marking the inner ring] ever prompted you to any act or word on which, in the cold small hours of a wakeful night, you can look back with satisfaction? If so, your case is more fortunate than most.

[We hope to gain material advantages "from every Inner Ring we penetrate," Lewis says: "power, money, liberty to break rules, avoidance of routine duties, evasion of discipline. But all of these would not satisfy us if we did not get in addition the delicious sense of secret intimacy." It is this we unconsciously desire, and it is this which has the subtle power to corrupt us.]

. . . Unless you take measures to prevent it, this desire is going to be one of the chief motives of your life. . . . That will be the natural thing—the life that will come to you of its own accord. Any other kind of life, if you lead it, will be the result of conscious and continuous effort. If you do nothing about it, if you drift with the stream, you will in fact be an "inner ringer." I don't say you'll be a successful one; that's as may be. But whether by pining and moping outside Rings that you can never enter, or by passing triumphantly further and further in—one way or the other you will be that kind of man.

I have already made it fairly clear that I think it better for you not to be that kind of man. . . .

. . . Of all passions the passion for the Inner Ring is the most skilful in making a man who is not yet a very bad man do very bad things. . . .

And you will always find [a ring] hard to enter, for a reason you very well know. . . . your genuine Inner Ring exists for exclusion. There'd be no fun if there were no outsiders. . . . Exclusion is no accident: it is the essence.

The quest of the Inner Ring will break your hearts unless you break it. But if you break it, a surprising result will follow. If in your working hours you make the work your end, you will presently find yourself all unawares inside the only circle in your profession that really matters. You will be one of the sound craftsmen, and other sound craftsmen will know it. . . . And if in your spare time you consort simply with the people you like, you will again find that you have come unawares to a real inside: that you are indeed snug and safe at the centre of something which, seen from without, would look exactly like an Inner Ring. But the difference is that its secrecy is accidental, and its exclusiveness a by-product . . . : for it is only four or five people who like one another meeting to do things that they like. This is friendship. Aristotle placed it among the virtues. It causes perhaps half of all the happiness in the world, and no Inner Ringer can ever have it. ✦

In a sketch first published in the Daily News, *prolific British writer G. K. Chesterton uses a small incident in his life, an excursion to draw with chalk, to argue that virtue is much more than abstaining from iniquity. It is a presence, alive, vital, shimmering with energy.*

FROM "A PIECE OF CHALK"

But as I sat scrawling these silly figures on the brown paper, it began to dawn on me, to my great disgust, that I had left one chalk, and that a most exquisite and essential chalk, behind. I searched all my pockets, but I could not find any white chalk. Now, those who are acquainted with all the philosophy (nay, religion) which is typified in the art of drawing on brown paper, know that white is positive and essential. I cannot avoid remarking here upon a moral significance. One of the wise and awful truths which this brown-paper art reveals, is this, that white is a colour. It is not a mere absence of colour; it is a shining and affirmative thing, as fierce as red, as definite as black. When, so to speak, your pencil grows red-hot, it draws roses; when it grows white-hot, it draws stars. And one of the two or three defiant verities of the best religious morality, of real Christianity for example, is exactly this same thing; the chief assertion of religious morality is that white is a colour. Virtue is not the absence of vices or the avoidance of moral dangers; virtue is a vivid and separate thing, like pain or a particular smell. Mercy does not mean not being cruel or sparing people revenge or punishment; it means a plain and positive thing like the sun, which one has either seen or not seen.

Chastity does not mean abstention from sexual wrong; it means something flaming, like Joan of Arc. In a word, God paints in many colours; but He never paints so gorgeously, I had almost said so gaudily, as when He paints in white. In a sense our age has realised this fact, and expressed it in our sullen costume. For if it were really true that white was a blank and colourless thing, negative and non-committal, then white would be used instead of black and grey for the funeral dress of this pessimistic period. We should see city gentlemen in frock coats of spotless silver satin, with top hats as white as wonderful arum lilies. Which is not the case.

Meanwhile I could not find my chalk. ❧

It almost goes without saying that one who "rejoiceth not in iniquity" has no interest in the trash that bombards us on nearly every front. Even the home is vulnerable if it has a television set, a sound system, a mail box, a computer. Rather than catalogue the sleaze and slime, let us look for reassurance from lines in a powerful sermon delivered many centuries ago, by the prophet Mormon. His subject is the giving of gifts—one form of charity—and he treats that subject in relation to the morality of the giver. Of interest, too, is the fact that later in the sermon, Mormon turns his focus to the three incremental principles of faith, hope, and charity (see Moroni 7:32–48), further reinforcing the link Paul saw between charity and rejoicing not in iniquity.

For I remember the word of God which saith by their works ye shall know them; for if their works be good, then they are good also.

For behold, God hath said a man being evil cannot do that which is good; for if he offereth a gift, or prayeth unto God, except he shall do it with real intent it profiteth him nothing.

For behold, it is not counted unto him for righteousness.

For behold, if a man being evil giveth a gift, he doeth it grudgingly; wherefore it is counted unto him the same as if he had retained the gift; wherefore he is counted evil before God.

And likewise also is it counted evil unto a man, if he shall pray and not with real intent of heart; yea, and it profiteth him nothing, for God receiveth none such.

Wherefore, a man being evil cannot do that which is good; neither will he give a good gift.

For behold, a bitter fountain cannot bring forth good water; neither can a good fountain bring forth bitter water; wherefore, a man being a servant of the devil cannot follow Christ; and if he follow Christ he cannot be a servant of the devil. (Moroni 7:5–11.) ❧

Mormon goes on to elaborate on the power of discernment that is available to every mortal through the Holy Spirit or light of Christ. Therein lies the key to rejoicing in goodness. As Alma taught, "Wickedness never was happiness." (Alma 41:10.)

11

CHARITY REJOICETH
IN THE TRUTH

For the word of the Lord is truth, and whatsoever

is truth is light, and whatsoever is light is

Spirit, even the Spirit of Jesus Christ.

D & C   8 4 : 4 5

Untruth is the only thing that is impossible to God.

CLEMENT OF ROME

P aul's use of the term rejoiceth, *though a tongue-twister in King James English, suggests that the person who feels and exercises the pure love of Christ not only tells the truth and loves the truth but also finds great joy in the truth as a gift from God. By the same token, there is only misery in falsehood and sham. Leaders of The Church of Jesus Christ of Latter-day Saints, past and present, have made important statements about the nature of truth. In doing so, they have spoken of it in connection with personal testimony, guidance of the Holy Spirit, and the authentic calling of prophets—particularly of the Prophet Joseph Smith. I have elected to represent a number of such discourses here.*

One who has written forcefully about truth is Elder John A. Widtsoe. In his biography of Joseph Smith, he enumerates the truths established by Joseph's first vision, and at the same time he demonstrates how they overturn the misconceptions prevalent in many longstanding, even cherished, religious beliefs.

THE CHALLENGE OF THE FIRST VISION

The First Vision was a challenge to the religious vagaries of the day. It shattered many a false doctrine taught throughout the centuries. Yet it was plain and simple to the human understanding. There was no mysticism about it. Joseph saw, in full light, the personages of the vision and heard their words. The vision was beyond philosophic quibbling.

The vision struck first at atheism. The man-made definitions of God, inadequate for clear human thinking, had made atheists of many persons and near atheists of many more. Most of these people felt that there must be a moving power behind all natural phenomena, but many preferred to believe that the universe is driven by unknown, probably unintelligent, mechanistic forces. To such a conception, the vision made emphatic answer. God the Father with his Son stood before Joseph and instructed him. God, an intelligent being, does exist! That was the witness of the vision. Upon the certainty of the existence of God, the life labors of Joseph Smith were built.

Further, the vision challenged the contradictory and confusing conceptions of the nature of God. For centuries men had thought, talked and philosophized about the nature of God, not only his powers but the essence of him, without reaching an agreement. Some of the ablest minds on earth, from Socrates to Ralph Waldo Emerson, had engaged in the discussion. The result was unutterable confusion to the rational mind.

A few, and a very few, had conceived God to be a person, not merely a personage. This view had ordinarily been laid aside, since it made God more nearly like man in body and powers. Men had held up their hands in horror at an anthropomorphic God, whatever that may have meant.

In early Christian days, more thinkers had accepted God as a personage, but one wholly different from man, usually a tenuous entity, indefinable, and incomprehensible.

Others, many of them Christians, taught that God was neither a person nor a personage, but a force, much like electricity or magnetism, permeating the universe, . . . a world spirit, a first cause, an unknowable source of all things, the immovable mover of the universe, pure energy, the spirit filling all men, the sole independent substance of the universe, a thought in the human mind, a spiritual substance, a monad, man's highest idea, universal reason and intelligence, and other equally useless and incomprehensible definitions![1]

The First Vision clarified this whole matter. It set these philosophic guesses at rest. It answered the centuries' old query about the nature of God. The Father and the Son had appeared to Joseph as persons, like men on earth in form. They spoke to him as persons. They were persons, not mental aberrations. To Joseph Smith, God was thenceforth a living, personal Being.

From the early days of Christianity, the erroneous doctrine of the nature of God had led to other equally false conclusions. Jesus of Nazareth had declared himself to be the Son of God. . . . He had also taught the existence, powers, and mission of the Holy Ghost. . . . Christian philosophers, departing from the simple truth in Christ's teachings, began to ask if there could be more than one God. Out of their thinking came the conception that the Father, the Son, and the Holy Ghost, the Godhead, were One, a unity. Therefore, though God is One, he is also Three Persons, or as some philosophers preferred to say, three emanations. . . .

This false doctrine was laid low by the First Vision. Two personages, the Father and the Son, stood before Joseph. The Father asked the Son to deliver the message to the boy. There was no mingling of personalities in the vision. Each of the personages was an individual member of the Godhead. Each one separately took part in the vision.

There was also the current heretical belief that God, whatever he was, was a faraway figure, who no longer had direct concern with earth. . . . He had placed men on earth and had no further concern with them until after death. In answer to the teaching that the day of revelation had ended, the First Vision was a declaration not only of the possibility of revelation but of a continuity of revelation. God . . . would not forget his children on earth,

---

1. S. E. Frost, The Basic Teachings of the Great Philosophers.

nor can he be divorced from the right to come on earth, to show himself to his children, or to set his work in order. . . .

It was astonishing to the lad, who had asked which of the contending religions was right, to hear that they had all fallen into error, that none had the full gospel. . . .

So, a restoration of the ancient truth, in doctrine and organization, was necessary. Indeed, the Personages in the First Vision declared that the true Church was to be re-established on earth. He, Joseph Smith, was to be the instrument through whom this was to be done. But he was to wait for further commands from the Lord. He was not to do it of himself.

This was another challenge to the practices of the world. Men who felt that they had an "inward call," had thought themselves at liberty to organize a church. The authority must come directly from the Lord or his appointed agents. . . .

The First Vision thus offered challenges at least to some existing dogmas: God exists as a glorious Personage; God and Christ are personal Beings; members of the Godhead may act individually as separate beings; all churches on earth had departed more or less from the pure gospel of Christ; God may reveal himself to man at any time; the church of God would be restored, but only by direct spoken authority of the Lord. . . .

In the grove at Palmyra on the sun-bathed spring day of 1820, the new age of continuous revelation of God's truth had dawned. ❧

John A. Widtsoe's next chapter discusses what truth seekers can learn from the first vision about the process of arriving at truth.

TRUTH SEEKERS MAY FIND THE WAY

. . . Joseph's desire for certain truth was the key that unlocked the door to heavenly visions. It was not conceivable that God would impose a knowledge of himself upon any person who cared indifferently for truth. Desire must precede any great accomplishment. Men may always be judged by their desires.

God deals only in truth and cannot palliate untruth. Error is always abominable. The sorrows of the world may be traced to untruth masquerading as truth. The noble spirit of truth seeking has in all ages brought light out of darkness.

The truth seeker is neither doubter, skeptic, nor unbeliever. The truth of a statement is not denied until it has been examined. The truth seeker always holds his judgment in abeyance until he has accumulated sufficient evidence on which to base a conclusion. He has an open mind; above all else he desires to know truth. The authority of superior knowledge or position is respected, but only after a full personal conviction that it is real authority and that it is properly exercised. In the end, truth followers must rest their convictions on personal experiences.

It was knowledge of God's truth that Joseph desired. Complying with the scriptural injunction that had inspired him, as well as the use of common sense, the boy proceeded to ask of the Lord. Every great work begins with a prayer to a master. The spirit of prayer runs through the whole accumulation of learning, profane and sacred. Every student in school may be said to be an asker for truth. Every leader of thought teaches only answers to the questions that he and others have asked.

Prayer, "the soul's sincere desire," must accompany the seeker in quest of truth. Without prayer he fails. . . . Every person who has set out in search of truth has had his prejudices, preconceived notions, doubts of success, and all sorts of apparently logical antagonisms rise up against him and his venture. Men all too often fail to realize the vast opposition heaped up within their own minds to anything contrary to their traditions and false teachings. . . .

In Joseph's case, however, more important opposition came from without. The forces of evil, angels of darkness, lie everywhere in waiting. Joseph's love of truth, his determination to find truth, and his willingness to follow the appointed way to truth, were challenges to evil. . . . Therefore, he was obliged to learn that the powers of darkness were real. The terrific struggle was not of an imaginary character. . . . This contest with evil was necessary. Knowledge comes by comparisons and contrasts. By light we know darkness, by good we know evil; by successive, comparative steps man moves into a larger knowledge. A person does not need to practice evil to know good. Evil is recognized by its effects without practicing it. Everyone must oppose it as Joseph did in the Sacred Grove. There was a fine pedagogic purpose in Joseph's battle with evil, as it gave him a contrast with the glory he was about to experience. Every seeker for truth must expect to battle with untruth.

The praying boy won. He vanquished the powers of darkness. Praying men are always victorious. . . . truth is revealed if the seeker fail not in his search. . . .

When the youthful prophet had fought off evil, the vision began. An effulgent light gradually filled the grove, until every leaf, twig, and branch stood out distinctly against the bright light. So it must be. Truth cannot dwell with mystery and superstition and darkness. Truth can always be recognized by the accompanying clearness of vision and peace of mind. Fear and doubt retreat from truth. Truth and light always travel together. . . .

When the heavenly beings had departed, Joseph found himself lying on his back, looking into heaven, with his physical strength largely spent.

It was his first realization of the fierce cost of truth. . . .

Many lessons came out of the First Vision for Joseph's future guidance, such as: the desire for truth unlocks heavenly visions, a sincere prayer is always heard and answered, the seeker for truth must be ready to battle with the forces of untruth, and the seeker for truth must pay a great cost in effort. Truth is often known by contrasts.

Every truth seeker could profitably learn the lessons which came out of Joseph Smith's First Vision. In one form or another they are always present when a person sets out to find truth. ❦

In his much earlier biography of the Prophet Joseph, George Q. Cannon cites a number of published responses to Joseph by interested nonmember observers. While none of them would admit to his divine calling, all of them were surprised and struck by the authenticity of his character and the fineness of his demeanor. Representative of the group from whom George Cannon quotes is Josiah Quincy, who, in a lengthy assessment, makes this comment:

History deals in surprises and paradoxes quite as startling as this. The man who established a religion in this age of free debate, who was and is today accepted by hundreds of thousands as a direct emissary from the Most High—such a rare human being is not to be disposed of by pelting his memory with unsavory epithets. Fanatic, imposter, charlatan, he may have been; but these hard names furnish no solution to the problem he presents to us. Fanatics and imposters are living and dying every day, and their memory is buried with them; but the wonderful influence which this founder of a religion exerted and still exerts throws him into relief before us, not as a rogue to be criminated, but as a phenomenon to be explained. ✦

But George Q. Cannon is not baffled. He knows wherein Joseph's authority lies, and the source of truth from which his people derive testimony and strength.

It cannot be expected that any non-believer will testify to the prophetic power of Joseph Smith. To admit it is to believe. And yet this power, too, can be proved by external evidence. Of his predictions not one word has failed. His inspiration may also be proved by external evidence. It is now admitted by every student of his life and work that the Book of Mormon came from or through him. This work could not have been originated by any man in the nineteenth century.

But the best evidence of the divine inspiration which had descended upon him is not external. It is like faith in Christ. It is the whisper of the Spirit. During Joseph Smith's lifetime many thousands of people bore solemn testimony that they knew he was a Prophet of God. Since his death many more thousands have declared the same knowledge. Such proof may be insufficient for the world, but it is enough for the Saints. The world says that men who knew him were deceived by his personal magnetism. But what shall be said of men who believe and yet never saw him? Very few of the Latter-day Saints living today ever met the Prophet. Magnetism has a limited circle and a limited duration. Inspiration is infinite and eternal. The men who never saw Jesus Christ believe on Him because the Holy Spirit inspires belief; the men who never saw Joseph Smith believe in him because the Holy Spirit inspires belief.

. . . If Christians were dependent today solely upon the history of Christ's work, their faith might be insecure; but they have that testimony of the Spirit which gives to the sincere seeker after truth a conviction so firm as to be unassailable by all the power of Satan. It is this same Spirit which convinces the Saints of latter days that as truly as Christ lived, God's only begotten Son, as truly as He performed a divine mission upon earth, as truly as He died upon Calvary a martyr to redeem a fallen world; just so truly was Joseph Smith ordained and inspired of God to reveal his truths and lead men back out of the darkness of ages, into communion with the heavens.

. . . No words of a believer can of themselves convince an unbeliever. There is but one power of demonstration, and that is to seek by humble prayer for the voice of the Holy Spirit. So surely as man prays in faith and meekness, so surely will the answer come. This answer is the testimony of Jesus Christ; it is the testimony to His servant Joseph Smith.

The world will not put this to the test. Only here and there an honest, humble soul, struggling to the light will bow before the general throne and make sincere petition for guidance.

By this testimony will the age be judged. We declare unto all whom these words shall come that Joseph Smith was a Prophet of God. Flesh and blood have not revealed it unto us, but our Father which is in heaven; and this holy revelation is the gift, exclusively, to no man and no class of men. It is free to all who will seek for it in obedience and sincere humility. ❧

One of many such testimonies is that of Emmeline B. Wells, who describes two instances in which the Spirit testified to her of the truth of the prophetic calling.

I feel that I have a testimony to bear, that I have always kept from the very day that I entered the City of Nauvoo and saw the Prophet Joseph. He came down to the boat to meet the saints who were coming from the eastern states and the middle states up to the west. . . .

When I came up the river on the boat, and standing on the top of the boat to see the Prophet on the landing from the boat, I knew instantly then that the gospel was true by the feeling that pervaded me from the crown of my head to the end of my fingers and toes, and every part of my body. I was sure then that I was right, that "Mormonism" was true and that I was fully paid for all the sacrifices that I had made to come to Nauvoo. I felt that just to see him would be worth it all. I had been prepared in a measure for seeing him, but I want to tell you I was not disappointed, because there never was a man like him.

The only incident where a man resembled him was when Brigham Young announced himself as president of the Church and the successor of the Prophet Joseph. I don't remember the words, but that was the announcement that he made in the grove on Temple Hill in the City of Nauvoo. There were but very few people that knew he had . . . returned [after the deaths of Joseph and Hyrum]. When he came forward and made that announcement, the whole company arose and exclaimed, in one voice, you might say, that it was the Prophet Joseph.

I was standing in a wagon box on wheels, so I did not have to rise, but those who were seated arose and made that exclamation. I could see very well, and every one of them thought it was really the Prophet Joseph risen from the dead. But after Brigham Young had spoken a few words, the tumult subsided, and the people really knew that it was not the Prophet Joseph, but the President of the quorum of the Twelve Apostles. It was the most wonderful manifestation, I think, that I have ever known or seen, and I have seen a very great number.

Helen Mar Whitney adds her witness.

I can bear witness, with hundreds of others who stood that day under the sound of Brigham's voice, of the wonderful and startling effect that it had upon us. If Joseph had risen from the dead and stood before them, it could hardly have made a deeper or more lasting impression. It was the very voice of Joseph himself. This was repeatedly spoken of by the Latter-day Saints. And surely it was a most powerful and convincing testimony to them that he was the man, instead of Sidney Rigdon, that was destined to become the "great leader," and upon whose shoulders the mantle of Joseph had fallen. ❖

Joseph Fielding Smith explains the power of such a witness from the Holy Ghost.

The Spirit of God speaking to the spirit of man has power to impart truth with greater effect and understanding than the truth can be imparted by personal contact even with heavenly beings. Through the Holy Ghost the truth is woven into the very fibre and sinews of the body so that it cannot be forgotten. ❧

Joseph F. Smith has also made a number of important statements about arriving at truth and testimony.

It is not by marvelous manifestations unto us that we shall be established in the truth, but it is by humility and faithful obedience to the commandments and laws of God. When I as a boy first started out in the ministry, I would frequently go out and ask the Lord to show me some marvelous thing, in order that I might receive a testimony. But the Lord withheld marvels from me, and showed me the truth, line upon line, precept upon precept, here a little and there a little, until He made me to know the truth from the crown of my head to the soles of my feet, and until doubt and fear had been absolutely purged from me. He did not have to send an angel from the heavens to do this, nor did He have to speak with the trump of an archangel. By the whisperings of the still small voice of the Spirit of the living God, he gave to me the testimony I possess.

And by this principle and power he will give to all the children of men a knowledge of the truth that will stay with them, and it will make them to know the truth, as God knows it, and to do the will of the Father as Christ does it. And no amount of marvelous manifestations will ever accomplish this. It is obedience, humility, and submission to the requirements of heaven and to the order established in the kingdom of God upon the earth, that will establish men in the truth. Men may receive the visitation of angels; they may speak in tongues; they may heal the sick by the laying on of hands; they may have visions and dreams; but except they are faithful and pure in heart, they become an easy prey to the adversary of their souls, and he will lead them into darkness and unbelief more easily than others. ❧

One other passage from Joseph F. Smith bears quoting here.

We believe in righteousness. We believe in all truth, no matter to what subject it may refer. No sect or religious denomination in the world possesses a single principle of truth that we do not accept or that we will reject. We are willing to receive all truth, from whatever source it may come; for truth will stand, truth will endure. No man's faith, no man's religion, no religious organization in all the world, can ever rise above the truth. The truth must be at the foundation of religion, or it is vain and it will fail of its purpose. I say that the truth is at the foundation, at the bottom and top of, and it entirely permeates this great work of the Lord that was established through the instrumentality of Joseph Smith, the prophet. God is with it; it is his work, not that of man; and it will succeed, no matter what the opposition may be. ✦

In writing of his first mission, as a young man, to the Hawaiian Islands, George Q. Cannon tells of using the truth rather than argument to confront falsehood.

When the Presbysterian missionary at Wailuku saw that I had come back there he was displeased. He used all his influence against me among his congregation, and one Sunday he came out in public and delivered a most abusive discourse against the Prophet Joseph and our principles, in which he gave an entirely false statement of the cause of his death, and also warned the people against me.

I happened to be present when this sermon was delivered. While listening to it a variety of emotions agitated me. My first impulse was to jump upon one of the seats as soon as he had got through, and tell the people he had told them a pack of falsehoods. But this I thought would produce confusion, and result in no good. When the services were over, I walked around to the pulpit where he stood. He knew how short a time we had been on the islands, and, I believed, had no idea that I could understand what he had said; when he saw me, therefore, his face turned pale, and to me he looked like a man who had been caught in a mean, low act.

I told him I wanted to give him correct information respecting the things he had told the people that morning, that he might remove the effect of the lies which he had repeated to them; for, I said, they were base lies, and I was a living witness that they were.

He said he did not believe they were lies, and he should not tell the people anything different to what he had said; he thought he had but done his duty, and if the people had been warned against Mahomet in his day, he would not have got so many disciples.

I bore him a solemn testimony respecting the Prophet Joseph, and the truth of the work, and said that I would stand as a witness against him at the judgment seat of God, for having told that people lies and for refusing to tell them the truth when it had been shown to him. . . .

This was the first occurrence of the kind in my experience in which I was personally prominent, and it had an importance in my eyes which it would scarcely have were it to happen today. ✦

Under very different circumstances, Oliver Cowdery, who was then disaffected from the Church, refused, in a court of law, to retract his witness to the truth and authenticity of the Book of Mormon. According to B. H. Roberts, one account of that event is recorded by Utah Judge C. M. Nielsen in an affidavit notarized by Salt Lake notary public A. A. Dixon, December 3, 1909. Nielsen declares that as a young missionary in Minnesota in 1884, he followed a spiritual prompting that led him to a man named Barrington, a man who claimed to have been present in that courtroom. As Barrington told it, Oliver was trying a case as prosecuting attorney, and the opposing attorney tried to discredit him by referring to his connection to "Joe Smith" and his "Mormon Bible." The effect in the courtroom was immediate, as those present wondered how Oliver would react. The eyewitness described his response in words to this effect:

He arose as calm as a summer morning, and in a low but clear voice which gradually rose in pitch and volume as he proceeded, said:

"If your honor please, and gentlemen of the jury, the attorney of the opposite side has challenged me to state my connection with Joseph Smith and the *Book of Mormon;* and as I cannot now avoid the responsibility, I must admit to you that I am the very Oliver Cowdery whose name is attached to the testimony, with others, as to the appearance of the angel Moroni; and let me tell you that it is not because of my good deeds that I am here, away from the body of the Mormon church, but because I have broken the covenants I once made, and I was cut off from the church; but, gentlemen of the jury, I have never denied my testimony, which is attached to the front page of the Book of Mormon, and I declare to you here that these eyes saw the angel, and these ears of mine heard the voice of the angel, and he told us his name was Moroni; that the book was true, and contained the fulness of the gospel, and we were also told that if we ever denied what we had heard and seen that there would be no forgiveness for us, neither in this world nor in the world to come."

Another account ends: "Now how can I deny it—I dare not; I will not!" The observer told Elder Nielsen that he had felt no peace since hearing Oliver testify to the truth of what he saw and heard, under circumstances in which a lie would have spared him ridicule and embarrassment. From that moment, the observer wanted to know more about the religion that prompted Oliver's reply.

Brigham Young's devotion to truth defined the man, as explained by Elder John A. Widtsoe.

FROM "WHEREIN LAY THE GREATNESS OF BRIGHAM YOUNG?"

Two basic qualities made Brigham Young capable of his tremendous world service. All other qualities utilized by him were derivatives of these two.

The first of these was his love of truth. Truth, the impelling passion of his life, was placed above all else. From his youth to the end of his days, he sought truth to guide him. When the Book of Mormon first came to him, with its attendant restoration, in its purity, of the gospel of Jesus Christ, he did not accept the offering at once. Through two long years he studied the book and examined the foundations of the newly organized Church. At last, convinced of the truth of the claims of Joseph Smith, he entered the waters of baptism. When he did so, he sacrificed much of a temporal nature. He became a humble member of a small, already hated group, with no prospects of earthly advancement. He could not then foresee that within three years he would be called to a position of leadership in the Church. But, all that did not count, for he had found the truth!

Throughout his life he spoke of truth with an exuberance of love that thrilled his hearers, and thrills the readers today. . . .

This surrender to truth with the existence of God as the supreme truth, is the first key to Brigham Young's achievements. There is really no other approach to lasting eminence in attainment or leadership. Fame based upon untruth is transient and worthless. This is confirmed by human history. Only those whose feet have rested upon truth, and whose weapon in every affair has been drawn from truth, are secure in the halls of fame.

The second quality that explains the remarkably successful career of Brigham Young was his strict and complete obedience to truth. He held, and correctly, that truth unused has no value in human life.

Truth once found was eagerly obeyed, that is, used. Obedience to truth, whether discovered by man, or received by revelation from God, became the pattern, practice, and concern of Brigham Young's life. His every act and decision squared with truth. He did not therefore choose the easiest path to personal welfare; he followed the way of truth though sometimes thorny.

He understood that many a man knows truth, but does not obey it. Many know that the restored gospel is true but fail to join the Church. Thousands violate the demands of truth, to satisfy their appetites or improper impulses. . . .

These two governing principles of his life—loving truth, as God's gift, above all else; and obeying truth at any cost—explain the success that attended Brigham Young. He cannot well be understood unless it is comprehended that these two principles gave power, to every motive and action of his life. That which he did, temporally and spiritually, was hammered out on the anvil of obeyed truth. ❦

The hunger for truth has persisted among mortals since a fallen Adam sought instruction from the Lord. Nobel Peace Prize recipient Elie Wiesel writes of his youthful desire for a teacher who could lead him to truths he only dimly apprehended. The experience he describes, of course, occurred before his incarceration in Nazi concentration camps.

Young Elie had asked his father to find a master who could guide him in studying the cabbala, but his father had refused, saying he was too young. Elie must study basic subjects before venturing into mysticism.

FROM *NIGHT*

He wanted to drive the notion out of my head. But it was in vain. I found a master for myself, Moshe the Beadle.

He had noticed me one day at dusk, when I was praying.

"Why do you weep when you pray?" he asked me, as though he had known me a long time.

"I don't know why," I answered, greatly disturbed.

The question had never entered my head. I wept because—because of something inside me that felt the need for tears. That was all I knew.

"Why do you pray?" he asked me, after a moment.

Why did I pray? A strange question. Why did I live? Why did I breathe?

"I don't know why," I said, even more disturbed and ill at ease. "I don't know why."

After that day I saw him often. He explained to me with great insistence that every question possessed a power that did not lie in the answer.

"Man raises himself toward God by the questions he asks Him," he was fond of repeating. "That is the true dialogue. Man questions God and God answers. But we don't understand His answers. We can't understand them. Because they come from the depths of the soul, and they stay there until death. You will find the true answers, Eliezer, only within yourself!"

"And why do you pray, Moshe?" I asked him.

"I pray to the God within me that He will give me the strength to ask Him the right questions."

We talked like this nearly every evening. We used to stay in the synagogue after all the faithful had left, sitting in the gloom, where a few half-burned candles still gave a flickering light.

One evening I told him how unhappy I was because I could not find a master in Sighet to instruct me in the Zohar, the cabbalistic books, the secrets of Jewish mysticism. He smiled indulgently. After a long silence, he said:

298

"There are a thousand and one gates leading into the orchard of mystical truth. Every human being has his own gate. We must never make the mistake of wanting to enter the orchard by any gate but our own. To do this is dangerous for the one who enters and also for those who are already there.

And Moshe the Beadle, the poor barefoot of Sighet, talked to me for long hours of the revelations and mysteries of the cabbala. It was with him that my initiation began. We would read together, ten times over, the same page of the Zohar. Not to learn it by heart, but to extract the divine essence from it.

And throughout those evenings a conviction grew in me that Moshe Beadle would draw me with him into eternity, into that time where question and answer would become *one*. ✦

Regardless of Wiesel's approach to it, his subject is revealed truth from a divine source.

That is the one eternal education: to be sure enough that something is true that you dare to tell it to a child. (G. K. Chesterton.) ✦

'Tis a great lesson, how mighty divine truth is, which passes through, though she be hemmed in ever so closely; the more she is read, the more she moves and takes possession of the heart. (Martin Luther.) ✦

In an address at Brigham Young University, S. Dilworth Young stressed the importance of truth-telling. To illustrate the point, he told of being pulled over by a patrol car as late one night he raced home from Provo to attend his ailing wife.

FROM "COURAGE TO BE RIGHTEOUS"

Going north on the highway—the moon was full, the light was bright, I could see as easily as in daylight and I was the only person on the road— I went quite rapidly until I got to Farmington Junction, where I was to turn off to go up over the mountain road toward home. I turned off on that road and I really hit it up. I had that car going 70 miles an hour, which was good for those days over that road, and I whipped past the road going over to

Hill Field, and down into Weber Canyon. I got about half way down the hill when through the rear view mirror I saw the flashing red light. The patrolman had been hiding up Hill Field road. So I pulled to a stop and got out. . . . It was now nearly one o'clock.

So I walked back a few yards and stood there and his headlights picked me up and he came to a stop about thirty yards away. He got out of his car and came up to me. He said, "May I see your driver's license and your car registration." . . .

I said, "Well, give me the ticket. I've got to get home; my wife is ill and helpless. I was speeding."

He said, "Yes, you were going faster than 60 miles an hour."

And I said, "I was going faster than 70 miles an hour."

He said, "Well, I'm not going to give you a ticket. I'm going to give you a *warning* ticket so you won't do it again." . . .

I couldn't imagine why he had given me just a warning ticket. He got the ticket written out and he handed it to me—then he smiled, and he stuck his hand out, which a cop seldom does, and he said to me, "My name is Bybee. I used to be one of your scouts at Camp Kiesel."

All the rest of the way home, every time the wheels turned, I said to myself, "What if I'd lied to him—what if I'd lied to him—what if I'd lied to him."

I've learned by what little experience I've had with lies that anyone who tells a lie, I can guarantee that that lie will last him all his life and he'll have it burn into his soul over and over again until he dies. ❧

THE SHEPHERD BOY AND THE WOLF

A Shepherd boy, who tended his flock not far from a village, used to amuse himself at times in crying out "Wolf! Wolf!" Twice or thrice his trick succeeded. The whole village came running out to his assistance; when all the return they got was to be laughed at for their pains. At last one day the Wolf came indeed. The Boy cried out in earnest. But his neighbors, supposing him to be at his old sport, paid no heed to his cries, and the Wolf devoured the Sheep. So the Boy learned, when it was too late, that liars are not believed even when they tell the truth. (Aesop.) ❧

Emily Dickinson had a lot to say about truth, and she describes her own unique perspective on the subject in this poem.

Tell all the Truth but tell it slant—
Success in Circuit lies
Too bright for our infirm Delight
The Truth's superb surprise

As Lightning to the Children eased
With explanation kind
The Truth must dazzle gradually
Or every man be blind.

Truth strikes us from behind, and in the dark, as well as from before and in broad day-light. (Henry David Thoreau.) ❧

The following dialogue by an unknown author offers a comical echo of Dickinson and Thoreau. The piece is editorially titled "How to Tell Bad News" (tell it slant, indeed).

MR. H. AND THE STEWARD

Mr. H.   HA! Steward, how are you, my old boy? How do things go on at home?

Steward.   Bad enough, your honor; the magpie's dead.

H.   Poor Mag! So he's gone. How came he to die?

S.   Overeat himself, sir.

H.   Did he? A greedy dog; why, what did he get he liked so well?

S.   Horseflesh, sir; he died of eating horseflesh.

H.   How came he to get so much horseflesh?

S.   All your father's horses, sir.

H.   What! are they dead, too?

S.   Ay, sir; they died of overwork.

H.   And why were they overworked, pray?

S.   To carry water, sir.

H.   To carry water! and what were they carrying water for?

S.   Sure, sir, to put out the fire.

H.   Fire! what fire?

S.   O, sir, your father's house is burned to the ground.

H.   My father's house burned down! and how came it to set on fire?

S.   I think, sir, it must have been the torches.

H.   Torches! what torches?

S.   At your mother's funeral.

H.   My mother dead!

S.   Ah, poor lady! she never looked up, after it.

H.   After what?

S.   The loss of your father.

H.   My father gone, too?

S.   Yes, poor gentleman! he took to his bed as soon as he heard of it.

H.   Heard of what?

S.   The bad news, sir, and please your honor.

H.   What! more miseries! more bad news!

S.   Yes, sir; your bank has failed, and your credit is lost, and you are not worth a shilling in the world. I made bold, sir, to wait on you about it, for I thought you would like to hear the news. ❦

It exercises the imagination to consider how this particular fellow might have reported Job's losses to him.

On the other hand, it is usually best to tell the truth and tell it head on. The Church essayed to do just that in April 1907 when it issued an official public declaration of its beliefs and principles. President Joseph F. Smith introduced it, Orson F. Whitney read it aloud to the congregation in General Conference, and Francis F. Lyman reported the Council of the Twelve's endorsement of the statement. He then moved that the Church body adopt the document the First Presidency had presented. The congregation approved it in a standing vote. Below are a few key excerpts from the fourteen-page treatise. (Note: As recently as the fall of 1995, the Church also issued a proclamation to the world at large, this one affirming its stand on principles of morality and family values. See the Ensign, November 1995.)

The Church of Jesus Christ of Latter-day Saints to the World
GREETING:

In the hope of correcting misrepresentation, and of establishing a more perfect understanding respecting ourselves and our religion, we, the officers and members of the Church of Jesus Christ of Latter-day Saints, in General Conference assembled, issue this Declaration.

Such an action seems imperative. Never were our principles or our purposes more widely misrepresented, more seriously misunderstood. Our doctrines are distorted, the sacred ordinances of our religion ridiculed, our Christianity questioned, our history falsified, our character traduced, and our course of conduct as a people reprobated and condemned.

In answer to the charges made against us, for ourselves and for those who, under divine direction, founded our religion and our Church; for our posterity, to whom we shall transmit the faith, and into whose keeping we shall give the Church of Christ; and before mankind, whose opinions we respect, we solemnly declare the truth to be:

Our religion is founded on the revelations of God. The Gospel we proclaim is the Gospel of Christ, restored to earth in this the dispensation of the fulness of times. The high claim of the Church is declared in its title— The Church of Jesus Christ of Latter-day Saints. Established by divine direction, its name was prescribed by Him whose Church it is—Jesus Christ.

The religion of this people is pure Christianity. Its creed is expressive of the duties of practical life. Its theology is based on the doctrines of the Redeemer.

If it be true Christianity to accept Jesus Christ in person and in mission as divine; to revere Him as the Son of God, the crucified and risen Lord, through whom alone can mankind attain salvation; to accept His teachings as a guide, to adopt as a standard and observe as a law the ethical code He promulgated; to comply with the requirements prescribed by Him as essential to membership in His Church, namely, faith, repentance, baptism by immersion for the remission of sins, and the laying on of hands for the gift of the Holy Ghost,—if this be Christianity, then we are Christians, and the Church of Jesus Christ of Latter-day Saints is a Christian church.

The theology of our Church is the theology taught by Jesus Christ and His apostles, the theology of scripture and reason. It not only acknowledges the sacredness of ancient scripture, and the binding force of divinely-inspired acts and utterances in ages past; but also declares that God speaks to man in this final Gospel dispensation.

We believe in the Godhead, comprising the three individual personages, Father, Son, and Holy Ghost.

We hold that man is verily the child of God, formed in His image, endowed with divine attributes, and possessing power to rise from the gross desires of earth to the ennobling aspirations of heaven.

We believe in the pre-existence of man as a spirit, and in a future state of individual existence, in which every soul shall find its place, as determined by justice and mercy, with opportunities of endless progression, in the varied conditions of eternity.

We believe in the free agency of man, and therefore in his individual responsibility.

We believe that salvation is for no select few, but that all men may be saved through obedience to the laws and ordinances of the Gospel.

We affirm that to administer in the ordinances of the Gospel, authority must be given of God; and that this authority is the power of the Holy Priesthood.

We affirm that through the ministration of immortal personages, the Holy Priesthood has been conferred upon men in the present age, and that under this divine authority the Church of Jesus Christ has been organized.

We proclaim the objects of this organization to be, the preaching of the Gospel in all the world, the gathering of scattered Israel, and the preparation of a people for the coming of the Lord. . . .

The Church of Jesus Christ of Latter-day Saints holds to the doctrine of the separation of church and state; the non-interference of church authority in political matters; and the absolute freedom and independence of the individual in the performance of his political duties. If, at any time, there has been conduct at variance with this doctrine, it has been in violation of the well settled principles and policy of the Church.

We declare that from principle and policy, we favor:

The absolute separation of church and state;

No domination of the state by the church;

No church interference with the functions of the state;

No state interference with the functions of the church, or with the free exercise of religion;

The absolute freedom of the individual from the domination of ecclesiastical authority in political affairs;

The equality of all churches before the law.

The reaffirmation of this doctrine and policy, however, is predicated upon the express understanding that politics in the states where our people reside, shall be conducted as in other parts of the Union; that there shall be no interference by the State with the Church, nor with the free exercise of religion. . . .

"Mormonism" is in the world for the world's good. Teaching truth, inculcating morality, guarding the purity of the home, honoring authority and government, fostering education, and exalting man and woman, our religion denounces crime, and is a foe to tyranny in every form. "Mormonism" seeks to uplift, not to destroy society. She joins hands with the civilization of the age. Proclaiming herself a special harbinger of the Savior's second coming, she recognizes in all the great epochs and movements of the past, steps in the march of progress leading up to the looked for millennial reign. "Mormonism" lifts an ensign of peace to all people. The predestined fruits of her proposed system are the sanctification of the earth and the salvation of the human family.

And now, to all the world: Having been commanded of God, as much as lieth in us, to live peaceably with all men—we, in order to be obedient to the heavenly commandment, send forth this Declaration, that our position upon the various questions agitating the public mind concerning us may be known. We desire peace, and will do all in our power on fair and honorable principles to promote it. Our religion is interwoven with our lives, it has formed our character, and the truth of its principles is impressed upon our souls. We submit to you, our fellow-men, that there is nothing in those principles that calls for execration, no matter how widely in some respects they may differ from your conceptions of religious truth. Certainly there is nothing in them that may not stand within the wide circle of modern toleration of religious thought and practice. To us these principles are crystalizations of truth. They are as dear to us as your religious conceptions are to you. In their application to human conduct, we see the world's hope of redemption from sin and strife, from ignorance and unbelief. Our motives are not selfish; our purposes not petty and earth-bound; we contemplate the human race, past, present and yet to come, as immortal beings, for whose salvation it is our mission to labor; and to this work, broad as eternity and deep as the love of God, we devote ourselves, now, and forever. Amen.

JOSEPH F. SMITH,

JOHN R. WINDER,

ANTHON H. LUND,

In behalf of the Church of Jesus Christ of Latter-day Saints, March 26, 1907

Adopted by vote of the Church, in General Conference, April 5, 1907. Salt Lake City, Utah ◀

The Nauvoo journal Times and Seasons *once carried a little poetic exchange between W. W. Phelps and Joseph Smith about postmortal existence. Joseph Smith replies to W. W. Phelps in a versified rendering of Doctrine and Covenants 76. One need only compare the man-made version with the scriptural text to realize that (1) no mortal could have independently composed the revelations Joseph received, and (2) revealed truth from the Lord is inherently (and poetically) beautiful. Joseph's subject is elevated, and even though his poetry is fairly good, the form does not do justice to the magnificent truths of divine utterance. Still, it was a monumental task, transcribing the section in verse.*

W. W. Phelps's "poem," addressed to the Prophet Joseph, appears first.

VADE MECUM, (TRANSLATED,) GO WITH ME

Go with me, will you go to the saints that have died,—
To the next, better world, where the righteous reside;
Where the angels and spirits in harmony be
In the joys of a vast paradise? Go with me.

Go with me where the truth and the virtues prevail;
Where the union is one, and the years never fail;
Not a heart can conceive, nor a nat'ral eye see
What the Lord has prepar'd for the just. Go with me.

Go with me where there is no destruction or war;
Neither tyrants, or sland'rers, or nations ajar;
Where the system is perfect, and happiness free,
And the life is eternal with God. Go with me.

Go with me, will you go to the mansions above,
Where the bliss, and the knowledge, the light, and the love,
And the glory of God do eternally be?—
Death, the wages of sin, is not there. Go with me.
Nauvoo, January, 1843

Below are a few excerpts from Joseph Smith's lengthy published response, taking nearly four pages (eight columns) in the February 1, 1843, issue of Times and Seasons. *The pieces received front-page display, including a commentary assessing Joseph's reply as unpolished but inspired poetry and indirectly classifying "the poetry of Mr. Smith" as a "scripture poem." The Puritans did this sort of thing as a matter of course, paraphrasing scripture in rhymed verse so that it could be memorized more easily. Early on, Joseph's numbered verses roughly correspond with the verses in Doctrine and Covenants 76, but later he collapses some together. He finishes with 78 verses, compared with 119 in Section 76. The subject is revealed truth.*

THE ANSWER

To W. W. Phelps, Esq.
A Vision
1. I will go, I will go, to the home of the Saints,
Where the virtue's the value, and life the reward;
But before I return to my former estate
I must fulfil the mission I had from the Lord.
2. Wherefore, hear, O ye heavens, and give ear O ye earth;
And rejoice ye inhabitants truly again;

For the Lord he is God, and his life never ends,
And besides him there ne'er was a Saviour of men.
3. His ways are a wonder; his wisdom is great;
The extent of his doings, there's none can unveil;
His purposes fail not; from age unto age
He still is the same, and his years never fail.

. . . .

11. I, Joseph, the prophet, in spirit beheld,
And the eyes of the inner man truly did see
Eternity sketch'd in a vision from God,
Of what was, and now is, and yet is to be.
12. Those things which the Father ordained of old,
Before the world was, or a system had run,—
Through Jesus the Maker and Savior of all;
The only begotten, (Messiah) his son.
13. Of whom I bear record, as all prophets have,
And the record I bear is the fulness,—yea even
The truth of the gospel of Jesus—*the Christ,*
With whom I convers'd, in the vision of heav'n.

. . . .

40. And again I bear record of heavenly things,
Where virtue's the value, above all that's pric'd—
Of the truth of the gospel concerning the just,
That rise in the first resurrection of Christ.

. . . .

76. Ev'ry man shall be judg'd by the works of his life,
And receive a reward in the mansions prepar'd;
For his judgments are just, and his works never end,
As his prophets and servants have always declar'd.
77. But the great things of God, which he show'd unto me,
Unlawful to utter, I dare not declare;
They surpass all the wisdom and greatness of men,
And only are seen, as has Paul, where they are.

78. I will go, I will go, while the secret of life,
Is blooming in heaven, and blasting in hell;
Is leaving on earth, and a budding in space:—
I will go, I will go, with you, brother, farewell.
JOSEPH SMITH
Nauvoo, Feb. 1843

By rendering scripture in verse, Joseph implied a connection between truth and beauty that artists inside the Church and outside the Church have long advanced. Orson F. Whitney expounded at length on the subject, in verse and in prose. Below are a few extracts from his writings.

FROM "THE GOSPEL'S ACCESSORIES"

Many Ways to the Heart.—There is only one way into the Kingdom of Heaven, but there are many ways into the human heart; and the Church of Christ, in its mission of promulgating truth and turning souls to righteousness, has legitimate use for every avenue to that heart. Poetry, music, art in general, as well as science and philosophy—all these can be utilized as auxiliaries in the carrying on of the Lord's manifold work. They may not be essential parts of the divine message, but they prepare the way for its acceptance and are forerunners of greater things. This, to my thinking, is the main reason why they are in the world. There is something purifying, ennobling, exalting, in all true poetry, true music, real science and genuine philosophy.

The Essence of Poetry.—The essence of poetry is in idealism, in thought, sentiment, symbolism, and the power of suggestion. The Creator has built his universe upon symbols, the lesser suggesting and leading up to the greater; and the poetic faculty—possessed in fulness by the prophet—recognizes and interprets them. "All things have their likeness" [Moses 6:63]. All creations testify of their creator. They point to something above and beyond. That is why poetry of the highest order is always prophetic or infinitely suggestive; and that is why the poet is a prophet. . . .

The Greatest Poet and Prophet.—Jesus Christ, the greatest of all prophets, was likewise the greatest of all poets. He comprehended the universe and its symbolism as no one else ever did or could. He knew it through and through. What wonder? Had he not created it, and was it not made to bear record of him? He taught in poetic parables, taking simple things as types of greater things, and teaching lessons that lead the mind upward toward the ideal, toward perfection. The Gospel of Christ is replete with poetry. It is one vast poem from beginning to end. ❦

Less known, perhaps, is a hymn Parley P. Pratt composed on the occasion of the Nauvoo Concert Hall dedication on December 20, 1844. It could have been titled "Ode to Truth."

> Truth is our theme, our joy, our song,
> How sweet its numbers flow,
> All music's charms to truth belong,
> To truth ourselves we owe.
>
> 'Twas truth that brought us from afar;
> 'Twas truth that placed us here;
> Union and truth without a jar,
> Our Halls and Temples near.
>
> 'Twas truth first formed our band and choir
> On Zion's western plains;
> 'Twas truth that tuned our earliest lyre
> In sweet harmonious strains.
>
> Sacred to truth this Hall shall be,
> While earth and time remains;
> Where the band and choir in harmony
> Shall sound their sweetest strains.
>
> By truth our union is complete,
> Our songs in concert rise,
> And by the power of truth we'll meet
> To sing amid the skies.

Hosannah to the Prince of Peace,
His truth has made us free;
All hail the day of full release,
The earth's grand jubilee.

Truth reflects upon our senses . . .

I died for Beauty—but was scarce
Adjusted in the Tomb
When One who died for Truth, was lain
In an adjoining Room—

He questioned softly "Why I failed"?
"For Beauty", I replied—
"And I—for Truth—Themself are One—
We Brethren, are", He said—

And so, as Kinsmen, met a Night—
We talked between the Rooms—
Until the Moss had reached our lips—
And covered up—our names—
(Emily Dickinson.)

Obert C. Tanner has written, "Religion is deeply concerned with the three spiritual realms of value—three eternal verities: goodness, truth, and beauty. But the third one, beauty, has been much neglected. For this neglect, religion has suffered." (Christ's Ideals for Living, 120.) Poet John Keats saw Beauty and Truth as synonymous. Keats said in his famous "Ode on a Grecian Urn," "'Beauty is truth, truth beauty'—that is all / Ye know on earth, and all ye need to know." As the Romantic poets were inclined to do, Keats overstated his case, but he made a good point nonetheless.

If we think of Creation as the expression of the power of the Word—"God said, Let there be light: and there was light"—an embodiment of divine truth, then we can more readily see that in some sense, untruth simply could never be beautiful.

In a March 1992 fireside address to Brigham Young University students, President Gordon B. Hinckley named and elaborated on what he called his ten *articles of belief. His second article was "belief in beauty," and he addressed it at some length, alluding to the beauty of nature and people, "the beauty of good music and art, of pleasing architecture, and of good literature untainted by profanity or verbal filth." He also referred to the contrasting ugliness present "in the scarred earth, the polluted waters, the befouled air," the "coarse language," "sloppy dress and manners," and "immoral behavior that mocks the beauty of virtue and always leaves a scar."* (BYU 1991–92 Devotional and Fireside Speeches, p. 78.)

The following poem illustrates one LDS poet's exquisite sensitivity to natural beauty and his anticipation of the effect of Christ's second coming on the cosmos He created.

AUTUMN LEAVES

Dust of the summer weeks appalled the evenings,
Settling like peace into the russet plain
As a leveller of hues:
                        now earthtone leavenings
Float into the hill, and the empress cloud
Rails, trailing rain—rain, dint of high storm
Reviving light, then the lancet diagnol spurts
Of rain into dust, taking from the spectrum
Rainbow gusts of light, and the rise and span
Of trees vanish in turbulence, the rainwind
Veering lower in the silver dusk.
                              Hours
Of rain wash the concourse of the autumn leaves
In hours of night, and as dawn fields visions
Of the arriving day the leaves, in that intensity,
Leave gray and assume the shine of water
Freshening fine in the diamonds of spray,
Then in the thrust of light their fire!

Matte and patina dull, as once they were,
Become from russet topaz, from rust carmine,
From saffron aureate gold, from dun emerald,

From azure amethyst blue, smooth as the lake
In the silence of light, smooth as the fielding
Sun in aureate of hours that modulate hues in flashings
Of ridges to rockwall promontories and heights
Of the sky: gems in the suddenness of dew,
Misting swatches of yellow-gold, gold in the lighter
Green, green in brown, brown at the edge, the cardinal
Vale there like a wing, violet in deeper mauve,
Mauve in gray stone, earthbrown sills higher and higher,
Spun in gestures of color, ambient as the breeze
Reveals outcropping stone:
      aspens awakening at the surge
Of the sun's early wind, turning and fluttering leaves
Across vertical white strands in the plenum
Of their stand against the mountain, the mail
Rain still there, but coasting over margents of blue
Into the freer blue of sky, the sound of paling light. . . .
Autumn! and this from the steel twilight of rain!

All this will fall into the matte earth's engendering
Loam, rich black annealing soil.
      Sails of color wander
Under the clouds beyond this immediacy of wind,
Shadowy dim in the heights of space. Where is
The ultimate variety from the reign that will rinse
The sheen of the spiritual stars, the blue-white gems
Of polar winds wherein all glory flickers
As the autumn of stars, leafing as highlights
Wend across the spectral forest of light?
(Clinton F. Larson.)

Any beautiful thing reminds us that there are truths of the heart as well as truths of the mind. Sometimes we seek truth in definition, only to discover that truth lies in meanings no dictionary reports, and that beauty lies in charitable traits of character.

12

CHARITY BEARETH
ALL THINGS

Bear ye one another's burdens,

and so fulfil the law of Christ. . . .

But let every man prove his own work,

and then shall he have rejoicing in himself alone,

and not in another.

For every man shall bear his own burden. . . .

And let us not be weary in well doing:

for in due season we shall reap, if we faint not.

As we have therefore opportunity,

let us do good unto all men, especially unto them

who are of the household of faith.

GALATIANS 6:2, 4–5, 9–10

This passage, which contains a multiple message, seems to relate importantly to Paul's statement in 1 Corinthians that charity "beareth all
things." In Galatians, Paul urges us to bear one another's burdens but at
the same time to "prove [our] own work" and "bear [our] own burden." After
promising that we will reap whatever we sow, and that we therefore should sow

"to the Spirit" rather than to the "flesh" (Galatians 6:7–8), he repeats his previous admonition. He tells us to be engaged in "well doing"—in good work—and he tells us to "do good" to others.

The Savior's invitation in Matthew adds still another dimension to the idea, assuring us that he will aid us in our labors and bear some of our burden. Thus, he helps us as we help each other, through the exercise of true charity. His yoke that he invites us to bear, he says, "is easy," and his "burden is light." (Matthew 11:30.) We should not forget, either, that Jesus took upon himself the burden of our sins, the ultimate act of charity, of pure love. Any burden we might be asked to bear in his service would, by comparison, be light indeed.

This chapter, therefore, reflecting the several sides of "bearing all things," will offer exempla of several kinds: models of taking on whatever life hands us and going at it with a will, and without serious complaint; of shouldering one another's burdens and attempting to assist as Christ would; of doing one's part in the world's work and making a useful contribution—but without losing the capacity for light-heartedness or for contemplation.

I note, incidentally, that one can reasonably see redundancy in Paul's description of the charitable person as one who "beareth all things," for the phrase is arguably synonymous with "suffereth long" or "endureth all things." I repeat, however, that thoughtful consideration of Paul's definitions of charity suggests some distinctions among the sixteen traits he names. I have described the distinctions that occur to me; the reader may see others. The first examples in this section relate to bearing responsibility, gamely taking on a challenge, making the most of one's lot. John Longden tells of a very young Matthew Cowley humbly and prayerfully rising to a significant challenge in fulfilling his calling in the kingdom.

I should like to give you . . . an experience that came to my attention two days after the passing of that great prophet of God, Elder Matthew Cowley. It was given to me by a man who some thirty-five or forty years before had been district president of Brother Cowley down in New Zealand as he labored with [the] Maori people. He had only been out for two and one half months, and a district missionary conference was called. In one of those sessions, the morning session, Brother Cowley had an opportunity to speak. As the story has been related to me, he spoke for fifteen or twenty minutes in a fluent Maori tongue, so much so that it amazed the older Maori people in the congregation.

After the meeting, the district president and Brother Cowley were walking to a Maori home to partake of food between sessions, and the district president said, "How did you do it?" Brother Cowley asked, "Do what?" "How did you master this Maori language in such a short time?" A young missionary, seventeen years of age!

Brother Cowley said, "When I came here I did not know one word of Maori, but I decided I was going to learn twenty new words each day, and I did. But when I came to put them together, I was not successful." By this time they were passing a cornfield, and Brother Cowley said, "You see that cornfield? I went out there, and I talked to the Lord, but before that, I fasted, and that night I tried again, but the words just didn't seem to jell. So the next day I fasted again, and I went out into that cornfield, and I talked to the Lord. Again, I tried that night with a little more success.

"On the third day I fasted again, and I went out into the cornfield, and I talked to the Lord. I told the Lord that I believed his Church and kingdom had been established upon the earth; that men had the authority to proclaim the fulness of the gospel of Jesus Christ which pertained to the salvation and exaltation of our Heavenly Father's children. I told him that I had been called by this same authority to fill a mission, but if this was not the mission in which I was to serve to please make it known because I wanted to serve where I could accomplish the greatest amount of good."

That was the spirit of Brother Cowley. He said, "The next morning, as we knelt in family prayer in that Maori home, I was called upon by the head of the household to be mouth. I tried to speak in English, and I could not. But when I tried in Maori, the words just flowed forth, and I knew that God had answered my prayer and this was where I should serve." A young lad seventeen years of age! ❧

Elder Cowley adds his own wrinkle to the story:

FROM "THEY SHALL SPEAK

WITH NEW TONGUES"

I was just turning seventeen when I was called to go to New Zealand as a missionary. My first appointment there was to a little place called Judea— a wonderful place to go for a young missionary. The first meeting I attended in Judea I didn't understand a word that was being said, and after the meeting a sister who could speak English said to me, "Do you know what they said in there, what they did?"

I said, "I couldn't understand a word."

She said, "Well, you were called and sustained as the secretary of the Relief Society of the Judea Branch."

And I made up my mind right there and then that the Relief Society was not going to take any liberty with my time as a missionary without my knowing something about it. And so I determined to get the gift of the Maori language even if I had to work for it. And I did have to work for it. I studied eleven hours every day for several weeks. I read the *Book of Mormon* in Maori. My studies were punctuated with fasting and prayer, and on my twelfth Sunday I delivered my first sermon in the Maori language. ❦

Oscar A. Kirkham tells of another man, a rather reluctant fellow, who was uncertain about his ability to fulfill a particular calling but took it on anyway.

I went down into one [of] the stakes of the Church, and the president of the stake asked a man to become a stake missionary. He'd no sooner spoken the word to the man . . . than the brother said to him, "Now wait a moment. For a long while I've wanted to put a cement walk around the chapel, our ward chapel. I'll have my men up there tomorrow with a cement mixer and trucks. I'll put it in. . . . It won't cost you a cent, and here's my check; I'll sign it, and you put in the amount, but don't call me on a mission. My goodness, I don't know a thing about missionary work. I don't know one line of scripture."

The president of the stake said to me, "You know, Brother Kirkham, the more he talked, the more I was assured that he'd make a grand missionary, so I said to him, taking him by the arm, 'Come on, my brother, come on downstairs with me'; and I started toward the stairway leading down under the Tabernacle, and he turned to me again and said, 'What's the idea?'" And the president of the stake said, "Why, I'm taking you downstairs to set you apart as a missionary."

Well, somehow God gives to men who hold the priesthood of God, an understanding; and this man somehow felt in these words, now that the president of his stake was speaking, a voice that he couldn't quite resist. Oh, what a precious thing it is when the Spirit of God falls upon men who have responsibility, and somehow the Lord gives us the language of understanding.

So they went downstairs. The brother was set apart, and then he went home. When he arrived home, his wife saw that he was a little bit different. He was pale. And she said, "Why, what's the matter, dear? You look pale."

"You'd be pale, too, if you had happen to you what's happened to me."

And then he told his wife, seeking sympathy, that he'd been called to become a stake missionary; and his wife said, "Well, I think you'll do quite well."

Some days went by. One morning he came out and said to himself, "Why, I haven't done any missionary work. I must get busy. I've been called on a mission."

He didn't know how to go about it. He didn't know how to start. It was all strange to him. He said, "I looked across the field and saw my neighbor. He was not a member of the Church. We'd raised our families together. I thought there's my chance. I know him well enough. I'll be easy with him. And I called to him, 'Frank, come over here,' and Frank came over to the old fence; and when he arrived he said, 'What is it?' I said, 'Frank, I haven't called you over here to talk about cleaning the ditch or mending this fence. Believe it or not, I am a missionary, and you're my first victim.'"

His friend, good-natured and understanding, said, "Well, go ahead."

"I didn't have a thing to say. I was really baffled, until finally I said to him, 'Well, I don't know just how it is over at your house, but when we have our meal, we generally thank the Lord for the food and ask his blessings upon it, and we have family prayer together in our home.'" And he told

CHARITY BEARETH ALL THINGS

two or three simple things like this, and he said to his friend, "Well, that's about all for today," and his friend thanked him and said he'd done well and went back to his home. And then the story went over into this home.

He said, "Frank told me this: 'When I got over home I was still thinking about what my neighbor had said. They had been waiting dinner for me. I started by passing some of the food around, and that was about all. I was still thinking about my neighbor and what he had said about saying grace, and I said to the family, "Wait a minute. I've been talking to my neighbor, this man we often speak about and love, and he's been telling me that one of the lovely things they do is thank the Lord for food and ask his blessing upon it.""'

"He saw his eldest son across the table, and he said to him, 'Son, you lead out.' His son looked back to the father, and he said, 'Now, Dad, if there's going to be any reform in this family, you lead out.'

"And he said, 'Of course I had to go through with it. I'd started it. I bowed my head, and in a few simple words I told the Lord we were grateful for the food, and we'd try and do the right thing, Amen.' He just stumbled through, he told me, but he said, ' . . . when I raised my eyes I saw something beautiful. My wife . . . was drying her eyes. She didn't say a word, but I could hear her; she said, "That was a lovely thing to do. You did a courageous thing. My, how I love you." All of that I heard, although she never spoke a word. I soon left, and I was out doing the chores. I'd fed the cattle. I put down the pitchfork, and I reached in my pocket of old habit, and I began to roll a cigarette. Just at that moment another of my boys went by the shed, and he saw me. He didn't say anything, but I could hear him. He said, "Dad, if there's going to be reform, you'd better lead out.""'

"He said, 'I threw that thing away; and as life unfolded day by day I went with my family up to the Manti Temple and there before the altar of the Lord dressed in lovely white robes, I and my wife and children were sealed together for time and for eternity.'"

"'Happiness and joy,' Frank said to me, 'the likes of which I have never experienced before.'"

When did it all happen? Why, it happened that day when this man called across the field, "Frank, come over here." ❧

David O. McKay tells of an early experience that made a lasting impression.

FROM "WHATE'ER THOU ART, ACT WELL THY PART"

I remember as a missionary in Scotland fifty-seven years ago, after having been in Stirling only a few weeks, I walked around Stirling Castle with my senior companion, Elder Peter G. Johnston of Idaho. We had not yet secured our lodging in Stirling. I confess I was homesick. I did not like the attitude of the people there as they were so suspicious that we were there for ulterior motives. We had spent a halfday around the castle, and the men out in the fields ploughing, that spring day, made me all the more homesick, and took me back to my old home town.

As we returned to the town, I saw an unfinished building standing back from the sidewalk several yards. Over the front door was a stone arch, something unusual in a residence, and what was still more unusual, I could see from the sidewalk that there was an inscription chiseled in that arch.

I said to my companion: "That's unusual! I am going to see what the inscription is." When I approached near enough, this message came to me, not only in stone, but as if it came from One in whose service we were engaged: "Whate'er Thou Art, Act Well Thy Part."

I turned and walked thoughtfully away, and when I reached my companion I repeated the message to him.

That was a message to me that morning to act my part well as a missionary of the Church of Jesus Christ of Latter-day Saints. ❧

Sometimes the part we have been asked to perform, the burden we have been given to bear, seems beyond our physical capacity, as in this experience of Wilford Woodruff:

FROM *LEAVES FROM MY JOURNAL*

Early upon the morning of the 8th of August, 1839, I arose from my bed of sickness, laid my hands upon the head of my sick wife, Phoebe, and blessed her. I then departed from the embrace of my companion, and left her almost without food or the necessaries of life.

She parted from me with the fortitude that becomes a Saint, realizing the responsibilities of her companion. I quote from my journal:

"Phoebe, farewell! Be of good cheer; remember me in your prayers. I leave these pages for your perusal when I am gone. I shall see thy face again in the flesh. I go to obey the commands of Jesus Christ."

Although feeble, I walked to the banks of the Mississippi river. There President Young took me in a canoe (having no other conveyance) and paddled me across the river.

When we landed, I lay down on a side of sole leather, by the post office, to rest.

Brother Joseph, the Prophet of God, came along and looked at me.

"Well, Brother Woodruff," said he, "you have started upon your mission."

"Yes," said I, "but I feel and look more like a subject for the dissecting room than a missionary."

Joseph replied: "What did you say that for? Get up, and go along; all will be right with you!" ❦

Women figure in a great many engaging stories of pioneer pluck and resourcefulness. They seem to have been as ready as their male counterparts to bear whatever burden presented itself, to meet life's challenges gamely, to put their trust in the Lord and their hands to the task. The following accounts testify to their capacity to "bear all things."

While many Saints made their preparations to leave Nauvoo, Louisa Barnes Pratt wondered what to do, as her husband, Addison, was on a Church mission in the Pacific Islands. Without his support and without any other relatives in town, she felt overwhelmed by the call to leave Nauvoo and asked Church leaders for advice. Brother Brigham responded cheerfully, but clearly, "Ox team salvation is the safest way."

Louisa questioned why "those who had sent my husband to the ends of the earth did not call to inquire whether I could prepare myself for such a perilous journey." She was told:

"Sister Pratt, they expect you to be smart enough to go yourself without help, and even to assist others." The reply awakened in me a spirit of self-reliance. I replied, "Well, I will show them what I can do."

Determined to go it alone, Louisa outfitted a wagon and drove out of Nauvoo feeling "comparatively happy." ✦

Another Louisa, Louisa Free, who would become the wife of Daniel H. Wells, was also called on to perform a difficult assignment.

Although exceedingly desirous of crossing the plains with the first company of that year [1848], her father was unable to do more than barely provide the two wagons necessary to carry his family and provisions, and the requisite number of oxen to draw them. The luxury of an extra teamster to care for the second wagon was out of the question; and so Louisa, although but twenty-two years of age, and although she had never driven an ox in her life, heroically undertook the task of driving one of the outfits, and caring for a younger brother and sister.

The picture of her starting is somewhat amusing. After seeing that her allotment of baggage and provisions, along with her little brother and sister, had been stowed in the wagon; with a capacious old-fashioned sun-bonnet on her head, a parasol in one hand and an ox-whip in the other, she placed herself by the side of her leading yoke of oxen and bravely set her face westward. Matters went well enough for a short distance, considering her inexperience with oxen; but the rain began to pour, and shortly her parasol was found to be utterly inadequate, so in disgust she threw it into the wagon, and traveled on in the wet grass amid the pouring rain. Presently the paste-board stiffeners of her sun-bonnet began to succumb to the persuasive moisture, and before night, draggled and muddy, and thoroughly wet to the skin, her appearance was fully as forlorn as her condition was pitiable.

This was truly a discouraging start, but nothing daunted she pressed on with the company, and never allowed her spirits to flag. Arrived at the Sweetwater, her best yoke of oxen died from drinking the alkali water, and for a substitute she was obliged to yoke up a couple of cows. Then came the tug of war; for so irregular a proceeding was not to be tolerated for a moment by the cows, except under extreme compulsion. More unwilling and refractory laborers were probably never found, and from that point onward Louisa proceeded only by dint of the constant and vigorous persuasions of her whip.

During the journey a Mrs. McCarthy was confined; and it was considered necessary that Louisa should nurse her. But it was impossible for her to leave her team during the day; so it was arranged that she should attend the sick woman at night. For three weeks she dropped her whip each night when the column halted, and leaving her team to be cared for by the brethren, repaired to Mrs. McCarthy's wagon, nursing her through the night, and then seizing her whip again as the company moved forward in the morning.

However, she maintained good health throughout the journey, and safely piloted her heterodox outfit into the valley along with the rest of the company.

On the journey, after wearing out the three pairs of shoes with which she was provided, she was obliged to sew rags on her feet for protection. But each day these would soon wear through, and often she left bloody tracks on the cruel stones.

It was on this journey that she first became acquainted with Gen. Wells, to whom she was married shortly after they reached the valley. As the senior wife of that distinguished gentleman, "Aunt Louisa" is well known throughout Utah; and as a most unselfish and unostentatious dispenser of charity, and an ever-ready friend and helper of the sick and needy, her name is indellibly engraved on the hearts of thousands. ✦

Just as resourceful in rising to whatever the occasion required was Harriet A. Snow, wife of Lorenzo Snow.

A woman had died on the way, leaving three little children—one of them a helpless infant. Sister Snow was so wrought upon by the pitiful condition of the infant, that she weaned her own child and nursed the motherless babe. By a stupid blunder of her teamster, also, she was one night left behind, alone, with two little children on the prairie. Luckily for her, a wagon had broken down and had been abandoned by the company.

Depositing the babes in the wagon box, she made search, and found that some flour and a hand-bell had been left in the wreck, and with this scanty outfit she set about making supper. She first took the clapper out of the bell, then stopped up the hole where it had been fastened in. This now served her for a water-pitcher. Filling it at a brook some distance away, she wet up some of the flour; then, with some matches that she had with her, started a fire, and baked the flour-cakes, herself and thirteen-months-old child making their supper upon them. She then ensconced herself in the wagon with her babes, and slept till early morning, when her husband found her and complimented her for her ingenuity and bravery. ✦

The attitude with which responsibility is assumed is most surely a measure of the doer's charity or virtue. Mormon women were joined by others not of their faith but similarly endowed with a capacity to "bear all things" and even to view frontier hardship as a happy challenge. Such a one was Elinore Pruitt Stewart, whose collected letters about her experience have become a classic in western American literature. Widowed when her daughter was but two years old, she was on her own to make both a living and a life. Eventually, she struck out for Wyoming, taking a position as housekeeper for an irascible Scotsman. The letters she wrote back to the woman she once served as a domestic servant evidence her enthusiasm for writing as well as for work. They also show that she graced her work with occasional happy diversions. Below is a section of one her letters.

September 11, 1909

Dear Mrs. Coney,—

This has been for me the busiest, happiest summer I can remember. I have worked very hard, but it has been work that I really enjoy. Help of any kind is very hard to get here, and Mr. Stewart [her employer at this point, but eventually her husband] had been too confident of getting men, so that haying caught him with too few men to put up the hay. He had no man to run the mower and the stacker, so you can fancy what a place he was in.

I don't know that I ever told you, but my parents died within a year of each other and left six of us to shift for ourselves. Our people offered to take one here and there among them until we should all have a place, but we refused to be raised on the halves and so arranged to stay at Grandmother's and keep together. Well, we had no money to hire men to do our work, so had to learn to do it ourselves. Consequently I learned to do many things which girls more fortunately situated don't even know have to be done. Among the things I learned to do was the way to run a mowing-machine. It cost me many bitter tears because I got sunburned, and my hands were hard, rough, and stained with machine oil, and I used to wonder how any Prince Charming could overlook all that in any girl he came to. For all I had ever read of the Prince had to do with his "reverently kissing her lily-white hand," or doing some other fool trick with a hand as white as a snowflake. Well, when my Prince showed up he did n't lose much time in letting me know that "Barkis was willing," and I wrapped my hands in my old checked apron and took him up before he could catch his breath.

Then there was no more mowing, and I almost forgot that I knew how until Mr. Stewart got into such a panic. If he put a man to mow, it kept them all idle at the stacker, and he just could n't get enough men. I was afraid to tell him I could mow for fear he would forbid me to do so. But one morning, when he was chasing a last hope of help, I went down to the barn, took out the horses, and went to mowing. I had enough cut before he got back to show him I knew how, and as he came back manless he was delighted as well as surprised. I was glad because I really like to mow, and besides that, I am adding feathers to my cap in a surprising way. When you see me again you will think I am wearing a feather duster, but it is only that I have been said to have almost as much sense as a "mon," and that is an honor I never aspired to, even in my wildest dreams.

I have done most of my cooking at night, have milked seven cows every day, and have done all the hay-cutting, so you see I have been working. But I have found time to put up thirty pints of jelly and the same amount of jam for myself. I used wild fruits, gooseberries, currants, raspberries, and cherries. I have almost two gallons of the cherry butter, and I think it is delicious. I wish I could get some of it to you, I am sure you would like it.

We began haying July 5 and finished September 8. After working so hard and so steadily I decided on a day off, so yesterday I saddled the pony, took a few things I needed, and Jerrine [her daughter] and I fared forth.

325

Baby can ride behind quite well. We got away by sunup and a glorious day we had. We followed a stream higher up into the mountains and the air was so keen and clear at first we had on our coats. There was a tang of sage and of pine in the air, and our horse was midside deep in rabbit-brush, a shrub just covered with flowers that look and smell like goldenrod. The blue distance promised many alluring adventures, so we went along singing and simply gulping in summer.

[The letter then describes her fashioning a fishing pole from a birch stick and catching and cooking trout before riding home at sunset.] ✦

Among the notable literary portraits of durable women whose love not only lightened the burden of labor but also transformed it into joie de vivre *is that of Great-grandma in Ray Bradbury's delightful fictional revisit to his childhood in Green Town, Illinois. Having been born before the midpoint of the nineteenth century, Great-grandma exhibits a hefty measure of the pioneer spirit.*

FROM *DANDELION WINE*

She was a woman with a broom or a dustpan or a washrag or a mixing spoon in her hand. You saw her cutting piecrust in the morning, humming to it, or you saw her setting out the baked pies at noon or taking them in, cool, at dusk. She rang porcelain cups like a Swiss bell ringer, to their place. She glided through the halls as steadily as a vacuum machine, seeking, finding, and setting to rights. She made mirrors of every window, to catch the sun. She strolled but twice through any garden, trowel in hand, and the flowers raised their quivering fires upon the warm air in her wake. She slept quietly and turned no more than three times in a night, as relaxed as a white glove to which, at dawn, a brisk hand will return. Waking, she touched people like pictures, to set their frames straight.

But, now . . . ?

"Grandma," said everyone. "Great-grandma."

Now it was as if a huge sum in arithmetic were finally drawing to an end. She had stuffed turkeys, chickens, squabs, gentlemen, and boys. She had washed ceilings, walls, invalids, and children. She had laid linoleum, repaired bicycles, wound clocks, stoked furnaces, swabbed iodine on ten thousand grievous wounds. Her hands had flown all around about and down, gentling this, holding that, throwing baseballs, swinging bright croquet mallets, seeding black earth, or fixing covers over dumplings, ragouts, and children wildly strewn by slumber. She had pulled down shades, pinched out candles, turned switches, and—grown old. Looking back on thirty billions of things started, carried, finished and done, it all summed up, totaled out; the last decimal was placed, the final zero swung slowly into line. Now, chalk in hand, she stood back from life a silent hour before reaching for the eraser.

"Let me see now," said Great-grandma, "Let me see . . ."

With no fuss or further ado, she traveled the house in an ever-circling inventory, reached the stairs at last, and, making no special announcement, she took herself up three flights to her room where, silently, she laid herself out like a fossil imprint under the snowing cool sheets of her bed and began to die.

Again the voices:

"Grandma! Great-grandma!"

The rumor of what she was doing dropped down the stair well, hit, and spread ripples through the rooms, out doors and windows and along the street of elms to the edge of the green ravine.

"Here now, here!"

The family surrounded her bed.

"Just let me lie," she whispered.

Her ailment could not be seen in any microscope; it was a mild but ever-deepening tiredness, a dim weighting of her sparrow body; sleepy, sleepier, sleepiest.

As for her children and her children's children—it seemed impossible that with such a simple act, the most leisurely act in the world, she could cause such apprehension.

"Great-grandma, now listen—what you're doing is no better than breaking a lease. This house will fall down without you. You must give us at least a year's notice!"

Great-grandma opened one eye. Ninety years gazed calmly out at her physicians like a dust-ghost from a high cupola window in a fast-emptying house. "Tom . . . ?"

The boy was sent, alone, to her whispering bed.

"Tom," she said, faintly, far away, "in the Southern Seas there's a day in each man's life when he knows it's time to shake hands with all his friends and say good-by and sail away, and he does, and it's natural—it's just his time. That's how it is today. I'm so like you sometimes, sitting through Saturday matinees until nine at night when we send your dad to bring you home. Tom, when the time comes that the same cowboys are shooting the same Indians on the same mountaintop, then it's best to fold back the seat and head for the door, with no regrets and no walking backward up the aisle. So, I'm leaving while I'm still happy and still entertained."

[Twelve-year-old] Douglas was summoned next to her side.

"Grandma, who'll shingle the roof next spring?"

Every April for as far back as there were calendars, you thought you heard woodpeckers tapping the housetop. But no, it was Great-grandma somehow transported, singing, pounding nails, replacing shingles, high in the sky!

"Douglas," she whispered, "don't ever let anyone do the shingles unless it's fun for them."

"Yes'm."

"Look around come April, and say, 'Who'd like to fix the roof?' And whichever face lights up is the face you want, Douglas. Because up there on that roof you can see the whole town going toward the country and the country going toward the edge of the earth and the river shining, and the morning lake, and birds on the trees down under you, and the best of the wind all around above. Any one of those should be enough to make a person climb a weather vane some spring sunrise." ❧

Elinore Stewart and Great-grandma are in good company, domestically and otherwise, with Latter-day Saint women. At age ninety-three, Rhoda Richards (sister of Willard Richards) wrote:

I would not have it understood . . . that I have been a weakly, sickly, useless individual all my life. Those who have known me can say quite to the contrary. Some of our ambitious little girls and working women would doubtless be interested in a simple sketch of some few things which I have accomplished by manual labor. When myself and my sisters were only small girls, our excellent mother taught us how to work, and in such a wise manner did she conduct our home education that we always loved to work, and were never so happy as when we were most usefully employed. We knit our own and our brothers' stockings, made our own clothes, braided and sewed straw hats and bonnets, carded, spun, wove, kept house, and did everything that girls and women of a self-sustaining community would need to do. The day that I was thirteen years old I wove thirteen yards of cloth; and in twenty months, during which time I celebrated my eightieth birthday, I carded twenty weight of cotton, spun two hundred and fifteen balls of candlewicking, and two hundred run of yarn, prepared for the weaver's loom; besides doing my housework, knitting socks, and making shirts for "my boys" (some of the sons of my brothers). I merely make mention of these things as samples of what my life-work has been. I never was an idler, but have tried to be useful in my humble way, "doing what my hands found to do with all my might." I now begin to feel the weight of years upon me, and can no longer do as I have done in former years for those around me; but, through the boundless mercies of God, I am still able to wash and iron my own clothes, do up my lace caps, and write my own letters. . . . In my young days I buried my first and only love, and true to that affiance, I have passed companionless through life. ❧

Mary Elizabeth Woolley Chamberlain tells of another seemingly tireless woman.

Aunt Rachel [Simmons] had a large family of ten children, and was left a widow at 36. Aunt Net [Rachel's sister] had three daughters and had buried two sons. Aunt Rachel took a course in obstetrics, and was set apart as a midwife, by Wilford Woodruff, and practiced until she was over 70 years of age, bringing many hundreds of children into the world. She was a wonderful woman in many respects, had a constitution of iron, and a will as strong. She and Aunt Net were left with these 13 children, almost penniless, but courageously they fought their way thru. Aunt Net rented her little house and she kept house for all of them at Aunt Rachel's home while the latter went out nursing. She was often called out in the night and had to walk thru snow up to her knees for miles to deliver some poor woman who was unable to send a conveyance for her (cars were unknown in those days), and many times she had had to wrap the new baby in her own shawl for want of anything else to cover it. After being out all night I have seen her come home and stand at the wash tub all day, then in the evening she would get down on her hands and knees and play with the children, letting them get on her back and ride all around the room, till each of the smaller ones had a turn. She never seemed to get tired. ✦

Typically, women of this bent not only labored and bore their own burdens, but they lightened the burdens of others as well. And they did it in a variety of ways, as Ardeth Greene Kapp's reported reminiscence of her mother, Julia (June) Leavitt Greene, illustrates.

To help the family economy, June opened a one-room general store that, as Ardeth remembers, "had everything from mousetraps to English bone china . . .

"My mom ran this little store with all the dignity and the professionalism that you would expect in the finest store in the country," Ardeth remembers. "No matter what the weather was, she opened the store on time. No matter what the circumstances were, she never closed a minute early for fear a customer would come. She treated every customer with the same dignity you would expect for the most important person. . . ."

June was not, by circumstance or nature, the "traditional kind of mother," according to Ardeth. "I don't ever remember that she had hot cookies in the oven when I came home from school, but I remember that I worked beside her and that I saw her put store-bought cookies into the bags of people who couldn't afford them. I don't remember her reading stories to me, but I remember that she started the first lending library in our town of 300 people. Mother loved to read and bought a few good books and loaned them out for ten cents a book. Many people were able to read good books because she started a lending library. I learned to love to read.

"I don't remember that my mom closed the store to come to our school plays, but I remember that she was instrumental in influencing the school district to get some very good teachers in our school and to organize people to get music teachers to come from neighboring towns.

"Mom wasn't one who went with us on camping trips; it wasn't her style. But she was one who promoted the Glenwood band, and from our little town we had a band that played in very prestigious parades, like the Calgary Stampede. She brought dignity and importance as a leader in a little town. She wasn't the traditional kind of mom, but she was the best kind of mom for me. From her I learned loyalty, dependability, industry, and endurance." ✦

Eliza R. Snow, who spent her last dime for a bottle of ink before leaving Winter Quarters, stands as a prototype for womanly pluck and industry. One wonders, in reading from her autobiography, what the pioneer church would have done without her.

FROM "SKETCH OF MY LIFE"

As I had been intimately associated with, and had officiated as Secretary for the first organization [of the "Female Relief Society"], Pres. Young commissioned me to assist the Bishops in organizing Branches of the Society in their respective Wards; for at that time, the Bishops had not acquainted themselves with the movement, and did not know how to proceed. To me it was quite a mission, and I took much pleasure in its performance. I felt quite honored and much at home in my associations with the Bishops, and they appreciated my assistance. . . .

Not long after the re-organization of the Relief Society, Pres. Young told me he was going to give me another mission. Without the least intimation of what the mission consisted, I replied, "I shall endeavor to fulfil it." He said, "*I want you to instruct the sisters.*" Altho' my heart went "*pit a pat*" for the time being, I did not, and could not then form an adequate estimate of the magnitude of the work before me. To carry into effect the President's requisition, I saw, at once, involved public meetings and public speaking—also travel abroad, as the Branches of the Society of the sisterhood extended at that time, through several Counties in Utah, and ultimately, all the vallies of the mountains—numbering, at present date, nearly three hundred; besides other Branches in the U.S., Europe, Asia, Islands of the sea, wherever the "Church of Jesus Christ of Latter-day-Saints" has established its Branches. . . .

As if the task were not large enough, Eliza R. Snow also (in 1867) "organized the first Society of Young Ladies, called 'Young Ladies' Retrenchment Association,' under the direction of Pres. B. Young." She was also instrumental in the conception and organization of the Primary Association just over a decade later. She reports:

I have traveled from one end of Utah Ter. to the other—into Nevada & Idaho, in the interests of these organizations—have organized hundreds of the Young Ladies' and Primary Associations since their introduction.

In company of Mrs. Z. D. H. Young, my 1st Coun. in R.S. Central Board, I spent the Autumn & Winter of 1880–1 in St. George, officiating in the Temple for the dead, and visiting and organizing Associations in that interesting City, and adjacent country—having traveled one thousand ms. by team over jolting rocks and through bedded sand, occasionally camping out at night on long drives, before I started for home, and returned to Salt Lake City in March.

In Nov. 1875 I was notified of an appointment, and not long after received my credentials from Philadelphia, requiring me to take charge of the Woman's Department in Utah for the Centennial Fair. I saw at once that the proportions of the work before me, compared better with the elephant than the butterfly, but I never had shrunk from duty, and it was too late to begin.

She formed a committee of both Mormons and non-Mormons, enlisted presidents of Relief Societies and Young Ladies Associations, and went to the Utah legislature for an appropriation "which, for reasons satisfactorily explained, was not granted." Undaunted, the group sent a small exhibit to Philadelphia "and directed our energies toward a Territorial Fair . . . which we kept open during the summer of 1876, with grand success."

After closing the Fair, Prest. Young told me he wished the sisters to start a home-industry Store in the building occupied for the Fair: He proposed for us to sell on commission & everything sold must be of Home

Manufacture. Of course this required a new organization, for all engaged in it must be "Mormon" women, and interested in the developement of Utah.

. . . But experience proved that, no matter how many were obligated to sustain the enterprise, the weight of care and responsibility slid on to my shoulders. . . .

And that was not all. It devolved upon Eliza R. Snow, as she says, to "inaugurate a Hospital," which she did. A Board of Directors was formed and, she reports,

. . . I was required to preside, which, although acknowledging the honor conferred, I accepted with the greatest reluctance—reluctance that approached nearly to obstinacy. I saw at once that we were grasping a Mammoth—that as we had to commence at the bed-rock—build additions—make repairs in the building [vacated by St. Mary's Hospital], and fit up in every department, much thought, labor, and time must be devoted in that direction.

She took on the task with the promise that when things were up and running, she would be relieved of the assignment.

In connexion with the "Board of Directors," which consisted of ten ladies, I spent very much time—calling, and attending Board meetings—consulting *etc. etc.,* and succeeded beyond our most sanguine anticipations. Although many of our patients were unable to pay expenses for treatment, by liberal donations we were enabled to fit up the building, supply each department, and pay our work-hands, nurses, *etc.* But *our* remuneration consisted in the consciousness of doing our duty, and in the sweet enjoyment which follows extending relief to suffering humanity—not one of us received one cent for our services—we were not hirelings—dollars and cents, with us personally, were out of the question. ✦

In both pioneer and later times, there has been much mutual sharing of burdens, as described in this poem by Orson Scott Card.

LOOKING WEST

1

Grandfather is home from Seattle.
He smiles as we turn him and we smile back,
trying not to remember that his wasted arms
once tossed us high or tickled us to tears;
memories must be thrust from this room,
for even the light ones are melting and dark.

His last years, looking westward to the sea,
he learned the faces of sunset through his window;
now there is no glass holding him back,
only the weight of his own life
that drags him to his bed,
that holds him home.

He speaks to his children and loves them patiently;
with his help we conceal our gathering grief,
praying against hope that we can hold him,
even while his feeble legs long to take another step.

2

Old Mother stands at the window.
Old Mother bathes in blue light,
rests her hands in the white water
as the last dusk drifts in the kitchen window;
the dishes are done.
She smiles at the window sill,
and the sill reflects all the evening.
It shines from her shining it.
The window is clear because she cleaned it.
Her face is loving because she etched it
with tears, creased it with laughter,
furrowed it with worry, then let it rest.

Old Mother faces west
because the window faces west.
She smiles to remember
the stone at Father's head.
On the right it tells Father's name,
his date of birth, the day he died;
on the left old Mother's name,
her date of birth, and a space.
Soon, she thinks. Not today,
because the petunias need thinning
and the carpet needs sweeping,
but it will be soon.

She takes the plug from the sink
and as the water drains
she dries her hands.

Hugh B. Brown spoke of carrying burdens in this address to Salt Lake Temple workers on January 12, 1964:

FROM "DO YOUR DUTY AND BE BLESSED"

God bless you, my brothers and sisters; by virtue of my office and the Priesthood I bear, I bless you collectively and individually. There are those who have come here this morning with some burdens on their hearts. There are those who are carrying some heavy crosses. There are those who are sorrowful and bereaved. There are those who are somewhat lacking in understanding of the reason for things. I had a call yesterday from Chicago, where a mother's little newborn babe, not properly formed, is doomed to die, and the mother said, "Why, why, should this happen?" There are those here this morning who have been asking, "Why, why is my lot what it is?" The only answer I can give is this: God, your Father, is all-wise and has a love for you beyond anything that any man can comprehend. In wisdom and all-pervading love, He is guiding us, and whatever happens to us we may eventually understand to be a blessing. In my own life, I find myself expressing gratitude to God for some of the things which, if I could, I would have avoided, but through those experiences I learned some lessons I could not have learned in any other way. And now, looking back, I thank God that He gave me strength enough to carry my cross. The greatest lesson He taught us while He was on the earth was how to carry a cross, and do it uncomplainingly. ✦

What we decide to do, in the process of bearing our own and each other's burdens, is of enormous importance, as explained by Viktor Frankl, who was imprisoned in a Nazi concentration camp.

FROM *MAN'S SEARCH FOR MEANING*

What was really needed [by those in the camp] was a fundamental change in our attitude toward life. We had to learn ourselves and, furthermore, we had to teach the despairing men, that *it did not really matter what we expected from life, but rather what life expected from us.* We needed to stop asking about the meaning of life, and instead to think of ourselves as those who were being questioned by life—daily and hourly. Our answer must consist, not in talk and meditation, but in right action and in right conduct. Life ultimately means taking the responsibility to find the right answer to its problems and to fulfill the tasks which it constantly sets for each individual. ✦

But be ye doers of the word, and not hearers only. (James 1:22.) ✦

Again, Hugh B. Brown expresses the need for us to carry on, regardless of our station in life.

FROM "IN SPITE OF EVERYTHING"

Each one of us must live with himself throughout eternity, and each one is now working on the kind of man he must live with throughout eternity. Let us determine for ourselves the kind of man our eternal companion is to be. I say now is the time to act, it is neither too early nor too late.

Some young men say, "When I get older I will do something worth while, but let me enjoy my carefree youth." Let me bring to your attention a few examples of young men who did things while they were young.

Jefferson was 33 years old when he drafted the Declaration of Independence.

Benjamin Franklin was 26 when he wrote *Poor Richard's Almanac.*

Dickens was 24 when he began his *Pickwick Papers* and 25 when he wrote *Oliver Twist.*

McCormack was only 23 when he invented the reaper, and Newton was 24 when he formulated the law of gravitation.

May I add to this quotation, Joseph Smith was less than 15 when he had his first vision, 24 when he translated the Book of Mormon, 25 when the Church was organized, and he died a young man—yet he left an imprint upon this world second only to that of Christ the Lord.

Jesus Christ, himself, was only 30 when He began His transcendent mission which lasted only three years but affected the whole world and will yet redeem it.

Well, now, you older men, has your chance passed? You high priests, seventies, and elders, is it too late for you to do something worth while? Let me bring you another set of figures:

Immanuel Kant was 74 when he wrote his finest philosophical work.

Verdi was 80 when he produced "Falstaff" and 84 when he produced "Ave Maria."

Goethe was 80 when he completed "Faust."

Tennyson was 80 when he wrote "Crossing the Bar."

Michelangelo completed his greatest work at 87.

Titian at 98, painted the historic picture, "The Battle of Lepantos."

Justice Holmes was 90 when he was still writing brilliant opinions. . . .

President David O. McKay, past 90, is recognized world-wide as a dynamic and inspired religious leader. He is carrying a load which would buckle the knees of many younger men. At his advanced age he still leads us, shows us the way, and sets the pace.

But perhaps some of you say, "Well, I have some handicaps." Sarah Bernhardt had as her motto, "In spite of everything." Paul Speicher, writing

. . . about what happens to men who refuse to be stopped, reminds us of some statistics, reminds us of what can happen to a man if he has the will to do, and knows what he wants to do.

"Cripple a man and you have a Sir Walter Scott; put him in prison and you have a Banyan; bury him in the snow at Valley Forge and you have a George Washington; have him born in abject poverty and you have an Abraham Lincoln; load him with bitter racial prejudice and you have a Disraeli; afflict him with asthma until as a boy he lies choking in his father's arms and you have a Theodore Roosevelt; stab him with rheumatic pains until for years he cannot sleep without an opiate and you have a Steinmetz; put him in a grease pit in a locomotive round house and you have a Walter P. Chrysler; make him a second fiddle in an obscure orchestra in South America and you have a Toscanni."

History rests on the shoulders of those who accepted the challenges of difficulties and drove through to victory in spite of everything. ❦

But he that received seed into the good ground is he that heareth the word, and understandeth it; which also beareth fruit, and bringeth forth, some an hundredfold, some sixty, some thirty. (Matthew 13:23.) ❦

In the priesthood address quoted above, President Brown also implies—through a lengthy story about a father remorseful over his earlier and prolonged impatience with his small son—that we must learn to "bear" one another, or "bear with" one another. We are asked not only to carry each other's burdens but actually to tolerate one another—the irritating habits and opinions, the preferences, the tastes, the needs—because we love one another. We must learn to accept and value others for what they are, and to resist the temptation to judge and condemn, or to remodel a loved one to fit our own preferred design.

The following good-natured satire of "woman's work" would probably never see print today, but it was entirely acceptable to the writer's eighteenth-century audience. The author intentionally stereotypes male and female roles, and just as intentionally trivializes housekeeping enterprises. Implicit in his banter is the assumption that men have to bear a good deal of foolishness in order to maintain domestic tranquility. Clearly, in his view, "woman's work" has less value than men's, is even trivial and must be borne with. It is, in fact, a nuisance to him—

largely because it is not important to him. Loving one another means valuing each other's contributions and gifts. Charitable or not, we can enjoy this bit of comedy as a quaint period piece. The obviously male author, Francis Hopkinson, describes spring housecleaning, which even in my childhood was as regular as May.

FROM "ON WHITEWASHING"

There is no season of the year in which the lady may not, if she pleases, claim her privilege; but the latter end of May is generally fixed upon for the purpose. The attentive husband may judge, by certain prognostics, when the storm is nigh at hand. If the lady grows uncommonly fretful, finds fault with the servants, is discontented with the children, and complains much of the nastiness of everything about her: these are symptoms which ought not to be neglected, yet they sometimes go off without any further effect. But if, when the husband rises in the morning, he should observe in the yard a wheelbarrow with a quantity of lime in it, or should see certain buckets filled with a solution of lime in water, there is no time for hesitation. He immediately locks up the apartment or closet where his papers, and private property are kept, and putting the key into his pocket, betakes himself to flight. A husband, however beloved, becomes a perfect nuisance during this season of female rage. His authority is superseded, his commission suspended, and the very scullion who cleans the brasses in the kitchen becomes of more importance than him. He has nothing for it but to abdicate, for a time, and run from an evil which he can neither prevent nor mol[l]ify.

The husband gone, the ceremony begins. The walls are stripped of their furniture—paintings, prints, and looking-glasses lie in huddled heaps about the floors; the curtains are torn from their testers, the beds crammed into windows, chairs and tables, bedsteads and cradles crowd the yard; and the garden fence bends beneath the weight of carpets, blankets, cloth cloaks, old coats, under petticoats, and ragged breeches. *Here* may be seen the lumber of the kitchen, forming a dark and confused mass for the fore-ground of the picture; gridirons and frying-pans, rusty shovels and broken tongs, joint stools, and the fractured remains of rush-bottomed chairs. *There* a closet has disgorged its bowels—rivetted plates and dishes, halves of china bowls, cracked

339

tumblers, broken wine-glasses, phials of forgotten physic, papers of unknown powders, seeds and dried herbs, tops of tea-pots, and stoppers of departed decanters—from the rag hole in the garret, to the rat hole in the cellar, no place escapes unrummaged. It would seem as if the day of general doom was come, and the utensils of the house were dragged forth to judgment.

In this tempest, the words of king *Lear* unavoidably present [themselves], and might with little alteration be made strictly applicable.

> Let the great gods,
> That keep this dreadful pudder o'er our heads,
> Find out their enemies now. Tremble thou wretch
> That hast within thee undivulged crimes
> Unwhipt of justice.
> Close pent-up guilt,
> Rive your concealing continents, and ask
> These dreadful summoners grace.

This ceremony completed, and the house thoroughly evacuated, the next operation is to smear the walls and ceilings with brushes, dipped in a solution of lime, called WHITE-WASH; to pour buckets of water over every floor; and scratch all the partitions and wainscots with hard brushes, charged with soft soap and stonecutter's sand.

. . . The misfortune is, that the sole object is to make things *clean*. It matters not how many useful, ornamental, or valuable articles suffer mutilation or death under the operation. . . .

I know a gentleman here who is fond of accounting for every thing in a philosophical way. He considers this, what I call a *custom*, as a real, periodical disease, peculiar to the climate. . . . he found the distemper to be incurable; but after much study, he thought he had discovered a method to divert the evil he could not subdue. For this purpose, he caused a small building, about twelve feet square, to be erected in his garden, and furnished with some ordinary chairs and tables, and a few prints of the cheapest sort. His hope was, that when the whitewashing frenzy seized the females of his family, they might repair to this apartment, and scrub, and scour, and smear to their hearts' content; and so spend the violence of the disease in this outpost, whilst he enjoyed himself in quiet at head-quarters. But the experiment did not answer his expectation. It was impossible it should, since a principal part of the gratification consists in the lady's having an uncontrolled right to torment her husband, at least once in every year; to turn him out of doors, and take the reins of government into her own hands. ⬥

The description of a virtuous woman in Proverbs 31, cited in a previous chapter, is a sound rebuttal to the attitudes playfully represented above. I am reminded, too, of a Peanuts *comic strip in which Linus concludes that love means playing a game with a friend when he wants to, even if you might prefer another activity.*

Doing one's part in the world of work, bearing one's share of the load (and then some), has been a favorite subject of children's and adults' literature alike, literature that appeals to all ages. I add here, for the reader's enjoyment, a number of choice writings, mainly secular, on the subject. There is among them, you will note, a minority report or two.

WHEN YOUNG MELISSA SWEEPS

When young Melissa sweeps a room
I vow she dances with the broom!
She curtsies in a corner brightly
And leads her partner forth politely.
Then up and down in jigs and reels,
With gold dust flying at their heels,
They caper. With a whirl or two
They make the wainscot shine like new;
They waltz beside the hearth, and quick
It brightens, shabby brick by brick.
A gay gavotte across the floor,
A Highland fling from door to door,
And every crack and corner's clean
Enough to suit a dainty queen.
If ever you are full of gloom,
Just watch Melissa sweep a room!
(Nancy Byrd Turner.)

CLEAN CLARA

WHAT! not know our Clean Clara?
Why, the hot folks in Sahara,
And the cold Esquimaux,
Our little Clara know!
Clean Clara, the Poet sings,
Cleaned a hundred thousand things!

She cleaned the keys of the harpsichord,
She cleaned the hilt of the family sword,
She cleaned my lady, she cleaned my lord;
All the pictures in their frames,
Knights with daggers, and stomachered dames—
Cecils, Godfreys, Montforts, Græmes,
Winifreds—all those nice old names!

. . . .

She cleaned the Dutch-tiles in the place,
She cleaned some very old-fashioned lace;
The Countess of Miniver came to her,
"Pray, my dear, will you clean my fur?"
All her cleanings are admirable;

To count your teeth you will be able,
If you look in the walnut table!

She cleaned the tent-stitch and the sampler;
She cleaned the tapestry, which was ampler;
Joseph going down into the pit,
And the Shunammite woman with the boy in a fit;

. . . .

She cleaned the cage of the cockatoo,
The oldest bird that ever grew;
I should say a thousand years old would do—
I'm sure he looked it; but nobody knew;

She cleaned the china, she cleaned the delf,
She cleaned the baby, she cleaned herself!

To-morrow morning she means to try
To clean the cobwebs from the sky;
Some people say the girl will rue it,
But my belief is she will do it.

So I've made up my mind to be there to see:
There's a beautiful place in the walnut-tree;
The bough is as firm as the solid rock;
She brings out her broom at six o'clock.
(William Brighty Rands.)

It should be no surprise that the prolific Puritan Cotton Mather had something to say on the subject too.

FROM BONIFACIUS

In moving for the *devices* of *good neighborhood,* a principal motion which I have to make is that you consult the *spiritual* interests of your neighborhood, as well as the *temporal.* Be concerned lest the *deceitfulness of sin* undo any of the neighbors. If there be any *idle persons* among them, I beseech you, cure them of their *idleness;* don't nourish 'em and harden 'em in that; but find *employment* for them. Find 'em *work;* set 'em to *work;* keep 'em to *work.* Then [give] as much of your other bounty to them as you please. ❦

There are, however, times, as Thoreau said, when the bloom of the moment cannot be sacrificed to labor of the hands; and others have echoed his sentiment. Debate will always ensue between the relative merits of the life of action as opposed to the life of contemplation.

On the latter side of the argument, Robert Louis Stevenson has written a delightful essay that he titles "An Apology for Idlers." If not taken as a rationale for abandoning all employment, the piece offers an interesting perspective on the "busyness" we sometimes mistake for well-doing. Idleness, as Stevenson defines the term, is the opposite of lazily doing nothing. The work drudge, not the active "idler," he says, may be the chronic waster of time. (The essay appears in The Lantern-Bearers and Other Essays, pp. 39–40.)

The truly contemplative life, especially if contemplation is prompted by the desire for truth and understanding, is anything but idle. The Savior himself taught that principle by his own example and by the example of others, particularly in the instance when Martha complained about her sister Mary's leaving off domestic duties to sit at the Master's feet. His teaching is echoed in an early thirteenth-century document, prepared by an unknown cleric, to instruct three women who had elected to become religious recluses.

FROM "UNSPOTTED FROM THE WORLD"

Mary and Martha were both sisters, yet their lives were different. Ye anchoresses have taken you to Mary's part, which our Lord Himself praised: . . . "Martha, Martha," said He, "thou art in great turmoil; Mary hath chosen better, and nothing shall take from her her part." Housewifeship is Martha's part, and Mary's part is stillness and rest from all the world's noise, that nothing may hinder her from hearing God's voice. And look what God saith, that nothing shall take from you this part. Martha had her office; let her be, and sit ye with Mary stonestill, at God's feet, and harken to Him alone. Martha's business is to feed and clothe poor men, like as doth a lady of the house; Mary ought not to meddle in this; and if anyone blame her, God himself will defend her for this, as holy writ maketh known. ✤

To some it falls to bear responsibility for needful action and change, and to some it falls to accept their given circumstances and seek instead a different level of thinking and being. And to all can come the refreshment of momentarily abandoning labor.

I MEANT TO DO MY WORK TODAY

I meant to do my work to-day—
But a brown bird sang in the apple-tree,
And a butterfly flitted across the field,
And all the leaves were calling me.

And the wind went sighing over the land
Tossing the grasses to and fro,
And a rainbow held out its shining hand—
So what could I do but laugh and go?
(Richard LeGallienne.)

Without work, however, play, and perhaps even contemplation, would lose the power to renew us; and good work is its own reward, as Thoreau also said.

The laborer is recompensed by his labor, not by his employer. Industry is its own wages. Let us not suffer our hands to lose one jot of their handiness by looking behind to a mean recompense, knowing that our true endeavor cannot be thwarted, nor we be cheated of our earnings unless by not earning them. ❧

Writers typically portray the well-lived life as an unpretentious one filled with good work. In his Autobiography, Benjamin Franklin tells of inscribing his parents' marble headstone with these words of tribute to their natural diligence:

Josiah Franklin
and
Abiah his Wife
Lie here interred.
They lived lovingly together in Wedlock
Fifty-five years.
Without an Estate or any gainful Employment,[1]
By constant labour and Industry,
With God's Blessing,
They maintained a large Family
Comfortably;
And brought up thirteen Children,
And seven Grand Children
Reputably.

---

1. That is, appointment of consequence, or inheritance.

From this Instance, Reader,
Be encouraged to Diligence in thy Calling,
And distrust not Providence.
He was a pious & prudent Man,
She a discreet and virtuous Woman.
Their youngest Son,
In filial Regard to their Memory,
Places this Stone.

Significantly, the epitaph Benjamin Franklin wrote for his own headstone identifies him by his trade as a printer rather than as a statesman, an inventor, a writer, or anything else.

The body of Benjamin Franklin, printer, like the cover of an old book, its contents torn out and stripped of its lettering and gilding, lies here, food for worms. But the work shall not be lost; for it will, as he believed, appear once more in a new and more elegant edition, revised and corrected by the Author. ❧

Ida M. Tarbell extolls the virtues of work in this essay:

FROM "WORK"

I have never in my life undertaken a fresh piece of work [as a writer] that I have not been obliged to take myself by the scruff of the neck and seat myself at my desk and keep my hand on the scruff until my revolt had subsided. That is, I know the difficulties in steady work. If there was nothing in it but the fruits of barter, I would rather trust myself to the road. . . .

Here on earth everything works—the grain of sand, the oaks, the clouds—works and incessantly changes, passing from one form to another, for nothing dies as a fact. The earth tolerates no dead beats; it keeps everything busy. If it did not it would be out of step in the universe in which it travels year in and year out, never behindhand, never off the track—sunrise and sunset, moonrise and moonset always on schedule.

If I am to be happy in this steady-working world I must work, too; otherwise I'll suffer discomfort, uneasiness akin to that which comes to me when in walking I cannot keep step with my companion, when in talking I cannot follow the argument or catch the meaning, when in singing I am off key.

There is a vast unhappiness, inexplicable to those it afflicts, which comes from idleness in a working world. The idle are self-destructive as would be a star which announced that it was going to stand still for an eon or two.

What the idler fails to understand is the beauty of rhythm, the beauty and the excitement of being in his place in the endless chain of creative motion which is the essential nature of this magnificent and incomprehensible universe. . . .

Work means health. The very urges of our bodies show that nature expects action of us if we are to be in health. From the time we kick our heels and try our lungs on being released from our mother's womb we cry for work. Watch the child—never still. It is obeying the order of nature to keep busy.

How defeated and restless the child that is not doing something in which it sees a purpose, a meaning. It is by its self-directed activity that the child, as years pass, finds its work, the thing it wants to do and for which it is finally willing to deny itself pleasure, ease, even sleep and comfort.

In such work comes perhaps the deepest of all work's satisfactions: the consciousness that you are growing, the realization that gradually there is more skill in your fingers and your mind. . . .

But work does more for you. It is the chief protection you have in suffering, despair, disillusionment, fear. There is no antidote to mental and spiritual uncertainty and pain like a regular job.

Here, then, is my philosophy of work—the reasons why after fifty-six years of unbroken trial I thank God for it. It is something which reaches the deepest needs, helps reconcile the baffling mystery of the universe, helps establish order in a disorderly society; which puts despair to sleep. ✦

Pervading LDS poet Marden Clark's reminiscence of his father's nightly prayer is the steadfastness of the man, his devotion to work and his sense of duty.

T O O   L A T E   O N   F A T H E R ' S   D A Y

"And may our sleep be sweet this night."
    The ritual words, resonant, clear,
    That ended every family prayer
Came as relief to us whose plight

You never seemed to feel. Your long
    And earnest prayer stretched forth
    Embracing everything of worth
And everyone: His mighty throng,

His tender care, his love, his birth,
    His bounteous blessings, all our health
    And strength, our heritage, our length
Of space and time on blessed earth,

Our onion patch, the dryfarm wheat,
    President Grant, our loved ones all,
    Leaders of nations, any who call
On him in pain or sorrow, the feet

Of missionaries that they be led
    To doors of honest in heart, the poor,
    The sick and afflicted, all those sore
In heart or mind, even our dead.

Thus you'd solicit blessings from
    An unseen power you'd never think
    To doubt: you knew how deep we drink
From wells we can't begin to plumb.

To us who knelt on hardwood floors
    And felt the creep of time across
    The grain that marked our knees, the loss
Of play on summer nights outdoors

Kept all but echoes of your words
    Along the surface of our minds.
    We felt few doubts about the kinds
Of beings and powers up there where birds

Could soar and sing, beyond our reach,
    Their bright evangels to our God;
    You'd taught us much about the word,
His rod, to let us know he'd teach

Us more. Content with that we'd keep
    A restless sense of all that flow
    Of words we knew, like us, must go
At last and finally down to sleep.

And sleep we did. Our work and play
    Would help your invocation hold
    —But benediction too: You'd fold
Us in your love: How could we stray?

Yes, we squirmed enough and more.
    But found your prayer fulfilled in us
    As now we find your life is just
Fulfilled in death. And now the store

Of fruit you brought, as mellow too
    As you'd become, will save us from
    The grief we can't but feel. You've come
To rest—the only kind you'd know.

And now you move through dark to light:
    We softly sing you on your way—
    You'd never stop, even with your day,
But may your sleep be sweet this night.

"The sleep of a labouring man is sweet." (Ecclesiastes 5:12.)

13

CHARITY BELIEVETH
ALL THINGS

Faith is the substance of things hoped for,

the evidence of things not seen.

HEBREWS 11:1

I never saw a Moor—
I never saw the Sea—
Yet know I how the Heather looks
And what a Billow be.

I never spoke with God
Nor visited in Heaven—
Yet certain am I of the spot
As if the Checks were given—
(Emily Dickinson.)

We believe in God, the Eternal Father, and in His Son, Jesus Christ, and in the Holy Ghost. (First Article of Faith.)

While Christianity certainly has no corner on goodness and charity, it would be difficult for a Christian to separate the charity Paul and Mormon describe, "the pure love of Christ" (Moroni 7:47), from the author and embodiment of that charity. As Paul specifically declares, charity "believeth all things." The word "all" should not be misconstrued to suggest gulli-

350

bility, lack of discernment, or any other such laxity of reason and judgment. More likely, it is meant to suggest a perspective willing to encompass all truth; willing to believe in God—that is, to trust him as well as to acknowledge that he exists; willing to believe in the goodness and purposefulness of life; willing to believe that the Lord is ultimately in charge of the earth's and our own destinies; willing to trust in the decency of other human beings. Therefore, the selections in this section speak of faith, in both its specific sense—faith in God—and its general sense.

Most of the stories in this book are stories of faith, and most could have been used in the present chapter. In view of this, I have chosen to represent here mainly—but not entirely—important treatises on faith, lightened by a little poetry. Like the numberless discourses on it, faith can be both simple and sophisticated, depending on the disposition, experience, and calling of the believer. Each writer brings a slightly different perspective to the subject. First, Alma:

Faith is not to have a perfect knowledge of things; therefore if ye have faith ye hope for things which are not seen, which are true. . . .

Now, as I said concerning faith—that it was not a perfect knowledge—even so it is with my words. Ye cannot know of their surety at first, unto perfection, any more than faith is a perfect knowledge.

But behold, if ye will awake and arouse your faculties, even to an experiment upon my words, and exercise a particle of faith, yea, even if ye can no more than desire to believe, let this desire work in you, even until ye believe in a manner that ye can give place for a portion of my words.

Now, we will compare the word unto a seed. Now, if ye give place, that a seed may be planted in your heart, behold, if it be a true seed, or a good seed, if ye do not cast it out by your unbelief, that ye will resist the Spirit of the Lord, behold, it will begin to swell within your breasts; and when you feel these swelling motions, ye will begin to say within yourselves—It must needs be that this is a good seed, or that the word is good, for it beginneth to enlarge my soul; yea, it beginneth to enlighten my understanding, yea, it beginneth to be delicious to me. . . .

But if ye neglect the tree [that has sprung up from the planted seed], and take no thought for its nourishment, behold it will not get any root;

and when the heat of the sun cometh and scorcheth it, because it hath no root it withers away, and ye pluck it up and cast it out.

Now, this is not because the seed was not good, neither is it because the fruit thereof would not be desirable; but it is because your ground is barren, and ye will not nourish the tree, therefore ye cannot have the fruit thereof.

And thus, if ye will not nourish the word, looking forward with an eye of faith to the fruit thereof, ye can never pluck of the fruit of the tree of life.

But if ye will nourish the word, yea, nourish the tree as it beginneth to grow, by your faith with great diligence, and with patience, looking forward to the fruit thereof, it shall take root; and behold it shall be a tree springing up unto everlasting life. (Alma 32:21, 26–28, 38–41.) ❖

James E. Talmage offers a thoughtful consideration of the nature of faith in his discussion of the fourth Article of Faith. Below are a few excerpts from his discourse:

FROM "FAITH AND REPENTANCE"

The predominating sense in which the term faith is used throughout the scriptures is that of full confidence and trust in the being, purposes, and words of God. Such trust, if implicit, will remove all doubt concerning things accomplished or promised of God, even though such things be not apparent to or explicable by the ordinary senses of mortality. . . .

. . . Belief, in one of its accepted senses, may consist in a merely intellectual assent, while faith implies such confidence and conviction as will impel to action. . . . Belief is in a sense passive, an agreement or acceptance only; faith is active and positive, embracing such reliance and confidence as will lead to works. Faith in Christ comprises belief in Him, combined with trust in Him. One cannot have faith without belief; yet he may believe and still lack faith. Faith is vivified, vitalized, living belief.

. . . Neither belief nor its superior, actual knowledge, is efficient to save; for neither of these is faith. If belief be a product of the mind, faith is of the heart; belief is founded on reason, faith largely on intuition.

We frequently hear it said that faith is imperfect knowledge; that the first disappears as the second takes its place; that now we walk by faith but some day we shall walk by the sure light of knowledge. In a sense this is true; yet it must be remembered that knowledge may be as dead and unproductive in good works as is faithless belief. Those confessions of the devils, that Christ was the Son of God, were based on knowledge; yet the great truth, which they knew, did not change their evil natures. . . .

. . . Knowledge is to wisdom what belief is to faith, one an abstract principle, the other a living application. ❧

Orson Pratt describes the general concept but defines the terms a little differently.

FROM "TRUE FAITH"

It is the intention of the author in this chapter to define and simplify the great principle, called FAITH. This is not an abstract principle, separate and distinct from mind, but it is a certain condition or state of the mind itself. When the mind believes or has confidence in any subject, or statement, or proposition, whether correct or incorrect, it is then in possession of faith. To have faith is simply to believe. Faith and belief, therefore, are synonymous terms, expressive of the same idea.

Faith or belief is the result of evidence presented to the mind. Without evidence, the mind cannot have faith in anything. We believe that a stone will fall, when unsupported, on the evidence of past observation in relation to the falling of heavy bodies. We believe that day and night will continue on the evidence of past experience in regard to the uniformity of nature's laws. We believe that space is boundless, and duration endless, on the evidence, presented by the mind itself, which at once perceives the absurdity of either space or duration being limited. We believe in all self-evident truths, on the evidence that all opposite propositions to these truths are absurd. We believe in all the great truths of science, either on the evidences of our own investigations, or on the researches of others. We believe in historical facts on the evidence of the historian. Faith in every fact, statement, truth, or proposition which we have confidence in, is, in all cases whatsoever, derived from evidence. Therefore, without evidence, faith can have no existence.

Faith is of two kinds, namely *false* and *true*. A false faith is the result of giving credence to false evidence: a true faith, the result derived from true evidence. ◆

In a series of discourses titled The Kingdom of God, *Orson Pratt again takes up the subject of faith, though somewhat more specifically. He quotes Paul and adds, "Faith, in a more extended sense, is the* assurance of the mind *in relation to what has been, what is or what will be." He stresses again that "this* faith *or* assurance of the mind *is obtained only through evidence," and he gives examples of the difference between faith and perfect knowledge, and between true and false faith. Faith, that essential step toward eternal life, is the starting place, not the end, he says:*

On the morning of the Day of Pentecost, the large multitude of the Jews who were assembled, considered Jesus an imposter, but after hearing the evidence of the Old Testament prophets, combined with the evidence of the apostles who stood as living witnesses of the resurrection of Jesus, three thousand of them believed that He was the Son of God; the faith of these three thousand was founded wholly upon the evidences then set before them. The faith they had in this fact, was not different from faith in any other fact. The faith that Jesus is the Son of God, is the same as the faith that Solomon is the son of David; faith in both of these facts comes by evidence, and in no other way. Devils, as well as men, believe that Jesus is the Son of God. Devils' faith is the result of evidence the same as men's; in this respect, the faith of devils and human beings is alike. But abstract faith alone can benefit no being. Devils believe that Christ is the Son of God, and tremble.

Sinners may believe the same, and yet be damned. Saints may have the same faith, and yet, Judas-like, become the sons of perdition; the angels of heaven may have strong faith, and yet be thrust down to hell; so that faith alone will save neither devils, angels, nor men. Faith is essential to salvation; without faith no one can be saved; no one can even repent without first having faith. If a man does not believe in the existence of God, he will not believe in His revealed laws; neither will he believe that it is sinful to disregard those laws; he will not believe himself to be a sinner, neither will he believe that he will be punished in a future state for transgressing laws which he does not believe emanated from God. Faith must, therefore, precede repentance. Before mankind can properly repent, there are several things necessary to be believed: they must believe not only in the existence of God, but in the revealed laws of God; that is, in the laws He has given against doing evil. ✦

In a published discourse on faith, Matthew Cowley reiterates what Orson Pratt said about faith coming from evidence, and he even repeats some of Elder Pratt's examples. Elder Cowley, too, uses the term assurance, *pointing out that Joseph Smith's inspired rendering of Paul's phrase employs the word* assurance *in place of the King James word* substance.

FROM "FAITH"

This assurance of things hoped for must come through some evidence, either of a character which can be demonstrated in a tangible manner, or through some impression which gives an assurance to the mind of the individual possessing it, if to no other. This faith prompts to action all intelligent beings.

[Elder Cowley then goes on to "draw the line of distinction between faith in its general sense, and faith as a principle of power as enjoyed and exercised by those who are truly the people of God."]

Let us first remember that it is one thing to believe in the power of God as manifested by revelation, prophecy, healing, etc., when presented to us merely as the events of history, and altogether another thing to be confronted with the testimony of living apostles, presenting to the world doctrines that are unpopular and with which the cherished creeds of men have never failed to conflict—apostles who ask us to believe them to be servants of God, called by new revelation, and testing our faith by the promise that "if you will repent and be baptized" with honest hearts, you shall know for yourselves the truth, and need not depend upon the assertions of any other man for your knowledge concerning it. It is an undeniable fact of history that God has never sent a prophet to warn the world but He found thousands professing belief in the dead prophets, yet ready to reject and slay the living. It cannot be said that this generation is an exception, for the religious education they receive from the so-called "Christian pulpit["] is that apostles and prophets, together with the ancient gifts and powers of the gospel, are no longer needed; and if any come professing the ancient apostleship, they may reject them without investigation as "false prophets." They apparently forget that it would be difficult, if not impossible, to produce a counterfeit coin unless the genuine existed. ✦

Orson F. Whitney explains the pervasive necessity of faith.

FROM "THE MAINSPRING OF POWER"

The Moving Cause.—All power springs from faith. It is "the moving cause of all action" and "the foundation of all righteousness." [Lectures on Faith, Lecture 1, pp. 1, 2; See also Hebrews 11.] God did not create the principle of faith, but by means of it he created the worlds, and by means of it he controls and continues to have dominion over them. It is the faith of Omnipotence that upholds the universe.

A Negative Opinion.—A Christian minister, not of the orthodox school, with whom I was conversing on the subject of faith, tried to convince me that it was anything but an admirable quality. He even called it contemptible, declaring that it consisted of a weak willingness to believe—to believe anything, however improbable or absurd. In short, that it was mere credulity, nothing more.

A Spiritual Force.—When I referred to faith as a spiritual force, a principle of power, he said I was attaching to the term a significance that it had never borne, and for which there was no warrant. I then reminded him of the Savior's words: "If ye have faith as a grain of mustard seed, ye shall say unto this mountain, 'Remove hence to yonder place,' and it shall remove, and nothing shall be impossible unto you." [Matthew 17:20.] Whereupon he remarked rather flippantly: "Oh, it takes picks and shovels to move mountains."

Picks and Shovels.—And so it does—if one has no better way of moving them. But what about the faith necessary to handle pick and shovel? All energy springs from faith, and whether mountains are moved by man or by his Maker, it is faith that precedes the action and renders it possible. Yet here

356

was a professed minister of Christ, ignoring the teachings of Christ, and denying what all true Christians believe—that the smallest as well as the greatest acts of our lives spring from the exercise of faith. . . .

An Impelling Force.—Faith is the beating heart of the universe. Without it nothing can be accomplished, small or great, commonplace or miraculous. No work ever succeeded that was not backed up by confidence in some power, human or superhuman, that impelled and pushed forward the enterprise.

Those Who Believe.—It was not doubt that drove Columbus across the sea; it was faith—the impelling force of the Spirit of the Lord. [1 Nephi, 13:12.] It was not doubt that inspired Washington, Jefferson, Franklin, and other patriot fathers to lay broad and deep the foundations of this mighty republic, a hope and a refuge for oppressed humanity. It is not doubt that causes nations to rise and flourish, that induces great and good men in all ages and in all climes to teach and toil and sacrifice for the benefit of their fellows. It is faith that does such things. Doubt only hinders what faith would achieve. The men and women who move the world are the men and women who believe. ❦

Bruce R. McConkie speaks powerfully to the subject of faith.

FROM "FAITH IN GOD"

No faith unto life and salvation can be exercised in any false doctrine, in any false ordinance, or in any false system of religion. If a man believes with all his heart that there will be no resurrection; if every hope in his heart cries out in favor of annihilation of both soul and body at death; if he believes with every fiber of his being and every thought of his mind that death ends all—it does not matter one particle in the eternal sense. He cannot have faith in a doctrine that denies the resurrection. The fact, the reality, the truth is, there will be a resurrection, and there is nothing any of us can do about it one way or the other. A hope in an unseen expectancy that is false does not bring into being a single scintilla of faith. There is no such thing as faith unto life and salvation in a false doctrine. No man can exercise the slightest faith in infant baptism, or in baptism by sprinkling, or in a sacramental ordinance that has departed from the primitive similitude established by the Lord Jesus. All such are contrary to the order of heaven. They are not based and grounded on eternal truth. And faith is a hope in that which is not seen which is true. ✦

FROM "FAITH IN THE LORD JESUS CHRIST"

Those who work by faith must first have faith; no one can use a power that he does not possess, and the faith or power must be gained by obedience to those laws upon which its receipt is predicated. These we have set forth. Those who work by faith must believe in the Lord Jesus Christ and in his Father. They must accept at face value what the revealed word teaches as to the character, attributes, and perfections of the Father and the Son. They must then work the works of righteousness until they know within themselves that their way of life conforms to the divine will, and they must be willing to lay their all on the altar of the Almighty. ✦

FROM "THE FRUITS OF FAITH"

Faith is known by its fruits—on earth, in heaven, everywhere. Where the fruits of faith are found, there is faith; where there are no fruits, there is no faith. It is an eternal law of the universe that like begets like, that every tree brings forth after its own kind, and that the tree of faith bears, always and everlastingly, the fruit of faith. It is no more possible to pick the fruit of faith from the tree of unbelief than it is to harvest grapes from bramble bushes or figs from thistles. . . .

God created all men in his own image—physically, mentally, morally, spiritually. His offspring inherited from him the power and ability to become like him. Men are patterned after their Eternal Father, and if they ever become as their Maker, they must gain the same faith or power embodied in the Deity. To the extent that fallen men gain faith, they become like God and exercise his power. To the extent that they live in unbelief, they are without God in the world, do not exercise his power, are not in process of becoming like him, and cannot and will not be saved. ✦

Below is an excerpt from Joseph Smith's first of seven lectures on faith.

FROM "LECTURE FIRST"

On the Doctrine of the Church of Jesus Christ of Latter-day Saints, originally delivered before a Class of the Elders, in Kirtland, Ohio.

. . . .

If men were duly to consider themselves, and turn their thoughts and reflections to the operations of their own minds, they would readily discover that it is faith, and faith only, which is the moving cause of all action in them; that without it both mind and body would be in a state of inactivity, and all their exertions would cease, both physical and mental.

Were this class to go back and reflect upon the history of their lives, from the period of their first recollection, and ask themselves what principle excited them to action, or what gave them energy and activity in all their lawful avocations, callings, and pursuits, what would be the answer? Would it not be that it was the assurance which they had of the existence of things which they had not seen as yet? Was it not the hope which you had, in consequence of your belief in the existence of unseen things, which stimulated you to action and exertion in order to obtain them? Are you not dependent on your faith, or belief, for the acquisition of all knowledge, wisdom, and intelligence? Would you exert yourselves to obtain wisdom and intelligence unless you did believe that you could obtain them? Would you have ever sown, if you had not believed that you would reap? Would you have ever planted, if you had not believed that you would gather? Would you have ever asked, unless you had believed that you would receive? Would you have ever sought, unless you had believed that you would have found? Or, would you have ever knocked, unless you had believed that it would have been opened unto you? In a word, is there anything that you would have done, either physical or mental, if you had not previously believed? Are not all your exertions of every kind, dependent on your faith? Or, may we not ask, what have you, or what do you possess, which you have not obtained by reason of your faith? Your food, your raiment, your lodgings, are they not all by reason of your faith? Reflect, and ask yourselves if these things are not so. Turn your thoughts on your own minds, and see if faith is not the moving cause of all action in yourselves; and, if the moving cause in you, is it not in all other intelligent beings?

And as faith is the moving cause of all action in temporal concerns, so it is in spiritual; for the Saviour has said, and that truly, that "He that *believeth* and is baptized, shall be saved." Mark xvi.16

As we receive by faith all temporal blessings that we do receive, so we in like manner receive by faith all spiritual blessings that we do receive. But faith is not only the principle of action, but of power also, in all intelligent beings, whether in heaven or on earth. ❦

LUCY MACK SMITH

My father wandered labyrinthine ways
Of wars and wealth, of sorrow, earth, and sea
For years, until he fled the darkened maze
To hear his Savior's call: "Come unto me."
My sister held the slightest trace of breath.
I trembled fears my faith could not control
Until she rose, so bright, unheld by death.
The Lord had healed her body and my soul.
And now my Joseph's coming, young and slim,
His brother's shirt too big, hair out of place,
And breathless he speaks, praising: "I've seen Him,"
The suns of planets glowing in his face.
No Gabriel is needed at my door.
I've seen such light come resting twice before.
(Linda Madsen Sheffield.)

Parley P. Pratt wrote:

I will now venture to say that a believer in the Bible would be something that very few men have ever seen in this generation, with all its boasted religion; for there is a great difference between believing the book to be true when shut, and believing the things therein written. ❦

The following lines of verse and prayer appeared as a reprint in The Times and Seasons *(on April 15, 1845) with this introduction: "We present a page, preceding Genesis, from an old Bible printed in 1582, which is 263 years old. We have no fac simile of the border or type, but follow the arrangement and spelling."*

Of the incomparable treasure of the holy Scriptures,
with a prayer for the true use of
the same.

Here is the spring where waters flowe,
to quenche our heate of sinne:
Here is the tree where trueth doth grow,
to leade our lives therein:
Here is the judge that stintes the strife,
when mens devices faile:
Here is the bread that feedes the life,
that death cannot assaile.
The tidings of salv ation deare,
comes to our eares from hence:
The fortresse of our faith is here,
and shield of our defence.
Then be not like the hogge that hath
a pearle at his desire,
And takes more pleasure of the trough
and wallowing in the mire.
Reade not this booke in any case,
but with a single eye:
Reade not but first desire Gods grace,
to understand thereby.
Pray stil in faith with this respect,
to fructifie therein,
That knowledge may bring this effect,
to mortifie thy sinne.
Then happie thou in all thy life,
what so to thee befalles:

Yea, double happie shalt thou be,
when God by death thee calles.

O Gracious God and most mercifull Father, which hast vouchsafed
us the rich and precious Jewel of thy holy word, assist us with
thy Spirit, that it may be written in our hearts to our everlasting
comfort, to reforme us, to renew us according to thine owne Image,
to build us up, and edifie us into the perfect building of thy Christ,
sanctifying and encreasing in us all heavenly vertues. Graunt this
O heavenly Father, for Jesus Christs sake. Amen.

*One of the most famous poetic expressions of religious faith is William Blake's
"The Lamb," with its companion piece of a different tone that begins, "Tiger, tiger,
burning bright":*

THE LAMB

Little Lamb, who made thee?
Dost thou know who made thee?
Gave thee life, and bid thee feed,
By the stream, and o'er the mead;
Gave thee clothing of delight,
Softest clothing, woolly, bright;
Gave thee such a tender voice,
Making all the vales rejoice?
Little Lamb, who made thee?
Dost thou know who made thee?

Little Lamb, I'll tell thee,
Little Lamb, I'll tell thee.
He is callèd by thy name,
For He calls Himself a Lamb.
He is meek, and He is mild,
He became a little child.
I a child, and thou a lamb,
We are callèd by His name.

Little Lamb, God bless thee!
Little Lamb, God bless thee!

The following poem is known to most of us as a hymn:

LEAD, KINDLY LIGHT

[At Sea] Month Five: Day Seventeen
Lead, kindly Light, amid the encircling gloom
Lead Thou me on!
The night is dark, and I am far from home—
Lead Thou me on!
Keep Thou my feet; I do not ask to see
The distant scene—one step enough for me.

I was not ever thus, nor pray'd that thou
Shouldst lead me on.
I loved to choose and see my path, but now
Lead Thou me on!
I loved the garish day, and, spite of fears,
Pride ruled my will: remember not past years.

So long Thy power hath blest me, sure it still
Will lead me on,
O'er moor and fen, o'er crag and torrent, till
The night is gone;
And with the morn those angel faces smile
Which I have loved long since, and lost awhile.
(John Henry [Cardinal] Newman.)

James E. Talmage tells a story about the light of faith.

In my student days I waited in a snowstorm for a train. Long after midnight the train arrived, in a terrific whirl of wind and snow. I lingered behind my companions, as they hurriedly clamored aboard, for I was attracted by the engineer, who bustled about the engine, oiling some parts, adjusting others, and generally overhauling the panting locomotive. I ventured to speak to him, busy though he was. I asked how he felt on such a night—wild, weird, and furious, when the powers of destruction seemed to be let loose, abroad and uncontrolled, when the storm was howling and when danger threatened from every side. I thought of the possibility—the probability even—of snowdrifts or slides on the track; of bridges and high trestles, which may have been loosened by the storm; of these and other possible obstacles. I realized that in the event of accident through obstruction on, or disruption of the track, the engineer would be the most exposed to danger. All of these thoughts and others I expressed in hasty questioning of the bustling, impatient engineer.

His answer was a lesson not yet forgotten. In effect, he said, "Look at the engine headlight. Doesn't that light up the track for a hundred yards or more? Well, all I try to do is cover that hundred yards of lighted track. That I can see, and for that distance I know the roadbed is open and safe. And," he added with a merry twinkle in his eye, "believe me, I've never been able to drive this old engine of mine—God bless her!—so fast as to outstrip that hundred yards of lighted track. The light of the engine is always ahead of me!"

I boarded the train satisfied. For a little distance the storm-swept track was lighted up; for that short space the engineer drove on!

We may not know what lies ahead of us in the future years, nor even in the days or hours immediately beyond. But for a few yards, or possibly only a few feet, the track is clear, our duty is plain, our course is illuminated. For that short distance, for the next step, lighted by the inspiration of God, go on! ❧

One day while conversing with a member of his office staff and two others, Brigham Young was asked why "the Lord is not always at our side promoting universal happiness and seeing to it that the needs of people are met, caring especially for His Saints? Why is it so difficult at times?" Reportedly, President Young replied, "Because man is destined to be a God, and he must be able to demonstrate that he is for God and to develop his own resources so that he can act independently and yet humbly." He then added a statement that vividly explains his idea: "It is the way it is because we must learn to be righteous in the dark." (Brigham Young's

Office Journal, January 28, 1857 [quoted in Carolyn J. Rasmus, "Spiritual Valleys," Ensign, October 1984, p. 51].)

Lord, I believe; help thou mine unbelief. (Mark 9:24.) ❦

Adam S. Bennion tells this little anecdote to illustrate the principle of faith.

A minister of that city [Denver] in walking out into the fields discovered [a] boy flying his kite. It was a cloudy day, and as the minister approached the lad he said, "Son, what brings you into the field on such a day?"

"Oh," said the boy, "I am flying my kite."

"What, flying your kite," said the minister. "I do not see any kite."

"No," said the boy. "Maybe you don't see it. It is too cloudy for you to see it, but I know there is a kite up there. I can tell by the pull of it."

And men who subscribe honestly to the recipe given by Jesus can and will discover that there is a pull up there, which is man's finest and final evidence that it is God who is "up there." ❦

C. S. Lewis writes of his personal test of faith after the death of his wife to cancer. He had met her comparatively late in life, and they shared four years of extraordinary happiness. Understandably, her loss was devastating to him. In a book-length essay that charts his struggle and reassertion of faith, Lewis says the following:

FROM A GRIEF OBSERVED

When I lay these questions before God [about the necessity to choose God over a beloved mortal] I get no answer. But a rather special sort of "No answer." It's not the locked door. It is more like a silent, certainly not uncompassionate, gaze. As though He shook His head not in refusal but waiving the question. Like, "Peace, child; you don't understand."

Can a mortal ask questions which God finds unanswerable? Quite easily, I should think. All nonsense questions are unanswerable. How many hours are there in a mile? Is yellow square or round? Probably half the questions we ask—half our great theological and metaphysical problems—are like that.

And now that I come to think of it, there's no practical problem before me at all. I know the two great commandments, and I'd better get on with them. ✦

A good many poets have written about anticipated reunions with loved ones in the next life, most notably, perhaps, Elizabeth Barrett and Robert Browning. Others have expressed faith in another kind of reunion—with their Maker.

CROSSING THE BAR

Sunset and evening star,
And one clear call for me!
And may there be no moaning of the bar,
When I put out to sea.

But such a tide as moving seems asleep,
Too full for sound and foam,
When that which drew from out the boundless deep
Turns again home.

Twilight and evening bell,
And after that the dark!
And may there be no sadness of farewell,
When I embark;

For tho' from out our bourne of Time and Place
The flood may bear me far,
I hope to see my Pilot face to face
When I have crost the bar.
(Alfred, Lord Tennyson.)

HOMECOMING

I'm ready, Lord—just say the summoning word
And I will come on swift and anxious wings.

I've peeked around the curtains; I have heard
Celestial music. When the choir sings
I scent the sweet white fruit—the tree of life
(Remembered cravings well up 'round my tongue,
Whetted by prophets) ready, ripe-and-rife,
The victor's trophy ancient seers have sung.

This is the mission I've looked forward to:
My spirit elevating out-of-bounds,
Fetters will fall away, I will renew
Old ties, old loves, ambitions, sights-and-sounds.

Death is no sudden, dismal, rude surprise.
I will lie down—and shall as surely rise.
(Ora Pate Stewart.)

In her eighties, Florida Scott-Maxwell fashioned a notebook of the thoughts engendered by life's experiences. Below is an entry she made one Easter Day:

I am in that rare frame of mind when everything seems simple. When I have no doubt that the aim and solution of life is the acceptance of God. It is impossible and imperative, and clear. To open to such unimaginable greatness affrights my smallness. I do not know what I seek, cannot know, but I am where the mystery is the certainty.

My long life has hardly given me time—I cannot say to understand—but to be able to imagine that God speaks to me, says simply—"I keep calling to you, and you do not come," and I answer quite naturally—"I couldn't, until I knew there was nowhere else to go." ❦

George Herbert, an early seventeenth-century poet who turned from a political career to become an Anglican priest, uses in this poem a flower as a metaphor for his own alternately flagging and revitalized faith:

THE FLOWER

How fresh, O Lord, how sweet and clean
Are Thy returns! ev'n as the flowers in Spring,

To which, besides their own demean,
The late-past frost tributes of pleasure bring;
Grief melts away
Like snow in May.
As if there were no such cold thing.

Who would have thought my shrivel'd heart
Could have recover'd greennesse? It was gone
Quite under ground; as flowers depart
To see their mother-root, when they have blown,
Where they together
All the hard weather,
Dead to the world, keep house unknown.

These are Thy wonders, Lord of power,
Killing and quickning, bringing down to Hell
And up to Heaven in an houre;
Making a chiming of a passing-bell.
We say amisse
This or that is;
Thy word is all, if we could spell.

O that I once past changing were,
Fast in Thy Paradise, where no flower can wither;
Many a Spring I shoot up fair,
Offring at Heav'n, growing and groning thither;
Nor doth my flower
Want Spring-showre,
My sinnes and I joyning together.

But while I grow in a straight line,
Still upwards bent, as if Heav'n were mine own,
Thy anger comes, and I decline;
What frost to that? what pole is not the zone
Where all things burn,
When Thou dost turn,

And the least frown of Thine is shown?

And now in age I bud again,
After so many deaths I live and write;
I once more smell the dew and rain,
And relish versing: O, my onely Light,
It cannot be
That I am he
On whom Thy tempests fell all night.

These are Thy wonders, Lord of love,
To make us see we are but flow'rs that glide;
Which when we once can find and prove,
Thou hast a garden for us where to bide;
Who would be more,
Swelling through store,
Forfeit their Paradise by their pride.

The essay that yields the following lines is a late nineteenth-century effort by Henry Drummond to reconcile Darwinism with religious faith.

FROM *NATURAL LAW IN THE SPIRIT WORLD*

Room is still left for mystery [in Natural Law]. Had no place remained for mystery it had proved itself both unscientific and irreligious. A Science without mystery is unknown; a Religion without mystery is absurd. This is no attempt to reduce Religion to a question of mathematics, or demonstrate God in biological formulae. The elimination of mystery from the universe is the elimination of Religion. However far the scientific method may penetrate the Spiritual World, there will always remain a region to be explored by a scientific faith. "I shall never rise to the point of view which wishes to 'raise' faith to knowledge. To me, the way of truth is to come through the knowledge of my ignorance to the submissiveness of faith, and then, making that my starting place, to raise my knowledge into faith."

Lest this proclamation of mystery should seem alarming, let us add that this mystery is also scientific. . . .

. . . Revelation never volunteers anything that man could discover for himself—on the principle, probably, that it is only when he is capable of discovering it that he is capable of appreciating it. ✦

As we saw in chapter 9, Blaise Pascal would concur with James E. Talmage that "faith is of the heart." Pascal adds:

For the knowledge of first principles, as space, time, motion, number, is as sure as any of those which we get from reasoning. And reason must trust these intuitions of the heart, and must base them on every argument. . . . And it is as useless and absurd for reason to demand from the heart proofs of her first principles, before admitting them, as it would be for the heart to demand from reason an intuition of all demonstrated propositions before accepting them.

This inability ought, then, to serve only to humble reason, which would judge all, but not to impugn our certainty, as if only reason were capable of instructing us. Would to God, on the contrary, that we had never need of it, and that we knew everything by instinct and intuition! But nature has refused us this boon. On the contrary, she has given us but very little knowledge of this kind; and all the rest can be acquired only by reasoning. . . .

Order—Against the objection that Scripture has no order.

The heart has its own order; the intellect has its own, which is by principle and demonstration. The heart has another. We do not prove that we ought to be loved by enumerating in order the causes of love; that would be ridiculous.

It is the heart which experiences God, and not the reason. This, then, is faith; God felt by the heart, not by the reason.

Faith is a gift of God; do not believe that we said it was a gift of reasoning. Other religions do not say this of their faith. They only give reasoning in order to arrive at it, and yet it does not bring them to it. . . .

The heart has its reasons, which reason does not know. We feel it in a thousand things. ✦

SONNET III

O World, thou choosest not the better part!
It is not wisdom to be only wise,
And on the inward vision close the eyes,
But it is wisdom to believe the heart.
Columbus found a world, and had no chart,
Save one that faith deciphered in the skies;
To trust the soul's invincible surmise
Was all his science and his only art.
Our knowledge is a torch of smoky pine,
That lights the pathway but one step ahead
Across a void of mystery and dread.
Bid, then, the tender light of faith to shine
By which alone the mortal heart is led
Unto the thinking of the thought divine.
(George Santayana.)

Below is a short extract from an essay prepared by Elder Boyd K. Packer, more than two decades ago, to illustrate the use of example in teaching. The principle illustrated, it so happens, is faith in God. Elder Packer tells of a long plane ride on which his anonymous but assertive seat mate not only borrowed his newspaper but also vocally expressed disgust with the contents of the front page.

FROM "A WORLD OF EXAMPLES"

He said the newspaper was typical of humanity and of life—miserable, meaningless, and in all ways useless and futile. Finally I had to protest and insist that life was purposeful, that there lives a God who loves His children, and that life is good indeed.

The young man introduced himself as an attorney. When he learned that I was a minister he said, with some emphasis, "All right, we have one hour and twenty-eight minutes on this flight, and I want you to tell me what business you or anyone else has traipsing about the earth saying that there is a God and that life has any substantial meaning."

He then confessed himself to be an atheist and pressed his disbelief so urgently that I finally said, "You are wrong, my friend. There is a God. He lives. I know He lives."

I then bore testimony to him that God lives and that Jesus is the Christ and that I knew it to be so. This testimony fell on doubtful ears. "You don't know," he said. "Nobody knows that. You can't *know* it."

I would not yield, and the attorney finally said, condescendingly, "All right, you say you know, then [inferring, 'if you are so smart']. Tell me *how* you know."

I felt helpless at this, perhaps the ultimate of questions. I said, "The Spirit of the Holy Ghost has borne witness to my soul."

The attorney said, "I don't know what you are talking about."

I found that the words *prayer, discernment,* and *faith* were meaningless to him, for they were outside his experience.

Seeing me helpless to explain how I knew, he finally said, "You see, you don't really know. If you did know, you'd be able to tell me how you know." (The implication of his words was that anything we know we can readily explain with words alone.)

I felt that I may have borne my testimony unwisely, and I prayed in my heart that if the young attorney could not understand my words, he could at least feel the sincerity of my declaration.

"All knowledge is not conveyed in words alone," I said. I then asked this question: "Do you know what salt tastes like?"

"Of course I do," was his reply.

"When did you taste salt last?"

"I had dinner a short time ago and I tasted salt then."

"You just think you know what salt tastes like," I said.

"I know what salt tastes like as well as I know anything," he insisted.

"If I gave you a cup of salt and a cup of sugar, and let you taste them both, could you tell the salt from the sugar?"

"Now you are becoming juvenile," was his reply. "Of course I could tell the difference. I know what salt tastes like!"

Then I asked one further question. "Assuming that *I* have never tasted salt, can you explain to me in words just what it tastes like?"

After some thought the attorney ventured, "Well, it is not sweet and it is not sour."

"You've told me what it isn't," was my answer, "not what it is."

After several attempts he admitted failure in the little exercise and found himself quite as helpless as I had been to answer his previous question: how I know the gospel is true.

As we walked into the terminal I bore testimony once again and said, "I claim to know there is a God. You ridiculed that testimony and said that if I did know I would be able to tell you exactly how I know. My friend, spiritually speaking, I have tasted salt. I am no more able to convey to you in words how this knowledge has come than you are able to perform the simple exercise of telling me what salt tastes like. But I say to you again, there is a God. He lives. Just because you don't know, don't try to tell me I don't know, for I do." ❧

But it is no lazy man's task—this getting knowledge by faith. It requires the bending of the whole soul, the calling up of the depths of the human mind, and linking them with God—the right connection must be formed. Then comes knowledge by faith. (B. H. Roberts.) ❧

TO A WATERFOWL

Whither, midst falling dew,
While glow the heavens with the last steps of day,
Far, through their rosy depths, dost thou pursue
Thy solitary way?

Vainly the fowler's eye
Might mark thy distant flight to do thee wrong,
As, darkly seen against the crimson sky,
Thy figure floats along.

Seek'st thou the plashy brink
Of weedy lake, or marge of river wide,
Or where the rocking billows rise and sink
On the chafed ocean-side?

There is a Power whose care
Teaches thy way along that pathless coast—
The desert and illimitable air—
Lone wandering, but not lost.

All day thy wings have fanned,
At that far height, the cold, thin atmosphere,
Yet stoop not, weary, to the welcome land,
Though the dark night is near.

And soon that toil shall end;
Soon shalt thou find a summer home, and rest,
And scream among thy fellows; reeds shall bend,
Soon, o'er thy sheltered nest.

Thou'rt gone, the abyss of heaven
Hath swallowed up thy form; yet, on my heart
Deeply has sunk the lesson thou has given,
And shall not soon depart.

He who, from zone to zone,
Guides through the boundless sky thy certain flight,
In the long way that I must tread alone,
Will lead my steps aright.
(William Cullen Bryant.)

*Implicit in the following short excerpt from her autobiography is the upbeat
faith of Bathsheba Wilson Bigler Smith, as she writes of leaving Nauvoo, the beautiful.*

On the 9th of February, 1846, in company with many others, my husband took me and my boy of three and a half years and my little girl of one

and a half years and some of the other members of our family (the remainder to follow as soon as the weather would moderate), and we crossed on the ice the Mississippi River and turned our faces toward the wilderness in which we were to seek out an abiding place.

We left a comfortable home, the accumulations of four years of labor and thrift and took away with us only a few much needed articles such as clothing, bedding and provisions. We left everything else behind us for our enemies. My last act in that precious spot was to tidy the rooms, sweep up the floor, and set the broom in its accustomed place behind the door. Then with emotions in my heart which I could not now pen and which I then strove with success to conceal, I gently closed the door and faced an unknown future, faced a new life, a greater destiny as I well knew, but I faced it with faith in God and with no less assurance of the ultimate establishment of the Gospel in the West and of its true, enduring principles, than I had felt in those trying scenes in Missouri. I, a girl of sixteen, had at that time declared to the weeping Saints, around the death-bed of David Patten, that God had established His church with the promise that it should never be thrown down and I testified that though we might some of us be called to give up our lives, yet the Kingdom of God should stand and His people would be preserved. Now I was going into the wilderness, but I was going with the man I loved dearer than my life. I had my little children. I had heard a voice, so I stepped into the wagon with a certain degree of serenity. ❧

14

CHARITY HOPETH ALL THINGS

FROM "AN ESSAY ON MAN"

Oh blindness to the future! kindly given,
That each may fill the circle marked by Heaven:
Who sees with equal eye, as God of all,
A hero perish, or a sparrow fall,
Atoms or systems into ruin hurled,
And now a bubble burst, and now a world.
　　Hope humbly then; with trembling pinions soar;
Wait the great teacher Death; and God adore.
What future bliss, he gives not thee to know,
But gives that hope to be thy blessing now.
Hope springs eternal in the human breast;
Man never is, but always to be blessed.
(Alexander Pope.)

F aith and hope are so closely related that it is difficult to imagine one without the other. It is true that faith often gives rise to hope, producing an
optimistic attitude toward life. In another sense, however, hope is more
tentative and less certain than faith and becomes a first step toward it. Then, too,
at first glance, the connection between hope and charity may seem a bit curious.
But when we remember that our ultimate hope resides in Christ and his redeeming love, we see that we have every reason to hope, to approach life with vigor and
gladness, to aspire to improve ourselves and the lives of others. The person who
hopes is a person with vision, foresight, and a sense of destiny.

In John Milton's magnificent poem Paradise Lost, a fallen Adam speaks for *all of us after the Archangel Michael teaches him that mortals may yet be redeemed and restored to a glory far exceeding that of Eden. Anticipating the conclusion of Christ's earthly ministry, Michael says:*

> Then to the Heav'n of Heav'ns he shall ascend
> With victory, triúmphing through the air
> Over his foes and thine; there shall he surprise
> The Serpent, Prince of air, and drag in Chains
> Through all his Realm, and there confounded leave;
> Then enter into glory, and resume
> His Seat at God's right hand, exalted high
> Above all names in Heav'n; and thence shall come,
> When this world's dissolution shall be ripe,
> With glory and power to judge both quick and dead,
> To judge th' unfaithful dead, but to reward
> His faithful, and receive them into bliss,
> Whether in Heav'n or Earth, for then the Earth
> Shall all be Paradise, far happier place
> Than this of *Eden,* and far happier days.
> So spake th' Arch-Angel *Michaël,* then paus'd,
> As at the World's great period; and our Sire [Adam]
> Replete with joy and wonder thus repli'd.
> O goodness infinite, goodness immense!
> That all this good of evil shall produce,
> And evil turn to good; more wonderful
> Than that which by creation first brought forth
> Light out of darkness! full of doubt I stand,
> Whether I should repent me now of sin
> By me done and occasion'd, or rejoice
> Much more, that much more good thereof shall spring,
> To God more glory, more good will to Men
> From God, and over wrath grace shall abound.

Brigham Young spoke frequently of that same eternal hope.

It is written that the greatest gift God can bestow upon man is the gift of eternal life. The greatest attainment that we can reach is to preserve our identity to an eternal duration in the midst of the heavenly hosts. We have the words of eternal life given us through the Gospel, which, if we obey, will secure unto us that precious gift. (*Journal of Discourses* 8:7.)

Suppose it possible that you have the privilege of securing to yourselves eternal life—to live and enjoy these blessings forever; you will say this is the greatest blessing that can be bestowed upon you, to live forever and enjoy the society of wives, children, and children's children, to a thousand generations, and forever; and also the society of brethren, sisters, neighbors, and associates, and to possess all you can ask for to make you happy and comfortable. What blessing is equal to this? What blessing is equal to the continuation of life— to the continuation of our organization? (*Journal of Discourses* 8:63.)

I am for life everlasting. I have a being and a life here; and this life is very valuable; it is a most excellent life! I have a future! I am living for another existence that is far above this sinful world, wherein I will be free from this darkness, sin, error, ignorance and unbelief. I am looking forward to a world filled with light and intelligence, where men and women will live in the knowledge and light of God. (*Journal of Discourses* 13:220.)

I expect, if I am faithful, with yourselves, that I shall see the time, with yourselves, that we shall know how to prepare to organize an earth like this—know how to people that earth, how to redeem it, how to sanctify it, and how to glorify it, with those who live upon it who hearken to our counsels. (*Journal of Discourses* 6:274–75.) ✦

Howard W. Hunter chose hope as the subject of his fireside address at Brigham Young University, February 7, 1993. He was then president of the Council of the Twelve Apostles. Below are excerpts from that important address.

FROM "AN ANCHOR TO THE SOULS OF MEN"

I am here tonight to tell you that Despair, Doom, and Discouragement are not an acceptable view of life for a Latter-day Saint. However high on the charts they are on the hit parade of contemporary news, we must not walk on our lower lip every time a few difficult moments happen to confront us.

I am just a couple of years older than most of you, and in those few extra months I have seen a bit more of life than you have. I want you to know that there have always been some difficulties in mortal life and there always will be. But knowing what we know, and living as we are supposed to live, there really is no place, no excuse, for pessimism and despair. . . .

Here are some actual comments that have been made and passed on to me in recent months. This comes from a fine returned missionary:

Why should I date and get serious with a girl? I am not sure I even want to marry and bring a family into this kind of a world. I am not very sure about my own future. How can I take the responsibility for the future of others whom I would love and care about and want to be happy?

Here's another from a high school student:

I hope I die before all these terrible things happen that people are talking about. I don't want to be on the earth when there is so much trouble.

And this from a recent college graduate:

I am doing the best I can, but I wonder if there is much reason to even plan for the future, let alone retirement. The world probably won't last that long anyway.

Well, isn't that a fine view of things? Sounds like we all ought to go and eat a big plate of worms.

I want to say to all within the sound of my voice tonight that you have every reason in this world to be happy and to be optimistic and to be confident. Every generation since time began has had some things to overcome and some problems to work out. Furthermore, every individual person has a particular set of challenges that sometimes seem to be earmarked for us individually. We understood that in our premortal existence. . . .

. . . God will cut short [the world's] unrighteousness in his own due time, but our task is to live fully and faithfully and not worry ourselves sick about the woes of the world or when it will end. Our task is to have the gospel in our lives and to be a bright light, a city set upon a hill that reflects the beauty of the gospel of Jesus Christ and the joy and happiness that will always come to every people in every age who keep the commandments.

In this last dispensation there will be great tribulation (Matthew 24:21). We know that from the scriptures. We know there will be wars and rumors of wars and that the whole earth will be in commotion (D&C 45:26). . . .

Inevitably, the natural result of some of these kinds of prophecies is fear, and that is not fear limited to a younger generation. It is fear shared by those of any age who don't understand what we understand.

But I want to stress that these feelings are not necessary for faithful Latter-day Saints, and they do not come from God. . . .

For Latter-day Saints this is a time of great hope and excitement—one of the greatest eras of the Restoration and therefore one of the greatest eras in any dispensation, inasmuch as ours is the greatest of all dispensations. We need to have faith and hope, two of the greatest fundamental virtues of any discipleship of Christ. . . .

Listen to this marvelous counsel given by President Joseph F. Smith nearly ninety years ago. It sounds as if young people in that day might have been a little anxious about their future as well. I quote:

You do not need to worry in the least, the Lord will take care of you and bless you. He will also take care of His servants, and will bless them and help them to accomplish His purposes; and all the powers of darkness combined in earth and in hell cannot prevent it. . . . [LDS Conference Report, October 1905]

More recently President Marion G. Romney counseled the Church. This was twenty-five years ago, when the world also knew some difficulty. An American president had been assassinated, communism was alive and menacing, and a war was building up in Southeast Asia. My sons were just exactly your age at that time, and they had some of the same anxieties you have about life and marriage and the future. Here's what President Romney said then:

Naturally, believing Christians, even those who have a mature faith in the gospel, are concerned and disturbed by the lowering clouds on the horizon. But they need not be surprised or frantic about their portent, for, as has already been said, at the very beginning of this last dispensation the Lord made it abundantly clear that through the tribulations and calamity that he foresaw and foretold and that we now see coming upon us, there would be a people who, through acceptance and obedience to the gospel, would be able to recognize and resist the powers of evil, build up the promised Zion, and prepare to meet the Christ and be with him in the blessed millenium. . . . [LDS Conference Report, 1966]

Let me offer a third example from yet another moment of difficulty in this century. In the midst of the most devastating international conflagration the modern world has ever seen, Elder John A. Widtsoe of the Council of the Twelve counseled people who were worried. Nazism was on the march, there was war in the Pacific, nation after nation seemed to be drawn into war. Mind you this was 1942, not 1992 or 1993. This is what Brother Widtsoe said:

Above the roar of cannon and airplane, the maneuvers and plans of men, the Lord always determines the tide of battle. So far and no farther does He permit the evil one to go in his career to create human misery. The Lord is ever victorious; He is the Master to whose will Satan is subject. Though all hell may rage, and men may follow evil, the purposes of the Lord will not fail. [LDS Conference Report, April 1942]

I promise you tonight in the name of the Lord whose servant I am that God will always protect and care for his people. . . . The Lord has power over his Saints and will always prepare places of peace, defense, and safety for his people. When we have faith in God we can hope for a better world— for us personally and for all mankind. . . .

The faith and hope of which I speak is not a Pollyanna-like approach to significant personal and public problems. I don't believe we can wake up in the morning and simply by drawing a big "happy face" on the chalkboard believe that is going to take care of the world's difficulties. But if our faith and hope is anchored in Christ, and in his teachings, commandments, and promises, then we are able to count on something truly remarkable, genuinely miraculous. . . . He who fears loses strength for the combat of life in the fight against evil. Therefore, the power of the evil one always tries to generate fear in human hearts. . . .

. . . [Joseph Smith] said about our time—yours and mine—that ours is the moment *"upon which prophets, priests and kings* [in ages past] *have dwelt with peculiar delight;* [all these ancient witnesses for God] *have looked forward with joyful anticipation to the day in which we live; and fired with heavenly and joyful anticipations they have sung and written and prophesied of this our day; . . . we are the favored people that God has* [chosen] *to bring about the Latter-day glory."* [History of the Church 4:609–10]

That is a thrilling statement to me: that the ancients whom we love and read and quote so much—Adam and Abraham, Joshua and Joseph, Isaiah and Ezekial and Ezra, Nephi and Alma, and Mormon and Moroni—all of these ancient prophets, priests, and kings focused their prophetic vision "with peculiar delight" on our day, on our time. It is this hour to which they have looked forward "with joyful anticipation," and "fired with heavenly and joyful anticipation they have sung and written and prophesied of this our day." They saw us as "the favored people" upon whom God would shower his full and complete latter-day glory, and I testify that is our destiny. What a privilege! What an honor! What a responsibility! And what joy! We have every reason in time and eternity to rejoice and give thanks for the quality of our lives and the promises we have been given. ❧

President Hunter reminds us that hope, perhaps even more than courage, is the opposite of fear. In making his point, he refers to several Book of Mormon passages, one of which yields his title:

Wherefore, ye must press forward with a steadfastness in Christ, having a perfect brightness of hope, and a love of God and of all men. Wherefore, if ye shall press forward, feasting upon the word of Christ, and endure to the end, behold, thus saith the Father: Ye shall have eternal life. (2 Nephi 31:20.) ❧

Wherefore, whoso believeth in God might with surety hope for a better world, yea, even a place at the right hand of God, which hope cometh of faith, maketh *an anchor to the souls of men,* which would make them sure and steadfast, always abounding in good works, being led to glorify God. (Ether 12:4; emphasis added.) ❧

Martin Luther implicitly confirms the link between faith, in its general sense, and hope.

FROM "TABLE TALK"

Everything that is done in the world is done by hope. No husbandman would sow one grain of corn if he hoped not it would grow up and become seed; no bachelor would marry a wife if he hoped not to have children; no merchant or tradesman would set himself to work if he did not hope to reap benefit thereby, &c. How much more, then, does hope urge us on to everlasting life and salvation? ◆

A prophet, by definition, is one who looks to the future, often shouldering tasks that to the casual onlooker appear impossible to achieve. Of his specific prophecy of a home for the Saints in the Rocky Mountains, Joseph Smith apparently said but a few words. Others, however, were aware of what a momentous thing it was, and they fell in step with high hopes. Below is the published record of Joseph's words, followed by Anson Call's statement of what transpired at the time of Joseph's prophecy.

I had a conversation with a number of brethren in the shade of the building on the subject of our persecutions in Missouri and the constant annoyance which has followed us since we were driven from that state. I prophesied that the Saints would continue to suffer much affliction and would be driven to the Rocky Mountains, many would apostatize, others would be put to death by our persecutors or lose their lives in consequence of exposure or disease, and some of you will live to go and assist in making settlements and build cities and see the Saints become a mighty people in the midst of the Rocky Mountains. ◆

In History of the Church, *B. H. Roberts adds the Call account in a footnote but comments that his source, volume 2 of Edward W. Tullidge's Histories, is very likely in error as to the date of the prophecy and a few other details. History of the Church gives the date of the prophecy as July 6, 1842, while Tullidge dates the Call statement a year and a week later. Despite the discrepancy, Roberts is*

383

convinced that the accounts describe the same event. Below is Anson Call's statement, preceded by commentary from Tullidge:

On the 14th of July, 1843, with quite a number of his brethren, [Joseph] crossed the Mississippi river to the town of Montrose, to be present at the installment of the Masonic Lodge of the "Rising Sun." A block schoolhouse had been prepared with shade in front, under which was a barrel of ice water. . . . Joseph, as he was tasting the cold water, warned the brethren not to be too free with it. With the tumbler still in his hand he prophesied that the Saints would yet go to the Rocky Mountains; and, said he, this water tastes much like that of the crystal streams that are running from the snow-capped mountains. We will let Mr. Call describe this prophetic scene:

I had before seen him in a vision, and now saw while he was talking his countenance change to white; not the deadly white of a bloodless face, but a living brilliant white. He seemed absorbed in gazing at something at a great distance, and said: "I am gazing upon the valleys of those mountains." This was followed by a vivid description of the scenery of these mountains, as I have since become acquainted with it. Pointing to Shadrach Roundy and others, he said: "There are some men here who shall do a great work in that land." Pointing to me, he said: "There is Anson, he shall go and shall assist in building up cities from one end of the country to the other, and you, rather extending the idea to all those he had spoken of, shall perform as great a work as has been done by man, so that the nations of the earth shall be astonished, and many of them will be gathered in that land and assist in building cities and temples, and Israel will be made to rejoice."

It is impossible to represent in words this scene which is still vivid in my mind, of the grandeur of Joseph's appearance, his beautiful descriptions of this land, and his wonderful prophetic utterances as they emanated from the glorious inspirations that overshadowed him. There was a force and power in his exclamations of which the following is but a faint echo: "Oh the beauty of those snow-capped mountains! The cool refreshing streams that are running down through those mountain gorges!" Then gazing in another direction, as if there was a change of locality: "Oh the scenes that this people will pass through! The dead that will lay between here and there." ❧

When the call finally did come to migrate west once again, this time way west, most of the Saints rose to the occasion, catching the vision of a new hope for peace and freedom of worship in the Rocky Mountains. No one was more eloquent on the subject than Heber C. Kimball, who picked up the theme in a conference address in October 1845. "I am glad the time of our exodus is come," he said, adding that he had "looked for it for years." He granted that some may "look at their pretty houses and gardens" and find it very difficult to leave. But, he exclaimed, "When we start, you will put on your knapsacks, and follow after us." (History of the Church 7:466.)

Even a single stanza from John Taylor's poem "The Valley" captures the radiance of his hope:

> Let me go to the Zion, which God hath prepared
> As the hope of the saints—as rest and reward,
> Where the fountains and rivers in purity flow,
> And the earth teems with plenty—oh! there let me go.

Less celebratory, but still founded in hope, is Emmeline B. Wells' poetic statement.

LEAVING NAUVOO

> Sad was the parting, weary was the way
> The Pilgrims trod while journeying along;
> Many the hardships borne from day to day,
> And yet at eve the merry dance and song
> The drooping spirits cheer'd, and hope grew bright;
> And when they knelt upon the ground to pray
> They seemed to see a resting place in sight,
> And holy angels guarding all the way.

As we have noted before, the personal writings of Latter-day Saint pioneer women contain many an account of heartbreak and grueling physical struggle. Given the circumstances of their lives, it is easy to forget that few of the early Saints, men or women, retreated into permanent despair and surrender. Their capacity not only to endure but, in addition, to sustain "a perfect brightness of hope" is downright inspiring. One of those annalists was Mary Fielding Smith, who wrote these words to her brother, Joseph Fielding, from Commerce, Illinois, in June 1839:

As it respects myself, it is now so long since I wrote to you, and so many important things have transpired, and so great have been my affliction[s], etc., that I know not where to begin; but I can say, hitherto has the Lord preserved me, and I am still among the living to praise him, as I do to-day. I have, to be sure, been called to drink deep of the bitter cup; but you know, my beloved brother, this makes the sweet sweeter.

[She then tells of her husband's (Hyrum's) imprisonment and return, and expresses a desire that her other brothers and sisters might "embrace the fullness of the gospel."]

As to myself, I can truly say, that I would not give up the prospect of the latter-day glory for all that glitters in this world. O, my dear brother, I must tell you, for your comfort, that my hope is full, and it is a glorious hope; and though I have been left for near six months in widowhood, in the time of great affliction, and was called to take, joyfully or otherwise, the spoiling of almost all our goods . . . , yet I do not feel in the least discouraged; no, though my sister and I are here together in a strange land, we have been enabled to rejoice, in the midst of our privations and persecutions, that we were counted worthy to suffer these things, so that we may, with the ancient saints who suffered in like manner, inherit the same glorious reward. If it had not been for this hope, I should have sunk before this; but, blessed be the God and rock of my salvation, here I am, and am perfectly satisfied and happy, having not the smallest desire to go one step backward. ❧

Eliza R. Snow tells of lodging "over night at what was called the Halfway House" on the way to Far West, an "almost shelterless shelter" that on this occasion served "seventy-five or eighty souls" in "perhaps twenty feet square" of space. It was late December, and what food they had "was frozen hard." Despite the hardship, she says:

But, withal, that was a very merry night. None but saints can be happy under every circumstance. About twenty feet from the house was a shed, in the centre of which the brethren built a roaring fire, around which some of them stood and sang songs and hymns all night, while others parched corn and roasted frosted potatoes, etc. Not a complaint was heard—all were cheerful, and judging from appearances, strangers would have taken us to be pleasure excursionists rather than a band of gubernatorial exiles. ✦

This same buoyancy characterizes Eliza R. Snow's autobiography throughout, but especially memorable are her accounts of trail life, such as the following:

Much of the time we journeyed on untrod ground, but occasionally we struck the track of the Pioneers [she refers to members of the first companies as "Pioneers"] and read the date of their presence, with an "*All well*" accompaniment inscribed on a bleached buffalo skull, and had a general time of rejoicing. Those skulls were duly appreciated. . . .

We had many seasons of rejoicing in the midst of privation and suffering—many manifestations of the loving kindness of God. In very many instances the sick were healed, and those who by accidents were nigh unto death, made speedily whole. . . .

Many, yes many were the star and moonlight evenings, when, as we circled around the blazing fire and sang our hymns of devotion and songs of praise to Him who knows the secrets of all hearts—when with sublime union of hearts, the sound of united voices reverberated from hill to hill; and echoing through the silent expanse, apparently filled the vast concave above, while the glory of God seemed to rest on all around us.

[She includes a four-stanza poem "Song of the Desert," prompted by "one of those soul-inspiring occasions."] ✦

My favorite passage from Eliza R. Snow's life sketch, however, is her description of her "delightful" first winter in the Salt Lake Valley, in a hut with a leaky roof. She shared the home of Clara Decker Young, and with them was an Indian girl who had been "purchased" from a tribe who had threatened to kill her (as they had previously killed a boy) unless the Mormons ransomed her.

This hut, like most of those built the first year, was roofed with willows and earth, with very little inclination. . . . We suffered no inconvenience until about the middle of March, when a long storm of snow, sleet, and rain occurred, and then for several days, the sun did not make its appearance. Mrs. Clara Young happened to be on a visit to her mother. . . .

. . . One evening as several were sitting socially conversing in my room [the driest], the water commenced dropping in one place and then in another, and so on: they dodged it for a while, but it increased so rapidly, they concluded to return to their own wet houses. After they left, Sally [the Indian girl] wrapped herself in her buffalo robe on the floor, and I spread my umbrella over my head and shoulders as I ensconced myself in bed, the lower part being unshielded, was wet enough before morning. During the night, despite all discomfitures, I laughed involuntarily while alone in the darkness of the night I lay reflecting the ludicrous scene. ❧

The same upbeat tone enlivens the journal of Louisa Barnes Pratt. Without ignoring hardships, she finds reason to rejoice.

The company was generally healthy; even those who started on beds were soon able to enjoy the amusements accessible to all, such as climbing mountains and picking wild fruit. The gloom on my mind wore gradually away. When I had been three weeks on the way there was not a more mirthful woman in the whole company. The grandeur of nature filled me with grateful aspirations. The beautiful camping grounds were so clean that one was led to conclude no human foot had ever trodden there.

. . . Sometimes the whole camp of six hundred wagons would be within visiting distance, then indeed it was like a city of tents and wagons. The cheerful campfires blazing at night, far away from the civilized world, reminded us that our trust must be in the Lord.

When we came to the buffalo country, we were full of wonder and admiration. Nothing could be more exciting than to see them in large herds, marching as orderly as a company of soldiers; nothing seemed to daunt them. If they were headed towards our traveling companies, we would make a wide passage for them to cross our path [Eliza R. Snow, incidentally, found these forced detours a nuisance.] They would march along so majestically, with their great bushy heads, turning neither to the right nor left, not seeming to notice us at all, while we would stare at them with breathless anxiety. . . .

The Platte River country was beautiful. The women, in small companies, were often seen walking on its banks by moonlight, or bathing in its waters. Our hearts, at the same time, glowed with wonder and admiration at the beauty and sublimity of the scenery, alone in a great wilderness far from the haunts of civilization, with none but an occasional red man wandering along in search of game. . . .

Then we travelled miles without seeing a tree. When, at length, we came to a lone cedar tree, we stopped our teams, alighted, and many of the company walked quite a distance for the pleasure of standing a few moments under its branches. . . .

Aug. 20th, 1848—This morning arose with cheerful spirits, anticipating the arrival of our camp in the desired haven. We begin to think of green corn, cucumbers; how delicious they will be to the poor fasting pilgrims. We have ascended an eminence, where, with a spyglass we can see the great Salt Lake, in the valley of which the Saints are located. Our hearts leap for joy! ❧

These writings demonstrate repeatedly that perspective, outlook, and attitude go a long way toward defining quality of life, regardless of circumstances. In my view, Zina Diantha Huntington Jacobs's one-line entry for August 20, 1845, takes the prize: "Washing. A beautiful day, and may my heart be clean."

> Be like the bird who, halting in his flight on a limb too slight
> Feels it give way beneath him,
> Yet sings knowing he hath wings.
> (Victor Hugo.)

The first of several "Little Ditties" by William Brighty Rands laughs gently at an attitude opposite to hope.

WINIFRED WATERS sat and sighed
Under a weeping willow;
When she went to bed she cried,
Wetting all the pillow;

Kept on crying night and day,
Till her friends lost patience;
"What shall we do to stop her, pray?"
So said her relations.

Send her to the sandy plains,
In the zone called torrid:
Send her where it never rains,
Where the heat is horrid!

Mind that she has only flour
For her daily feeding;
Let her have a page an hour
Of the driest reading,—

Navigation, logarithm,
All that kind of knowledge,—
Ancient pedigrees go with 'em,
From the Heralds' College.

When the poor girl has endured
Six months of this drying,
Winifred will come back cured,
Let us hope, of crying.

Then she will not day by day
Make those mournful faces,
And we shall not have to say,
"Wring her pillow-cases."

John Lyman Smith, who as a youngster lived with the Prophet Joseph's family for several months, tells this charming story of the Prophet's contagious optimism:

In my early years I used to often eat at the table with Joseph the Prophet. At one time he called us to dinner. I being at play in the room with his son Joseph, he called us to him, and we stood one on each side of him. After he had looked over the table he said, "Lord, we thank Thee for this Johnny cake, and ask Thee to send us something better. Amen." The corn bread was cut and I received a piece from his hand.

Before the bread was all eaten, a man came to the door and asked if the Prophet Joseph was at home. Joseph replied he was, whereupon the visitor said, "I have brought you some flour and a ham."

Joseph arose and took the gift, and blessed the man in the name of the Lord. Turning to his wife, Emma, he said, "I knew the Lord would answer my prayer." ❦

I can imagine a twinkle in Joseph's eye as he spoke those words. A similar story is told of young Heber J. Grant, who, with his mother, lived in Bishop Edwin Woolley's ward.

One day, after hearing a powerful sermon from Bishop Woolley on the Lord's fourfold generosity to those who were generous with Him, Heber walked up to Edwin and gave him $50 he had just acquired. Edwin took $5 and handed the rest back. Heber said, "Didn't you preach here today that the Lord rewards fourfold? My mother is a widow and she needs $200." Edwin replied, "My boy, do you believe that if I take this other $45, you will get your $200 quicker?" "Yes I do." Edwin took the money. The next day Heber came by to tell the bishop that he had earned $218.50 from an idea he had while walking home from that meeting. Heber was a little disappointed that he hadn't made $2.35 more to fully cover the tithing on his $218.50. ❦

Parley P. Pratt seems also to have been endowed with a healthy portion of spunk, humor, and hopefulness—even downright ingenuity. He tells of one occasion when he was interrupted in his preaching, arrested on trumped-up charges, and taken before a corrupt judge.

I was soon ordered to prison, or to pay a sum of money which I had not in the world. It was now a late hour, and I was still retained in court, tantalized, abused and urged to settle the matter, to all of which I made no reply for some time. This greatly exhausted their patience. It was near midnight. I now called on brother Petersen to sing a hymn in the court. We sung, "O how happy are they." This exasperated them still more, and they pressed us greatly to settle the business, by paying the money.

I then observed as follows: "May it please the court, I have one proposal to make for a final settlement of the things that seem to trouble you. It is this: if the witnesses who have given testimony in the case will repent of their false swearing, and the magistrate of his unjust and wicked judgment and of his persecution, blackguardism and abuse, and all kneel down together, we will pray for you, that God might forgive you in these matters."

[Parley was then "conducted to a public house" and locked in for the night, for the prison was some miles away and could not be reached until morning. Parley's companions were freed, and he promised to join them soon.]

After sitting awhile by the fire [next morning] in charge of the officer, I requested to step out. I walked out into the public square accompanied by him. Said I, "Mr. Peabody, are you good at a race?" "No," said he, "but my big bull dog is, and he has been trained to assist me in my office these several years; he will take any man down at my bidding." "Well, Mr. Peabody, you compelled me to go a mile, I have gone with you two miles. You have given me an opportunity to preach, sing, and have also entertained me with lodging and breakfast. I must now go on my journey; if you are good at a race you can accompany me. I thank you for all your kindness—good day, sir."

I then started on my journey, while he stood amazed and not able to step one foot before the other. Seeing this, I halted, turned to him and again invited him to a race. He still stood amazed. I then renewed my exertions, and soon increased my speed to something like that of a deer. He did not awake from his astonishment sufficiently to start in pursuit till I had gained, perhaps, two hundred yards. I had already leaped a fence, and was making my way through a field to the forest on the right of the road. He now came hallooing after me, and shouting to his dog to seize me. The dog, being one of the largest I ever saw, came close on my footsteps with all his fury; the officer behind still in pursuit, clapping his hands and hallooing, "stu-boy, stu-boy—take him—watch—lay hold of him, I say—down with him," and pointing his finger in the direction I was running. The dog was fast over-taking me, and in the act of leaping upon me, when, quick as lightning, the thought struck me, to assist the officer, in sending the dog with all fury to the forest a little distance before me. I pointed my finger in that direction, clapped my hands, and shouted in imitation of the officer. The dog hastened past me with redoubled speed towards the forest; being urged by the officer and myself, and both of us running in the same direction.

Gaining the forest, I soon lost sight of the officer and the dog, and have not seen them since. . . . A church of about sixty members was soon orga-nized in the place where I had played such a trick of deception on the dog. ❦

When Ruth May Fox was called at age seventy-five to be general president of the young women's organization (YLMIA), she expressed reservations about her call to President Heber J. Grant. His response was to hand her a bit of verse:

> Age is a quality of mind;
> If your dreams you've left behind,
> If hope is cold;
> If you no longer look ahead,
> If your ambition's fires are dead—
> Then you are old.

> But if from life you take the best,
> And if in life you keep the zest,
> If love you hold;
> No matter how the years go by,
> No matter how the birthdays fly—
> You are not old.

Emily Dickinson writes:

> "Hope" is the thing with feathers—
> That perches in the soul—
> And sings the tune without the words—
> And never stops—at all—

And sweetest—in the Gale—is heard—
And sore must be the storm—
That could abash the little Bird
That kept so many warm—

I've heard it in the chillest land—
And on the strangest Sea—
Yet, never, in Extremity,
It asked a crumb—of Me.
(Emily Dickinson.)

REQUIEM

Under the wide and starry sky,
Dig the grave and let me lie.
Glad did I live and gladly die,
And I laid me down with a will.

This be the verse you grave for me:
Here he lies where he longed to be,
Home is the sailor, home from the sea,
And the hunter home from the hill.
(Robert Louis Stevenson.)

PROSPICE

Fear death?—to feel the fog in my throat,
The mist in my face,
When the snows begin, and the blasts denote
I am nearing the place,
The power of the night, the press of the storm,
The post of the foe;
Where he stands, the Arch Fear in a visible form,
Yet the strong man must go:
For the journey is done and the summit attained,
And the barriers fall,

Though a battle's to fight ere the guerdon be gained,
The reward of it all.
I was ever a fighter, so—one fight the more,
The best and the last!
I would hate that death bandaged my eyes, and forbore,
And bade me creep past.
No! let me taste the whole of it, fare like my peers
The heroes of old,
Bear the brunt, in a minute pay glad life's arrears
Of pain, darkness and cold.
For sudden the worst turns the best to the brave,
The black minute's at end,
And the element's rage, the fiend-voices that rave,
Shall dwindle, shall blend,
Shall change, shall become first a peace, out of pain,
Then a light, then thy breast,
O thou soul of my soul! I shall clasp thee again,
And with God be the rest!
(Robert Browning.)

William Wordsworth's "Ode: Intimations of Immortality from Recollections of Early Childhood" is known mainly for a few lines commonly lifted from context in the poem's midsection ("Our birth is but a sleep and a forgetting . . ."). The poem's principal subject, however, is the distancing of heaven as one ages and becomes increasingly entrenched in the world. The poet is able to work through the sense of loss and change, and by the final sections he rekindles hope in the fact that in the wisdom of maturity "our Souls have sight of that immortal sea which brought us hither":

. . . Though nothing can bring back the hour
Of splendour in the grass, of glory in the flower;
We will grieve not, rather find
Strength in what remains behind;
In the primal sympathy
Which having been must ever be;

In the soothing thoughts that spring
Out of human suffering;
In the faith that looks through death,
In years that bring the philosophic mind.

And O, ye Fountains, Meadows, Hills, and Groves,
Forbode not any severing of our loves!
Yet in my heart of hearts I feel your might;
I only have relinquished one delight
To live beneath your more habitual sway.
I love the Brooks which down their channels fret,
Even more than when I tripped lightly as they;
The innocent brightness of a new-born Day
Is lovely yet;
The Clouds that gather round the setting sun
Do take a sober colouring from an eye
That hath kept watch o'er man's mortality;
Another race hath been, and other palms are won.
Thanks to the human heart by which we live,
Thanks to its tenderness, its joys, and fears,
To me the meanest flower that blows can give
Thoughts that do often lie too deep for tears.

GOD'S GRANDEUR

The world is charged with the grandeur of God.
It will flame out, like shining from shook foil;
It gathers to a greatness, like the ooze of oil
Crushed. Why do men then now not reck his rod?
Generations have trod, have trod, have trod;
And all is seared with trade; bleared, smeared with toil;
And wears man's smudge and shares man's smell: the soil
Is bare now, nor can foot feel, being shod.

And for all this, nature is never spent;
　　There lives the dearest freshness deep down things;
And though the last lights off the black West went
　　Oh, morning, at the brown brink eastward, springs—
Because the Holy Ghost over the bent
　　World broods with warm breast and with ah! bright wings.
(Gerard Manley Hopkins.)

TO THE FRINGED GENTIAN

Thou blossom bright with autumn dew,
And colored with the heaven's own blue,
　　That openest when the quiet light
　　Succeeds the keen and frosty night.

Thou comest not when violets lean
O'er wandering brooks and springs unseen,
　　Or columbines, in purple dressed,
　　Nod o'er the ground-bird's hidden nest.

Thou waitest late and com'st alone,
When woods are bare and birds are flown,
　　And frosts and shortening days portend
　　The aged year is near his end.

Then doth thy sweet and quiet eye
Look through its fringes to the sky,
　　Blue—blue—as if that sky let fall
　　A flower from its cerulean wall.

I would that thus, when I shall see
The hour of death draw near to me,
　　Hope, blossoming within my heart,
　　May look to heaven as I depart.
　　　　(William Cullen Bryant.)

Certainly, the ability to find joy in life, to make the best of whatever circumstances present themselves, to laugh easily—especially at oneself—to be cheerful rather than sour, blesses both the cheerful and the people whose lives intersect theirs. In that sense, even if in no other, living hopefully is a charity.

THE POBBLE WHO HAS NO TOES

The Pobble who has no toes
Had once as many as we;
When they said, "Some day you may lose them all,"—
He replied,—"Fish fiddle de-dee!"
And his Aunt Jobiska made him drink,
Lavendar water tinged with pink,
For she said, "The World in general knows
There's nothing so good for a Pobble's toes!"
The Pobble who has no toes,
Swam across the Bristol Channel;
But before he set out he wrapped his nose,
In a piece of scarlet flannel.
For his Aunt Jobiska said, "No harm
Can come to his toes if his nose is warm;
And it's perfectly known that a Pobble's toes
Are safe, . . . provided he minds his nose."
The Pobble swam fast and well,
And when boats or ships came near him
He tinkledy-binkledy-winkled a bell
So that all the world could hear him.
And all the Sailors and Admirals cried,
When they saw him nearing the further side—
"He has gone to fish, for his Aunt Jobiska's
Runcible Cat with crimson whiskers!["]
But before he touched the shore,
The shore of the Bristol Channel,
A sea-green Porpoise carried away

His wrapper of scarlet flannel.
And when he came to observe his feet
Formerly garnished with toes so neat
His face at once became forlorn
On perceiving that all his toes were gone!
And nobody ever knew
From that dark day to the present,
Whoso had taken the Pobble's toes,
In a manner so far from pleasant.
Whether the shrimps or crawfish gray,
Or crafty Mermaids stole them away—
Nobody knew; and nobody knows
How the Pobble was robbed of his twice five toes!
The Pobble who has no toes
Was placed in a friendly Bark,
And they rowed him back, and carried him up,
To his Aunt Jobiska's Park.
And she made him a feast at his earnest wish
Of eggs and buttercups fried with fish;—
And she said,—"It's a fact the whole world knows,
That Pobbles are happier without their toes."
(Edward Lear.)

Almost invariably, the person who joys in the present moment is also the person who anticipates the future with hope. In a "Spoken Word" sermonette, Richard L. Evans offers this counsel:

Sometimes we become impatient with the present. We see its evils, its uncertainties, its imperfections, and eagerly we wish for the day when things will be different. It is proper and expected that immortal man would hope for and have faith in a finer future—but of utmost importance also is the power to appreciate the present. No matter what far futures lie before us (and we earnestly believe that they are limitless and everlasting), yet always we live in the present. We may sometimes rebel at all the uncertainties and at all the undisclosed events, but those who would always force the

399

future, who are overly impatient for it to unfold, may let the happiness and opportunities and obligations of the present pass them by. . . . And one of the great gifts of life—one of the surest sources of happiness—is the power to appreciate the present. ❧

An unknown author wrote:

He has achieved success who has lived well, laughed often and loved much; who has gained the respect of intelligent men and the love of little children; who has filled his niche and accomplished his task, who has left the world better than he found it, whether by an improved poppy, a perfect poem or a rescued soul; who has never lacked appreciation of earth's beauty, or failed to express it; who has always looked for the best in others and given the best he had; whose life was an inspiration; whose memory is a benediction. ❧

Anthropologist Loren Eiseley tells of encountering on a stormy seashore the hope that is charity.

FROM "THE STAR THROWER"

The beaches of Costabel are littered with the debris of life. Shells are cast up in windrows; a hermit crab, fumbling for a new home in the depths, is tossed naked ashore, where the waiting gulls cut him to pieces. Along the strip of wet sand that marks the ebbing and flowing of the tide death walks hugely and in many forms. . . .

In the end the sea rejects its offspring. They cannot fight their way home through the surf which casts them repeatedly back upon the shore. The tiny breathing pores of starfish are stuffed with sand. The rising sun shrivels the mucilaginous bodies of the unprotected. The seabeach and its endless war are soundless. Nothing screams but the gulls. . . .

. . . I made my way around the altered edges of the cove and proceeded on my morning walk up the shore. Now and then a stooping figure moved in the gloom or a rain squall swept past me with light pattering steps. . . .

. . . Ahead of me, over the projecting point, a gigantic rainbow of incredible perfection had sprung shimmering into existence. Somewhere toward its foot I discerned a human figure standing, as it seemed to me, within the rainbow, though unconscious of his position. He was gazing fixedly at something in the sand.

Eventually he stooped and flung the object beyond the breaking surf. I labored toward him over a half mile of uncertain footing. By the time I reached him the rainbow had receded ahead of us, but something of its color still ran hastily in many changing lights across his features. He was starting to kneel again.

In a pool of sand and silt a starfish had thrust its arms up stiffly and was holding its body away from the stifling mud.

"It's still alive," I ventured.

"Yes," he said, and with a quick yet gentle movement he picked up the star and spun it over my head and far out into the sea. It sank in a burst of spume, and the waters roared once more.

"It may live," he said, "if the offshore pull is strong enough." He spoke gently, and across his bronzed worn face the light still came and went in subtly altering colors.

"There are not many come this far," I said, groping in a sudden embarrassment for words. "Do you collect?"

"Only like this," he said softly, gesturing amidst the wreckage of the shore. "And only for the living." He stooped again, oblivious of my curiosity, and skipped another star neatly across the water.

"The stars," he said, "throw well. One can help them."

He looked full at me with a faint question kindling in his eyes, which seemed to take on the far depths of the sea.

"I do not collect," I said uncomfortably, the wind beating at my garments. "Neither the living nor the dead. I gave it up a long time ago. . . ." I nodded and walked away, leaving him there upon the dune with that great rainbow ranging up the sky behind him.

I turned as I neared a bend in the coast and saw him toss another star, skimming it skillfully far out over the ravening and tumultuous water. For a moment, in the changing light, the sower appeared magnified, as though casting larger stars upon some greater sea. He had, at any rate, the posture of a god. . . .

Somewhere far up the coast wandered the star thrower beneath his rainbow. Our exchange had been brief because upon that coast I had learned that men who ventured out at dawn resented others in the greediness of their compulsive collecting. I had also been abrupt because I had, in the terms of my profession and experience, nothing to say. The star thrower was mad, and his particular acts were a folly with which I had not chosen to associate myself. I was an observer and a scientist. Nevertheless, I had seen the rainbow attempting to attach itself to earth.

On a point of land, as though projecting into a domain beyond us, I found the star thrower. In the sweet rain-swept morning, that great many-hued rainbow still lurked and wavered tentatively beyond him. Silently I sought and picked up a still-living star, spinning it far out into the waves. I spoke once briefly. "I understand," I said. "Call me another thrower." Only then I allowed myself to think, He is not alone any longer. After us there will be others. . . .

I picked and flung another star. Perhaps far outward on the rim of space a genuine star was similarly seized and flung. I could feel the movement in my body. It was like a sowing—the sowing of life on an infinitely gigantic scale. I looked back across my shoulder. Small and dark against the receding rainbow, the star thrower stooped and flung once more. I never looked again. The task we had assumed was too immense for gazing. I flung and flung again while all about us roared the insatiable waters of death. ✦

15

CHARITY ENDURETH
ALL THINGS

Fear thou not; for I am with thee:

be not dismayed; for I am thy God:

I will strengthen thee; yea, I will help thee;

yea, I will uphold thee with the right hand

of my righteousness.

ISAIAH 41:10

When Paul speaks of the love that endures all things, I think he is talking about moral courage, about gathering strength and weathering difficult times, about surviving loss, about standing up for and living what we profess to believe—regardless of the opposition. How durable are we? How courageous, how hardy, how strong? Just as faith and hope are closely related, so are faith and endurance, or courage. In 2 Timothy as in 1 Corinthians, Paul links enduring courage with charity—love—and with good sense and strength, too.

For God hath not given us the spirit of fear; but of power, and of love, and of a sound mind. (2 Timothy 1:7.) ❖

In the preceding section, I suggested that fearfulness is antithetical to hope. But debilitating and unfounded fear is antithetical to courageous endurance, too, for the paralysis of fear can dissipate both strength and will. Joseph F. Smith has

403

offered impressive counsel about exercising what he calls "the courage of faith," standing up for what we believe.

The Gospel Causes Disturbance. In truth the gospel is carrying us against the stream of passing humanity. We get in the way of purely human affairs and disturb the current of life in many ways and in many places. People who are comfortably located and well provided for, do not like to be disturbed. It angers them, and they would settle things once for all in the most drastic manner. . . . Those who defend us, do so not infrequently with an apologetic air. The Saints are never safe in following the protests and counsels of those who would have us ever and always in harmony with the world. We have our particular mission to perform; and that we may perform it in consonance with divine purposes, we are running counter to the ways of man. We are made unpopular. The contempt of the world is on us, and we are the unloved child among the peoples of the earth.

"Having Done All, Stand." There are people who are courageous in doing all they can to bring about certain results. They will combat evils and resist the wrongs that are inflicted upon them and upon others; but when they have been defeated, when they see a just cause suffer, and evilly disposed men triumphant, they give up. What is the use? That is the question uppermost in their minds. They see wicked men apparently successful. They see men of evil repute honored by their fellowmen until they are almost persuaded that fate has her rewards for wrong doing. With them, what appears to be a lost cause inspires no hope. It is lost, they say, and we shall have to make the best of it, and let it go. They are at heart discouraged. Some almost question the purposes of Providence. They have the courage of men who are brave at heart, but they have not the courage of faith.

How different it was with Paul! He had labored fearlessly, he had delivered a divine message, he had resisted the enemy, and they apparently triumphed over him. He was taken prisoner and subjected to humiliating treatment by the administrators of the law. He was in bonds, and death awaited him, but he was still courageous. His was the courage of faith. Read these stirring words of his sent to the Ephesians, recorded in Ephesians 6:13, sent when most men would have thought their cause lost: "Wherefore

404

take unto you the whole armour of God, that ye may be able to withstand in the evil day, and having done all, to stand."

After we have done all we could do for the cause of truth, and withstood the evil that men have brought upon us, and we have been overwhelmed by their wrongs, it is still our duty to stand. We cannot give up; we must not lie down. Great causes are not won in a single generation. To stand firm in the face of overwhelming opposition, when you have done all you can, is the courage of faith. The courage of faith is the courage of progress. Men who possess that divine quality go on; they are not permitted to stand still if they would. They are not simply the creatures of their own power and wisdom; they are instrumentalities of a higher law and a divine purpose.

Others would quit, they would avoid trouble. When it comes, it is to them most unfortunate. It is really too bad. In their minds, it might have been avoided. They want to square themselves with the world. The decree of the world has gone forth, why withstand it? "We have withstood evil," they say, "and it has overwhelmed us. Why stand longer?" Such men read history, if at all, only as they make it; they cannot see the hand of God in the affairs of men, because they see only with the eye of man and not with the eye of faith. All resistance is gone out of them—they have left God out of the question. They have not put on his whole armor. Without it they are loaded down with fear and apprehension, and they sink. To such men everything that brings trouble seems necessary. As Saints of God, it is our duty "to stand," even when we are overwhelmed by evil. ❧

Jesus sometimes spoke in paradoxical terms, telling his listeners on one occasion that he brought not peace but the sword, and on another that they should turn the other cheek rather than strike back at one who has wronged them. Just so, the counsel of Brigham Young on a number of occasions might seem contradictory to Joseph F. Smith's words above. A close analysis, however, reveals their ultimate consistency. Brigham Young is denouncing neither courage nor a firm stand for the right; rather, he is denouncing the foolish bravado that sometimes masquerades as righteous courage. In fact, as explained by Hugh Nibley, to endure rather than always to come out swinging is one kind of courage, one kind of charity.

FROM "BRIGHAM YOUNG AS A LEADER"

There was, in Brigham's philosophy and his actions, no place for heroics and hysterics. This sounds like a strange thing for the Lion of the Lord to say. "I have always acknowledged myself a coward, and hope I always may be, to make me cautious enough to preserve myself and my brethren from falling ignobly by a band of Indians" (*JD* 1:106). Be a coward, keep clear of them. Don't go out and stir up something. He says again, "I am a great coward myself, I do not wish to rush into danger imprudently" (*JD* 1:105). . . .

"I should have more fear in consequence of the ignorant and foolish audacity of the Elders, than of their being afraid" (*JD* 1:165). . . . And he said there were many courageous characters. This was a danger he always had to watch, that the elders didn't go out and start something. Look out, he said—"they would rush into danger like an unthinking horse into battle. So I will not find fault with regard to their courage. On that point, I am a coward myself, and if people would do as I tell them, I would not only save my own life, but theirs likewise" (*JD* 1:165).

Standing firmly for the right, as President Young did on many occasions, demonstrates true courage. Impulsive aggression or retaliation, on the other hand, has nothing to do with courage. It is, in fact, an enemy to charity, which is the exercise of love. Hugh Nibley speaks of true patriotism and courage, and the violation of them that is also a violation of charity.

FROM "THE USES AND ABUSES OF PATRIOTISM"

For most people, patriotism is a matter of forms and ceremonies. How far can we externalize a noble emotion? Like charity, it vaunteth not itself; the true patriot does not covet medals and badges to be seen of men, fearful less his heroism go unrecognized and unrewarded. . . .

Clichés and heroics can lead to disastrous excesses. . . . The tradition [of assassination and terror] still reverberates in the Middle East, where millions ecstatically hail acts of the most brutal, cowardly, and underhanded terrorism as patriotism of the highest and holiest order. . . .

While military action sometimes demands of the patriot a high order of courage, we must not forget that patriotism requires at least all four of the

Platonic virtues, and valor is only one of them. The one most likely to be overlooked, and actually the most demanding of these virtues in the patriot, is moderation—restraint and self-control. "We shall go on from victory to victory, and from conquest to conquest; *our* evil passions will be subdued, *our* prejudices depart; we shall find no room in our bosoms for hatred." It is those who "reject milder counsels" who bring "death and sorrow upon the Church . . ." (*Teachings of the Prophet Joseph Smith,* 179, emphasis added; 136). "Some of the Elders would much rather fight for their religion than live it. If any one thinks to get into the kingdom by fighting, . . . they will find themselves mistaken" (*Millenial Star* 33:433). ✦

Alfred Noyes ("The Highwayman") and Sir Walter Scott ("Lochinvar") have written stirring narrative poems about daring lovers, but daring is not the same as true courage.

OPPORTUNITY

This I beheld, or dreamed it in a dream:—
There spread a cloud of dust along a plain;
And underneath the cloud, or in it, raged
A furious battle, and men yelled, and swords
Shocked upon swords and shields. A prince's banner
Wavered, then staggered backward, hemmed by foes.
A craven hung along the battle's edge,
And thought, "Had I a sword of keener steel—
That blue blade that the king's son bears,—but this
Blunt thing—!" He snapt and flung it from his hand,
And lowering, crept away and left the field.
Then came the king's son, wounded, sore bestead,
And weaponless, and saw the broken sword,
Hilt-buried in the dry and trodden sand,
And ran and snatched it, and with battle-shout
Lifted afresh, he hewed his enemy down,
And saved a great cause that heroic day.
(Edward Rowland Sill.)

I learned a lasting lesson from a sign tacked to the log wall in the Exxum climbing school near Jackson, Wyoming. It said something like this: "When the summit is only a few hundred yards away, and a storm is threatening, it takes more courage to turn back than to go on." A hearty respect for forces we cannot control, a recognition of our very real limitations, is healthy, and it may even save our lives. The connection between love and courage, as opposed to braggadocio— which is only cowardice dressed up—is demonstrated in this fanciful children's poem. And since we are drawing morals, why not remark on the related virtue of modesty?

THE TALE OF CUSTARD THE DRAGON

Belinda lived in a little white house,
With a little black kitten and a little gray mouse,
And a little yellow dog and a little red wagon,
And a realio, trulio, little pet dragon.

Now the name of the little black kitten was Ink,
And the little gray mouse, she called her Blink,
And the little yellow dog was sharp as Mustard,
But the dragon was a coward, and she called him Custard.

Custard the dragon had big sharp teeth,
And spikes on top of him and scales underneath,
Mouth like a fireplace, chimney for a nose,
And realio, trulio daggers on his toes.

Belinda was as brave as a barrel full of bears,
And Ink and Blink chased lions down the stairs,
Mustard was as brave as a tiger in a rage,
But Custard cried for a nice safe cage.

Belinda tickled him, she tickled him unmerciful,
Ink, Blink and Mustard, they rudely called him Percival,
They all sat laughing in the little red wagon
At the realio, trulio, cowardly dragon.

Belinda giggled till she shook the house,
And Blink said *Weeck!,* which is giggling for a mouse,
Ink and Mustard rudely asked his age,
When Custard cried for a nice safe cage.

Suddenly, suddenly they heard a nasty sound,
And Mustard growled, and they all looked around.
Meowch! cried Ink, and Ooh! cried Belinda,
For there was a pirate, climbing in the winda.

Pistol in his left hand, pistol in his right,
And he held in his teeth a cutlass bright,
His beard was black, one leg was wood;
It was clear that the pirate meant no good.

Belinda paled, and she cried Help! Help!
But Mustard fled with a terrified yelp,
Ink trickled down to the bottom of the household,
And little mouse Blink strategically mouseholed.

But up jumped Custard, snorting like an engine,
Clashed his tail like irons in a dungeon,
With a clatter and a clank and a jangling squirm
He went at the pirate like a robin at a worm.

The pirate gaped at Belinda's dragon,
And gulped some grog from his pocket flagon,
He fired two bullets, but they didn't hit,
And Custard gobbled him, every bit.

Belinda embraced him, Mustard licked him;
No one mourned for his pirate victim.
Ink and Blink in glee did gyrate
Around the dragon that ate the pyrate.

Belinda still lives in her little white house,
With her little black kitten and her little gray mouse,

And her little yellow dog and her little red wagon,
And her realio, trulio, little pet dragon.

Belinda is as brave as a barrel full of bears,
And Ink and Blink chase lions down the stairs,
Mustard is as brave as a tiger in a rage,
And Custard keeps crying for a nice safe cage.
(Ogden Nash.)

Elder John H. Groberg tells a moving story of quiet initiative, strength, and endurance, one of many he witnessed on his first mission to Tonga some forty years ago:

THE LORD'S WIND

Finding someone willing to listen to the discussions was like finding a piece of gold, especially if a member had referred them. One day we received such a referral. We were told that if we would be at a certain harbor on a particular island when the sun set the next day, a family would meet us there and listen to the discussions.

What joy such news gives to missionaries! I quickly found four members who were experienced sailors to take me to the island.

Early the next morning, after prayer, the five of us started out in our sailboat. There was a nice breeze, and we moved swiftly along the coast, through the opening in the reef, and out into the wide expanse of the open ocean. We made good progress for a few hours. Then as the sun climbed higher in the sky and the boat got farther from land, the wind played out and soon quit completely, leaving us bobbing aimlessly on a smooth sea.

Those familiar with sailing know that to get anywhere, you must have wind. Sometimes there are good breezes without storms and heavy seas, but often they go together. An experienced sailor does not fear storms or heavy seas, for they contain the lifeblood of sailing—wind. What experienced sailors fear is no wind, or being becalmed!

Time passed and the sun got higher, the sea calmer. Nothing moved. We soon realized that unless something changed, we would not arrive at our appointment by sundown. I suggested that we pray and plead again with the Lord to send some wind so we could get to the harbor. What more righteous desire could a group of men have? We wanted to get to a family to teach the gospel. I offered a prayer. When I finished, things seemed calmer than ever. When it was obvious nothing was happening, I said, "Okay, which one of you is like Jonah? Who lacks faith? We'll throw you overboard so the Lord can send the wind and we can get on with our journey." No one would admit to being like Jonah, so we just drifted.

Then one of the older men suggested that everyone kneel and all unite their faith and prayers, each one offering a silent prayer at the same time, which we did. There was great struggling of spirit, but when the last person opened his eyes, nothing! No movement at all. The sails hung limp and listless. Even the slight ripple of the ocean against the side of the boat had ceased. The ocean seemed like a sea of glass.

Time was moving, and we were getting desperate. Then this same older man suggested that everyone kneel again in prayer, and each person in turn offer a vocal prayer for the whole group. Many beautiful, pleading, faithful prayers ascended to heaven. But when the last one finished and everyone opened their eyes, the sun was still burning down with greater intensity than before. The ocean was like a giant mirror. It was almost as though Satan was laughing, saying, "See, you can't go anywhere. There is no wind. You are in my power."

I thought, "There is a family at the harbor that wants to hear the gospel. We are here and we want to teach them. The Lord controls the elements. All that stands between getting the family and us together is a little wind. Why won't the Lord send it? It's a righteous desire."

As I was thinking, I noticed this faithful older man move to the rear of the boat. I watched as he unlashed the tiny lifeboat, placed two oars with pins into their places, and carefully lowered the lifeboat over the side.

Then the old man looked at me and softly said, "Get in."

I answered, "What are you doing? There is hardly room for two people in that tiny thing!"

The old man responded, "Don't waste any time or effort. Just get in. I

411

am going to row you to shore, and we need to leave right now to make it by sundown."

I looked at him incredulously, "Row me *where?*"

"To the family that wants to hear the gospel. We have an assignment from the Lord. Get in."

I was dumbfounded. It was miles and miles to shore. The sun was hot and this man was old. But as I looked into the face of that faithful brother, I sensed an intensity in his gaze, an iron will in his very being, and a fixed determination in his voice as he said, "Before the sun sets this day, you will be teaching the gospel and bearing testimony to a family who wants to listen."

I objected, "Look, you're over three times my age. If we're going to do it this way, fine, but let me row."

With that same look of determination and faith-induced will, the old man replied, "No leave it to me. Get in the boat. Don't waste time talking or moving unnecessarily. Let's go!" We got into the boat with me in the front and the old man in the middle with his feet stretching to the rear of the boat, his back to me.

The glazed surface of the ocean was disturbed at the intrusion of this small boat and seemed to complain, "This is my territory. Stay out." Not a wisp of air stirred, not a sound was heard except the creaking of oars and the rattling of pins as the small craft began to move away from the side of the sailboat.

The old man bent his back and began to row—dip, pull, lift, dip, pull, lift. Each dip of the oar seemed to break the resolve of the mirrorlike ocean. Each pull of the oar moved the tiny skiff forward, separating the glassy seas to make way for the Lord's messenger.

Dip. Pull. Lift. The old man did not look up, rest, or talk. But hour after hour he rowed and rowed and rowed. The muscles of his back and arms, strengthened by faith and moved by unalterable determination, flexed in a marvelous cadence like a fine-tuned watch. We moved quietly, relentlessly toward an inevitable destiny. The old man concentrated his efforts and energy on fulfilling the calling he had from the Lord—to get the mission-

412

ary to the family that wanted to hear the gospel. He was the Lord's wind that day.

Just as the sun dipped into the ocean, the skiff touched the shore of the harbor. A family *was* waiting. The old man spoke for the first time in hours and said, "Go. Teach them the truth. I'll wait here."

I waded ashore, met the family, went to their home, and taught them the gospel. As I bore testimony of the power of God in this Church, my mind seemed to see an old man rowing to a distant harbor and patiently waiting there. I testified with a fervor as great as any I have ever felt that God does give power to men to do His will if they have faith in Him. I said, "When we exercise faith in the Lord Jesus Christ, we can do things we could not otherwise do. When our hearts are determined to do right, the Lord gives us the power to do so."

The family believed and eventually was baptized.

In the annals of Church history, few will be aware of this small incident. Hardly anyone will know about this insignificant island, the family who waited, or the obscure, old man who never once complained of fatigue, aching arms, a painful back, or a hurting body. He never talked about thirst, the scorching sun, or the heat of the day as he relentlessly rowed uncomplainingly hour upon hour and only referred to the privilege of being God's agent in bringing a missionary to teach the truth to those who desired to hear. But God knows! He gave him the strength to be His wind that day, and He will give us the strength to be His wind when necessary.

How often do we not do more because we pray for wind and none comes? We pray for good things and they don't seem to happen, so we sit and wait and do no more. We should always pray for help, but we should always listen for inspiration and impressions to proceed in different ways from those we may have thought of. God does hear our prayers. God knows more than we do. He has had infinitely greater experience than we have. We should never stop moving because we think our way is barred or the only door we can go through is seemingly closed.

No matter what our trials, we should never say, "It is enough." Only

God is entitled to say that. Our responsibility, if we are faithful, is to ask, "What more can I do?" then listen for the answer and do it!

I'll never forget the example of that old man. ✦

Wars fought on principle have a way of spawning acts of singular courage, courage based on love; and those acts capture the poet's imagination. Whose pulse does not quicken to the beat of lines penned in honor of courageous patriots of the American Revolution and the American Civil War? The first two stanzas of "Paul Revere's Ride," by Henry Wadsworth Longfellow, have been recited in many a schoolroom. I also cite the final stanza:

FROM "PAUL REVERE'S RIDE"

Listen, my children, and you shall hear
Of the midnight ride of Paul Revere,
On the eighteenth of April, in Seventy-five;
Hardly a man is now alive
Who remembers that famous day and year.
He said to his friend, "If the British march
By land or sea from the town to-night,
Hang a lantern aloft in the belfry arch
Of the North Church tower as a signal light,—
One, if by land, and two, if by sea;
And I on the opposite shore will be,
Ready to ride and spread the alarm
Through every Middlesex village and farm,
For the country folk to be up and to arm."

. . . .

So through the night rode Paul Revere;
And so through the night went his cry of alarm
To every Middlesex village and farm,—
A cry of defiance and not of fear,
A voice in the darkness, a knock at the door,
And a word that shall echo forevermore!
For, borne on the night-wind of the Past,

Through all our history, to the last,
In the hour of darkness and peril and need,
The people will waken and listen to hear
The hurrying hoof-beats of that steed,
And the midnight message of Paul Revere.

*Equally enduring and inspiriting is the courage of old Barbara Frietchie,
immortalized in verse by John Greenleaf Whittier.*

BARBARA FRIETCHIE

Up from the meadows rich with corn,
Clear in the cool September morn,
The clustered spires of Frederick stand
Green-walled by the hills of Maryland.
Round about them orchards sweep,
Apple and peach tree fruited deep,
Fair as the garden of the Lord
To the eyes of the famished rebel horde,
On that pleasant morn of the early fall
When Lee marched over the mountain-wall,—
Over the mountains winding down,
Horse and foot, into Frederick town.
Forty flags with their silver stars,
Forty flags with their crimson bars,
Flapped in the morning wind: the sun
Of noon looked down, and saw not one.
Up rose old Barbara Frietchie then,
Bowed with her fourscore years and ten;
Bravest of all in Frederick town,
She took up the flag the men hauled down;
In her attic window the staff she set,
To show that one heart was loyal yet.
Up the street came the rebel tread,
Stonewall Jackson riding ahead.

Under his slouched hat left and right
He glanced: the old flag met his sight.
"Halt!"—the dust-brown ranks stood fast.
"Fire!"—out blazed the rifle-blast.
It shivered the window, pane and sash;
It rent the banner with seam and gash.
Quick, as it fell, from the broken staff
Dame Barbara snatched the silken scarf.
She leaned far out on the window-sill,
And shook it forth with a royal will.
"Shoot, if you must, this old gray head,
But spare your country's flag," she said.
A shade of sadness, a blush of shame,
Over the face of the leader came;
The nobler nature within him stirred
To life at that woman's deed and word:
"Who touches a hair of yon gray head
Dies like a dog! March on!" he said.
All day long through Frederick street
Sounded the tread of marching feet:
All day long that free flag tost
Over the heads of the rebel host.
Ever its torn folds rose and fell
On the loyal winds that loved it well;
And through the hill-gaps sunset light
Shone over it with a warm good-night.
Barbara Frietchie's work is o'er,
And the Rebel rides on his raids no more.
Honor to her! and let a tear
Fall, for her sake, on Stonewall's bier.
Over Barbara Frietchie's grave,
Flag of Freedom and Union, wave!
Peace and order and beauty draw

Round thy symbol of light and law;
And ever the stars above look down
On thy stars below in Frederick town!

Although we would not care to embrace everything Pericles espouses in his famous funeral oration, he articulates an ideal of courage unique to his time and place. The occasion is a state funeral honoring the Athenians who fell in the Peloponnesian War between Athens and Sparta (431–404 B.C.). Following is an extract from that oration.

When you find [Athens] a great city remember that men won that greatness for her by their boldness, their ability to grasp what was required of them, and the sense of honor with which they carried it out. . . .

. . . the real tomb of famous men is the whole earth; they are marked out not merely by the inscription over a grave in their own country but in other lands also by an unwritten memory, recording their spirit more than their actions, which lives on in the minds of men. Emulate them, then, in your own lives; learn from them that the key to happiness is freedom, the key to freedom a stout heart, and do not set a false value on the dangers of war. It is not the unfortunate, those with no hope of anything better, who have most reason to sacrifice their lives freely, but those who face the danger of a change for the worse if they go on living and, if they come to disaster in any undertaking, risk the greatest loss. To a man of any spirit the suffering and humiliation that go with cowardice are more painful to endure than a quick death, coming unnoticed in the full flush of strength and common hopes. ❧

Mormon history tells many stories of quiet courage, the kind born of enduring faith. Even imminent death cannot shake such courage. The following accounts demonstrate that bravado is no match for genuine courage, which endures in faith and charity. The first event took place in Missouri; the mob spirit was rampant.

Louisa [Free, later Wells] and her sister Emeline, with their cousin, Eliza Free, stood guard, on a ridge near the house, for three weeks, night and day, to warn the families of the approach of the mob. . . . [Their father had gone to the defense of Far West, then under serious seige.]

417

While thus standing guard, one day, the girls saw a troop of horsemen near, marching with a red flag and the beating of drums. They had with them a prisoner, on foot, whom they were thus triumphantly marching to their camp. They were a troop of the mob. The prisoner was grandfather Andrew Free, though at the time the sisters knew it not.

It was almost night. The horsemen made direct for their camp with their "prisoner of war," whom they had taken, not in arms, for he was aged, yet was he a soldier of the cross, ready to die for his faith.

Already had the veteran disciple been doomed by his captors. He was to be shot; one escape only had they reserved for him.

Before the mob tribunal stood the old man, calm and upright in his integrity, and resolved in his faith. No one was near to succor him. He stood alone, face to face with death, with those stern, cruel men, whose class had shown so little mercy in Missouri, massacring men, women and children, at Haun's Mill, and elsewhere about the same time.

Then the captain and his band demanded of the old man that he should swear there and then to renounce Jo. Smith and his d——d religion, or they would shoot him on the spot.

Drawing himself up with a lofty mien, and the invincible courage that the Mormons have always shown in their persecutions, the veteran answered: "I have not long to live. At the worst you cannot deprive me of many days. I will never betray or deny my faith which I know to be of God. Here is my breast, shoot away, I am ready to die for my religion!"

At this he bared his bosom and calmly waited for the mob to fire.

But the band was abashed at his fearless bearing and answer. For a time the captain and his men consulted, and then they told their prisoner that they had decided to give him till the morning to reconsider whether he would retract his faith or die.

Morning came. Again the old man was before the tribunal, fearless in the cause of his religion as he had been the previous night. Again came from him a similar answer, and then he looked for death, indeed, the next moment.

But he had conquered his captors, and the leader declared, with an oath: "Any man who can be so d—d true to any d—d religion, deserves to live!"

Thereupon the mob released the heroic disciple of Mormonism, and he returned to his home in safety. ❦

Lucy Mack Smith tells of her own encounter with armed men, and of her son Joseph's courageous and peaceful defusing of their evil intent. The "visit" described below occurred subsequent to an altercation between Mormons and non-Mormons, at an election polling place in Daviess County, Missouri.

FROM *HISTORY OF JOSEPH SMITH*

Joseph was at our house writing a letter. While he was thus engaged, I stepped to the door, and looking toward the prairie, I beheld a large company of armed men advancing towards the city, but, as I supposed it to be training day, said nothing about it.

Presently the main body came to a halt. The officers dismounting, eight of them came into the house. Thinking they had come for some refreshment, I offered them chairs, but they refused to be seated, and, placing themselves in a line across the floor, continued standing. I again requested them to sit, but they replied, "We do not choose to sit down; we have come here to kill Joe Smith and all the 'Mormons.'"

"Ah," said I, "what has Joseph Smith done, that you should want to kill him?"

"He has killed seven men in Daviess County," replied the foremost, "and we have come to kill him, and all his Church."

"He has not been in Daviess County," I answered, "consequently the report must be false. Furthermore, if you should see him, you would not want to kill him."

"There is no doubt that the report is perfectly correct," rejoined the officer; "it came straight to us, and I believe it; and we were sent to kill the Prophet and all who believe in him, and I'll be d—d if I don't execute my orders."

"I suppose," said I, "you intend to kill me, with the rest?"

"Yes, we do," returned the officer.

"Very well, I continued, "I want you to act the gentleman about it, and do the job quick. Just shoot me down at once, then I shall be at rest; but I should not like to be murdered by inches."

"There it is again," said he. "You tell a 'Mormon' that you will kill him, and they always tell you, 'that is nothing—if you kill us, we shall be happy.'"

Joseph just at this moment finished his letter, and, seeing that he was at liberty, I said, "Gentlemen, suffer me to make you acquainted with Joseph Smith, the Prophet." They stared at him as if he were a spectre. He smiled, and stepping towards them, gave each of them his hand, in a manner which convinced them that he was neither a guilty criminal nor yet a hypocrite.

Joseph then sat down and explained to them the views, feelings, etc., of the Church, and what their course had been; besides the treatment which they had received from their enemies since the first. He also argued, that if any of the brethren had broken the law, they ought to be tried by the law, before anyone else was molested. After talking with them some time in this way, he said, "Mother, I believe I will go home now—Emma will be expecting me." At this two of the men sprang to their feet, and declared that he should not go alone, as it would be unsafe—that they would go with him, in order to protect him. Accordingly the three left together, and, during their absence, I overheard the following conversation among the officers, who remained at the door:

1st Officer. "Did you not feel strangely when Smith took you by the hand? I never felt so in my life."

2nd Officer. "I could not move. I would not harm a hair of that man's head for the whole world." ✦

The portrait of Moroni, commander of the Nephite armies in the days of Helaman, is a model of righteous courage. He favored decisive action, but he was never cruel or self-serving.

And now it came to pass that when Moroni, who was the chief commander of the armies of the Nephites, had heard of these dissensions, he was angry with Amalickiah.

And it came to pass that he rent his coat; and he took a piece thereof, and wrote upon it—In memory of our God, our religion, and freedom, and our peace, our wives, and our children—and he fastened it upon the end of a pole.

And he fastened on his headplate, and his breastplate, and his shields, and girded on his armor about his loins; and he took the pole, which had on the end thereof his rent coat, (and he called it the title of liberty) and he bowed himself to the earth, and he prayed mightily unto his God for the blessings of liberty to rest upon his brethren, so long as there should a band of Christians remain to possess the land—. . . .

And therefore, at this time, Moroni prayed that the cause of the Christians, and the freedom of the land might be favored. . . .

And when Moroni had said these words, he went forth among the people, waving the rent part of his garment in the air, that all might see the writing which he had written upon the rent part, and crying with a loud voice, saying:

Behold, whosoever will maintain this title upon the land, let them come forth in the strength of the Lord, and enter into a covenant that they will maintain their rights, and their religion, that the Lord God may bless them. (Alma 46:11–13, 16, 19–20.)

Now it came to pass that while Amalickiah had thus been obtaining power by fraud and deceit, Moroni, on the other hand, had been preparing the minds of the people to be faithful unto the Lord their God.

Yea, he had been strengthening the armies of the Nephites, and erecting small forts, or places of resort; throwing up banks of earth round about to enclose his armies, and also building walls of stone to encircle them about, round about their cities and the borders of their lands; yea, all round about the land.

And in their weakest fortifications he did place the greater number of men; and thus he did fortify and strengthen the land which was possessed by the Nephites.

And thus he was preparing to support their liberty, their lands, their wives, and their children, and their peace, and that they might live unto the Lord their God, and that they might maintain that which was called by their enemies the cause of Christians.

And Moroni was a strong and a mighty man; he was a man of a perfect understanding; yea, a man that did not delight in bloodshed; a man whose soul did joy in the liberty and the freedom of his country, and his brethren from bondage and slavery;

Yea, a man whose heart did swell with thanksgiving to his God, for the many privileges and blessings which he bestowed upon his people; a man who did labor exceedingly for the welfare and safety of his people.

Yea, and he was a man who was firm in the faith of Christ, and he had sworn with an oath to defend his people, his rights, and his country, and his religion, even to the loss of his blood. (Alma 48:7–13.) ✦

The final three verses cited above describe the person, not just the warrior, of abiding courage, faith, charity, and endurance. Moroni thought only of the people and the God he served. He concentrated on fortification and protection rather than destruction of others, and his weapon of choice was his mind. Many a "battle" was won by strategem rather than slaughter—sometimes without a single fatality.

Life and literature present stirring accounts of endurance and courage that reach beyond valor. Viktor E. Frankl writes of almost unfathomable courage that wedged up, like a mariposa lily, through the cracks of grief and horror to bloom in the moral desert of Nazi concentration camps. This is the charity of enduring.

FROM MAN'S SEARCH FOR MEANING

The experiences of camp life show that man does have a choice of action. There were enough examples, often of a heroic nature, which proved that apathy could be overcome, irritability suppressed. Man *can* preserve a vestige of spiritual freedom, of independence of mind, even in such terrible conditions of psychic and physical stress.

We who lived in concentration camps can remember the men who walked through the huts comforting others, giving away their last piece of bread. They may have been few in number, but they offer sufficient proof that everything can be taken from a man but one thing: the last of the human freedoms—to choose one's attitude in any given set of circumstances, to choose one's own way.

And there were always choices to make. Every day, every hour, offered the opportunity to make a decision which determined whether you would or would not submit to those powers which threatened to rob you of your very self, your inner freedom; which determined whether or not you would become the plaything of circumstance, renouncing freedom and dignity to become molded into the form of the typical inmate.

. . . Even though conditions such as lack of sleep, insufficient food and various mental stresses may suggest that the inmates were bound to react in certain ways, in the final analysis it becomes clear that the sort of person the prisoner became was the result of an inner decision, and not the result of camp influences alone. Fundamentally, therefore, any man can, even under such circumstances, decide what shall become of him—mentally and spiritually. ❦

Thomas Carlyle writes in praise of Martin Luther's courage in Luther's attack on the practice of selling religious indulgences, and his refusal at the Diet of Worms (April 17, 1521) to recant and accede to the Pope's corrupt authority on the matter.

It is, as we say, the greatest moment in the modern history of men. English puritanism, England and its parliaments, Americas, and vast work these two centuries; French revolution, Europe and its work everywhere at present; the germ of it all lay there; had Luther in that moment done other, it had all been otherwise! . . .

. . . Luther did what every man that God has made has not only the right, but lies under the sacred duty, to do; answered a falsehood when it questioned him, Dost thou believe me? No! At what cost soever, without counting of costs, this thing behooved to be done. . . .

. . . Laughter was in this Luther, as we said; but tears also were there. Tears also were appointed him; tears and hard toil. . . . I will call this Luther a true great man; great in intellect, in courage, affection and integrity; one of our most lovable and precious men. Great, not as a hewn obelisk; but as an Alpine mountain—so simple, honest, spontaneous, not setting up to be great at all; there for quite another purpose than being great! Ah yes, unsubduable granite, piercing far and wide into the heaven; yet in the clefts of it fountains, green beautiful valleys with flowers! A right spiritual hero and

423

prophet; once more, a true son of nature and fact, for whom these centuries and many that are to come yet, will be thankful to heaven. ✦

Carlyle would have appreciated the courage of another defender of the faith, this one who lived more than three centuries later than Luther, on the American continent. Many of Carlyle's words apply equally well to his contemporary, Joseph Smith. Parley P. Pratt has described a moving episode of courage, one of many, in the Prophet's life. Parley, Joseph, and others were imprisoned during the Missouri persecutions and placed under "an unruly guard" that was "composed generally of the most noisy, foul-mouthed, vulgar, disgraceful rabble that ever defiled the earth." Here is Parley's account of what transpired:

FROM *AUTOBIOGRAPHY OF PARLEY P. PRATT*

In one of those tedious nights we had lain as if in sleep till the hour of midnight had passed, and our ears and hearts had been pained, while we had listened for hours to the obscene jests, the horrid oaths, the dreadful blasphemies and filthy language of our guards, Colonel Price at their head, as they recounted to each other their deeds of rapine, murder, robbery, etc., which they had committed among the "*Mormons*" while at Far West and vicinity. They even boasted of defiling by force wives, daughters and virgins, and of shooting or dashing out the brains of men, women and children.

I had listened till I became so disgusted, shocked, horrified, and so filled with the spirit of indignant justice that I could scarcely refrain from rising upon my feet and rebuking the guards; but had said nothing to Joseph, or anyone else, although I lay next to him and knew he was awake. On a sudden he arose to his feet, and spoke in a voice of thunder, or as the roaring lion, uttering, as near as I can recollect, the following words:

"*SILENCE, ye fiends of the infernal pit. In the name of Jesus Christ I rebuke you, and command you to be still; I will not live another minute and hear such language. Cease such talk, or you or I die THIS INSTANT!*"

He ceased to speak. He stood erect in terrible majesty. Chained, and without a weapon; calm, unruffled and dignified as an angel, he looked upon the quailing guards, whose weapons were lowered or dropped to the ground; whose knees smote together, and who, shrinking into a corner, or crouching at his feet, begged his pardon, and remained quiet till a change of guards.

I have seen the ministers of justice, clothed in magisterial robes, and criminals arraigned before them, while life was suspended on a breath, in the Courts of England; I have witnessed a Congress in solemn session to give laws to nations; I have tried to conceive of kings, of royal courts, of thrones and crowns; and of emperors assembled to decide the fate of kingdoms; but dignity and majesty have I seen but *once*, as it stood in chains, at midnight, in a dungeon in an obscure village of Missouri. ✦

The courage of the early Saints is aptly characterized in a letter written by Irene Hascall Pomeroy to her cousin in Massachusetts. The letter, sent from Salt Lake City and dated in the spring of 1848, illustrates not only her plucky enjoyment of the journey—most of which she made on foot—but also her courageous faith. This one statement reveals the woman:

What I say to one I say to all who shall here it, and read it to every one you can (this part if nothing more) for I say it again I know it is truth and I say it by the spirit of God. I would die in one minute for this gospel if necessary or required of the Lord. ✦

LONE WOMAN: CHARITY (ARMS) EVERTS

> She must have been whip-thin to make that trek
> Across the continent, her body taut
> As wet rawhide, her courage ramrod stiff.
> How else to leave those little graves behind,
> Six of the ten she bore, one slashed to death
> By peccaries, in shallow slits of earth,
> That one long gash beneath a spreading oak
> From one black, fatal day in Illinois
> Before they reached Nauvoo to join the Saints.
> The solemn workmen brought her Joshua,
> Her life, her love, the husband half of her,
> His body shattered by a falling tree,

To live but briefly, dying in her arms.
Through ashen, urgent lips he begged her go.
"Go with the Saints. Let nothing interfere.
To Zion, to The Kingdom—for our sakes."
(Alice Morrey Bailey.)

The Wanlass family papers tell a courageous story of fourteen-year-old Mary, whose mother had died and whose father, Jackson, had suffered a stroke. Later her stepmother also died, leaving Mary to care for the family.

FROM "THEY CAME ALONE"

[Mary's family consisted of] twins four years of age, a little sister of six, her brother nine and a bedridden father. However, with all this added responsibility, she never lost sight of the fact that they had left their home and comforts in England to go to Zion, and up 'til now, they had gotten only as far as Missouri. She couldn't forget how her stepmother had pleaded to go on, and even on her death bed she turned to Mary and said: "Don't give your father any peace until he goes to the Rocky Mountains." So she vowed within herself to take the children to the Rockies even if she had to go alone.

She told her father what she intended to do with such earnestness that he believed she meant it. So in spite of pleadings of Maj. Sievere, who even offered him half interest in the coal holdings, the father sold all he had for enough money to buy a wagon, a yoke of young steers, a yoke of cows, and a few provisions. Aunt Ellen Sharp made the children some new clothes, and helped them with their arrangements.

Finally, when all was in readiness, they bade goodbye to their loved ones and started the journey west. An immigrant train of non-Mormon settlers going to Oregon to escape the ravages of war, had been up to St. Louis, and Jackson made arrangements to go with them as far as Iowa. Here he expected to join a company of Saints. Soon after they started, the father suffered another partial stroke of the left side, which made him entirely bedfast and it necessary for them to drop behind until he was able to travel. They were detained for more than a week, and by the time they were able to continue their journey, they were so far behind they never did catch up with anyone, so they pressed on alone. The three small children were placed on the backs of the oxen, and the nine-year-old boy acted as co-pilot.

Day after day they trudged through a country overrun by lawless renegades—men who had deserted both armies and were foraging for themselves. They pushed on until the last settlement was left behind, and nothing but treeless and trackless wilderness lay before them. When they reached the Platte River, they should have crossed it, but instead they continued on the west side which unknowingly isolated them from the whites and led them through hostile country.

They saw Indians every day. Sometimes they were talkative and friendly, while other times they were sullen and painted with war paint. On several occasions young warriors would rush upon them, shout, and wave blankets at the cattle to stampede them, but the cattle only shook their heads, blinked eyes and plodded on. Then [the] Indians would laugh and ride away. Many times the cattle would be driven off in the night, but in the morning they were always found in a nearby wash, or behind a hill. When they made camp at night, the Indians would come from every direction and sit around their fire, or on the wagon tongue. Mary's only fear was that the tongue might break under their weight, then they would surely be stalled.

The hand of the Lord was manifest in their behalf throughout the whole journey, but more especially so on several occasions. The Indians knew her father was bedfast because they would raise the wagon cover and look in. In poor English they asked if her pappy was sick. When she nodded, they would ride away, only to return with rabbits or wild ducks for her to cook for him.

Whirlwinds are very common on the plains, and one evening, when they were camped on the banks of the Platte, they encountered an extra strong one. It picked up Annie, one of the twins, and dropped her in the middle of the river. The other children screamed, and Mary, who was getting supper, turned around just in time to see Annie drop. She immediately plunged in, clothes and all, and brought her out. How, she did not know, because she knew nothing about swimming, and her brother was busy tending the cattle. Whenever they camped by the water they let the cattle drink as often and as much as they could because sometimes it was a long time between drinks.

The little black heifer, that helped pull the wagon each day, was the one that supplied the twins with milk, and the only feed she got was what she could forage at night. After the twins were fed, the remainder was put in a jar, and at the end of the day it was taken out in the form of butter; thus the rough roads did the churning. [Despite increasingly difficult circumstances and a badly worn wagon, the courageous little group reached Echo Canyon where "they met the first white man they'd seen since they left Missouri." From there, they followed the Provo River and were reunited with relatives in Lehi.] ❦

It also required courage as well as faith for the early Saints to accept and live the principle of plural marriage. In her autobiography, printed serially in the Woman's Exponent, *Elizabeth Ann Whitney writes of her personal reconciliation to that principle. "Among that number" who "remained firm and immovable" in their acceptance of plural marriage, she says, "were my husband [Newel K. Whitney] and myself." There is charity in her words.*

FROM "A LEAF FROM AN AUTOBIOGRAPHY"

Although my husband believed and was firm in teaching this Celestial order of Marriage, he was slow in practice. Joseph repeatedly told him to take a wife, or wives, but he wished to be so extremely cautious not to do what would probably have to be undone, that in Joseph's day he never took a wife. When he did so, he did it to fulfill a duty due to the principles of divine revelation as he understood his duty, and believing sincerely that every man should prove his faith by his works; but he afterwards took several wives, and with one or two exceptions, they came into the same house with me, and my children; therefore, I believe I am safe in saying that I am intimately acquainted with the practical part of polygamy.

We learn to understand human nature, by being brought into close connection with each other, and more especially when under trying and difficult circumstances; and we seldom think more unkindly of persons from gaining an insight into their real hearts and character. Instead of my opinion of women being unfavorable or my feelings unkindly in consequence of being intimately associated in family relationship with them, I am more favorably disposed to women as a class, learning more of the true nature of woman-kind than I ever could without this peculiar experience; and I am willing and ready to defend enthusiastically those of my sisters who have been genuine enough and who possessed sufficient sublimity of character, to practically live the principles of divine faith, which have been revealed in these last days, in the establishing of the kingdom of God upon the earth. It has required sterling qualities indeed to battle with the opposition on every hand, and not be overcome.

That this is God's work and not man's should be apparent to all those who are acquainted with the history of the saints, their persecutions, their trials, their difficulties, and the marvelous means of their deliverance,— when dangerous and various untoward circumstances environed them. ❧

In what he calls "nonlecture one," the first of six "nonlectures" cited earlier, poet e e cummings draws touching portraits of his parents, both of whose courage and capacity for love leave me a little dazed. Here, a story about his father.

Thirty-five years ago, a soiled envelope with a French stamp on it arrived at 104 Irving Street, Cambridge. The envelope contained a carefully phrased scrawl; stating (among other things) that I was interned in a certain concentration camp, with a fine friend named Brown whom I'd met on the boat going to France—he, like myself, having volunteered as an ambulance driver [World War I] with Messers Norton (not Charles Eliot) and Harjes. Immediately my father—than whom no father on this earth ever loved or ever will love his son more profoundly—cabled his friend Norton; but Mr. Norton hadn't even missed us, and consequently could do less than nothing. Next, through a mere but loyal acquaintance, my father set the American army on our trail; forcefully stipulating that my friend and I must be rescued together. Many days passed. Suddenly the telephone rang—top brass demanding Reverend Edward Cummings. "Hello" my father said. "This is Major Soandso" an angry voice sputtered. "That friend of your son is no damned good. May even be a spy. Unpatriotic anyhow. He deserves what's coming to him. Do you understand?" "I understand" said my deeply

429

patriotic father. "We won't touch Brown" the sputter continued "so it's your son or nothing. And I guarantee that your son alone will be out of that hell-hole in five days—what do you say about that?" "I say" replied my father "don't bother." And he hung up.

Incidentally, the major bothered; and as a result, my friend Slater Brown is also alive.

Let me only add that while my father was speaking with the American army, my mother was standing beside him; for these two wonderful human beings, my father and my mother, loved each other more than themselves—

if there are any heavens my mother will (all by herself) have
one. It will not be a pansy heaven or
a fragile heaven of lilies-of-the-valley but
it will be a heaven of blackred roses

my father will be (deep like a rose
tall like a rose)

standing near my

(swaying over her
silent)
with eyes which are really petals and see

nothing with the face of a poet really which
is a flower and not a face with
hands
which whisper
This is my beloved my

    (suddenly in sunlight)
he will bow,

(and the whole garden will bow)

—as for me, I was welcomed as no son of any king and queen was ever welcomed. Here was my joyous fate and my supreme fortune. If somehow a suggestion of this illimitable blessing should come to you from me, my existence here and now would be justified: otherwise, anything I may say to you will have not the slightest significance. ✦

Cummings goes on to relate the story of his mother's self-masterful courage following an accident in which her husband was killed and she suffered severe injuries. (See his account quoted above, in chapter 6 of this volume.) Cummings cites these lines from Shelley as an epilogue to his sixth nonlecture, and thus to his book. The lines affirm the charity of courageous endurance.

THE CONCLUSION

TO *PROMETHEUS UNBOUND*

This is the day, which down the void abysm
At the Earth-born's spell yawns for Heaven's despotism,
And Conquest is dragged captive through the deep:
Love, from its awful throne of patient power
In the wise heart, from the last giddy hour
Of dread endurance, from the slippery, steep,
And narrow verge of crag-like agony, springs
And folds over the world its healing wings.

Gentleness, Virtue, Wisdom, and Endurance,—
These are the seals of that most firm assurance
Which bars the pit over Destruction's strength;
And if, with infirm hand, Eternity,
Mother of many acts and hours, should free
The serpent that would clasp her with his length;
These are the spells by which to re-assume
An empire o'er the disentangled doom.

To suffer woes which Hope thinks infinite;
To forgive wrongs darker than death or night;
To defy Power, which seems omnipotent;
To love, and bear; to hope till Hope creates
From its own wreck the thing it contemplates;

Neither to change, nor flatter, nor repent;—
This, like thy glory, Titan, is to be
Good, great and joyous, beautiful and free;
This is alone Life, Joy, Empire, and Victory.
(Percy Bysshe Shelley.)

16

CHARITY NEVER FAILETH

Therefore, I would that ye should be steadfast

and immovable, always abounding in good works,

that Christ, the Lord God Omnipotent, may seal you

his, that you may be brought to heaven, that ye

may have everlasting salvation and eternal life,

through the wisdom, and power, and justice,

and mercy of him who created all things, in heaven

and in earth, who is God above all.

MOSIAH 5:15

In saying that charity "never faileth," Paul is extolling the staying power of love, the pure love of Christ. Very likely, the phrase has more to do with endurance—in the sense of enduring to the end—than has the phrase discussed in the foregoing chapter, "endureth all things." And here, as with the other attributes of charity, Paul's brief phrase invites expansion. In the passage above, the wise and noble King Benjamin seems to have provided that expansion. He uses the words steadfast, immovable, always, and everlasting, and he makes five allusions to the Lord Jesus Christ. Together, the references call up some aspects of what Paul may have meant by the phrase "never faileth." As Christ never fails us, so are we never to fail him or each other. We are to persevere in our duty and commitments, to trust him and to be ourselves trustworthy and loyal.

Reaching a bit, but perhaps not overstretching Paul's meaning, we might also see a relationship to the continuity of remembrance, the stability of memory. The charity or love that does not fail remembers both divine and mortal ties, and their attendant blessings and responsibilities. These words of Brigham Young seem especially pertinent to the theme "charity never faileth":

While speaking the other day to the people, I observed that "the race was not to the swift, nor the battle to the strong," neither riches to men of wisdom. I happened to cast my eyes upon Ira Ames, who was sitting in the congregation. I knew he had been in the Church a considerable length of time, I have been personally acquainted with him for twenty years. My eye also caught many more of the first Saints at the same time. These men know that "Mormonism" is true, they have moved steadily forward, and have not *sought* to become noted characters, as many have; but, unseen as it were, they have maintained their footing steadily in the right path. I could place my hand upon many in this congregation, who will win the race, though they are not very swift, to outward appearance, and they make no great pretensions; they are found continually attending to their *own business.* They do not appear to be great warriors, or as if they were likely to win the battle. But what is their true character? They have faith to-day, they are filled with faith, their words are few, but they are full of integrity. You will find them to-morrow as they were yesterday, or are to-day. Visit them when you will, or under whatever circumstances, and you find them unalterably the same; and finally when you have spent your life with them, you will find that their lives throughout have been well spent, full of faith, hope, charity, and good works, as far as they have had the ability. These are the ones who will win the race, conquer in the battle, and obtain the peace and righteousness of eternity. (*Journal of Discourses* 1:89.) ◄

In seeking a simple narrative exemplum for the truism that the race of life is more often won by perseverance than by swiftness, we turn to the story of the tortoise and the hare. Its concluding line echoes still in my ears: "Slow and steady wins the race." Lord Dunsany, early twentieth-century Irish writer with a taste for political satire, gives the story a different spin.

THE TRUE HISTORY
OF THE HARE AND THE TORTOISE

For a long time there was doubt with acrimony among the beasts as to whether the Hare or the Tortoise could run the swifter. Some said the Hare was the swifter of the two because he had such long ears, and others said that the Tortoise was the swifter because any one whose shell was so hard as that should be able to run hard too. And lo, the forces of estrangement and disorder perpetually postponed a decisive contest.

But when there was nearly war among the beasts, at last an arrangement was come to and it was decided that the Hare and the Tortoise should run a race of five hundred yards so that all should see who was right.

"Ridiculous nonsense!" said the Hare, and it was all his backers could do to get him to run.

"The contest is most welcome to me," said the Tortoise. "I shall not shirk it."

O, how his backers cheered.

Feeling ran high on the day of the race; the goose rushed at the fox and nearly pecked him. Both sides spoke loudly of the approaching victory up to the very moment of the race.

"I am absolutely confident of success," said the Tortoise. But the Hare said nothing, he looked bored and cross. Some of his supporters deserted him then and went to the other side, who were loudly cheering the Tortoise's inspiriting words. But many remained with the Hare. "We shall not be disappointed in him," they said. "A beast with such long ears is bound to win."

"Run hard," said the supporters of the Tortoise.

And "run hard" became a kind of catch-phrase which everybody repeated to one another. "Hard shell and hard living. That's what the country wants. Run hard," they said. And these words were never uttered but multitudes cheered from their hearts.

Then they were off, and suddenly there was a hush.

The Hare dashed off for about a hundred yards, then he looked round to see where his rival was.

"It is rather absurd," he said, "to race with a Tortoise." And he sat down and scratched himself. "Run hard! Run hard!" shouted some.

"Let him rest," shouted others. And "let him rest" became a catch-phrase too.

And after a while his rival drew near to him.

"There comes that cursed Tortoise," said the Hare, and he got up and ran as hard as he could so that he should not let the Tortoise beat him.

"Those ears will win," said his friends. "Those ears will win; and establish upon an incontestable footing the truth of what we have said." And some of them turned to the backers of the Tortoise and said: "What about your beast now?"

"Run hard," they replied. "Run hard."

The Hare ran on for nearly three hundred yards, nearly in fact as far as the winning-post, when it suddenly struck him what a fool he looked running races with a Tortoise who was nowhere in sight, and he sat down again and scratched.

"Run hard. Run hard," said the crowd, and "Let him rest."

"Whatever is the use of it?" said the Hare, and this time he stopped for good. Some say he slept.

There was desperate excitement for an hour or two, and then the Tortoise won.

"Run hard. Run hard," shouted his backers. "Hard shell and hard living: that's what has done it." And then they asked the Tortoise what his achievement signified, and he went and asked the Turtle. And the Turtle said: "It is a glorious victory for the forces of swiftness." And then the Tortoise repeated it to his friends. And all the beasts said nothing else for years. And even to this day "a glorious victory for the forces of swiftness" is a catch-phrase in the house of the snail.

And the reason that this version of the race is not widely known is that very few of those that witnessed it survived the great forest-fire that happened shortly after. It came up over the weald by night with a great wind. The Hare and the Tortoise and a very few of the beasts saw it far off from a high bare hill that was at the edge of the trees, and they hurriedly called a meeting to decide what messenger they should send to warn the beasts in the forest.

They sent the Tortoise. ✦

Stories abound that exemplify perseverance of the sort Brigham Young describes, many of them designed specifically to instruct and delight the young. One, titled "The Little Engine That Could," was a staple in my childhood and may still be a favorite with children. How many times we repeated with mother, and the little engine, "I think I can, I think I can." And we grew up thinking that indeed we could, whatever it happened to be.

I doubt that any "Mormon" story has been told more often than that of Heber J. Grant's perseverance. Actually, there are two stories, one he told about learning to throw a baseball and the other about learning to sing.

Being an only child, my mother reared me very carefully; indeed, I grew more or less on the principle of a hot-house plant, the growth of which is "long and lanky," but not substantial. I learned to sweep, and to wash dishes, but did little stone throwing, and little indulging in those sports which are interesting and attractive to boys, and which develop their physical frames; therefore, when I joined a base ball club, the boys of my own age, and a little older, played in the first nine; those younger than myself played in the second, and those still younger in the third and I played with them. One of the reasons for this was that I could not throw the ball from one base to the other; another reason was that I lacked physical strength to run or bat well. When I picked up a ball, the boys would generally shout, "Throw it here, sissy!" So much fun was engendered on my account by my youthful companions that I solemnly vowed that I would play base ball in the nine that would win the championship of the Territory of Utah.

My mother was keeping boarders at the time for a living, and I shined their boots until I saved a dollar which I invested in a base ball. I spent hours and hours throwing the ball at a neighbor's barn, (Edwin D. Wool[l]ey's) which caused him to refer to me as the laziest boy in the Thirteenth Ward. Often my arm would ache so that I could scarcely go to sleep at night. But I kept on practicing, and eventually played in the nine that won the championship of the Territory. Having thus made good my promise to myself, I retired from the base ball arena. ❧

There are several personal accounts of President Grant's relentless efforts to learn to carry a tune well enough to sing hymns. In speeches, he frequently made jokes about his singing, and he sometimes demonstrated his point by singing a few lines. He published one account in the Improvement Era *(August 1900); another, excerpted below, he delivered as part of an impromptu general conference address:*

I have a letter clear from the Philippine Islands, in which I was told, among other things, "Don't try to sing." The writer says: "I am in earnest." He is one of my nearest friends, too. . . . I have had a great many of my friends come to me and beg me not to sing. Six months ago one of my fellow Apostles said to me, "Come in, Heber, but don't sing." The same Apostle last night [in response to Elder Grant's asking him to "tell me how I will learn to sing without singing] . . . said, "Sing every chance you get, Brother Grant, but do your first singing down in Mexico or Arizona or somewhere a long way off." . . . I propose to sing the "Holy City" in the big Tabernacle before I get through with it, and I propose to sing it without a mistake. I do not say this boastingly, because I believe what Alma of old said, in the twenty-ninth chapter of his book, that "God granteth unto men according to their desires, whether they be for good or for evil, for joy or remorse of conscience." I desire to sing, and I expect to work at it and stay right with it until I learn. The most I ever worked was to sing 400 songs in four days; that is the biggest amount of work I have ever done in the singing line. There are a great many people that can learn to sing very easily. When I started to learn to sing, it took me four months to learn a couple of simple hymns, and recently I learned one in three hours by the watch and then sang it without a mistake.

"That which we persist in doing becomes easier for us to do; not that the nature of the thing itself is changed, but that our power to do is increased." I propose to keep at it until my power to do is increased to the extent that I can sing the songs of Zion. Nobody knows the joy I have taken in standing up in the Tabernacle and other places and joining in the singing, because it used to be a perfect annoyance to me to try and to fail, besides annoying those around me, because I loved the words of the songs of Zion.

I am very sorry now for having persecuted people as I used to. In our meetings in the Temple, the brethren would say, "That is as impossible as it is for Brother Grant to carry a tune," and that settled it; everybody acknowledged that was one of the impossibilities. I believe what the Lord says, "My soul delighteth in the song of the heart, yea, the song of the righteous is a prayer unto me, and it shall be answered with a blessing upon their head." I desire to serve the Lord, and pray unto him in the songs of Zion; and I know that it produces a good influence. ✦

Robert Louis Stevenson speaks of the discipline required in learning to write.

FROM "A COLLEGE MAGAZINE"

All through my boyhood and youth, I was known and pointed out for the pattern of an idler; and yet I was always busy on my own private end, which was to learn to write. I kept always two books in my pocket, one to read, one to write in. As I walked, my mind was busy fitting what I saw with appropriate words; when I sat by the roadside, I would either read, or a pencil and a penny version-book would be in my hand, to note down the features of the scene or commemorate some halting stanzas. Thus I lived with words. And what I thus wrote was for no ulterior use, it was written consciously for practice. It was not so much that I wished to be an author (though I wished that too) as that I had vowed that I would learn to write. That was a proficiency that tempted me; and I practised to acquire it, as men learn to whittle, in a wager with myself. Description was the principal field of my exercise; for to any one with senses there is always something worth describing, and town and country are but one continuous subject. But I worked in other ways also; often accompanied my walks with dramatic dialogues, in which I played many parts; and often exercised myself in writing down conversations from memory.

This was all excellent, no doubt; so were the diaries I sometimes tried to keep, but always and very speedily discarded, finding them a school of posturing and melancholy self-deception. And yet this was not the most

439

efficient part of my training. Good though it was, it only taught me (so far as I have learned them at all) the lower and less intellectual elements of the art, the choice of the essential note and the right word: things that to a happier constitution had perhaps come by nature. And regarded as training, it had one grave defect; for it set me no standard of achievement. So that there was perhaps more profit, as there was certainly more effort, in my secret labours at home. Whenever I read a book or a passage that particularly pleased me, in which a thing was said or an effect rendered with propriety, in which there was either some conspicuous force or some happy distinction in the style, I must sit down at once and set myself to ape that quality. I was unsuccessful, and I knew it; and tried again, and was again unsuccessful and always unsuccessful; but at least in these vain bouts, I got some practice in rhythm, in harmony, in construction and the co-ordination of parts. . . .

. . . Before he can tell what cadences he truly prefers, the student should have tried all that are possible; before he can choose and preserve a fitting key of words, he should long have practised the literary scales; and it is only after years of such gymnastic that he can sit down at last, legions of words swarming to his call, dozens of turns of phrase simultaneously bidding for his choice, and he himself knowing what he wants to do and (within the narrow limit of a man's ability) able to do it. ✦

Perseverance, dutifulness, dependability—what Eudora Welty called "the habit of love"—characterize the charity that never fails. Welty used the phrase to describe the compulsion of an ancient (she was more than elderly) southern grandmother to make a periodic and hazardous foot-journey to get medicine for her ailing little grandson. The story follows Phoenix Jackson over hill, across creek, and through woods, on a trek so arduous for her old bones that when she arrives at her destination in Natchez, she momentarily forgets why she has come. Her feet know the way, however, and she perseveres. Her sense of mission defines her character. One nurse at the clinic identifies the old woman as "a charity case." The term works both ways, for Phoenix does more than receive free medicine. In her unsentimental affection and sacrifice, she embodies the pure love of Christ.

FROM "A WORN PATH"

Her name was Phoenix Jackson. She was very old and small and she walked slowly in the dark pine shadows, moving a little from side to side in her steps, with the balanced heaviness and lightnesss of a pendulum in a grandfather clock. She carried a thin, small cane made from an umbrella, and with this she kept tapping the frozen earth in front of her. This made a grave and persistent noise in the still air, that seemed meditative like the chirping of a solitary little bird.

She wore a dark striped dress reaching down to her shoe tops, and an equally long apron of bleached sugar sacks, with a full pocket: all neat and tidy, but every time she took a step she might have fallen over her shoelaces, which dragged from her unlaced shoes. She looked straight ahead. Her eyes were blue with age. . . .

Now and then there was a quivering in the thicket. Old Phoenix said, "Out of my way, all you foxes, owls, beetles, jack rabbits, coons and wild animals! . . . Keep out from under these feet, little bob-whites. . . . Keep the big wild hogs out of my path. Don't let none of those come running my direction. I got a long way."

[When old Phoenix finally arrives at the clinic and remembers her errand, she says,]

"My little grandson, he sit up there in the house all wrapped up, waiting by himself. . . . We is the only two left in the world. He suffer and it don't seem to put him back at all. He got a sweet look. He going to last." ✦

If the boy has any of his grandmother's perseverance, he will indeed "last." The bit of whimsy below is about someone who always faileth—to close the door, that is.

Godfrey Gordon Gustavus Gore—
No doubt you have heard the name before—
Was a boy who never would shut a door!

The wind might whistle, the wind might roar,
And teeth be aching and throats be sore,
But still he never would shut the door.

441

His father would beg, his mother implore,
"Godfrey Gordon Gustavus Gore,
We really *do* wish you would shut the door!"

Their hands they wrung, their hair they tore;
But Godfrey Gordon Gustavus Gore
Was deaf as the buoy out at the Nore.

When he walked forth the folks would roar,
"Godfrey Gordon Gustavus Gore,
Why don't you think to shut the door?"

They rigged out a Shutter with sail and oar,
And threatened to pack off Gustavus Gore
On a voyage of penance to Singapore.

But he begged for mercy, and said, "No more!
Pray do not send me to Singapore
On a Shutter, and then I will shut the door!"

"You will?" said his parents; "then keep on shore!
But mind you do! For the plague is sore
Of a fellow that never will shut the door,
Godfrey Gordon Gustavus Gore!"
(William Brighty Rands.)

Oscar A. Kirkham tells of a young man's quiet perseverance in his calling as a missionary.

I am grateful for a young missionary this year whom I met in the mission field. He told me of an incident that happened just a few days before. He said, "Brother Kirkham, I had a rather interesting experience just the other day. My companion and I were going out tracting. We had been instructed always to be prayerful as we approached a house, and when I came to the door the woman said to me, 'I understand you are a Mormon missionary. Well, I don't want anything to do with you. I know something about your people. You're just a menace. Leave this place.' Then," said the young missionary, "I had been told to be prayerful, so I continued in my heart to pray as I stood listening to what she had to say. The woman continued telling me what she thought of me and our people, and asked me again to leave. I continued to pray. In a few moments she turned abruptly and said, 'Well, why don't you come in?'" Thank God for the stability of the generation that's marching on to the greatest destiny of our people. They have taught me many helpful lessons. ❧

Sometimes the fruits of missionary perseverance are delayed, as the next two stories illustrate, the first told by W. W. Cluff, the second by Charles A. Callis.

When young Elders are sent on missions and meet with opposition, prejudice and indifference, so general in the world, they often feel more or less discouraged. They often travel days and weeks without apparently having made a single convert; are refused a night's lodging, or even a meal of victuals, and are possibly reviled and threatened with violence. Under these circumstances they are sometimes inclined to feel that their labors are in vain.

The labors of an elder who diligently bears a faithful testimony, warning the people to repent, will in time yield fruit. "Cast thy bread upon the waters: for thou shalt find it after many days." I call to mind an instance which proves the truth of the above saying, and which came under my own observation while laboring in the Scandinavian Mission, thirty-eight years ago.

A young elder, weary and foot-sore, called at the humble cottage of a lowly peasant and asked for a drink of water. He met with a kind hospitable reception from the honest man and his wife; the elder preached the Gospel, and bore his testimony to the unassuming occupants of that simple cottage; and, taking his departure, left some tracts, which he told them would more fully and clearly explain the principles of the doctrine of Christ.

Months after this, another elder by chance called at the same peasant's home. On learning that the stranger was an elder of the Church, the man said: "I have been praying to the Lord that he might send one of his inspired servants to our humble home, as myself and wife believe in the truth of the Gospel as set forth in some pamphlets left with us some months ago by a

Mormon missionary and we wish to be baptized and become members of the Church." And so this second elder had the pleasure of baptizing that man and his wife, both of whom proved faithful to the covenants which they then made. Thus, the "bread cast upon the waters" by that footsore and half discouraged, humble servant of the Lord, who first bore testimony to those honest people, was found by his successor, and the first elder really filled an important mission, even though he himself never baptized a single person. That he did a noble work, the following results will prove. This family, consisting of father, mother and several sons and daughters, all gathered to Zion, and have proved faithful Latter-day Saints. . . .

Three of their sons and several of their grandsons have filled honorable missions to the nations of the earth, and were the means of bringing many to a knowledge of the Gospel. Thus we see that the seed sowed by that servant of the Lord who first visited and bore testimony to that family, thirty-eight years ago in far off Denmark, has borne fruit an hundred, yea, possibly a thousand fold, in the redemption and salvation of the children of our Heavenly Father. ❖

When I was president of the Southern States Mission, I had each missionary come into the office before he was released. One day a young man came in and I said, "What have you accomplished?"

He said, "Nothing, and I am going home."

"What do you mean you have accomplished nothing?"

"Well," he said, "I baptized one man in the backwoods of Tennessee. He didn't know enough or have enough sense to wear shoes. And that's all I've done. I have wasted my time and my father's money, and I'm going home."

I went up into that area six months later to check on that man. The sense of failure with which that boy went home disturbed me, and I decided to check on the man he had baptized. I found he had been ordained a deacon and he had some small assignments in the branch in which he lived. Later he was ordained an elder and was given further responsibilities. He moved off the tenant farm on which he had lived and bought a little piece of ground of his own. Later he was made branch president. He later sold his farm, moved to Idaho and bought a farm there. He reared his family; his sons and daughters went on missions and their sons and daughters. I have just completed a survey which indicates, according to the best information I can find, that over 1100 people have come into the Church as a result of the baptism of that one man by a missionary who thought he had failed. ❧

Such incidents illustrate the importance of never failing in one's duty and service to the Lord. In a general conference priesthood session, President Harold B. Lee spoke of religious perseverance and of unfailing mutual trust between us and the Lord.

I sat in a class in Sunday School in my own ward one day, and the teacher was the son of a patriarch. He said he used to take down the blessings of his father, and he noticed that his father gave what he called "iffy" blessings. He would give a blessing, but it was predicated on "if you will not do this" or "if you will cease doing that." And he said, "I watched these men to whom my father gave the 'iffy' blessings, and I saw that many of them did not heed the warning that my father as a patriarch had given, and the blessings were never received because they did not comply."

You know, this started me thinking. I went back into the Doctrine and Covenants and began to read the "iffy" revelations that have been given to the various brethren in the Church. If you want to have an exercise in something that will startle you, read some of the warnings that were given through the Prophet Joseph Smith to Thomas B. Marsh, Martin Harris, some of the Whitmer brothers, William E. McLellin—warnings which, had they heeded, some would not have fallen by the wayside. But because they did not heed, and they didn't clear up their lives, they fell by the wayside, and some had to be dropped from membership in the Church.

Now, there is one thing that I think we should all be mindful of. I was with a group of missionaries in the temple one day. A question was asked by one of the sisters about the Word of Wisdom, concerning the promise made that if one would keep the Word of Wisdom he should run and not be weary and should walk and not faint. And she said, "How could that promise be realized if a person were crippled? . . ."

I answered her, "Did you ever doubt the Lord? The Lord said that."

The trouble with us today, there are too many of us who put question

445

marks instead of periods after what the Lord says. I want you to think about that. We shouldn't be concerned about why he said something, or whether or not it can be made so. Just trust the Lord. We don't try to find the answers or explanations. We shouldn't try to spend time explaining what the Lord didn't see fit to explain. . . .

If you would teach our people to put periods and not question marks after what the Lord has declared, we would say, "It is enough for me to know that is what the Lord said."

Elder Gordon B. Hinckley told a story after going into Vietnam that to me was a great lesson. There was a young man, as I remember it, who was in the military service in Vietnam and who joined the Church and was now about to go back to his home country in Southeast Asia.

Brother Hinckley said to him, "What is it going to do to you when you get back home now that you have joined the Church?"

"Oh," said the youth, "I will be cast out. My family will disown me. I will have difficulty in school. I will have no military rank."

Elder Hinckley then asked, "Isn't that a pretty big price to pay?"

And this young man looked at Elder Hinckley and said, "Well, the gospel is true, isn't it?"

That was a soul-searching question for Brother Hinckley, who replied: "Yes, my boy, with all my soul, the gospel is true."

And then this young man said, "Well, what else matters then?" ✦

The name of Mary Fielding Smith, wife of Hyrum and mother of Joseph F. Smith, is synonymous with perseverance. Who has not heard the stories of her exercising faith and prayer to accomplish the healing of her ailing ox on the long journey west, or to find a lost yoke of oxen? I will not repeat the oxen stories because they are readily available in a variety of sources, nor will I enumerate other hardships she endured. I will not recount instances of her dedicated service to the Lord and her success in the community once she reached Salt Lake City. Instead, I offer the belated obituary that served notice of her passing. It sketches with broad strokes, but even in general outline it tells much about the charity never fails:

Died, in this City, the 21st of September last. MARY, relict of the martyred Patriarch HYRUM SMITH, aged 51 years and 2 months.

The deceased was truly a "mother in Israel," and her name and deeds will be had in everlasting remembrance, associated as they are, with the persecutions of the Saints, and those tragic scenes that can never be forgotten. Possessed, in a superlative degree, of those peculiar qualifications that support and invigorate the mind in adversity, she endured afflictions and overcame difficulties with a degree of patience and perseverance worthy of imitation.

By the massacre of Carthage, June 27, 1844, she was left the sole guardian of a large family of children and dependents, for whom, by her indefatigable exertions, she provided the means of support, and removal from Nauvoo to this peaceful valley of the mountains. And after providing for their future wants here, she has been called to leave them and a numerous circle of kindred and friends, to enjoy the society of her martyred husband, and of the Prophet and Saints that have gone before, in another state of existence.

Her last illness, of about two months' continuance, she bore with her usual fortitude and patience, and only wished to live to do good to her family and those around her. She has entered into rest, and may the example she set, during her sojourn on earth, not be forgotten by those she has left behind to follow her. ❦

Ruth M. Anderson writes of her father, who never failed in love and good works.

DAD'S SLIPPERS

My father was a remarkable person who had a great love for his fellowman. He manisfested this by the consistent service he gave to others. When he passed from this life, my oldest brother assumed responsibility as our family patriarch.

When we met for our next annual family reunion, my brother, who had received a pair of my father's favorite house slippers, gave some good counsel to all of us concerning the need for each of us to pattern our lives after our father's life. He presented the slippers that had belonged to my father to one of us, with the challenge to "walk in Dad's shoes" for a year, and then make a report at our next reunion.

We did not know then that within a month this brother, our oldest, would be taken from us in death. With his passing, the nine of us decided to continue his challenge and each year pass Dad's slippers on to someone in the family. This year it is my turn. I have them hanging in my closet, where I see them every day, reminding me to "walk in Dad's shoes."

The challenge has already had a great impact on my life. Dad attended the temple often, loading his car with widows or others needing rides or encouragement. I have excused myself in the past as being too busy, but I am now attending the temple once a week. Dad sought out the unfortunate and helped wherever he could, often without being identified. I am trying each day to do something for someone outside my immediate family.

Can a pair of house slippers change your life? I think so. Each day as I see these shoes, I resolve anew to do the things I have seen my father do. ✦

Below is the story of another parent whose life was a pattern of unfailing perseverance. Called to the hospital room of her stricken mother, Aline R. Petit writes of a long anxious night in which only mumbled sounds issued from her mother's restless lips. Then, family members recognized what the elderly woman, Lydia Knudsen Rawson, was saying.

FROM "A BEAUTIFUL JOURNEY"

She was repeating the [twenty-third] Psalm and it was word perfect. By the time she came to the last line, "I will dwell in the house of the Lord forever," the words were completely understandable. She turned to us and smiled. Her mind seemed to clear. Her eyes brightened. She knew we were with her.

. . . How typical that she should repeat the Twenty-third Psalm!

Vivid in our memories was Mother busying herself about the house reciting a favorite poem or giving a special thought or bit of scripture that especially appealed to her. Mother not only read voraciously, she memorized. As she read she always had pencil and paper nearby, and when she found something that appealed to her, she wrote it down, not to be filed away but to be memorized. . . .

Mother was active in Relief Society for forty-eight consecutive years. Most of that time she taught theology and literature. Teaching meant giving the lesson as outlined, *plus* memorizing all the scripture or literary works offered. . . .

Mother was never an onlooker on life. On the contrary she was always in the middle of it. When she was in her late seventies, and alone, my brother built her a lovely little house at the rear of his home. She went there to live, but she refused to settle down to being an old lady. Relief Society in her new ward needed her and she needed them she would say.

One day several years after Mother moved to her little home, my sister-in-law found her crumpled on the lawn where she had collapsed while hanging out some clothes. She was hurrying to get her washing done so she could go visiting teaching with her partner.

Later, when the doctors examined her at the hospital, she asked: "Will I be able to go home in a week? I'm scheduled to give a lesson in my Church next Wednesday."

She was visiting teacher message leader at the time. The fact that she was then eighty-eight years old, and that perhaps her body was beginning to fail, did not dawn on her. Her illness was more serious than she had thought.

Mother will be ninety next July. At the time of my last visit, she was elated because her Camp of the Daughters of the Pioneers had transferred their meeting place to her convalescent home so she could share in the lessons with them.

"Can you hear the lessons as they give them, Mother?" I asked.

"No, I can't hear them because my hearing is almost gone, but that doesn't matter. You see, I've been asked to give a poem at each meeting and that is such a joy to me."

"But, Mother," I said, "how can you read a poem when your eyes are so dim?"

I should have known better than to ask that question.

"Of course I don't read the poems! One of the ladies here helps me and I memorize them."

"You memorize a new poem for each monthly meeting?"

"Certainly," she answered. "I surely can't remain here and do nothing!" ❦

In contrast, Belle Spafford tells of meeting a group of women who had certainly survived, but who in an important sense had perhaps failed to persevere. The occasion was a Relief Society meeting held in a residential care center for the elderly.

FROM "THOSE WHO ENDURE TO THE END"

The members were between 75 and 90 years of age. They were ambulatory, bright of mind, and enthusiastic over their Society. The lesson was from the Doctrine and Covenants and was followed by testimony bearing. The sisters contributed intelligently to the lesson discussions. Their offerings reflected a knowledge of Church doctrine and familiarity with the gospel, as well as rich life experiences. It was a delightful meeting. Then came the testimony period. Each sister who spoke, one by one, prayed that she would endure to the end. As I contemplated their intelligent understanding of the gospel as demonstrated in the discussion, and as I considered how late in life it was for most of them, I thought, why would they pray that they might endure to the end? Surely they have already proved themselves.

Later, however, in private conversation with some of them, I was made aware that they were not entirely above reproach, that they had a tendency to excuse themselves for failures to comply with the laws of the gospel because of age and circumstances.

These are a few comments made by these sisters as I talked with them:

One sister said, "We have sacrament meeting here at the home, as well as Relief Society, but I never go to sacrament meeting. I am too old to be preached to." I inquired, "Don't you feel a need to partake of the sacrament?" "No," the sister indifferently replied. "I don't think it matters at my age."

Another sister said, "I want to move to a little better home. I have enough money to do so. I have no one on whom to spend my money but myself. My family does not need it, and I am no longer interested in doing things for others that cost money. I don't even pay tithing. I don't think the Lord expects it of one my age."

Still another sister, who was drinking tea as I called, said, "I almost live on tea. When I was a younger woman, you couldn't have hired me to drink a cup of tea, but I don't think it will be held against me now."

Yet another said, as we heard footsteps near the door, "I hope that's not my daughter. She only comes because she fears criticism if she doesn't. She has very little love for me, and I have very little for her."

One more comment: "I seem to be growing weaker every day, suffering as I do with pain. I used to have the elders administer to me, but I don't believe in that anymore."

Attendance at sacrament meeting, partaking of the sacrament, renewing one's covenants, the payment of tithing, observance of the Word of Wisdom, love of family, priesthood administration—all basic laws of the gospel—had been abandoned by one or the other of these sisters with a feeling of justification; yet each had earnestly prayed that she might endure to the end.

Sympathetic as we may be toward these sisters and toward their circumstances, and understanding as we may be of their actions, yet we must recognize that with clear minds they were justifying the nonobservance of God's laws. I am led to ask also, "Has the Lord ever set a retirement age for keeping his commandments?"

Nor is it during the later years of life only that people grow careless. During the younger years there are those who violate their covenants, weaken in defense of right, disobey commandments which they know to be important, and rationalize their nonallegiance to Church teachings. ❧

President Hugh B. Brown also discusses the virtue of endurance in the following two selections:

451

FROM "WELL DONE, CARRY ON"

While life lasts, one must look upon each new achievement as a challenge and a beginning. Mile posts marking the way were not intended for camping grounds.

The gospel is a challenge to finish the course, not simply to begin it. All the fine accomplishments of a worth-while life may be defeated by a poor ending.

He was able to pass through Gethsemane and with full knowledge of the road ahead, go on to Calvary, and not until then did He say, "It is finished." To have stopped at any point of great achievement along the way, in the temple, his victory when he said to Satan "get thee behind me," the matchless sermon on the mount, on the mount of transfiguration, or even in the valley of Gethsemane, would have been to fail.

Always when missionaries are released they are admonished to carry on, for completing a mission is not by any means a final goal. There still remain many battles to be won. There is no final goal. That which appears so may be attained only by undiscouragable effort. It in turn will prove to be another guidepost to the future. ❧

FROM "THE PROPHET JOSEPH SMITH"

I am greatly impressed by the courage of the Prophet Joseph Smith. Dr. Heidenreich, a former minister from New York who joined the Church came to see me yesterday for a few moments. He said, "The thing that I am grateful for is that the Prophet Joseph Smith had the courage to finish his job in the face of the most difficult situations and circumstances." I have thought of this often and have tried to put myself in his place. He was a young man full of life and hope and expectations, hounded and persecuted and driven, beaten, mobbed, imprisoned, murdered, when at any time he could have said, "It is a hoax, it is not true, I am sorry I said it, I withdraw what I said." If he had said those things, the persecution would have stopped, he would have been turned loose to do as he pleased and would have had no more notice from the public, and he would have not died as he did. ❧

I have fought a good fight, I have finished my course, I have kept the faith. (2 Timothy 4:7.) ❧

Joseph Smith, who never failed in his faith or his calling, merited the unfailing trust and loyalty of his people and his fellow servants in the work. Some, however, did fail him, while others never swerved in their love and faith. George Q. Cannon writes:

From that day [of mutual reception of spiritual gifts] Joseph and Brigham were friends, attached to each other by a tie stronger and closer than that of earthly kinship. From that time on for twelve years Brigham gave earnest help to Joseph and demonstrated by his consideration and devotion that he knew the authority under which the younger man was acting. There was a time to come when Oliver Cowdery—the fellow apostle of Joseph, who, with him, had received the Aaronic Priesthood under the hands of John the Baptist, and the Melchisedec Priesthood under the hands of the Apostles Peter, James and John, heavenly messengers sent expressly to confer these two Priesthoods upon them—would waver in his fidelity to the truth and would oppose Joseph and leave the Church.

Not many years from the time of which we write Sidney Rigdon, the trusted counselor, the eloquent spokesman of the Prophet, who with him had beheld in vision the glories of the eternal world and borne solemn testimony that he had seen the Savior and knew that He lived, would turn his back upon and be ready to desert Joseph and to conspire against the Church. But not so with Brigham Young; but not so with the Prophet's brother Hyrum, and many others less eminent than these two. Hyrum Smith was the embodiment of unswerving fidelity and fraternal love. . . . When death stood in the pathway and menaced with its fearful terrors Joseph and those who stood by him, the Prophet besought Hyrum to stand aside and not accompany him. But, however obedient he might be to the slightest wish of his brother in other directions, upon this point he was immovable. If Joseph died, they would die together. As in his life, so in his death, Hyrum Smith exhibited the perfection of human love.

With similar fidelity and unshaken integrity Brigham Young, from the time of this meeting in Kirtland, cordially sustained the Prophet Joseph in all his ministrations up to the day of his martyrdom. Many times during the ensuing twelve years, and especially during the great defection and apostasy at Kirtland, he had occasion, because of his devotion to Joseph, to exhibit the decision of character and moral courage for which he was so distinguished in after life. When hesitation and doubt were far too common, and many leading men faltered and fell away, Brigham stood in the midst of the storm of opposition like a tower of strength. . . .

But it was not in Joseph's lifetime alone that Brigham manifested his admiration for and devotion to his great friend. During the long period—thirty-three years—which he outlived the Prophet (when a common man under his circumstances might have been tempted to criticise the acts or peculiarities of his predecessor, or to contrast his own management of affairs with that of Joseph's) no one ever heard a word drop from his lips that was not worthy of the two men. His own success and great world-wide prominence never diminished nor obscured the deep-rooted love and loyalty he felt towards the man whom God had chosen to hold the keys of this last dispensation and to be his file-leader in the Priesthood. ◆

Joseph, and those loyal to him, had yet a higher love and loyalty than that to each other, and a higher trust. They never failed the Lord, and they knew he would never fail them.

But to fulfill the law is to do with willingness and love the works which the law requires, and freely and without constraint of the law to lead an upright and godly life, as if there were no law and no penalty for disobedience. (Martin Luther.) ◆

John Calvin wrote about the need to endure in our prayers.

PERSEVERANCE IN PRAYER

We must not wish to bind God to certain circumstances, because in this very prayer [the Lord's prayer] we are taught not to put on him any law, nor to impose upon him any condition. For, before making any prayer for ourselves, before all things, we ask that his will be done; whereby we submit beforehand our will to his, in order that, as if it were caught and retained by a rein, our will may not presume to wish to range and to submit him under our will. If, having the heart formed in this obedience, we permit ourselves to be governed according to the good pleasure of the divine providence, we shall easily learn to persevere in prayer and wait with patience upon the Lord, while deferring the fulfillment of our desires to the hour set by his will; being assured that, although he does not show himself to us, yet he is always present to us and at his own time will reveal that he did not at all have his ears deaf to our prayers, though they seemed to men to be despised by him.

And even if at the end, after long waiting, our mind cannot understand the profit of our praying, and our senses feel no fruit thereof, nevertheless our faith will certify unto us what our mind and sense will not be able to perceive, that is, we shall have obtained [from God] all that which was good for us, for he will make us in poverty to possess abundance and in affliction to have consolation. For, even if all things should fail us, yet God will never leave us, inasmuch as he cannot disappoint the expectation and patience of his own. And he alone will be sufficient unto us for all things, inasmuch as he contains in himself all goods, which in the time to come he will fully reveal to us. ✦

In speaking of perseverance in prayer, Orson Pratt enlarged the subject to include the habit of charity.

FROM "HOW THE FAITHFUL SHOULD PRAY"

The great secret in obtaining favors from God, is to form, modify, and cultivate such characters and dispositions as will correspond in every respect with the teachings of the word and spirit of Christ. Condescend to men of low estate. Despise not the poor because of his poverty; and when you prepare a feast invite in "the poor, the halt, the maimed, and blind; for they cannot recompense you again in this life, but you shall receive your recompense at the resurrection of the just." Feed the hungry, clothe the naked, administer to the widow and the fatherless in their afflictions; visit the sick. Let your love abound unto all men; endeavor to reclaim men from the error of their ways by telling them the plain, unvarnished truth in meekness and with sobriety, remembering that you yourselves were once in gross darkness, because of the traditions and false religions with which you are surrounded; therefore have compassion upon the millions of deluded beings who have deceived themselves with the pomp and vain show of modern Christianity. Be upright and honest before all men. Practice virtue and holiness continually. Such should be the disposition and character of all the children of God, in order to qualify themselves for usefulness in this world, and to inherit eternal life in the world to come. ❖

Elder John A. Widtsoe expanded the discussion to include testimony.

FROM "HOW IS A TESTIMONY KEPT? LOST?"

How may a testimony be kept?

Since a testimony is a compound of knowledge and the use of knowledge, it is much as a living thing. It is never static, like a stone. The small testimony may grow larger, the large testimony become smaller. Therefore, it must be cared for, as any other type of life. Our treatment of it is of prime importance.

First, to keep our testimony we must feed it, regularly and plentifully. The steps that lead to testimony: desire, prayer, study, and practice, must be trodden continuously. The desire for truth should stamp our every act; help from God in all things must be invoked; the study of the gospel, which has not been plumbed to its depth by any man, should be continued; and the practice of gospel principles, in all our labors, must never be forgotten.

He who would retain his testimony is required to give constant study to the gospel. He cannot live forever on that which he learned yesterday. By a little such study every day, light will follow light, and understanding will increase. This is doubly important since we live in a changing world, which requires continuous applications of gospel truth to new conditions.

To keep his testimony, a person must increase in the use of gospel principles. There must be stricter conformity with the higher as well as the lesser laws of life—more activity in Church service; increasing charity and kindness; greater sacrifice for the common good; more readiness to help advance the plan of salvation; more truth in all we do. And as our knowledge of gospel law increases, our activity under gospel law must increase.

By such feeding, a testimony may be kept; may remain whole and sound; and may grow to become an increasingly certain guide, and a constant joy in life. There is no other way to preserve a testimony. Look about you. Have you not seen people who have fed their testimonies? Is it not good to be with them?

How may a testimony be lost?

A testimony, being a living thing, may die. Sorrowfully, all of us may have seen such a passing. Witness the life of any apostate. Refuse to do the things that lead to a testimony, and, gradually, it will starve, wither, and perish. It does not matter how strong it may have been. It must be fed to be kept alive. ❖

The passage above is filled with words that suggest never-failing perseverance—"continuous/continuing/continued," "every," "keep/kept," "constant," "forever," "remain," "preserve," and so on. And words like "increase" and "grow" suggest the positive outcomes of persistence in faith.

Richard Cracroft tells the story of a young Swedish woman who learned a powerful lesson about trusting the Lord, who never fails.

FROM "'WE'LL SING

AND WE'LL SHOUT' . . . "

Sister Ingrid Olsen (not her real name) was a recently divorced mother of a young son and was almost as recently a convert to the Church. The divorce had alienated Ingrid from part of her family, and her conversion to Mormonism had alienated her from her friends. The resulting personal anguish had dampened her initial joy in joining the Church. She felt alone and abandoned and overwhelmed before an uncertain future. In the midst of such turmoil, her prayers seemed futile, and what had initially been a time of spiritual refreshing had become a season of despair.

Bewildered by it all, she welcomed one afternoon the opportunity to visit a cousin in a neighbouring village, nearly ninety minutes away by bicycle. She planned to devote the trip to prayer, hoping to receive some indication that her Heavenly Father understood her plight and would give her some needed direction and solace. As she rode her bicycle toward her destination, she was miserably aware that the darkening day and threatening clouds matched her own darkened spirits, and she felt that her prayers were rebounding, unheard and unanswered, from the leaden heavens.

In this state of mind, Ingrid at length reached the distant village and made her visit. Starting on her return trip, she rode her bicycle up a long incline in the face of an increasingly strong wind before which she could hardly make progress. Seeing in her difficulty an opportunity to test the reality of the Lord, she went into a grove of trees and prayed that the Father would manifest his presence in a simple way: He would stop the wind. And she would know that he heard her prayers and knew her predicament. Mustering her faith, she resumed her journey—in the face of an ever-increasing head wind. She rode, hard, into that wind, becoming more disillusioned and bitter with each kilometer, for it seemed apparent that God, if after all there was really such a Being, had neither heard nor answered her heartfelt pleas. Arriving at last at the hill above her village, a bitter Sister Olsen dismounted before coasting down the hill toward her home. Looking to the lowering heavens, she uttered a sardonic, "Thanks, Lord; now I know."

Then it happened, the surprise of the Spirit. Suddenly Ingrid Olsen was filled with an intense, powerful, commanding voice that sounded through her being and thrilled her with the words, "I did not still the wind; instead, I gave you strength to overcome." Then stillness, and that was all! But God had changed her life.

She was stunned by the reality of what she had just experienced. Her whole soul reverberated with the Hosanna Shout, and she stood all amazed at this tangible answer to her prayers. Wondering about the meaning of the words, she glanced at her watch and was surprised to realize that she had made the ninety-minute return trip, in the face of the heaviest wind she had ever encountered, in less than sixty minutes. She knew immediately the truth of the words of the Holy Spirit—he had not stilled the wind; he had instead given her strength to overcome. She knew, as well, that this revelation described his pattern in dealing with all of his mortal children, and it becomes a revelation to all of us who listen with spiritually attuned ears: God will not diminish the adversity or the obstacles of our lives—there must need be such; that is the nature of our probation. However, he will be with us "always, even unto the end of the world" to guide and direct and give succor, through his minister, the Holy Spirit (see Matthew 28:20). ❖

When we speak in a serious sense of never failing, we speak of stability and, I think also, of the continuity of experience. Scripture admonishes us to remember the Savior, to remember the commandments, to remember the words of prophets. As human beings, we are blessed with more than genetic or instinctive memory. In remembering our past, we remember who we are and what we must do. Madeleine L'Engle speaks of stability as her reading in the work of another prompts an appreciative allusion to her own solid home.

Far too often houses are built without love and without excellence, houses that are not expected to stand for hundreds of years, houses that will have no history and little personality. . . .

Our family doesn't have the "hundreds of acres" of [Mary Ellen Chase's] Windswept, but we do have a house which is over two hundred years old and was built by people of deep faith in God. Building a house used to be a community affair; raising the rooftree itself would take several strong men. Some of the planks in the walls and floors of our house are over two feet wide. The original doors are the "cross and Bible" doors, and the original hardware is all HL, "Help Lord," hardware. Men and women have made love in this house, babies have been born, birthdays celebrated, deaths mourned. It is a house full of story, and that, too, was one of the good things we did for our children: let them grow up in a house full of story.

We were in the country on the day of the Bicentennial, and that afternoon we saw a double rainbow stretch across the house to the old trees of the orchard, a double rainbow for the country's double birthday, and these two may never come together again this side of the tomb. But they have come, and we were there. ❖

LDS author Elouise Bell writes of life-enriching memories.

FROM "HIGH ON HUCKLEBERRY HILL"

But the real nostalgia food of my childhood was huckleberries. Huckleberries and blueberries are first cousins—same family but different genus. One of the earliest memories of my life centers on cool summer mornings in northern Pennsylvania, before the sun had warmed the day, when a swarthy woman known only as "Huckleberry Mary" came sauntering through the alleys of our childhood calling that wonderful chant, "Huckle-berries!" On her head she balanced a large dishpan filled with berries she and her children had picked before sunrise that day. My grandmother would give me a peck measure, and I would scoot out and get our morning's supply. The deep-purple berries were rinsed in cold water, covered with sugar and milk (not today's 1-percent or even 2-percent), and slowly, almost meditatively, consumed. You could put them on cereal, of course, or in muffins or pancakes, but to me, such arrangements always obscured the point, which was the plump, perfect berries themselves. No fruit I know of is plumper than a ripe huckleberry—you might almost call it over-inflated. To feel the berries burst on your tongue and yield up their sweetness—that was a pleasure that never lost its delight.

Now, in actuality, huckleberries have a rather . . . what can I say that will be honest yet not disloyal? . . . a simple flavor. I know that objectively, strawberries and peaches and other fruits are more impressive. But beauty is in the taste-buds of the beholder, so to speak. The other day at Albertson's I saw cups of blueberries for sale. Not quite huckleberries, but family is family. I took them home, washed them lovingly, and poured on some half-and-half. I expected a degree of disappointment. But no. Suddenly, I was five years old again, and the morning was cool, the world fresh, and Huckleberry Mary's street-chant was strong and alluring as ever, unmuffled by time's long corridor. ❦

Elouise Bell has written about religious remembrance, too.

"THIS DO IN REMEMBRANCE OF ME"

Blinking out into the April brightness
One Sabbath after church,
I heard a Saint expound to a politely listening friend,
"With us, the sacrament is just a symbol."

"Just a symbol."
All the sunlong day and starlong night
Those slippery words shadowed me.

True enough: the bread but bread.
Yet the body offered
up was real,
Its shattered nerves most verifiable
As pain spiked along the net.

Right enough: the water nothing more.
But the shed blood pulsed power-poor,
Streamed swift, then slow, to dry and cake
Down racked arms and flanks.

How pallid the bread when pale the memory.
Yet sweet the nourishment when we his Spirit summon
By rich remembering.

Every symbol has two halves.
But to us falls the matching.
What match we, then, in sacramental token?
What fit we to the water, and the bread?

RECESSIONAL

1897

God of our fathers, known of old,
Lord of our far-flung battle-line,
Beneath whose awful Hand we hold

Dominion over palm and pine—
Lord God of Hosts, be with us yet,
Lest we forget—lest we forget!

The tumult and the shouting dies;
The Captains and the Kings depart:
Still stands Thine ancient sacrifice,
An humble and a contrite heart.
Lord God of Hosts, be with us yet,
Lest we forget—lest we forget!

Far-called, our navies melt away;
On dune and headland sinks the fire:
Lo, all our pomp of yesterday
Is one with Nineveh and Tyre!
Judge of the Nations, spare us yet,
Lest we forget—lest we forget!

If, drunk with sight of power, we loose
Wild tongues that have not Thee in awe,
Such boasting as the Gentiles use,
Or lesser breeds without the Law—
Lord God of Hosts, be with us yet,
Lest we forget—lest we forget!

For heathen heart that puts her trust
In reeking tube and iron shard,
All valiant dust that builds on dust,
And guarding, calls not Thee to guard,
For frantic boast and foolish word—
Thy mercy on Thy People, Lord!
(Rudyard Kipling.)

FROM *ULYSSES*

Come, my friends,
'Tis not too late to seek a newer world.
Push off, and sitting well in order smite
The sounding furrows; for my purpose holds
To sail beyond the sunset, and the baths
Of all the western stars, until I die.
It may be that the gulfs will wash us down:
It may be we shall touch the Happy Isles,
And see the great Achilles, whom we knew.
Though much is taken, much abides; and though
We are not now that strength which in old days
Moved earth and heaven, that which we are, we are;
One equal temper of heroic hearts,
Made weak by time and fate, but strong in will
To strive, to seek, to find, and not to yield.
(Alfred, Lord Tennyson.)

EPILOGUE

And faith, hope, charity and love, with an eye single

to the glory of God, qualify him for the work.

Remember faith, virtue, knowledge, temperance,

patience, brotherly kindness, godliness,

charity, humility, diligence.

D & C 4 : 5 – 6

J*ohn Ruskin provides a fitting capstone to this volume about the sixteen virtues of charity, of pure love.*

FROM "THE MYSTERY OF LIFE AND ITS ARTS"

And now, returning to the broader question, what these arts and labors of life have to teach us of its mystery. . . .

. . . The second [lesson they teach] is a very plain, and greatly precious one: namely—that whenever the arts and labors of life are fulfilled in this spirit of striving against misrule, and doing what we have to do, honorably and perfectly, they invariably bring happiness, as much as seems possible to the nature of man. In all other paths, by which that happiness is pursued there is disappointment, or destruction; for ambition and for passion there is no rest—no fruition; the fairest pleasures of youth perish in a darkness greater than their past light; and the loftiest and purest love too often does but inflame the cloud of life with endless fire of pain. But, ascending from lowest to highest, through every scale of human industry, that industry, worthily followed, gives peace. Ask the laborer in the field, at the forge, or in the mine; ask the patient, delicate-fingered artisan, or the strong-armed, fiery-hearted worker in bronze, and in marble, and with the colors of light; and none of these, who are true workmen, will ever tell you, that they have found the law of heaven an unkind one—that in the sweat of their face they should eat bread, till they return to the ground; nor that they ever found it an unrewarded obedience, if, indeed, it was rendered faithfully to the command, "Whatsoever thy hand findeth to do—do it with thy might."

. . . Is it all a dream then—the desire of the eyes and the pride of life— or, if it be, might we not live in nobler dream than this? The poets and prophets, the wise men, and the scribes, though they have told us nothing about a life to come, have told us much about the life that is now. They have had—they also,—their dreams, and we have laughed at them. They have dreamed of mercy, and of justice; they have dreamed of peace and good-will; they have dreamed of labor undisappointed, and of rest undisturbed; they have dreamed of fulness in harvest, and overflowing in store; they have dreamed of wisdom in council, and of providence in law; of gladness of parents, and strength of children, and glory of grey hairs. And at these visions of theirs we have mocked, and held them for idle and vain, unreal and unaccomplishable. What have we accomplished with our realities? Is this what has come of our worldly wisdom, tried against their folly? this, our mightiest possible, against their impotent ideal? or, have we only wandered among the spectra of a baser felicity, and chased phantoms of the tombs, instead of visions of the Almighty; and walked after the imaginations of our evil hearts, instead of after the counsels of Eternity, until our lives—not in the likeness of the cloud of heaven, but of the smoke of hell—have become as "a vapor, that appeareth for a little time, and then vanisheth away"? . . .

And whatever our station in life may be, at this crisis, those of us who mean to fulfill our duty ought first, to live on as little as we can; and, secondly, to do all the wholesome work for it we can, and to spend all we can spare in doing all the sure good we can.

And sure good is, first in feeding people, then in dressing people, then in lodging people, and lastly in rightly pleasing people, with arts, or sciences, or any other subject of thought.

I say first in feeding; and, once for all, do not let yourselves be deceived by any of the common talk of "indiscriminate charity." The order to us is not to feed the deserving hungry, nor the industrious hungry, nor the amiable and well-intentioned hungry, but simply to feed the hungry. . . .

. . . We once taught [our youths] to make Latin verses, and called them educated; now we teach them to leap and to row, to hit a ball with a bat, and call them educated. Can they plow, can they sow, can they plant at the right time, or build with a steady hand? Is it the effort of their lives to be chaste, knightly, faithful, holy in thought, lovely in word and deed? Indeed it is, with some, nay, with many, and the strength of England is in them, and the hope; but we have to turn their courage from the toil of war to the toil of mercy; and their intellect from dispute of words to discernment of things; and their knighthood from the errantry of adventure to the state and fidelity of a kingly power. And then, indeed, shall abide, for them and for us, an incorruptible felicity, and an infallible religion; shall abide for us Faith, no more to be assailed by temptation, no more to be defended by wrath and by fear;—shall abide with us Hope, no more to be quenched by the years that overwhelm, or made ashamed by the shadows that betray;—shall abide for us, and with us, the greatest of these; the abiding will, the abiding name of our Father. For the greatest of these is Charity. ✦

Authors, Titles, and Sources

Introduction

Talmage, James E. Excerpt from *A Study of the Articles of Faith.* Salt Lake City: LDS Church, Deseret News Press, 1962, p. 429. (1890)

Smith, Joseph. Excerpt from letter to Twelve Apostles, Dec. 15, 1840. Quoted in James B. Allen, Ronald K. Esplin, and David J. Whittaker. *Men with a Mission.* Salt Lake City: Deseret Book, 1992, p. 414.

Prologue

Cowley, Matthew. "Charity." *Cowley's Talks on Doctrine.* Chattanooga, TN: Ben E. Rich, 1902, pp. 157–61.

Chapter 1: Charity Suffereth Long

Smith, Joseph. Excerpt from Address to the Twelve. *History of The Church of Jesus Christ of Latter-day Saints* 3:383 (hereinafter cited as *History of the Church*). Salt Lake City: LDS Church, Deseret News Press, 1949.

Smith, Joseph. Letter to W. W. Phelps. *History of the Church* 4:162–64. See above. Also commentary by B. H. Roberts.

Chamberlain, Mary Elizabeth Woolley. Excerpt from *A Sketch of My Life.* Typescript, p. 13. Courtesy of Diane Chamberlain.

Grant, Heber J. Story about John Taylor. *Improvement Era,* 1942, 43:522; slightly altered in *Gospel Standards.* Salt Lake City: Improvement Era, 1943, pp. 286–87.

Kirkham, Oscar A. "The Worth of a Boy." *Say the Good Word.* Salt Lake City: Deseret Book, 1958, pp. 23–24.

Kimball, Spencer W. Quotation from LDS Conference Report, October, 1949.

Bacon, Francis. Quotation from "Of Revenge."

Blake, William. "A Poison Tree." *Blake: The Complete Poems,* 2d ed., ed. W. H. Stevenson. New York: Longman, 1971/1989, pp. 212–13.

Buddha, Gautama. Excerpt from *The Dhammapada.* In *Man and Spirit: The Speculative Philosophers,* eds. Saxe Commins and Robert N. Linscott. New York: Random House, 1947, p. 166.

Franklin, Benjamin. Quotation from *Poor Richard's Almanac.*

Hanks, Marion D. Quoted in *Notes to Quote,* comp. Albert L. Zobell, Jr. Salt Lake City: Bookcraft, 1965, pp. 76–78.

Ekken, Kaibara. Excerpt from "Social Intercourse," trans. Ken Hoshino. In *An Anthology of World Prose,* ed. Carl Van Doren. New York: Literary Guild, n.d., pp. 65–66.

Smith, Joseph F. Excerpts from LDS Conference Report, October 1907, and *Juvenile Instructor,* January 1911, p. 16. Rptd. in *Gospel Doctrine.* Salt Lake City: Deseret Book, 1919/1939, pp. 337–38; 339.

Cleary, Thomas, trans./ed. "Shame and Conscience." *Zen Antics: A Hundred Stories of Enlightenment.* Boston: Shambhala Press, 1993, pp. 19–20.

Avila, Teresa of, trans. Henry W. Longfellow. Excerpt rptd. in *Women in Praise of the Sacred,* ed. Jane Hirshfield. New York: HarperCollins, 1994/1995, p. 144.

Wycliffe, John. Excerpt from "Of Virtuous Patience." *The Poor Caitiff,* mod. trans. In *Great Voices of the Reformation,* ed. Henry Emerson Fosdick. New York: Modern Library, 1942, pp. 32–33.

Silverstein, Shel. "The Crocodile's Toothache." *Where the Sidewalk Ends.* New York: Harper & Row, 1974, p. 66.

Thomas, Edith M. "To Cancel Wrong." In *One Thousand Beautiful Things,* comp. Marjorie Barrows. New York: Spencer Press, 1947, p. 149.

Turner, Nancy Bird. "Enigma." *Star in a Well.* New York: Dodd, Mead,

1935/1939, p. 22; *Poems Selected and New.* Manchester Center, VT: Golden Quill Press, 1965, p. 96.

Twain, Mark. "My Watch." *Sketches New and Old.* New York: Harper & Brothers, 1917, pp. 11–15. (1875)

Milton, John. "Sonnet XIX." *John Milton: Complete Poems and Major Prose,* ed. Merritt Y. Hughes. New York: Odyssey, 1957, pp. 168–69.

Lindbergh, Anne Morrow. Excerpts from *Gift from the Sea.* New York: Vintage, 1983, pp. 15–17, 114–15. (1955)

Green, Louisa Lula. Excerpts from journal, LDS Church archives. Transcription courtesy of Maureen Ursenbach Beecher.

Kimball, Heber C. Quoted in Orson F. Whitney. *The Life of Heber C. Kimball.* Salt Lake City: Bookcraft, 1992, p. 69. (1888)

Larson, Clinton F. "Granddaughter." *Sunwind,* ed. David L. Evans. Geneva Steel Corp., 1990, p. 3. Courtesy of Naomi B. Larson.

Donne, John. Excerpt from "Meditation XVII." *Devotions upon Emergent Occasions,* mod. trans. In *Toward Liberal Education,* 5th ed., eds. Louis G. Locke, William M. Gibson, and George Arms. New York: Holt, Rinehart and Winston, 1967, pp. 659–60.

Schweitzer, Albert. Excerpt from *Memoirs of Childhood and Youth,* trans. C. T. Campion. New York: Macmillan, 1950, pp. 77–78.

CHAPTER 2: CHARITY IS KIND

Spinoza, Baruch. Quotation from *Foundations of the Moral Life.*

Nye, E. H. Excerpt from *Stories About Joseph Smith the Prophet,* comp. Edwin F. Parry. Salt Lake City: Deseret News Press, 1951, pp. 100–102. (1934)

Grant, B. F. Excerpt from *Faith Promoting Stories,* comp. Preston Nibley. Salt Lake City: Deseret Book, 1943, pp. 147–48.

Woodruff, Wilford. Excerpt from *Leaves from My Journal,* 2d ed. Salt Lake City: Juvenile Instructor Office, 1882, pp. 9–10. Rptd. in *Missionary Experiences,* comp. Preston Nibley. Salt Lake City: Deseret News Press, 1942; *Three Mormon Classics,* comp. Preston Nibley. Salt Lake City: Bookcraft, 1988, pp. 14–15.

Morrell, Jeanette McKay. Excerpt from "Kindness to Animals." *Highlights* *in the Life of President David O. Mckay.* Salt Lake City: Deseret Book, 1966, pp. 294–95.

Burgess, Margaret McIntyre. Excerpts from *Stories About Joseph Smith the Prophet,* comp. Edwin F. Parry. Salt Lake City: Deseret News Press, 1951, pp. 23–27.

Arrington, Leonard J. *From Quaker to Latter-day Saint: Bishop Edwin D. Woolley.* Salt Lake City: Deseret Book, 1976, p. 321. Arrington also quotes from Nathaniel George Stringham. *Briant Stringham and His People.* Salt Lake City: Stevens and Wallis, 1949, p. 21.

Longfellow, Henry Wadsworth. "The Children's Hour." *The Poems of Henry Wadsworth Longfellow.* Boston: Houghton Mifflin, 1882/1983, pp. 225–26.

Lewis, J. S. "Oh, I had such a pretty dream, mamma." *Deseret Sunday School Songs.* Salt Lake City: Deseret Sunday School Union, 1909, no. 184.

Ignatius. Excerpt from letter to Polycarp. In *Early Christian Writings: The Apostolic Fathers,* trans. Maxwell Staniforth. New York: Dorset Press, 1968, p. 127.

McKay, Emma Ray Riggs. Excerpt from "The Art of Rearing Children Peacefully" (Talk at BYU, April 12, 1952). Provo: BYU Press, 1966, pp. 10–11. Rptd. as a YWMIA brochure.

cummings, e e. Excerpt from *six nonlectures.* Cambridge, MA: Harvard University Press, 1953, p. 30.

Aesop. "The Wind and the Sun." *Aesop's Fables,* trans. Thomas James. Philadelphia: J. B. Lippincott, 1949, p. 58.

Belloc, Hilaire. "The Frog." *Cautionary Verses.* New York: Alfred A. Knopf, 1962, pp. 197–99. (1931)

Ballif, Arta Romney. "A Wedding Night." *Literature and Belief* 2 (1982):37–42.

Browning, Elizabeth Barrett. "Sonnet 43." *Sonnets from the Portuguese.*

Hunt, Leigh. "Abou Ben Adhem." *Stories in Verse.* London and New York: Geo. Routledge, 1855, n.p.

Lake, Louise. Excerpt from *Each Day a Bonus*. Salt Lake City: Deseret Book, 1971, pp. 11–12.

Schweitzer, Albert. Excerpt from *On the Edge of the Primeval Forest*. In *A Treasury of Albert Schweitzer*, ed. Thomas Kiernan. New York: Grammercy Books, 1965, p. 116.

Neruda, Pablo. Excerpt from "Childhood and Poetry." *Neruda and Vallejo: Selected Poems*, ed./trans. Robert Bly. Boston: Beacon Press, 1971, pp. 12–13.

Arrington, Janell R. "Psalm of Gratitude and Service." *Ensign*, April 1984, p. 7.

Harrah, Madge. "I've Come to Clean Your Shoes." *Reader's Digest* 123 (December 1983):21–22, 24; cond. from "The Man Who Came to Help," *Guidepost Magazine*, May 1981.

Richards, Stayner. Excerpt from LDS Conference Report, October 1951, pp. 71–72.

Buddha, Gautama. Excerpt from "The Sermon at Benares." In *Toward Liberal Education*, 5th ed, eds. Louis G. Locke, William M. Gibson, and George Arms. New York: Holt, Rinehart and Winston, 1967, p. 642.

"Damon and Pythias." In *A Story to Tell*. Salt Lake City: Deseret Book, 1945, pp. 203–4.

Young, S. Dilworth. "The Brothers, June 24, 1844." *The Long Road: from Vermont to Nauvoo*. Salt Lake City: Bookcraft, 1967, pp. 175–78.

Hassan, Mahammed Abdille. "To a Friend Going on a Journey," trans. M. Laurence. In *A World Treasury of Oral Poetry*, ed. Ruth Finnegan. Bloomington: Indiana University Press, 1978, pp. 102–3.

Luther, Martin. Excerpt from "Concerning Christian Liberty." In *Great Voices of the Reformation*, ed. Harry Emerson Fosdick. New York: Modern Library, 1942, p. 93.

CHAPTER 3: CHARITY ENVIETH NOT

Schweitzer, Albert. Excerpt from *Memoirs of Childhood and Youth*, trans. C. T. Campion. New York: Macmillan, 1950/1955, pp. 65–66.

Lake, Louise. Excerpt from *Each Day a Bonus.* Salt Lake City: Deseret Book, 1971, pp. 74–75.

Young, Sylvia Probst. "Gifts From My Mother." *Relief Society Magazine,* May 1965, pp. 339–40.

L'Engle, Madeleine. Excerpt from *Trailing Clouds of Glory: Spiritual Values in Children's Literature.* Philadelphia: Westminster Press, 1985, p. 121.

Richards, George F. Excerpt from *Storyteller's Scrapbook,* comp. Albert L. Zobell, Jr. Salt Lake City: Bookcraft, 1948, pp. 95–96.

Turner, Nancy Byrd. "First Thanksgiving of All." In *Favorite Poems Old and New,* ed. Helen Ferris. Garden City, NY: Doubleday, 1957, pp. 410–11.

Cornaby, Hannah. Excerpt from "Autobiography." *Autobiography and Poems,* 1881, pp. 41–42.

Lincoln, Abraham. "Proclamation of Thanksgiving." *Abraham Lincoln: Speeches and Writings 1859–1865.* New York: Library of America, 1989, pp. 520–21.

Brown, James. Excerpt from "Brigham Young's Predictions." In *Pioneer Stories,* comp. Preston Nibley. Salt Lake City: Bookcraft, 1976, p. 47. Also Church archives.

Stapley, Delbert L. Excerpt from LDS Conference Report, April 1953, pp. 117–18.

Pratt, Parley P. Excerpt from *Autobiography of Parley P. Pratt,* ed. Parley P. Pratt, II. Salt Lake City: Deseret Book, 1938/1985, pp. 16–17.

Excerpt from *The Passover Haggadah: Legends and Customs,* interp. Rabbi Menachim Hacohen. Adama Books, 1987, p. 84.

Thoreau, Henry David. Excerpt from "Where I Lived and What I Lived for." *Walden.* New York: Random House, 1937/1950, p. 82.

Marshall, Donald R. "The Preparation." *The Rummage Sale.* Provo: Press Publishing, 1972, pp. 23–25; Salt Lake City: Deseret Book, 1985, pp. 18–22.

Thoreau, Henry David. Excerpt from "Conclusion." *Walden.* New York: Random House, 1937/1950, p. 292.

Chamberlain, Mary Elizabeth Woolley. Excerpt from *A Sketch of My Life.* Typescript, pp. 16–17. Courtesy of Diane Chamberlain.

Lyman, Eliza Maria Partridge. Excerpt from personal journal, p. 21. Courtesy of Maureen Ursenbach Beecher.

Wright, Frank Lloyd. Excerpt from "Modern Architecture: The Cardboard House." *The Future of Architecture.* New York: Horizon Press, 1953, pp. 142–43.

Tsu, Lao. Quotation from "Forty-Four." *Tao Te Ching.*

Spinoza, Baruch. Quotation from *Foundations of the Moral Life,* XXIX.

Wilcox, Ella Wheeler. "The Story of Grumble Tone." *The Beautiful Land of Nod.* Chicago: W. B. Conkey, 1892, pp. 98–99.

Rands, William Brighty. "The Discontented Yew Tree." *Lilliput Lyrics,* ed. R. Brimley Johnson. London and New York: John Lane, 1899, pp. 52–54.

Hazlitt, William. Quotation from *Characteristics.*

Okazaki, Chieko. Excerpt from *Lighten Up!* Salt Lake City: Deseret Book, 1993, pp. 108–9.

Aesop. "The Goose with the Golden Eggs." *Aesop's Fables,* trans. Thomas James. Philadelphia: J. B. Lippincott, 1949, p. 67.

"Poor Cat, Rich Cat" from the Persian of *The Fables of Pilpay. The Lights of Canopus,* adapted from a trans. by Edward B. Eastwick. Hertford: Stephen Austin, 1854, pp. 55–58.

Aesop. "The Fox and the Grapes." *Aesop's Fables,* trans. Thomas James. Philadelphia: J. B. Lippincott, 1949, p. 139.

Howard, Henry. Earl of Surrey. "The Means to Attain a Happy Life." *Selections from English Literature,* eds. Leonidas Warren Payne, Jr. and Nina Hill. New York: Rand McNally, 1922, pp. 114–15.

CHAPTER 4: CHARITY VAUNTETH NOT ITSELF

Nibley, Hugh. Quotations from Joseph Smith, and commentary. *Brother Brigham Challenges the Saints,* eds. Don E. Norton and Shirley S. Ricks.

Provo and Salt Lake City: FARMS with Deseret Book, 1994, pp. 224–25.

"Let Each Man Learn to Know Himself." *Hymns: Church of Jesus Christ of Latter-day Saints.* Salt Lake City: LDS Church, 1948/1954, no. 91.

Smith, George Albert. "The Story of a Generous Man." *Improvement Era,* June 1947, p. 357.

Snow, Lorenzo. Excerpts from his autobiography. In *Biography and Family Record of Lorenzo Snow,* comp. Eliza R. Snow. Salt Lake City: Deseret News Company, 1884, pp. 15, 16.

Spafford, Belle S. Excerpt from "The Qualities Needed for Greatness." *Women in Today's World.* Salt Lake City: Deseret Book, 1971, p. 75.

Whitney, Helen Mar. Excerpts from "Scenes in Nauvoo After the Martyrdom of the Prophet and Patriarch." *Woman's Exponent,* February 1, 1883, p. 130.

Rands, William Brighty. Section VI from "Little Ditties." *Lilliput Lyrics,* ed. R. Brimley Johnson. London and New York: John Lane, 1899, pp. 207–9.

Noyes, Alfred. "The New Duckling." *Collected Poems.* Philadelphia: J. B. Lippincott, 1920, pp. 208–9.

Fields, James T. "The Owl-Critic." In *The Best Loved Poems of the American People,* ed. Hazel Felleman. Garden City, NY: Doubleday, pp. 496–97.

Dickinson, Emily. "I'm Nobody! Who are you?" *The Complete Poems of Emily Dickinson,* ed. Thomas H. Johnson. Boston: Little, Brown, 1960, p. 133.

Clement of Rome. Excerpt from "An Exhortation to Amendment of Life." In *Early Christian Writings: The Apostolic Fathers,* trans. Maxwell Staniforth. New York: Dorset Press, 1968, pp. 38–39.

Reynolds, Charlotte Teresa. "Indian Grandmother." *Ensign,* March 1979, p. 61.

Schweitzer, Albert. Excerpt from "The Ethics of Reverence for Life." In *A Treasury of Albert Schweitzer,* ed. Thomas Kiernan. New York: Grammercy Books, 1965, p. 62.

Rossetti, Christina. "Hurt No Living Thing." *Sing-Song: A Nursery Rhyme*

Book and Other Poems for Children. New York: Macmillan, 1924/1940, p. 81.

Reeder, Bertha S. Excerpt from "If I Were in My Teens." *Improvement Era,* June 1954, p. 478. Rptd. in Janet Peterson and LaRene Gaunt. *Keepers of the Flame.* Salt Lake City: Deseret Book, 1993, p. 75.

Berry, Wendell. Excerpt from "The Rise." *The Long-Legged House.* Rptd. in Berry's *Recollected Essays 1965–1980.* San Francisco: North Point Press, 1981, p. 13.

Kimball, Spencer W. Excerpts from "Fundamental Principles to Ponder and Live." LDS Conference Report, *Ensign,* November 1978, pp. 43–45.

Woolman, John. Excerpt from *The Journal of John Woolman.* In *Anthology of American Literature,* vol 1. 4th ed., gen. ed. George McMichael. New York: Macmillan, 1989, p. 230.

Jeshua, son of Sirach. Excerpt from "The Wisdom of Sirach" 42:15–25. In *The Apocrypha,* trans. Edgar J. Goodspeed. New York: Vintage Books, 1938/1959, p. 307.

Hopkins, Gerard Manley. "Pied Beauty." *The Poetical Works of Gerard Manley Hopkins,* ed. Norman H. MacKenzie. Oxford: Clarendon Press, 1990, p. 144.

Magee, John Gillespie, Jr. "High Flight." *Poetry of the World Wars,* ed. Michael Foss. New York: Peter Bedrick Books, 1990, p. 114.

McQuarrie, John G. "Worship." *Talks to the Saints* (Eastern States Mission). New York, 1906, pp. 13–14.

Simpson, Robert L. "Temples." In *Notes to Quote,* comp. Albert L. Zobell, Jr. Salt Lake City: Bookcraft, 1965, pp. 119–20.

Talmage, James E. "What is Worship?" *A Study of The Articles of Faith.* Salt Lake City: LDS Church, 1962 ed., pp. 395–98.

McConkie, Bruce R. Excerpts from LDS Conference Report, October 1971, pp. 167–69.

Doddridge, Philip. "On the Power and Beauty of the New Testament." In *The World's Best Essays: from the Earliest Period to the Present Time,* vol. 4, ed. David J. Brewer. St. Louis: Ferd P. Kaiser, 1900, pp. 1,431–34.

Brown, Hugh B. Excerpt from "Prayer" (radio address). *Messages of Inspiration.* Salt Lake City: Deseret Book, 1957, p. 245.

Chapter 5: Charity Is Not Puffed Up

Snow, Eliza Roxcy. "Mental Gas." *Poems, Religious, Historical, and Political.* vol. 1. Liverpool: F. D. Richards; London: Latter-day Saints' Book Depot, 1856, pp. 49–50.

Maeser, Karl G. Excerpts from his personal narrative. In Reinhard Maeser, *Karl G. Maeser: A Biography.* Provo: Brigham Young University, 1928, pp. 18–21. Also statement by Karl's son, Reinhard, p. 23.

Sandburg, Carl. Excerpt from *Abraham Lincoln: The Prairie Years and the War Years.* London: Jonathan Cape, 1955, p.406.

McCord, David. "Glowworm." *One at a Time.* Boston: Little, Brown, 1974, p. 214.

Simmons, Rachel E. Excerpt from Reminiscences, 1904, typescript, Church archives, p. 1. Cited in Leonard J. Arrington. *From Quaker to Latter-day Saint: Bishop Edwin D. Woolley.* Salt Lake City: Deseret Book, 1976, p. 65. Arrington is also quoted, p. 65.

Schweitzer, Albert. Excerpt from *Memoirs of Childhood and Youth,* trans. C. T. Campion. New York: Macmillan, 1950, p. 21.

Trebonius, John. Quoted in Roland H. Bainton. *Here I Stand: A Life of Martin Luther.* Nashville: Abington Press, 1950, p. 25.

Whitney, Orson F. Excerpt from "The Educator." *Voices from the Mountains.* Liverpool, 1922, pp. 85–86.

Scott-Maxwell, Florida. Excerpt from *The Measure of My Days.* New York: Penguin Books, 1979, p. 59; Alfred A. Knopf, 1968.

Lincoln, Abraham. Quoted in Carl Sandburg. *The Prairie Years and the War Years.* London: Jonathan Cape, 1955, p. 406.

Lincoln, Abraham. Quotation from a letter. *Selections from the Letters, Speeches, and State Papers of Abraham Lincoln,* ed. Ida M. Tarbell. Boston: Ginn, 1911, p. 97.

Lincoln, Abraham. "Proclamation for a National Fast Day." *Selections from* the Letters, Speeches, and State Papers of Abraham Lincoln. See above, pp. 95–96.

Thayer, Ernest L. "Casey at the Bat: A Ballad of the Republic, Sung in the Year 1888." *San Francisco Examiner,* June 3, 1888, p. 4. Rptd. in *The Annotated Casey at the Bat,* ed. Martin Gardner. New York: Clarkson N. Potter, 1967, pp. 21–23.

Grant, Heber J. Story. In *Classic Stories from the Lives of Our Prophets,* comp. Leon R. Hartshorn. Salt Lake City: Deseret Book, 1971, pp. 201–2.

Aesop. "The Tree and the Reed." Adapted from trans. by William Caxton in *The Subtyl Historyes and Fables of Esope,* 1483. Rptd. San Francisco: Grabhorn Press, 1930, pp. 92–93.

Grant, Heber J. Excerpt from "A Remarkable Manifestation." *Improvement Era,* December 1918, pp. 97–99.

L'Engle, Madeleine. Excerpts from *Trailing Clouds of Glory: Spiritual Values in Children's Books.* Philadelphia: Westminster Press, 1985, pp. 82–83.

Christiansen, Elray L. Excerpts from LDS Conference Report, April 1953, pp. 35–36.

Benson, Ezra Taft. Excerpts from "Beware of Pride." LDS Conference Report, *Ensign,* May 1989, pp 4–7.

Whitney, Orson F. Excerpt from "The Law of Obedience." *Saturday Night Thoughts: A Series of Dissertations on Spiritual, Historical and Philosophic Themes,* rev. ed. Salt Lake City: Deseret Book, 1927, pp. 232–34. (1921)

Excerpt from "Abraham and Isaac." In *Medieval English Verse and Prose,* eds. Sherman Loomis and Rudolph Willard. New York: Appleton-Century-Crofts, 1948, pp. 253–55.

Riley, James Whitcomb. "Little Orphant Annie." *The Complete Poetical Works of James Whitcomb Riley.* New York: P. F. Collier & Son, 1883–1932, pp. 370–71.

Snow, LeRoi C. Excerpt from "The Lord's Way Out of Bondage." *Improvement Era,* July 1938, p. 439.

Teasdale, George. Excerpt from LDS Conference Report, April 1900, p. 19.

Cowley, Matthew. Excerpts from "Obedience." *Cowley's Talks on Doctrine.* Chattanooga, TN: Ben E. Rich, 1902, pp. 153–54, 156.

Lawrence, D. H. Excerpts from "The Spirit of Place." *Studies in Classic American Literature.* New York: Viking Press, 1964/1966, pp. 3, 4, 5–6. (1923)

Whitney, Orson F. "Thy Will Be Done." *The Poetical Writings of Orson F. Whitney.* Salt Lake City: Juvenile Instructor Office, 1889, p. 112.

CHAPTER 6: CHARITY DOTH NOT BEHAVE ITSELF UNSEEMLY

Kimball, Heber C. Excerpt from "Address to My Children." In Orson F. Whitney. *The Life of Heber C. Kimball.* Salt Lake City: Bookcraft, 1992 p. 514. (1888)

Woodruff, Wilford. Excerpt from *Journal of Discourses* 22:330, October 8, 1881. *The Discourses of Wilford Woodruff,* ed. G. Homer Durham. Salt Lake City: Bookcraft, 1946/1990, p. 183.

Spafford, Belle S. "Good Manners." *Women in Today's World.* Salt Lake City: Deseret Book, 1971, pp. 127–28.

Hyde, Orson. Excerpt from a letter to his wife, dated from Preston, England, September 14, 1837. In *Men With a Mission,* eds. James B. Allen, Ronald K. Esplin, and David J. Whittaker. Salt Lake City: Deseret Book, 1992, p. 349.

Taylor, John. Excerpt from LDS Conference Report, April 1880, p. 77.

Wells, Emmeline B. Excerpt from *Young Woman's Journal* 16:555–56. Rptd. in *L.D.S. Stories of Faith and Courage,* comp. Preston Nibley. Salt Lake City: Bookcraft, 1957, p. 143.

Burgess, Gelett. "The Goops." In *The World Treasury of Children's Literature,* vol. 1, ed. Clifton Fadiman. Boston: Little, Brown, 1984, p. 102.

English nursery rhyme. In *The World Treasury of Children's Literature,* vol. 1. See above, p. 19.

[Longfellow, Henry Wadsworth?]. "Jemima." In *The Golden Treasury of Poetry,* ed. Louis Untermeyer. New York: Golden Press, 1959, p. 101.

Anthony, Edward. "Character Building." In *The Golden Treasury of Poetry.* See above, p. 26.

Snow, Eliza Roxcy. Excerpts from "To My Dear Pupils." *The Personal Writings of Eliza Roxcy Snow,* ed. Maureen Ursenbach Beecher. University of Utah Press, 1995, pp. 68–70.

Kapp, Ardeth Greene. Excerpts from *My Neighbor, My Sister, My Friend.* Salt Lake City: Deseret Book, 1990, pp. 178, 174.

Spafford, Belle S. Excerpts from "The Power of Composure." *Women in Today's World.* Salt Lake City: Deseret Book, 1971, pp. 115–17.

Young, Brigham. Excerpts from *Journal of Discourses.* Quoted, with commentary, in Hugh Nibley, *Brother Brigham Challenges the Saints,* eds. Don E. Norton and Shirley S. Ricks. Provo and Salt Lake City: FARMS with Deseret Book, 1994, pp. 201–4.

Kirkham, Oscar A. Story from *Say the Good Word.* Salt Lake City: Deseret Book, 1958, p. 211.

Macy, Arthur. "The Peppery Man." In *Favorite Poems Old and New,* ed. Helen Ferris. New York: Bantam Doubleday Dell, 1957, p. 319.

Anthony, Edward. Verse from *Oddity Land.* Garden City, NY: Doubleday, n.d., p. 27.

Hinckley, Gordon B. Excerpt from LDS Conference Report, April 1973, p. 73.

cummings, e e. Excerpt from *six nonlectures.* Cambridge, MA: Harvard University Press, 1953, pp. 12–13.

Earle, John. "A Young Man." *Microcosmography,* ed. Harold Osborne. London: University Tutorial Press, 1933; rptd. Scholarly Press, 1978, pp. 39–41.

Swift, Jonathan. Resolutions "When I come to be old." In *Jonathan Swift,* eds. Angus Ross and David Woolley. Oxford; New York: Oxford University Press, 1984, p. 23. (1699)

Carroll, Lewis. Excerpt from "Advice from a Caterpillar." *Alice's Adventures in Wonderland.* New York: Random House, 1946, pp. 52–55. (1865)

Scott-Maxwell, Florida. Excerpt from *The Measure of My Days.* New York: Penguin Books, 1979, pp. 142–43; Alfred A. Knopf, 1968.

Hawthorne, Nathaniel. Adaptation of "The Artist of the Beautiful." *The*

Portable Hawthorne, ed. Malcolm Cowley. New York: Viking Press, 1948, pp. 210–40.

Bacon, Francis. Excerpts from "On Studies." *Essays.* New York: E. P. Dutton, 1906; London: J. M. Dent & Sons; rptd. 1946, pp. 150–51.

Widtsoe, John A. Excerpt from LDS Conference Report, April 1950, p. 127.

Whitney, Orson F. "The Redemption of Zion." *The Poetical Writings of Orson F. Whitney.* Salt Lake City: Juvenile Instructor Office, 1889, p. 195.

Da Vinci, Leonardo. Excerpt from "Notes on Human Life." In *An Anthology of World Prose,* ed. Carl Van Doren. New York: Literary Guild, n.d., p. 508.

Chapter 7: Charity Seeketh Not Her Own

Whitney, Orson F. Excerpts from *Saturday Night Thoughts: A Series of Dissertations on Spiritual, Historical and Philosophic Themes,* rev. ed. Salt Lake City: Deseret Book, 1927, p. 77.

Smith, Joseph. Excerpt from "Lecture Sixth." In *A Compilation Containing the Lectures on Faith as Delivered at the School of the Prophets at Kirtland, Ohio,* comp. N. B. Lundwall. Salt Lake City: Bookcraft, n.d., p. 58.

Stegner, Wallace. Excerpt from *The Gathering of Zion.* Lincoln: University of Nebraska Press, 1992, p. 13. (1964)

Smith, Amanda. Personal story. In Edward W. Tullidge. *The Women of Mormondom.* New York: Tullidge & Crandall, 1877. Lithog. rpt. Salt Lake City, 1957–75, pp. 121–23.

Whitney, Elizabeth Ann. Excerpt from "A Leaf from an Autobiography." Printed serially in the *Woman's Exponent.* This section from vol. 7, October 1, 1878, p.71.

Wells, Emmeline B. Excerpt from "A Tribute of Respect" (to Elizabeth Ann Whitney). *Musings and Memories,* 2d ed. Salt Lake City: Deseret News Press, 1915, p. 134.

Jacobs, Zina Diantha Huntington. Excerpt from typescript of "The Nauvoo Diary of Zina Diantha Huntington Jacobs," ed. Maureen Ursenbach Beecher. Rptd. *BYU Studies* 19 (Spring 1979):285–320.

Pay, Mary Goble. Excerpts from her "Autobiography." In *Pay-Goble Pioneers of Nephi, Juab County, Utah,* comp. Arthur D. Coleman. Printed at Salt Lake City, 1968, pp. 79, 80, 81.

Browne, Edna S. "A Widow's Lullaby at Winter Quarters, 1846." *Ensign,* July 1984, p. 7.

Chamberlain, Mary Elizabeth Woolley. Excerpt from *A Sketch of My Life.* Typescript, pp. 3–4. Courtesy of Diane Chamberlain.

Kirkham, Oscar A. Excerpt from LDS Conference Report, April 1950; rptd. in *Say the Good Word.* Salt Lake City: Deseret Book, 1958, pp. 190–91.

Cowley, Matthew. Excerpt from LDS Conference Report, October 1948, pp. 159–60.

Ivins, Antoine R. Excerpt from LDS Conference Report, October 1947, pp. 88–89.

Hinckley, Gordon B. Excerpt from "Let Us Move This Work Forward." LDS Conference Report, *Ensign,* November 1985, p. 84.

Thayne, Emma Lou. "To a Daughter About to Become a Missionary: For Dinny." *As for Me and My House.* Salt Lake City: Bookcraft, 1989, pp. 82–84.

Ballard, Martha. Excerpts from her diary. In Laurel Thatcher Ulrich. *A Midwife's Tale: The Life of Martha Ballard, Based on Her Diary, 1785–1812.* New York: Vintage Books, 1990/1991, pp. 36–38. Also excerpt from Ulrich, p. 40.

Winters, Mae R. Excerpts from "The Apron." *Relief Society Magazine,* November 1968, p. 841.

Huff, Barbara A. "Afternoon with Grandmother." In *Favorite Poems Old and New,* ed. Helen Ferris. Garden City, NY: Doubleday, 1957, pp. 42–43.

Cather, Willa. Excerpt from "Old Mrs. Harris." *Obscure Destinies.* New York: Alfred A. Knopf, 1932, pp. 92–93.

Alden, Raymond MacDonald. Adaptation of his story "Why the Chimes Rang." *Why the Chimes Rang and Other Stories.* New York: Bobbs-Merrill, 1906/1945, pp. 11–18.

"Abram and Zimri." *The Contributor* 1 (June 1880):212–13.

Stockton, Frank R. Adaptation of his story "The Lady or the Tiger." *The Lady or the Tiger and Other Stories.* New York: Charles Scribner's Sons, 1907, pp. 3–12.

Aesop. Fable "of the envious dog," adapted from trans. by William Caxton. *Caxton's Aesop,* ed. R. T. Lenaghan. Cambridge: Harvard University Press, 1967, p. 153.

Barton, Bruce. "There Are Two Seas." *McCall's Magazine,* April 1928, p. 7.

Chapter 8: Charity Is Not Easily Provoked

Snow, Eliza Roxcy. Excerpt from her Nauvoo diary. *The Personal Writings of Eliza Roxcy Snow,* ed. Maureen Ursenbach Beecher. Salt Lake City: University of Utah Press, 1995, p. 80; also Carol Cornwall Madsen. *In Their Own Words: Women and the Story of Nauvoo.* Salt Lake City: Deseret Book, 1994, p. 63.

Excerpt from *Notes to Quote,* comp. Albert L. Zobell, Jr. Salt Lake City: Bookcraft, 1965, pp. 15–16.

Tsu, Lao. Excerpt from "Seventy-six." *Tao Te Ching,* trans. Gia-Fu Feng and Jane English. New York: Vintage Books, 1989, p. 78.

Excerpt from *Notes to Quote,* comp. Albert L. Zobell, Jr. Salt Lake City: Bookcraft, 1965, pp. 92–93.

Smith, Joseph. Excerpt from *History of the Church* 6:317; also *Times and Seasons,* August 15, 1844, p. 17.

Woodruff, Wilford. Excerpt from *Leaves from My Journal,* 2d. ed. Juvenile Instructor Office. Rptd. in *Three Mormon Classics,* comp. Preston Nibley. Salt Lake City: Bookcraft, 1988/1990, pp. 80–81.

Woodruff, Wilford. Excerpt from *Journal of Discourses* 17:194, October 7, 1874. Rptd. in *The Discourses of Wilford Woodruff,* ed. G. Homer Durham. Salt Lake City: Bookcraft, 1946/1990, pp. 328–29.

"There were once two cats . . . " In *Golden Treasury of Poetry,* ed. Louis Untermeyer. New York: Golden Press, 1959, p. 231.

Welch Lullaby. "All Through the Night." Adaptation from several versions.

White, E. B. Excerpts from "Walden—1954." *Yale Review* 44

(September 1954):13, 20. Rptd. in White's *The Points of My Compass.* New York: Harper & Row, n.d.

Thoreau, Henry David. Excerpt from "Higher Laws." *Walden.* New York: Modern Library, 1937/1950, pp. 194–95.

Yeats, William Butler. "The Lake Isle of Innisfree." *The Collected Poems of W. B. Yeats.* New York: Macmillan, 1959, p. 39. (1890)

Wylie, Elinor. "Velvet Shoes." *Collected Poems of Elinor Wylie.* New York: Alfred A. Knopf, 1954, p. 40. (1921)

Seneca. Excerpts from "On Noise," trans. Robin Campbell. In *The Art of the Personal Essay,* ed. Phillip Lopate. New York: Anchor Books/Doubleday, 1994/1995, pp. 5–8.

Pearson, Ranae. "My Sacred Place." *Ensign,* August 1983, p. 7.

Oaks, Stella. Excerpt from "Thy Will Be Done." In *Remarkable Stories from the Lives of Latter-day Saint Women,* vol. 2, comp. Leon R. Hartshorn. Salt Lake City: Deseret Book, 1975, pp. 183–84.

Snow, Eliza Roxcy. "Lines for Mrs. Wooley's Album." In combined sources: Leonard J. Arrington, *From Quaker to Latter-day Saint: Bishop Edwin D. Woolley.* Salt Lake City: Deseret Book, 1976, pp. 179–80; and *The Personal Writings of Eliza Roxcy Snow,* ed. Maureen Ursenbach Beecher. Salt Lake City: University of Utah Press, 1995, pp. 158–59.

Hoole, Daryl V., and Donette V. Ockey. Story retold in *The Art of Teaching Children.* Salt Lake City: Deseret Book, 1972, pp. 21–22.

Hamblin, Jacob. Excerpt from *Jacob Hamblin: A Narrative of His Personal Experience, as a Frontiersman, Missionary to the Indians and Explorer.* Salt Lake City: Deseret News Press, 1909, pp. 28–30.

Washington, George. Excerpts from "Farewell Address," September 17, 1796. In *A Compilation of the Messages and Papers of the Presidents,* vol. 1. New York: Bureau of National Literature, 1897, pp. 210–11.

Lincoln, Abraham. Excerpt from "First Inaugural Address," March 4, 1861. In *Inaugural Addresses of the Presidents of the United States.* Washington, D.C.: U.S. Government Printing Office, 1974, p. 126.

Kennedy, John F. Excerpts from "Inaugural Address," January 20, 1961.

In *Inaugural Addresses of the Presidents of the United States.* See above, pp. 268–70.

Dame Julian of Norwich. Excerpts from *Revelations of Divine Love,* ed. Grace Warrack. London: Methuen & Company, 1901/1907, pp. 103–5. (1373)

Clement of Rome. Excerpt from "Harmony and Cooperation Are Lessons Which Nature Itself Teaches Us," no. 19 from an epistle to the Church of God at Corinth. In *Early Christian Writings: The Apostolic Fathers,* trans. Maxwell Staniforth. New York: Dorset Press, 1968, p. 33.

Thayne, Emma Lou. "Where Can I Turn for Peace?" *Hymns of the Church of Jesus Christ of Latter-day Saints.* Salt Lake City: LDS Church, 1985, no. 129. (1973)

CHAPTER 9: CHARITY THINKETH NO EVIL

Richards, Stephen L. Excerpt from "Tried and Not Found Wanting." *Where Is Wisdom?* Salt Lake City: Deseret Book, 1955, pp. 79–81.

Kimball, J. Golden. Excerpt from LDS Conference Report, April 1909, p. 37.

Brown, Hugh B. Excerpt from "You Are an Original." *The Abundant Life.* Salt Lake City: Bookcraft, 1955, p. 162.

Tanner, J. M. Excerpt from LDS Conference Report, April 1900, pp. 63–64.

Smith, George Albert. "The Product of My Thoughts." *Church News,* February 16, 1946, p. 1. Rptd. in *Classic Stories from the Lives of Our Prophets,* comp. Leon R. Hartshorn. Salt Lake City: Deseret Book, 1971, p. 240.

"The Magic Mask." In *A Story to Tell,* comp. Primary and Deseret Sunday School Boards. Salt Lake City: Zion's Press, Deseret Book, 1945, pp. 205–7.

Kirkham, Oscar A. Excerpt from *Say the Good Word.* Salt Lake City: Deseret Book, 1958, p. 167.

White, Susannah. "A Frightening Experience," submitted by Hortense Munson. *Children's Friend,* September 1943, p. 433.

Richards, Stephen L. Excerpt from "Tried and Not Found Wanting." *Where Is Wisdom?* Salt Lake City: Deseret Book, 1955, p. 81.

Richards, Stephen L. Excerpt from LDS Conference Report. Rptd. in *Where Is Wisdom?* See above, pp. 405–6.

Lee, Harold B. Excerpt from "Doing the Right Things for the Right Reasons." *Ye Are the Light of the World.* Salt Lake City: Deseret Book, 1974, pp. 30–31.

Clark, J. Reuben. Excerpt from LDS Conference Report. Rptd. in *Behold the Lamb of God.* Salt Lake City: Deseret Book, 1962/1991, p. 292.

Smith, Joseph F. Excerpt from *Gospel Doctrine.* Salt Lake City: Deseret Book, 1939, pp. 111–13. Rptd. from *Improvement Era,* March 1903, p. 388. Second excerpt, p. 254, rptd. from LDS Conference Report, *Improvement Era,* April 1913, p. 8.

Young, S. Dilworth. Excerpt from "Courage to Be Righteous" (May 7, 1968). In *Brigham Young University Speeches of the Year* (Provo, 7 May 1968), pp. 6–7.

Arrington, Leonard J. Excerpt from *From Quaker to Latter-day Saint: Bishop Edwin D. Woolley.* Salt Lake City: Deseret Book, 1976, p. 338.

Sirach. Excerpt from "The Wisdom of Sirach" 28:13–18. In *The Apochrypha,* trans. Edgar J. Goodspeed. New York: Vintage Books, 1938/1959, p. 277.

Unknown author. Excerpt from "There are ten things . . ." In *Notes to Quote,* comp. Albert L. Zobell, Jr. Salt Lake City: Bookcraft, 1965, p. 49.

Carroll, Lewis. Excerpt from "The Walrus and the Carpenter." *The Collected Verse of Lewis Carroll.* New York: Macmillan, 1933, pp. 89–93.

Pratt, Parley P. Excerpt from "A Dialogue between Joseph Smith and the Devil." The *New York Herald,* January 1, 1844. Later publ. as a pamphlet. Rptd. in *A Believing People,* eds. Richard H. Cracroft and Neal E. Lambert. Provo: BYU Press, 1974, p. 335.

Smith, Joseph F. Excerpt from *Gospel Doctrine.* Salt Lake City: Deseret Book, 1939, p. 114. Rptd. from *Improvement Era,* 1910, 14:72.

Thoreau, Henry David. Entry for April 20, 1841. *Journal,* vol. 1, gen. ed. John C. Broderick. Princeton, NJ: Princeton University Press, 1981, p. 302.

Pascal, Blaise. Excerpts from *Pensées,* nos. 28, 30, 32, 33. In *Man and Spirit: The Speculative Philosophers,* eds. Saxe Commins and Robert N. Linscott. New York: Random House, 1947, pp. 226–28.

Herbert, George. "Virtue." In *Selections from English Literature,* eds. Leonidas Warren Payne, Jr., and Nina Hill. Chicago: Rand McNally, 1927, p. 134.

Byron, Lord (George Gordon). "She Walks in Beauty." *The Poetical Works of Lord Byron,* ed. Ernest Hartley Coleridge. London: John Murray, 1905/1972, p. 340.

MacMurray, Maryann Olsen. "Winter Day and Night." *Ensign,* February 1979, p. 19.

Buddha, Gautama. "The Twin-Verses." *The Dhammapada.* In *Man and Spirit: The Speculative Philosophers,* eds. Saxe Commins and Robert N. Linscott. New York: Random House, 1947, pp. 155–56.

Jacobsen, Virginia Budd. Excerpt from *Cherished Experiences,* comp. Claire Middlemiss. Salt Lake City: Deseret Book, 1955, pp. 55–56.

Woodruff, Wilford. Excerpts from *Millenial Star* (1891) 53:642–44. Rptd. in *The Discourses of Wilford Woodruff,* ed. G. Homer Durham. Salt Lake City: Bookcraft, 1946/1990, pp. 293–96.

CHAPTER 10: CHARITY REJOICETH NOT IN INIQUITY

Thoreau, Henry David. Entry for July 1, 1840. *Journal,* vol. 1., gen. ed. John C. Broderick. Princeton, NJ: Princeton University Press, 1981, p. 146.

Young, Brigham. Excerpts from LDS Conference Report, October 1900, pp. 43–44.

Tanner, Obert C. Excerpt from "Integrity." *Christ's Ideals for Living.* Salt Lake City: Obert C. and Grace A. Tanner Foundation, 1981, p. 107.

"The Whale's Nature," from *The Bestiary.* In *Medieval English Verse and Prose,* eds. Roger Sherman Loomis and Rudolph Willard. New York: Appleton-Century-Crofts, 1948, pp. 74–75. Text from J. Hall, *Selections from Early Middle English,* vol. 1, 1920.

Roberts, Elizabeth Madox. "Mumps." *Under the Tree.* New York: Viking, 1956, p. 44. (1922)

Briggs, Kay W. Excerpt from *Brother Joseph: Stories and Lessons from the Life of the Prophet.* Salt Lake City: Bookcraft, 1994, pp. 109–10.

Smith, John Henry. Excerpt from LDS Conference Report, April 1907, p. 107.

Kimball, Heber C. Excerpt from "Address to My Children." In Orson F. Whitney. *The Life of Heber C. Kimball.* Salt Lake City: Bookcraft, p. 514.

Cicero. Excerpts from *On Friendship.* In *The Norton Book of Friendship,* eds. Eudora Welty and Ronald A. Sharp. New York: W. W. Norton, 1991, pp. 71, 74.

Johnson, Samuel. Quotation from *The Rambler,* no. 64. In *The Norton Book of Friendship.* See above, p. 90.

Confucius. Excerpt from *Analects* 12:23. *The Essential Confucius,* ed. Thomas Cleary. New York: HarperCollins, 1992, p. 135.

Aesop. "Birds of a Feather." *Fables of Aesop,* trans. S. A. Handford. Baltimore: Penguin Books, 1954/1966, p. 104.

Spafford, Belle S. Excerpts from "The Latter-day Saint Price Tag" and "Let Every Man Deal Honestly." *A Woman's Reach.* Salt Lake City: Deseret Book, 1974, pp. 129–30, 141.

Tolstoy, Leo. Excerpt from *What Is Art?,* trans. Aylmer Maude. London: Oxford University Press, 1939, pp. 287–88.

Gardner, John. Excerpts from *On Moral Fiction.* New York: Basic Books, 1978, pp. 22, 82.

Brown, James S. Excerpt from *Life of a Pioneer.* Geo. Q. Cannon & Sons Co., 1900, pp. 27–28.

[Maeser, Karl G.]. Quotation in *Notes to Quote,* comp. Albert L. Zobell, Jr. Salt Lake City: Bookcraft, 1965, p. 24.

Goldsmith, Oliver. "An Elegy on That Glory of Her Sex, Mrs. Mary Blaize." *The Poems and Plays of Oliver Goldsmith,* ed. Austin Dobson. London: J. M. Dent, 1891, pp. 77–78.

Fox, Ruth May. Cited in Janet Peterson and Larene Gaunt. *Keepers of the Flame.* Salt Lake City: Deseret Book, 1993, p. 49.

Brooks, Juanita. Excerpts from *Quicksand and Cactus*. Logan: Utah State University Press, 1992, pp. 153–54, 155, 157. Courtesy of Karl F. Brooks.

Woodruff, Wilford. Excerpt from *Wilford Woodruff: History of His Life and Labors as Recorded in His Daily Journals,* ed. Matthias F. Cowley. Salt Lake City: Bookcraft, 1964, pp. 476–77.

Adaptation of an anonymous story from *Storyteller's Scrapbook,* comp. Albert L. Zobell, Jr. Salt Lake City: Bookcraft, 1948, p. 85.

Lincoln, Abraham. Quotation from *The Lincoln Treasury,* comp. Caroline Thomas Harnsberger. Chicago: Wilcox & Follett, 1950, p. 196.

Kimball, J. Golden. Quotation from LDS Conference Report, October 1932.

Aurelius, Marcus. Excerpt from *The Meditations of Marcus Aurelius Antoninus.* In *Man and Man: The Social Philosophers,* eds., Saxe Commins and Robert N. Linscott. New York: Random House, 1947, p. 289.

Brown, Hugh B. Excerpt from "Building Mansions." *Millenial Star,* October 5, 1939. Rptd. in *The Abundant Life.* Salt Lake City: Bookcraft, 1965, pp. 323–25.

Holmes, Oliver Wendell. Excerpt from "The Chambered Nautilus." In *Anthology of American Literature,* vol. 1, ed. George McMichael. New York: Macmillan, 1989, p. 1786. (1858)

à Kempis, Thomas. Excerpt from "The Exercises of a Good Religious." *The Imitation of Christ.* Grand Rapids, MI: Zondervan, 1967, p. 28. (1441)

Manuel, Juan. "A King and Three Imposters." *Book of Count Lucanor,* trans. James York. In *An Anthology of World Prose,* ed. Carl Van Doren. New York: Library Guild, 1935, pp. 559–61.

Lincoln, Abraham. Quotation from *The Lincoln Treasury,* comp. Caroline Thomas Harnsberger. Chicago: Wilcox & Follett, 1950, p. 200.

Hazlitt, William. Quotation from *Characteristics.*

Eliot, George. Excerpts from "Moral Swindlers." *The Impressions of Theophrastus Such.* New York: Harper & Brothers, 1848, pp. 187–89.

Lewis, C. S. Excerpts from "The Inner Ring." *The Weight of Glory.* Grand Rapids, MI: William B. Eerdmans, 1965, pp. 61–65. (1949)

Chesterton, G. K. Excerpt from "A Piece of Chalk." *Tremendous Trifles.* New York: Dodd, Mead, 1909/1925, pp. 13–15.

CHAPTER 11: CHARITY REJOICETH IN THE TRUTH

Widtsoe, John A. Excerpts from "The Challenge of the First Vision" and "Truth Seekers May Find the Way." *Joseph Smith: Seeker After Truth, Prophet of God.* Salt Lake City: Bookcraft, 1993, pp. 5–9, 10–14. (1951)

Cannon, George Q. Excerpts from *The Life of Joseph Smith the Prophet,* 2d ed. Salt Lake City: Deseret News Press, 1907, pp. 338–39, 352–54. (1888)

Wells, Emmeline B. Excerpts from "My Testimony." In *Faith-Promoting Stories,* comp. Preston Nibley. Independence, MO.: Zion's Printing and Publishing, 1943; Deseret Book, 1943, pp. 136–37.

Whitney, Helen Mar. Excerpt from "Scenes in Nauvoo After the Martyrdom of the Prophet and Patriarch." *Woman's Exponent,* February 1, 1883, p. 130.

Smith, Joseph Fielding. Excerpt from *Doctrines of Salvation,* vol. 1, p. 48. Rptd. in *Discourses on the Holy Ghost,* comp. N. B. Lundwall. Salt Lake City: Bookcraft, 1959, p. 26.

Smith, Joseph F. Excerpts from two talks. (1) LDS Conference Report, April 1900, pp. 40–41; rptd. in *Gospel Doctrine,* 1st ed. 1919, p. 9; 5th ed., Deseret Book, 1939, p. 7. (2) LDS Conference Report, April 1909, p. 7; rptd. in *Gospel Doctrine,* p. 1.

Cannon, George Q. Excerpt from *My First Mission.* In *Three Mormon Classics,* comp. Preston Nibley. Salt Lake City: Bookcraft, 1988/1990, pp. 152–53. (1879)

Nielsen, C. M. Account of Oliver Cowdery's testimony in court. In B. H. Roberts. *A Comprehensive History of the Church of Jesus Christ of Latter-day Saints,* vol. 1. Provo: LDS Church, BYU Press, 1965, p. 142. (Nielsen affidavit on file in Church Historian's Office.)

Widtsoe, John A. Excerpt from "Wherein Lay the Greatness of Brigham Young?" *Evidences and Reconciliations.* Salt Lake City: Bookcraft, 1960/1987/1995, pp. 382–85.

Wiesel, Elie. Excerpt from *Night,* trans. Stella Rodway. New York: Bantam, 1982, pp. 2–3; Hill & Wang, 1960.

Chesterton, G. K. Quotation from *What's Wrong with the World.*

Luther, Martin. Quotation from *Table Talk.*

Young, S. Dilworth. Excerpt from "Courage to Be Righteous." In *Brigham Young University Speeches of the Year* (Provo, 7 May 1968), pp. 4–6.

Aesop. "The Shepherd Boy and the Wolf." *Aesop's Fables,* trans. Thomas James. Philadelphia: J. B. Lippincott, 1949, p. 76. (1848)

Dickinson, Emily. "Tell all the Truth . . . " *The Complete Poems of Emily Dickinson,* ed. Thomas H. Johnson. Boston: Little, Brown, 1960, p. 506.

Thoreau, Henry David. Quotation from *Journal,* vol. 1, gen. ed. John C. Broderick. Princeton, NJ: Princeton University Press, 1981, p. 10.

"Mr. H. and the Steward." In *McGuffey's Fifth Eclectic Reader.* Christian School Edition. N.p., n.d., pp. 81–82.

Smith, Joseph F., John R. Winder, and Anthon H. Lund, in behalf of the Church. Excerpts from "An Address: The Church of Jesus Christ of Latter-day Saints to the World." LDS Conference Report, April 1907, pp. 3–4, 14–16.

Phelps, W. W. "Vade Mecum, (translated,) Go With Me." *Times and Seasons,* February 1, 1843, pp. 81–82.

Smith, Joseph. Excerpts from "A Vision." *Times and Seasons,* February 1, 1843, pp. 82–85.

Whitney, Orson F. Excerpts from "The Gospel's Accessories." *Saturday Night Thoughts: A Series of Dissertations on Spiritual, Historical and Philosophic Themes,* rev. ed. Salt Lake City: Deseret Book, 1921/1927, pp. 263, 265–66, 267.

Pratt, Parley P. Hymn printed in a continuation of Helen Mar Whitney's "Scenes in Nauvoo After the Martydom of the Prophet and Patriarch" cited earlier. *Woman's Exponent,* February 15, 1883, p. 138.

Dickinson, Emily. "I died for Beauty . . . ." *The Complete Poems of Emily Dickinson,* ed. Thomas H. Johson. Boston: Little, Brown, 1960, p. 216.

Hinckley, Gordon B. Phrases from "This I Believe," March 1, 1992. *BYU 1991–92 Devotional and Fireside Speeches,* p. 78.

Larson, Clinton F. "Autumn Leaves." *Centennial Portraits.* Provo: BYU Press, 1976, pp. 6–7. Courtesy also of Naomi Larson.

CHAPTER 12: CHARITY BEARETH ALL THINGS

Longden, John. Excerpt from LDS Conference Report, April 1955, p. 59.

Cowley, Matthew. Excerpt from "They Shall Speak with New Tongues." In *Faith Like the Ancients,* comp. N. B. Lundwall. Manti: Mountain Valley Publishing, 1950, pp. 56–57.

Kirkham, Oscar A. Excerpt from *Say the Good Word.* Salt Lake City: Deseret Book, 1958, pp. 160–63.

McKay David O. Excerpt from dedicatory address (Sauniatu, Upolu, Samoa, January 15, 1955). In *Cherished Experiences from the Writings of President David O. McKay,* comp. Clare Middlemiss. Salt Lake City: Deseret Book, 1955, pp. 174–75.

Woodruff, Wilford. Excerpt from *Leaves from My Journal.* In *Three Mormon Classics,* comp. Preston Nibley. Salt Lake City: Bookcraft, 1988/1990, p. 83. (1881)

Holzapfel, Richard and Jenny. Louisa Barnes Pratt incident. *Women of Nauvoo.* Salt Lake City: Bookcraft, 1992, p. 165.

Tullidge, Edward W. Stories of Louisa Free Wells and Harriet A. Snow. *The Women of Mormondom.* New York: Tullidge & Crandall, 1877. Lithog. rpts. Salt Lake City, 1957–1975, pp. 336–38; p. 439.

Stewart, Elinore Pruitt. Excerpt from *Letters of a Woman Homesteader.* Atlantic Monthly Co., 1914. Rptd. Boston: Houghton Mifflin, 1988, pp. 15–18.

Bradbury, Ray. Excerpt from *Dandelion Wine.* New York: Doubleday, 1957–58; Bantam Books, 1959–68, pp. 138–40.

Richards, Rhoda. Excerpts from personal account. In Edward W. Tullidge. *The Women of Mormondom.* New York: Tullidge & Crandall, 1877. Lithog. rpts. Salt Lake City, 1957–1975, pp. 421–22.

Chamberlain, Mary Elizabeth Woolley. Excerpt from *A Sketch of My Life.* Typescript, p. 10. Courtesy of Diane Chamberlain.

Kapp, Ardeth Greene. Personal reminiscence. In Janet Peterson and LaRene Gaunt. *Keepers of the Flame.* Salt Lake City: Deseret Book, 1993, pp. 138–39.

Snow, Eliza Roxcy. Excerpts from "Sketch of My Life." *The Personal Writings of Eliza Roxcy Snow,* ed. Maureen Ursenbach Beecher. Salt Lake City: University of Utah Press, 1995, pp. 35–38, 41–42.

Card, Orson Scott. "Looking West." *Ensign,* July 1977, p. 59.

Brown, Hugh B. Excerpt from "Do Your Duty and Be Blessed" (address, January 12, 1964). Rptd. in *The Abundant Life.* Salt Lake City: Bookcraft, 1965, pp. 123–24.

Frankl, Viktor E. Excerpt from *Man's Search for Meaning.* New York: Washington Square Press (Simon & Schuster), 1985, p. 98. First publ. in Austria in 1946; this trans. first publ. by Beacon Press in 1959.

Brown, Hugh B. Excerpt from "In Spite of Everything" (talk, General Priesthood Meeting, October 5, 1963). Rptd. in *The Abundant Life.* Salt Lake City: Bookcraft, 1965, pp. 137–39.

Hopkinson, Francis. Excerpts from "On Whitewashing," in "A Letter from a Gentleman in America, to His Friend in Europe." *The Miscellaneous Essays and Occasional Writings of Francis Hopkinson, Esq.,* vol. 2. Philadelphia: T. Dobson, 1792, pp. 150–53, 154–56.

Turner, Nancy Byrd. "When Young Melissa Sweeps." *Magpie Lane.* New York: Harcourt, Brace, 1927, pp. 80–81.

Rands, William Brighty. Excerpts from "Clean Clara." *Lilliput Lyrics,* ed. R. Brimley Johnson. London and New York: John Lane, 1899, pp. 188–90.

Mather, Cotton. Excerpt from *Bonifacius.* In *Anthology of American Literature,* vol. 1, ed. George McMichael. New York: Macmillan, 1989, p. 190.

Excerpt from "Unspotted from the World," *The Rule of Anchoresses (Ancrene Riwle).* In *Medieval English Verse and Prose,* eds. Roger Sherman Loomis and Rudolph Willard. New York: Appleton-Century-Crofts, 1948, p. 50.

LeGallienne, Richard. "I meant to do my work today . . . ." *The Lonely Dancer and Other Poems.* New York and London: John Lane, 1913, p. 67.

Thoreau, Henry David. Entry July 1, 1840, from *Journal,* vol. 1, gen. ed. John C. Broderick. Princeton, NJ: Princeton University Press, 1981, p. 147.

Franklin, Benjamin. Epitaph for his parents' headstone. From *The Autobiography of Benjamin Franklin,* ed. Thomas Yosaloff. New Haven: Yale University Press, 1964, p. 56.

Franklin, Benjamin. Epitaph for his own headstone. Included as an epigraph to another edition of *The Autobiography,* New York: Fine Editions Press, 1957.

Tarbell, Ida M. Excerpts from "Work." *Cosmopolitan,* December 1936, pp. 19, 82.

Clark, Marden. "Too Late on Father's Day." *Ensign,* July 1977, p. 60.

CHAPTER 13: CHARITY BELIEVETH ALL THINGS

Dickinson, Emily. "I never saw a moor . . ." *The Complete Poems of Emily Dickinson,* ed. Thomas H. Johnson. Boston: Little, Brown, 1960, p. 480.

Talmage, James E. Excerpts from "Faith and Repentance." *A Study of The Articles of Faith.* Salt Lake City: LDS Church, Deseret News Press, 1962, pp. 96–100.

Pratt, Orson. Excerpt from "True Faith." In *A Compilation Containing the Lectures on Faith as Delivered at the School of the Prophets at Kirtland, Ohio,* comp. N. B. Lundwall. Salt Lake City: Bookcraft, n.d., p. 70.

Pratt, Orson. Excerpt from "The Nature and Character of the Laws of Adoption, or the Invariable Rule by which Aliens Are Admitted into the Kingdom as Citizens," from *The Kingdom of God.* In *A Series of Pamphlets on the Doctrines of the Gospel by the late Elder Orson Pratt.* Chattanooga, TN, 1899, p. 21.

Cowley, Matthew. Excerpts from "Faith." *Cowley's Talks on Doctrine.* Chattanooga, TN: Ben E. Rich, 1902, pp. 84, 86–87.

Whitney, Orson F. Excerpts from "The Mainspring of Power." *Saturday Night Thoughts: A Series of Dissertations on Spiritual, Historical and Philosophic Themes,* rev. ed. Salt Lake City: Deseret Book, 1921/1927, pp. 281–82, 283–84.

McConkie, Bruce R. Excerpts from "Faith in God," "Faith in the Lord Jesus Christ," and "The Fruits of Faith." *A New Witness for the Articles of Faith.* Salt Lake City: Deseret Book, 1985/1993, pp. 192, 193, 195.

Smith, Joseph. Excerpt from "Lecture First" of his *Lectures on Faith.* In *A Compilation Containing the Lectures on Faith as Delivered at the School of the Prophets at Kirtland, Ohio,* comp. N. B. Lundwall. Salt Lake City: Bookcraft, n.d. , pp. 7–8.

Sheffield, Linda Madsen. "Lucy Mack Smith." *Ensign,* March 1978, p. 43.

Pratt, Parley P. Excerpt from *A Voice of Warning and Instruction to All People.* Independence: Zion's Printing and Publishing Co., 1837. N.d., n.p. on pamphlet edition, p. 29.

Lines from an old Bible. Rptd. in *Times and Seasons,* April 15, 1845, p. 875.

Blake, William. "The Lamb." *The Poetical Works of William Blake,* ed. John Sampson. London: Oxford University Press, 1914, p. 67.

Newman, (Cardinal) John Henry. "Lead, Kindly Light." *Prayers, Poems Meditations,* ed. A. N. Wilson. New York: Crossroad, 1990, p. 147.

Talmage, James E. Personal reminiscence. In *Storyteller's Scrapbook,* comp. Albert L. Zobell, Jr. Salt Lake City: Bookcraft, 1948, pp. 54–55.

Bennion, Adam S. Anecdote. In *Inspirational Talks for Youth,* comp. Preston Nibley. Salt Lake City: Deseret News Press, 1948, p. 57.

Lewis, C. S. Excerpts from *A Grief Observed.* New York: Bantam Books, 1976, pp. 80–81; Seabury Press, New York, 1963; Faber and Faber, London, 1961.

Tennyson, (Alfred) Lord. "Crossing the Bar." *The Poetical Works of Alfred Lord Tennyson.* New York: Thomas Y. Crowell, n.d., p. 687.

Stewart, Ora Pate. "Homecoming." *Ensign,* June 1978, p. 29.

Scott-Maxwell, Florida. Excerpt from *The Measure of My Days.* New York: Penguin Books, 1979, pp. 106–7; Alfred A. Knopf, 1968.

Herbert, George. "The Flower." In Wayne Booth. *The Art of Growing Older.* New York: Poseidon Press, 1992, pp. 272–73.

Drummond, Henry. Excerpts from introductory essay to *Natural Law in the Spiritual World.* In *The World's Best Essays,* vol. 4, ed. David J. Brewer. St. Louis: Ferd P. Kaiser, 1900, pp. 1475, 1476.

Pascal, Blaise. Excerpts from *Pensées,* nos. 30–34. In *Man and Spirit: The Speculative Philosophers,* eds. Saxe Commins and Robert N. Lincott. New York: Random House, pp. 227–28.

Santayana, George. "Sonnet III." *Sonnets and Other Verses.* New York: Duffield, 1906, p. 5.

Packer, Boyd K. Excerpt from "A World of Examples." In *Teach Ye Diligently.* Salt Lake City: Deseret Book, 1975, pp. 48–50.

Roberts, B. H. Excerpt from an address (Salt Lake Tabernacle, January 23, 1932). *Discourses of B. H. Roberts.* Rptd. in *A Believing People,* eds. Richard H. Cracroft and Neal E. Lambert. Provo: BYU Press, 1974, p. 193.

Bryant, William Cullen. "To A Waterfowl." *The Poetical Works of William Cullen Bryant.* New York: AMS Press, 1969/1972, pp. 26–27; rptd. from 1903 edit.

Smith, Bathsheba Wilson. Excerpt from her autobiography. In *In Their Own Words: Women and the Story of Nauvoo,* ed. Carol Cornwall Madsen. Salt Lake City: Deseret Book, 1994, pp. 212–13.

Chapter 14: Charity Hopeth All Things

Pope, Alexander. Excerpt from *An Essay on Man* I:85–96. In *Eighteenth Century Poetry and Prose,* 2d ed., eds. Louis I. Bredvold, Alan D. McKillop, and Lois Whitney. New York: Ronald Press, 1939/1956, p. 371.

Milton, John. Excerpt from *Paradise Lost,* Book XII:451–78. *John Milton:*

Complete Poems and Major Prose, ed. Merritt Y. Hughes. New York: Odyssey Press, 1957, pp. 464–65.

Hunter, Howard W. Excerpts from "An Anchor to the Souls of Men," in *BYU 1992–93 Devotional and Fireside Speeches* (Provo: Brigham Young University Press, 1994), pp. 68–73.

Luther, Martin. Excerpt from "Table-Talk," trans. William Hazlitt. In *Anthology of World Prose,* ed. Carl Van Doren. New York: Literary Guild, n.d., p. 788.

Smith, Joseph, and Anson Call and B. H. Roberts. Intermingled statements from *History of the Church* 5:85–86. Salt Lake City: LDS Church, Deseret News Press, 1949.

Taylor, John. Excerpt from "The Valley." Appendix to *The Gospel Kingdom.* Salt Lake City: Bookcraft, 1943, p. 384.

Wells, Emmeline B. "Leaving Nauvoo." *Musings and Memories,* 2d ed. Salt Lake City: Deseret News Press, 1915, p. 77.

Smith, Mary Fielding. Excerpts from a letter. In Edward W. Tullidge. *The Women of Mormondom.* New York: Tullidge & Crandall, 1877. Lithog. rpts. Salt Lake City, 1957–1975, pp. 255–56, 257–58.

Snow, Eliza Roxcy. Excerpts from "Sketch of My Life." *The Personal Writings of Eliza Roxcy Snow,* ed. Maureen Ursenbach Beecher. Salt Lake City: University of Utah Press, 1995, pp. 13–14, 27–28, 29–31.

Pratt, Louisa Barnes. Excerpts from her journal. In *Heart Throbs of the West,* comp. Kate B. Carter. Salt Lake City: Daughters of Utah Pioneers, 1947, pp. 244, 245.

Jacobs, Zina Diantha Huntington. Entry from her journal. Typescript, courtesy of Maureen Ursenbach Beecher. Also publ. *BYU Studies* 19 (Spring 1979).

[Hugo, Victor.] Quotation attributed to Hugo by Louise Lake in "Manna on a Window Sill." *Each Day a Bonus.* Salt Lake City: Deseret Book, 1971, p. 35.

Rands, William Brighty. "Winifred Waters." *Lilliput Lyrics,* ed. R. Brimley Johnson. London and New York: John Lane, 1899, pp. 195–97.

Smith, John Lyman. Anecdote. In John A. Widtsoe. *Joseph Smith: Seeker*

After Truth, Prophet of God. Salt Lake City: Bookcraft, 1993, p. 353. (1951) Rptd. from *The Juvenile Instructor* 27:172–73.

Arrington, Leonard J. Excerpt from *From Quaker to Latter-day Saint: Bishop Edwin D. Woolley.* Salt Lake City: Deseret Book, 1976 p. 464; cites Bryant Hinckley's biography, *Heber J. Grant..*

Pratt, Parley P. Excerpt from *Autobiography of Parley P. Pratt.* Salt Lake City: Deseret Book, 1938/1985, pp. 36–39.

Verse by an unknown author, given to Ruth May Fox by Heber J. Grant. Rptd. in Janet Peterson and LaRene Gaunt. *Keepers of the Flame.* Salt Lake City: Deseret Book, 1993, p. 44.

Dickinson, Emily. "Hope is the thing with feathers." In *The Complete Poems of Emily Dickinson,* ed. Thomas H. Johnson. Boston: Little, Brown, 1960, p. 116.

Stevenson, Robert Louis. "Requiem." *The Complete Poems of Robert Louis Stevenson.* New York: Charles Scribner's Sons, 1923, p. 88.

Browning, Robert. "Prospice." *The Poems and Plays of Robert Browning,* eds. Bennett A. Cerf and Donald S. Klopfer. New York: Modern Library, 1934, p. 318.

Wordsworth, William. Excerpt from "Ode: Intimations of Immortality from Recollections of Early Childhood." *William Wordsworth: The Poems,* vol. 1. New Haven: Yale University Press, 1981, pp. 528–29.

Hopkins, Gerard Manley. "God's Grandeur." *Poems by Gerard Manley Hopkins,* ed. Norman H. MacKenzie. London: The Folio Society, 1974, p. 62.

Bryant, William Cullen. "To the Fringed Gentian." *Poetical Works of William Cullen Bryant.* New York: D. Appleton, 1904, p. 144. (Bryant collected and arranged this volume himself.)

Lear, Edward. "The Pobble Who Has No Toes." *The Pobble Who Has No Toes and Other Nonsense.* London: Collins, 1968, n.p.

Evans, Richard L. Excerpt from "The Spoken Word" sermonette. LDS Conference Report, October 1950, p. 106.

"He has achieved success . . ." Variously attributed to "Mrs. A. J. Stanley" (in

Distilled Wisdom) and Robert Louis Stevenson (in *Storyteller's Scrapbook*), and perhaps others.

Eiseley, Loren. Excerpts from "The Star Thrower." *The Unexpected Universe.* New York: Harcourt, Brace & World, 1964–69, pp. 69–72, 89–90.

CHAPTER 15: CHARITY ENDURETH ALL THINGS

Smith, Joseph F. Excerpt from *Gospel Doctrine.* Salt Lake City: Deseret Book, 1939, pp. 119–20. Rptd. from *Juvenile Instructor,* August 15, 1904, pp. 496–497.

Nibley, Hugh. Excerpts from "Brigham Young as a Leader" (address at BYU, June 6, 1967) and "The Uses and Abuses of Patriotism" (American Heritage course syllabus, BYU, 1977). *Brother Brigham Challenges the Saints.* Provo and Salt Lake City: FARMS and Deseret Book, pp. 472–73; 252–54.

Sill, Edward Rowland. "Opportunity." *The Poetical Works of Edward Rowland Sill.* Boston: Houghton Mifflin, 1867–1906, p. 277.

Nash, Ogden. "The Tale of Custard the Dragon." *The Face is Familiar: The Selected Verse of Ogden Nash.* New York: Garden City Publishing, 1941, pp. 240–42.

Groberg, John H. "The Lord's Wind." *In The Eye of the Storm.* Salt Lake City: Bookcraft, 1993, pp. 198–201.

Longfellow, Henry Wadsworth. Excerpts from "Paul Revere's Ride," The Landlord's Tale; from *Tales of a Wayside Inn. The Poems of Henry Wadsworth Longfellow.* New York: Modern Library, n.d., pp. 275–76, 279.

Whittier, John Greenleaf. "Barbara Frietchie." *The Complete Poetical Works of John Greenleaf Whittier.* Boston: James R. Osgood, 1876, pp. 196–97.

Pericles. Excerpts from "Funeral Oration." Thucydides' *History,* trans. Gerald F. Else. In *Classics in Translation,* vol. 1, eds. Paul L. MacKendrick and Herbert M. Howe. Madison: University of Wisconsin Press, 1952/1959, p. 242.

Tullidge, Edward W. Story. *The Women of Mormondom.* New York: Tullidge & Crandall, 1877. Lithog. rpts. Salt Lake City, 1957–1975, pp. 156–58.

Smith, Lucy Mack. Excerpt from *History of Joseph Smith by His Mother, Lucy Mack Smith,* ed. Preston Nibley. Salt Lake City: Bookcraft, 1979, pp. 254–56. First publ. 1901, with introd. by Joseph F. Smith.

Frankl, Viktor E. Excerpts from *Man's Search for Meaning.* New York: Washington Square Press (Simon & Schuster), 1985, pp. 86–87. (See earlier entry for publ. history.)

Carlyle, Thomas. Excerpt from *Lecture on Martin Luther.* Salt Lake City: Deseret News Press, 1926, pp. 34–35, 44–45.

Pratt, Parley P. Excerpt from *Autobiography of Parley P. Pratt.* Salt Lake City: Deseret Book, 1938/1985, pp. 179–80.

Pomeroy, Irene Hascall. Excerpt from letter. In *A Believing People,* eds. Richard H. Cracroft and Neal E. Lambert. Provo: BYU Press, 1974, p. 116.

Bailey, Alice Morrey. "Lone Woman: Charity (Arms) Everts." *Ensign,* March 1984, p. 56.

Jackson Wanlass family. Excerpt from family story "They Came Alone." Typescript, pp. 4–6. Courtesy of Bert Wanlass.

Whitney, Elizabeth Ann. Excerpts from two continuous serial segments of "A Leaf from an Autobiography." *Woman's Exponent,* December 15, 1878, p. 105; January 1, 1879, p. 115.

cummings, e e. Excerpt from *six nonlectures.* Cambridge: Harvard University Press, 1953, pp. 9–11.

Shelley, Percy Bysshe. The concluding stanzas (spoken by Demogorgon) from *Prometheus Unbound* IV:554–78. *Shelley's Prometheus Unbound,* ed. Lawrence John Zillman. Seattle: University of Washington Press, 1959, pp. 299–300.

CHAPTER 16: CHARITY NEVER FAILETH

Dunsany, Lord. "The True History of the Hare and the Tortoise." *Fifty-One Tales.* New York: Mitchell Kennerly, 1915, pp. 66–70.

Grant, Heber J. Personal story. In *Inspirational Talks for Youth.* Salt Lake City: Deseret News Press, 1948, pp. 241–42.

Grant, Heber J. Excerpts from LDS Conference Report, April 1901, pp. 63–64.

Stevenson, Robert Louis. Excerpts from "A College Magazine." *Memories and Portraits.* New York: Charles Scribner's Sons, 1900. Rptd. Grosse Pointe, MI: Scholarly Press, 1968, pp. 57–59, 62–63.

Welty, Eudora. Excerpt from "A Worn Path." *A Curtain of Green and Other Stories.* New York: Harcourt, Brace & World, 1936–1970, pp. 275–76, 288.

Rands, William Brighty. "Godfrey Gordon Gustavus Gore." *Lilliput Lyrics,* ed. R. Brimley Johnson. New York and London: John Lane, 1899, pp. 201–2.

Kirkham, Oscar A. Excerpt from *Say the Good Word.* Salt Lake City: Deseret Book, 1958, p. 217.

Cluff, W. W. Story. In *Inspirational Talks for Youth,* comp. Preston Nibley. Salt Lake City: Deseret News Press, 1948, pp. 35–37.

Callis, Charles A. Story as retold by Gordon B. Hinckley in "The Consequences of Conversion," *Brigham Young University Speeches of the Year* (Provo, 18 January 1959), pp. 4–5.

Lee, Harold B. Excerpt from LDS Conference Report, October 1972, pp. 130–31.

Obituary of Mary Fielding Smith. *Deseret News,* December 11, 1852. Rptd. in *Life of Joseph F. Smith,* comp. Joseph Fielding Smith. Salt Lake City: Deseret News Press, 1938, p. 161.

Anderson, Ruth M. "Dad's Slippers." *Ensign,* July 1985, p. 71.

Petit, Arline R. Excerpt from "A Beautiful Journey." *Relief Society Magazine,* May 1970, pp. 324–25, 328.

Spafford, Belle S. Excerpt from "Those Who Endure to the End." *Women in Today's World.* Salt Lake City: Deseret Book, 1971, pp. 46–48.

Brown, Hugh B. Excerpt from "Well Done, Carry On." *The Millennial Star,* October 19, 1939. Rptd. in *The Abundant Life.* Salt Lake City: Bookcraft, 1965, p. 254.

Brown, Hugh B. Excerpt from "The Prophet Joseph Smith" (Christmas address to Church employees, December 22, 1961). Rptd. in *The Abundant Life*. See above, p. 337.

Cannon, George Q. Excerpt from *Life of Joseph Smith*, 2d ed. Salt Lake City: Deseret News Press, 1907, pp. 121–23.

Luther, Martin. Quotation from "Preface to St. Paul's Epistle to the Romans." In *Great Voices of the Reformation*, ed. Harry Emerson Fosdick. New York: Modern Library, 1952, p. 120.

Calvin, John. "Perseverance in Prayer," from *Instruction in Faith*. In *Great Voices of the Reformation*. See above, pp. 230–31.

Pratt, Orson. Excerpt from "How the Faithful Should Pray." *Elder's Journal* 1:82. Rptd. in *Faith Like the Ancients*, comp. N. B. Lundwall. Manti: Mountain Valley Publishers, 1950, p. 136.

Widtsoe, John A. Excerpt from "How Is a Testimony Kept? Lost?" *Evidences and Reconciliations*. Salt Lake City: Bookcraft, 1960/1987, pp. 39–40.

Cracroft, Richard H. Excerpt from "'We'll Sing and We'll Shout': A Mantic Celebration of the Holy Spirit," *BYU 1992–93 Devotional and Fireside Speeches* (Provo: Brigham Young University Press, 1994), pp. 124–25.

L'Engle, Madeleine. Excerpts from *Trailing Clouds of Glory*. Philadelphia: Westminster Press, 1985, pp. 113–14.

Bell, Elouise. Excerpt from "High on Huckleberry Hill." *Only When I Laugh*. Salt Lake City: Signature Books, 1990, p. 10.

Bell, Elouise. "This Do in Remembrance of Me." *Ensign*, April 1980, p. 9.

Kipling, Rudyard. "Recessional 1897." *Rudyard Kipling The Complete Verse*. London: Kyle Cathie, 1990, p. 266.

Tennyson, (Alfred) Lord. Conclusion from *Ulysses*. *The Poems of Tennyson*, vol. 1, ed. Christopher Ricks. Essex: Longman Group, 1969/1987, pp. 619–20.

EPILOGUE

Ruskin, John. Excerpts from "The Mystery of Life and Its Arts." *Sesame and Lilies and The King of the Golden River*, ed. Herbert Bates. New York: Macmillan, 1900; rptd. 1901–1916, pp. 113, 114, 117, 120, 124–25.

PERMISSIONS

The author and Deseret Book sincerely thank the following authors, publishers, and agents whose interest, assistance, and permission to reprint selections have made possible the publication of *Pure Love: Readings on Sixteen Virtues*. All possible care has been taken to trace the ownership of every selection still under copyright that would not fall under "fair use" exemption. Every effort has also been taken to make full acknowledgment of the sources of all materials included. If any errors have inadvertently occurred, they will be corrected in subsequent editions, provided notification is sent to the publisher.

Beacon Press and Robert Bly, for excerpt from NERUDA AND VALLEJO: SELECTED POEMS. Copyright © 1971 by Robert Bly.

Bookcraft for excerpts from THE ABUNDANT LIFE, by Hugh B. Brown, copyright © 1965; from BROTHER JOSEPH: STORIES AND LESSONS FROM THE LIFE OF THE PROPHET, by Kay W. Briggs, copyright © 1994 by Family Library Guild; from A COMPILATION CONTAINING THE LECTURES ON FAITH AS DELIVERED AT THE SCHOOL OF THE PROPHETS AT KIRTLAND, OHIO, comp. by N. B. Lundwall, copyright © n.d.; from THE DISCOURSES OF WILFORD WOODRUFF, ed. G. Homer Durham, copyright © 1946, 190; from EVIDENCES AND RECONCILIATIONS, by John A. Widstoe, copyright© 1960, 1987; from IN THE EYE OF THE STORM, by John H. Groberg, copyright © 1993; from HISTORY OF JOSEPH SMITH BY

INDEX OF AUTHORS

509

INDEX OF SUBJECTS